THIS DAY IN MUSIC'S GUIDE TO
IRON MAIDEN

JOE SHOOMAN

IRON MAIDEN

This Day in Music's Guide To Iron Maiden

All rights reserved. No part of this publication may be reproduced, stored in a retrieval system, or transmitted in any form or by any means, electronic, electrostatic, recording, magnetic tape, mechanical, photocopying or otherwise, without prior permission in writing from the publisher.

The publisher makes no representation, express or implied, with regard to the accuracy of the information contained in this publication and cannot accept any responsibility in law for any errors or omissions.

The right of Joe Shooman to be identified as author of this work has been asserted by him in accordance with sections 77 and 78 of the Copyright, Designs and Patents Act 1988.

A catalogue record for this book is available from the British Library

This edition © This Day In Music Books 2018
Text ©This Day In Music Books 2018

ISBN: 978-1999592752

Front and back cover concept by Liz Sanchez

Cover design by Oliver Keen

Book design by Gary Bishop

Printed and bound by CPI Group (UK) Ltd, Croydon, CR0 4YY

This Day In Music Books
2B Vantage Park
Washingley Road
Huntingdon
PE29 6SR

www.thisdayinmusic.com

Email: editor@thisdayinmusic.com
Exclusive Distributors:
Music Sales Limited
4/15 Berners St
London
W1T 3JL

THIS DAY IN MUSIC BOOKS

CONTENTS

Credits and Acknowledgements — 5
Paul Mario Day — 7
Michael Kiske — 9
Introduction — 11

PART ONE: THE STORY

Early Days — 15
Paul Di'Anno — 31
Bruce Dickinson, Part One — 48
Blaze Bayley — 64
Bruce Dickinson, Part Two — 71

PART TWO: THE MUSIC

The Albums — 89
   Compilations — 121
   Live Albums — 122
   Bootlegs — 124
A Top 50 of Iron Maiden Songs — 129
Solo Careers — 143
   Steve Harris — 143
   Paul Mario Day — 148
   Dennis Willcock — 150
   Dave Murray — 151
   Paul Di'Anno — 152
   Dennis Stratton — 158
   Clive Burr — 160
   Adrian Smith — 164
   Bruce Dickinson — 173
   Nicko McBrain — 190
   Michael Kenney — 194
   Janick Gers — 195
   Blaze Bayley — 199
   The Nearly-Men — 206

IRON MAIDEN

PART THREE: MAIDENOLOGY

Rod Smallwood	213
Eddie	215
The Killer Krew	220
Maiden on Film	222
The Chemical Wedding	228
Scream for me Sarajevo	229
Maiden Books	232
Maiden Video Games	241
Maiden Ale	243
Maiden on the Ball	245
Fen-singer	248
Fly to Live	251
The Fans	253
Iron Who?	256
The Tribute Acts	258
Iron Maiden: The Next Generation	265
Websites	268
Index	271

CREDITS AND ACKNOWLEDGEMENTS

CREDITS AND ACKNOWLEDGEMENTS

All direct quotes in this book were taken from original interviews with the author during 2017 and 2018. The interviewees were:

Musicians

Paul Mario Day (Iron Maiden)
Paul Di'Anno (Iron Maiden)
Blaze Bayley (Iron Maiden)
Dennis Stratton (Iron Maiden)
Doug Sampson (Iron Maiden)
Mimi Burr (partner of Clive, Iron Maiden)
Dennis Willcock (Iron Maiden)
Terry Wapram (Iron Maiden)
Terry Rance (Iron Maiden)
Bob 'Angelo' Sawyer (Iron Maiden)
Ron 'Rebel' Matthews (Iron Maiden)
Paul Cairns (Iron Maiden)
Tony Moore (Iron Maiden)
Barry 'Thunderstick' Purkis (Iron Maiden/Samson)
Tony Parsons (Iron Maiden)
David Ingraham (Bruce Dickinson solo)
Chris Dale (Skunkworks/Bruce Dickinson solo)
Alex Elena (Skunkworks)
Robin Guy (Bruce Dickinson solo)
Bob Verschoyle (Gypsy's Kiss)
Paull Sears (Gypsy's Kiss)
John Hoye (Evil Ways/Urchin)
Maurice Coyne (Evil Ways/Urchin)
Alan Levett (Urchin)
Cliff Evans (Killers)
Michael Kiske (Helloween)
Doogie White (Rainbow/Praying Mantis)
Damian Wilson (Rick Wakeman/Praying Mantis)
Hans-Olav Solli (Psycho Motel)
Jamie Stewart (Untouchables)
Mikee Goodman (Primal Rock Rebellion)
Ian Gillan (Deep Purple/Black Sabbath/solo)
Fish (Marillion/solo)
Martin Connolly (Rhythms of the Beast)
Tony Miles (V1/Gibraltar)
John Dexter-Jones (Jump/moiderer)

Producers, engineers, crew

Tony Platt (Iron Maiden/Samson, producer)
Steve 'Loopy' Newhouse (Iron Maiden, Killer Krew)
Dave 'Lights' Beazley (Iron Maiden, Lighting/Stage Designer)
Rob Grain (Samson/various crew)
Jack Endino (Bruce Dickinson, producer)
Keith Olsen (Bruce Dickinson, producer)
Andy Griffin (Skunkworks/Wolfsbane engineer)
Jeff Williams (Iron Maiden, stage tech/Skunkworks bass tech/Eddie on stilts)

Writers, researchers, journalists, authors, movie makers, Top 50

Stjepan Juras
Erwin Lucas
Brigitte Shoen
Neil Daniels
Raziq Rauf
Mike Diver
Adrian Tierney-Jones (Beer writer of the year)
Jasenko Pasic (Scream for Me, Sarajevo idea/screenwriter/research)
Tatjana Bonny (Scream for Me, Sarajevo associate producer)
Keith Wilfort (Iron Maiden fan club)
Roland Hyams (Iron Maiden PR)
Brian Wright

THIS DAY IN MUSIC'S GUIDE TO **IRON MAIDEN** 5

IRON MAIDEN

Michelle Ferreira Sanches
Tim Jones
Henrik Johanssen
Everyone who contributed with their personal Top 50 lists

Tribute bands

Linda McDonald and The Iron Maidens, USA
The Duellists, Italy
Mihaly Beviz and Iron Maidenem, Hungary
Lennon Harris and the Best Maiden Tribute, Brazil
Gregory Wall and Powerslave, South Africa

Miscellaneous

Dr. Freya Roe, MRes, certMRCSLT
Dr. David Jones (retired GP)
Jed Houghton (competitive fencer)
Stuart Bailie (fencer, journalist)
William 'Merm' Mermelstein (Aviation Management Services, Cayman)

Facilitators, fact checkers, general heroes

Chop Pitman
Lindsey Kent
Clinton Cawood
Ben McFarland

Mark Wallace
Adrian Read
Sally Long
Jon Beeston
Joel McIver
Steve Parsons
Karim Bashir
Mark Sutherland
Elaine Todd
Mark (BLACKLAKE Design)
Born Again Heavy Metal Soundhouse
Jan Bayati
Kosta Zafiriou
The extremely splendid Claire Harris
Special thanks to countless members of the extended Iron Maiden family, who have been as helpful and brilliant as anyone could imagine. Take a bow, folks.
As for Steve 'Loopy' Newhouse – a man more helpful you will never meet. Buy his books immediately! www.loopyworld.com
And thanks to Malcolm Wyatt for the edit. Nice one!

Finally
Special thanks to Suzy as ever and to Neil Cossar at This Day in Music Books. If I've missed anyone in this list I am truly sorry and assure you it's only due to me being a fuckwit.
Bangor Comrades: Hanes a Balchder.

PAUL MARIO DAY

PAUL MARIO DAY

I've got good vibes about Maiden.

It all started when I saw this band called Gypsy's Kiss at Canning Town Bridge House. I fancied myself as a singer but hadn't done much aside from bedroom bands. I'd hardly ever worked with a drum-kit even. But I thought Gypsy's Kiss were good.

A few weeks later, I saw them walk past. I went up to Steve Harris - we didn't know each other - and said, "I'd like to have a sing, can I try out?" But he said, "Nah, we're all sorted out." They weren't looking for another member.

As it turned out, I came back a few months later and said, "Well, I am interested." So I sang. I can't remember what songs, but It was in a place Dave Lights had. He was living in a nunnery or something, where we always rehearsed, and that's how it all started.

It was a case of getting the songs that were already there tight, then starting to write new stuff. And the band changed from one thing to another thing, which was Iron Maiden. We thought, 'That's a pretty cool name.' Later, Thatcher was known as the Iron Maiden - it was a torture device, regardless.

Steve Harris introduced me to Judas Priest's music and straight away I was knocked out. I really, really was knocked out. I started trying to emulate Rob Halford wherever possible. I was absolutely blown away with it. It was a change, 'cause I couldn't find anything outside of Sabbath and Purple, Led Zeppelin. I liked The Who before anything else.

We did it 'cause we loved it. We were playing pubs; I never thought I was gonna be a rock star, I was just a kid from the East End of London, you know? What was I gonna do? I was 18, maybe 19, never came from a musical background. It was good. We were guys who got together for the love of the music, the love of playing, and maybe there was a possibility that we could make a few quid out of it too. Maybe become big enough so that the stars who inspired us would turn around and say, "Good job, mate." How can I sugar-coat that? It's just life.

There wasn't a huge audience in my day; I was bugging Steve to do a few more covers, get a few more people in, but he said, "No, I'm sticking to it." And he was right – although I didn't think he was at the time. Looking in retrospect, he had the right attitude. I didn't see that coming, although I was warned about it a bit, to try and up my game. But I didn't know what the game was that I had to step up.

I wasn't experienced enough at the time, and that was my downfall. Also, I was deep in having to do the work thing – believe it or not I wasn't allowed to have time off work. I also had a girlfriend, and that, with the inexperience, Steve let me go. It was a bit sad, but life went on. The band More came up later for me and I took that Judas Priest style with me - we did really well. We ended up supporting Iron Maiden, which was sort of, 'Now I can show Steve Harris how much better I've got!' I went out there to show off towards the audience, and it was a great European tour with them.

I even ended up doing spotlights for Maiden, as Dave Lights wanted someone who could speak English. It's funny, I got paid for my own gig and then for the spotlights, so got paid twice!

IRON MAIDEN

I did my bit, I was with the audience, and it was doubling my income. I saved up my money and bought a graphic equaliser – unfortunately that was a waste of money. I've never bought another one since.

Bruce Dickinson sounded a lot like one of my other musical influences, Ian Gillan, when Bruce was in Samson. A brilliant voice and a brilliant muso; that's Bruce. He's very different from Paul Di'Anno, and in a way Bruce took back up what I'd left the band with: that Judas Priest energy and injection of enthusiasm.

I moved Down Under after a while singing for The Sweet. I was quite envious of Maiden in the 1980s, doing so well and doing it the way I'd wanted to do it. Even living in Australia, the band was starting to get more and more well-known. I was like, 'I can't get away from them!' It kept on reminding me of what I wasn't doing. It was a shame that inexperience cost me that chance, but then again that's not worth the paper it's written on, 'cause who knows what might have happened?

A lot of bands change with the times, different styles, different fashions, but Maiden always stayed with it. I wish Zeppelin had stayed with it! That's why people fell in love with them, from the first album on. They kept the formula. Eddie had a lot to do with it too in the old days: he was a trademark, there was nothing like him and he was never forgettable.

Iron Maiden's continued success is a bit of everything: them as people, their talent, being in the right place at the right time – and those little choices you make in your career that then become big ones. I can only speak for Steve, cause he's the only one still there from when I was in the band, but I can say that he made a lot of them decisions, right at the start. He was very focused, never cocky or over-confident: he was the business.

I'm just enjoying musical retirement these days, doing the day-job and pursuing my hobbies. Being the singer in Iron Maiden gave me a warm feeling. I never thought I was gonna be a rock star – of course I would have liked it to have happened. But it was good, and the experience put me on the road to doing it properly with the likes of More, Wildfire and The Sweet. It's all about the crowd: if they are really loving you, you can do amazing things. I've felt, some nights, like I could walk on water. I was just that in tune with everything. At other times when it's not working, you can't wait for it to be over. There are no guarantees as to what happens. Music has the biggest highs and biggest lows in any trade I've been involved with. And no matter what sort of musical performance, it's the same.

I saw Maiden in 2017 in Sydney and they still play like it's new. I hadn't seen them for, say, 35 years and they were still powering on like it was all brand new. That really impressed me. I think that's why they've done so well for so long – they always stay true to themselves. That's not a bad motto for life, is it? If you love it, give it everything, and who knows what can happen.

/ Paul Mario Day, vocalist, Iron Maiden.

MICHAEL KISKE

MICHAEL KISKE

I always wanted to make music. Elvis was my entry into music at around nine, and I played only Elvis, Simon & Garfunkel, and Beatles songs on an acoustic guitar. But that was all to change.

One of my best friends was already into AC/DC, Priest, Kiss, Motorhead and Iron Maiden. I was around 14 when I heard 'Run to the Hills' on the radio. It blew me away. It had these high-pitched energetic vocals with all those harmonies. The energy really struck me, and that's when I started to ask my friend about that band. So metal started for me with Iron Maiden.

After that I began to play louder music. I got an electric guitar and formed a school band trying to play songs by Maiden and Judas Priest. Especially Maiden, who were always at the centre of my world. Later it was also Queensryche and anything Ronnie James Dio laid vocals on. But Maiden changed a lot for me.

Another friend, a singer and guitar player who isn't so famous but very passionate about his music, told me once there are those types of bands or artists you just like a lot; you listen to their music and enjoy it. Then there are those artists or bands that leave such an impression on you, that you want to do this for yourself. Maiden was that type of band for me; they had the passion and energy that just made me think, 'Wow, that's a cool thing to do!'

The great thing about music is that it knows no nationalities and boundaries. It strikes you on an emotional chord. Even if you don't understand the lyrics, you get the energy. Music is universal. As a teenager you suck it all in and it has a huge impact. You are a flexible mass and everything strong leaves strong marks, not the same in later years.

I will always be a Maiden fan; I don't think that will ever go away. If you grow up with a band like that, it's always there, no matter what you do for yourself.

I have two special things I'll always remember about Maiden and like to share. One is that when I was at school, Maiden were playing in Hamburg and I had an exam the next day. This was the *Piece of Mind* tour. I was there in the front row, Adrian Smith was in front of me on stage and at the end I made a sign pointing at my wrist, because I wanted his sweatband. He had red sweatbands at the time. He took it off, threw it to me, and I kept it. Things like that mean a lot for a metal-teenager. A few years later, when Adrian wasn't in Maiden anymore and I wasn't in Helloween, I found myself in his house for a week or so, fooling around with songs. I told him about the wristband and he said, 'Oh I need it back now!' It's a huge thing to start as a fan of a band, then years later write songs with a guy from that band. Two of those songs were on my first solo album, *Instant Clarity*.

The other great thing I remember was the 1988 tour Helloween did with Maiden. It was the time of *Keeper of the Seven Keys Part II* and we were pretty successful. We were all big fans and had the same management, so opened for them. And it couldn't have gone down any better! It was a great tour, the audience was amazing and it was a perfect combination looking back. Experiences like that make musicians' lives richer. I got to know the guys and wasn't disappointed. It was another thing I always liked about Maiden: What you see is what they are; *real*.

There were rumours later that I was up for the job when Bruce left. Funny thing is that it was

IRON MAIDEN

never discussed. We had the same management [Sanctuary], so it would've been easy to talk about it, but it never came up. I even heard the news on a TV-Show - *Hard and Heavy* or something like that - hosted by a good-looking lady, who revealed, 'It's a fact that Michael Kiske is going to be the new singer of Iron Maiden.' I thought, 'Oh, that's interesting. I haven't heard about that yet; I better start rehearsing!' It makes you realise you can hardly believe anything you see on TV.

It was flattering of course; but I don't want to see Maiden without Bruce. Who does? The same way I don't want to see Judas Priest without Robert Halford. It's just the way it is. Bruce is a miracle to me anyway; how he can always come back like that, full of energy, no matter what. I don't know anyone else with that energy. His powerful vocals draw me to Maiden in the first place.

Maiden were often trying to have some sort of concept for every record, not just the lyrics but also the artwork. I remember *Powerslave* in particular; an impressive cover. For a band to become big it's important to have trademarks. For Helloween it was the pumpkin-stuff, the humour and the comics. With Iron Maiden there was the humour, and also the logo for the name is very strong; then there's Eddie. That combination was a huge part of their success commercially.

Before I even knew Iron Maiden, I knew the *Killers* cover. Around the time, the heavy metal wave from Britain had just started. Maiden were a huge part of it, together with Judas Priest and Saxon. I'd seen this cover a few times before and it stuck in my mind; also in a 'disturbing' way. I didn't know it belonged to a band — I just connected it with heavy metal. It was different to the pretty, cute stuff you saw in music by that time — cruel, disturbing and challenging at the same time - and as a teenager you remember that. It gets to you, leaves a mark and is something to confuse your parents with: very important! I even drew that cover in art school.

Every band goes through changes, having to discover new ground from time to time to keep the fire burning. I always say if you want to try out something new as an artist, go for it! If you don't, just don't. The only thing that really matters in the end is that you never do what you don't want to. You should never bow down to trends or fashions or follow other people's dogma artistically; this will eat your soul. There is nothing wrong with being inspired and learning from other musicians or bands, we all do; but don't follow trends to be fashionable — you should rather try to *set* them, if you can. The ones that really meant something in the music world always had something unique to say; and influence other artists that follow them later. Go your own way, make your own statement, create your own sound, your own niche - even if it isn't always easy. In the end it pays off.

Iron Maiden don't have to excuse anything, and don't have to please any musical direction that isn't their own. I often say to younger musicians you have to be true to yourself; no one will believe in your music unless it's really yours. And this is totally independent from the style of music you do; it's generally true, and all real musicians know that. It's important to be open and learn and explore, but if you want others to believe in what you're doing, you've got to be true and do what you believe in.

That is what Maiden always did and that's why they are where they are today, fully deserved. Long may they continue. Up the Irons!

Michael Kiske, Helloween

INTRODUCTION

Iron Maiden are the most successful heavy metal band in UK history; perhaps the world. They came from London over 40 years ago. They've seen off fashions, genre explosions, line-up changes, several prime ministers and presidents. The one consistent link is founder and driving force Steve Harris. They also have their own pet monster/zombie, the instantly-recognisable Eddie. They still wear horrible trousers sometimes. Rinky-dink pop poppets try and look cool by wearing Maiden T-shirts. They succeed.

Iron Maiden's singer flies them around the world on jumbo jets. The band play to tens of thousands in stadiums across the globe as a matter of course. They have sold hundreds of millions of records along the way.

Not bad for a group that took five years and many, many changes of personnel to get off the ground enough to make any real dent in the music world. Lesser personalities would have given up long before the band's breakthrough.

But Maiden are special, as we're going to find out.

First, let's get something straight. There are thousands upon thousands of websites, social media groups, and online places where you can read about lists of gigs, all the songs the band has ever played and when, haircuts, homes, family members, bootlegs, different editions of albums, artwork and endless discussion of wider meanings.

If you're after the lowdown on what colour pants Pyro Pete had on when Dave Lights called him up for a chat one night in 1982, you might not find it here. But online, yes, perhaps: all anyone needs is a web browser and a few hundred years to surf and speculate. Books, however, have finite numbers of pages to play with. Not to mention that there are also numerous excellent tomes available, including Bruce Dickinson's own and the official history. You are encouraged to read them. After this one, obviously.

This Day in Music's Guide to Iron Maiden, then, presents the Iron Maiden tale courtesy of exclusive interviews with as many ex-members, crew, collaborators, experts, fans, lunatics and commentators we could get our claws on. Given that there's four-and-a-bit decades of history to catch up on, numerous people's memories often contradict each other. Such is the beautiful frustration of life; were it any different it would indeed be dull. We have tried our best to speak with everyone connected to the band that we were able to get access to. Otherwise, what would be the point?

It is intended to be a companion piece to the official history, or the history that

IRON MAIDEN

has become a generally accepted one. But sometimes there are nuances that are lost, forgotten, perhaps even deliberately misplaced along the way. You can find some of those nuances here, in the words of the people that were there at the actual time. There are myths aplenty about Maiden; we're trying not to add to them.

There's also an in-depth look at all the band's albums and overviews of the important solo projects, plus an incredibly unscientific survey of the group's top 50 tracks. That was fun to do. Please direct all angry letters to complaints@ThisDayIronMaiden.com (it's not a real email address, but might make you feel better).

We've also included a whole section dedicated to *Maidenology*, which is where you can find the more left-field articles and angles.

We hope you find it illuminating, thought-provoking and fun. We enjoyed putting it together.

But don't listen to me blathering on. Make like Bruce Dickinson himself and *Dive! Dive! Dive!* Into the text.

Splashing, dive-bombing and heavy petting are all encouraged.

Joe Shooman, UK, November 2018

Photo credit: Ami Barwell

PART ONE: THE STORY

IRON MAIDEN

1

"Steve Harris is a bloody genius"

Paul Di'Anno

PART ONE: **EARLY DAYS**

PART ONE: THE STORY

Early days

The popular version of the Iron Maiden story pegs their formation as Christmas Day, 1975. Steve Harris, bassist, had cut his teeth with Gypsy's Kiss and Smiler, learning both how to play his instrument and a fair bit about what being in a band involved along the way. By the time he gathered a group around him he was keen to write and perform his own material and very driven to try and make a success of his new venture.

Dave 'Lights' Beazley was the gent who'd put on that Battle of the Bands where he and Harris first met.

"About a year later he went out with a girl called Lorraine, who was a school friend of my first wife," says Beazley. "She said, 'There's this guy, he's got a new band, can they come and rehearse at the vicarage [where Lights was staying].' And that's how I first met Steve and the original Maiden line-up.

"I had my own little band at the time, but I wasn't that great a singer and can't remember lyrics – so that went nowhere! We never had a name. We used to rehearse in the church: it was me, Jimmy Rotters, Micky Burroughs, and we tried to learn 'Smoke on the Water'. We got through the first bit of it, and then it just went mad. I always remember Harris saying to me, 'cos punk was big at the time, 'You'd be a great punk singer.' And I was like, 'Fucking punk, are you having a laugh?'"

Ron Matthews' take on how it all came together is rather different from some of the generally accepted stories about Maiden's genesis. The drummer recalls that in the early mid-'70s he was rehearsing with a three-piece band, the bass player of which had a rather interesting moniker.

"We used to call him 'trippy-eyed Steve,' because he always looked like he was tripping [on LSD]," says the drummer. "And he taught Steve Harris how to play. Trippy-eyed Steve met a new girl, was infatuated with her, and couldn't commit to this rehearsing band with no name. He said he knew another bass player – Steve Harris. So he came around, had a go and I thought, this could work, this could be alright. So we did several rehearsals.

"Steve [Harris] then said he wasn't happy with the guitarist [Matthews couldn't recall his name in our interview]. The guitarist was

IRON MAIDEN

1

throwing his head back, posing in the studio, lots of long hair. He said that was never going to get us anywhere. So me, my wife, Steve and his girlfriend at the time, Lorraine, met in a pub in Canning Town to work out what we were going to do."

Matthews said that he really would like to make a living out of rock'n'roll as a proper job. Music to Harris' ears.

"He said he felt exactly the same. We had a real unity. After that me and Steve had quite a few rehearsals, just me and him."

Further, Steve Harris didn't drive but Ron Matthews did, and had a vehicle.

"Steve has said that without my maroon Mini van, Iron Maiden would never have existed," Matthews laughs. "And that's true! I used to have to pick him up."

The world wasn't quite ready for drum 'n' bass, however: more players were needed.

Original guitarist Terry Rance remembers how he joined the band.

"It all started by me answering an advertisement Steve had placed in a [weekly UK] music magazine called the *Melody Maker*," he says. "We started by having a drink at his local pub in Leyton - I can't remember the name of the pub. We had a long chat about types of music and influences. It seemed that we were both into the likes of Stray and Wishbone Ash."

He quickly brought his mate into the band with him.

"Steve asked me if I knew of another guitarist. I had been working with Dave Sullivan, writing songs for about two years, and he seemed the ideal choice. So I got him onboard. Steve got the other members, Paul and Ron."

In late 1975/early 1976, the first line-up was a five-piece, with Paul Mario Day on vocals, Ron 'Rebel' Matthews on drums, Harris on bass, with Dave Sullivan and Terry Rance on guitars.

Matthews even recalls how the band got its name.

"Terry Rance said, 'What about something like a mask, kind of thing?' and [Steve Harris] said he didn't really know. But then Steve came back [another day] and said, 'Let's call it Iron Maiden.' But really and truly it was Terry that planted the seed there."

The ambition, Rance remembers, was to 'create a great hard rock band using a twin harmony-style lead, like a heavier version of Wishbone Ash.'

Writing songs was obviously key to the future of the band and they got straight down to it.

"We used to go around Steve's house in Leyton and sit in his bedroom bouncing ideas around," Rance says, "Until we would come up with something that we could rehearse with - which never seemed to take us long. In them days we would rehearse at least three nights a week; sometimes on a Sunday as well. Then we would all have a drink in the pub across the road."

The nascent Maiden spent about a year to a year and a half rehearsing at the vicarage, recalls Dave Lights.

"Then Steve said they had a couple of pub gigs and asked me if I wanted to be a roadie for them. I said, "I'll do better than that, I'll make you up some lightboxes." I was quite involved in the church at that time, in pantomimes and stuff where I did the lighting. The first lightboxes I had were flowerpots; I just emptied out the dirt, put lights in and some [coloured plastic sheets used in lighting] gels on them. I also made pyrotechnics.

"What I didn't realise was that these pubs

PART ONE: **EARLY DAYS**

1

where we were playing didn't have any lights in them. It was quite a big thing for a band to come along with a show. I just added, added, and added to it. I was a painter and decorator at that point, and in them days paint tins were made of metal. I used to collect the empty ones, paint them black, stick a light in the back, put a blanket on them, and that was the closest we had to proper Parcan [stage lights]."

"I had to leave the vicarage 'cause they were selling it off, and I moved down to Wapping. I used to have parties for any reason and he was the only one who had a car, a little Mini. One Christmas it was snowing. We used to go to a pub called the Town of Ramsgate, just up from St Catherine's Dock, and we all got on top of the car.

"Ron was a bit older than the rest of us and came across as a bit of a Jack-the-lad type vibe. That's why I named him Ron Rebel. We got on really well — I always got on well with drummers because that's the backbone of the music and when you're doing lighting you follow that beat. Everything else comes on top of that."

The first gig, Rance remembers, wasn't in the most salubrious of venues.

"I think it was a church hall - I think we were up for a percentage of the door takings. We only got about five quid and we had to sweep up the dancefloor afterwards. I suppose you're got to start somewhere!"

The band was well-rehearsed, Matthews says, and thus the debut went pretty well.

"It was all original material, apart from one or two numbers. That is always difficult — people have never heard your stuff. There we were, up and running with a band. We started to play gigs in East London."

There is a legend that says one John Northfield stepped in for Dave Sullivan at two gigs in late 1976; 40 years later, despite all our efforts, we couldn't verify whether his supposed gigs on 5 and 16 September at Merry Fiddlers, Dagenham and Cart & Horses respectively, did indeed feature him. Harris' diary from the *Early Days Part 1* DVD certainly seems clear. Dave Lights for one does recall Northfield.

"The guy I was sharing the vicarage with was Jim Northfield, whose brother John stood in for Dave Murray for a few gigs at one time," he recalls.

Other names that have been bandied about as either rehearsing with Maiden or being considered around this time include guitarists Jeff Summers and Martin Bushell. There is also a strange story about Charlie Borg — later of V1 — filling in on bass for at least one gig. Filling in for Steve Harris? Do me a favour.

We asked Terry Wapram about it and he was unequivocal: "I have also heard this, many times," he says of that odd rumour. "It is completely wrong. Charlie Borg never played bass at any point for Maiden." So now we know the truth.

Back to verifiable reality. Though Paul Mario Day was a good singer, his tenure as frontman was a short one.

"It was basically his image," says Matthews. "He didn't have that right. He was a good vocalist, but his jeans would be a little bit too short, which in them days looked really naff."

Rance takes up the story: "Paul was a great singer, however we felt that the band needed someone with more stage presence to make it edgier."

Matthews can still remember the day that the band sacked their first vocalist.

"I remember it like it was yesterday. He

IRON MAIDEN

was so gutted," the drummer says. "Then we met Denny Willcock. He was a completely different character; loads of long blond, permed hair, loads of confidence. He was a couple of years older than us, which makes such a difference when you're in your early 20s. He had all the panache onstage and all the rest of it."

Willcock-y new singer

Dennis Willcock had been in a band with Harris already: Smiler, a blues-rock outfit. Contrary to some versions of how he joined Maiden, he is adamant that he needed no audition.

"I'd already been in a band with Steve. So why would I audition?" he asks. "He phoned me up on the pretence, initially, of attending their auditions as a vocalist, so I could give my opinion on the guys they were seeing."

Auditions took place in the rehearsal studios Maiden used in Walthamstow; the would-be vocalists had applied following another ad in the music papers. At 40 years' distance, the names of the auditionees have long faded – if they were even known at all.

"You could get a hundred guys [responding], or none," says Willcock. "There were [various] vocalists there, we went through their issues, and at the end of the day Steve asked if I was prepared to join. I went off, had a think and decided to join them in the band. That is how that happened. I didn't have to audition. It's one of the folklores that are around. That is my cut on it."

At the time, the band's set was what Willcock describes as 'a mishmash of numbers.'

"It was very much a general rock band; they did Thin Lizzy and things like that, plus some original material written by Dave Sullivan and Terry Rance and Steve as well. It was a low-key band; nothing different to anyone else that was doing the pub circuit in those days. A mediocre rock band, but potentially there was good, original stuff in there which I related to, which is why I joined. It was far from what I'd call an exciting level, you might say."

Willcock lifted everything, says Ron Matthews, with the band now picking up an extremely loyal following around their antics.

"We did the Cart and Horses, The Bridgehouse, and we were packing the place out. People couldn't even get in through the door. The funny thing is that none of us really realised we were going somewhere. It was only the second band I'd been in, so I thought that was how it always was! Of course, it isn't like that. We were really pulling them in.

"Steve was pretty much an amateur player and often he would say he couldn't do it, that he wasn't cut out for this. I remember on many occasions cuddling him, putting my arm around him and saying, 'Come on, fuck it, let's go out there, do it and go fucking crazy.' He used to get so terribly nervous. He was about 19 at the time, very young."

At that stage, comments the ever-strident Willcock, Steve Harris wasn't seen as the 'augmenter or orchestrator of the band.'

"He was just learning off-pat and playing. He wasn't up to the capacity of his writing prowess of his subsequent 40 years in Maiden. He was just another, run-of-the-mill bassist. In Smiler he was very much a beginner. He got more into it. Maiden were an amateur band, in my opinion, in those days. You had to be really on your game. There were lots of bands; Slowbone [for

PART ONE: **EARLY DAYS**

example]. You had to really try to get to that level of playing.

"Like everyone, Maiden wanted to be professional musicians. The band needed taking hold of."

Another character central to the Maiden story is Dave Beazley – better known as Dave Lights, for reasons that will become evident in due course.

"Dave was there pretty much from the beginning," says Matthews. "I was very close to Dave – he was the one who gave me the name Ron Rebel. In those days, playing-wise, I used to really hit the kit hard, big-time. I guess it came out of that."

One of the reasons Dennis Willcock was approached for the band was his noted sense of theatrics and stage presence. It has been said that his vocals weren't as strong as Day's, but that is only one part of what it takes to front a band trying to stand out from the crowd.

"I'd played in other bands; Warlock, Nitro with Bob Sawyer," Willcock says. "People would go away [from gigs] remembering numbers, but especially remembering what we did onstage. There were too many bands coming out plying their wares, going onstage, job done. There was no excitement, reaction or anything there.

"So, let's give them something they would not actually see in a pub. So they would be walking away saying, 'Bloody hell, what have we seen here?' We had to make changes; I used [fake] blood with swords. Again, [I've read] that Steve didn't like it, but they still used it, masks spurting blood and that, after I left. There must have been some significance. We used blood and the sword, a mask for 'Prowler,' which gave a lot more life to a band playing a bland circuit."

Unless you did something different, adds Willcock, you were just going to be another run-of-the-mill pub group. One of the singer's innovations was to wear that mask during the song 'Prowler.' The gnarled, wizened old man persona would add a layer of menace to his performance. Note well, folks, that this is the first time Maiden had a character onstage during a song to enhance it. Hey, that's a good idea...

Willcock, like Matthews, also had access to something that would be very useful for a new band.

"I had a massive PA system," he explains. "In those days people would go along with 100-Watt columns [of amps and speakers] whereas I was running 3,000 Watts of power. Which meant we could mic everything up, make the sound stronger. I brought in a mixing desk and engineer, which was unheard of. It made such a difference to the act."

As did the pyrotechnics that the singer claims he introduced.

Dave Lights explains how Maiden made a difference, and how Willcock had made a difference to the band.

"When we did the pubs, we were one of the only bands putting on a show," says Lights. "Most pubs didn't have any lights at all. A stage and maybe a few coloured bulbs. That was one of the main reasons I think Maiden stood out from all the other bands: they tried to put a show on. Dennis Willcock brought quite a bit of a theatrical element to the band, wearing masks, then in 'Iron Maiden' he would pull a sword through his mouth and fake blood would come out."

Tony Miles, a future bandmate of Willcock in Gibraltar, remembers Willcock very clearly.

"Back in the late '70s, early '80s, Dennis had the rock-star vibe going on," Miles says.

IRON MAIDEN

"He had the long curly hair, Robert Plant style. He drove around in a huge customised red Mustang. He had the big ego, big talk, the swagger, the confidence, a quick wit, and he pretty much commanded the stage as a result. But he was much more of a shouter than a singer and had a limited range, so his voice suited some songs better than others. He also would sing flat a lot of the time, but I don't think he realised it."

Kick out the jams (and the axemen, too)

Things were hotting up, but for some members of the band things were by contrast to come to an end. Dave Sullivan and Terry Rance both were to leave the group after Steve Harris decided that Maiden needed a third guitarist; one Dave Murray, to be exact.

"Me and Dave [Sullivan] both left at the same time due to the fact that the band wanted to bring in a third guitarist," Rance confirms. "So that would have been six of us. We felt it would be too over the top and sound messy and erratic."

Ron Matthews remembers it a bit differently.

"We had a meeting and decided we had to get rid of Terry Rance and Dave Sullivan," he offers. "Dave was struggling really as a guitarist. So, we brought in Bob Sawyer and Dave Murray from Urchin. That lifted it again; Bob Sawyer was very much a showman. Denny always thought Bob was upstaging him. You know what it's like, in rock'n'roll people get so fucking jealous it's unreal."

Sawyer remembers meeting Steve Harris at the New River Arms pub in Cheshunt, Hertfordshire around late 1975.

"He was with someone I knew," Sawyer says. "He seemed very dedicated to becoming a rock star. He seemed nice enough and we had the same musical interests; the major British bands at the time were UFO, Thin Lizzy, The Sweet, Nazareth, Bad Company.

"I joined in December 1976 through a chance meeting with Den Willcock, who I had previously been in Nitro with in 1975. There was no real game-plan at the time. We just enjoyed what we did."

A neat pre-echo of something Maiden were to do around 15 years later to rather less successful effect occurs at this stage.

"The first rehearsal was in an old lorry trailer in a field in Essex! It went well. I just played along with them and got into their songs."

Sawyer was what you'd call a front-stage guitarist, says Willcock.

"He would do all the antics; he had the drive, he had the moves, the looks, everything else. Dave Murray had [previously] auditioned for a band I did after Warlock and I was struck by his playing. He was a shit-hot player. Compared to the other two guitarists, he was worlds apart: much more skilled, much more innovative. Bob brought a number to the band, 'Sanctuary,' and the two guitarists changed the whole sound. Much more guitar-led, up-front and dynamic."

The first gig with the new line-up was at a private function somewhere in Hertfordshire, remembers Sawyer. It went well, he recalls, despite the audience not being what you might call conventional rock fans.

"It kicked it up a level," says Dennis Willcock of the changed line-up. "We didn't have a record company or anything like that.

PART ONE: **EARLY DAYS**

It was my personal cash, personal ideas, personal graphics."

Willcock warms to his theme: he had been asked in 2017 how he saw his role in Iron Maiden in those days.

"I was the director of the band. I had to take on a lot of responsibility for the band. People would contact me to do other gigs. To get the work. I directed the band and in fact, Barry Purkis – Thunderstick, who joined [later] – said to me a couple of days ago that even when he had been in the band for several weeks he thought that [Iron Maiden] was mine."

More of Thunderstick later, too.

"It wasn't; it was Steve's band idea, but he didn't have the inclination of being the runner of the band," Willcock comments. "If they'd carried on as they were, they would have melted into the background the same as 90 per cent of those bands did. That was it."

There were more line-up changes for Maiden. As Ron Matthews remembers it, there was jealousy at play.

"After gigs in Cart and Horses and so on I'd get quite a lot of people coming around and asking me for autographs," says Matthews. "My mum and dad used to come to the gigs to see me play in those days; my mum told me she'd seen Steve Harris in the corner, absolutely cowling at the fact I was getting all the attention and the autographs, and he was just the ordinary bass player. Nobody was really interested in him. You can ask my mum! It's true.

"I was at work, doing the middle shift of 5pm to 11pm. I came home, walked in through the front door and my drum-kit was there in its cases on the floor. I asked my wife what was happening, and she said Vic [Vella, long-time cohort of the band and Harris] and some manager geezer we had at the time dropped it round.

"Hang on a minute, I formed this fucking band! How can I be out of it?"

Matthews drove out to Edmonton to speak to Willcock, who he thought was the instigator of the unexpected firing.

"Dennis had a big car at the time; he was a flash man at the time. He was a bit of a geezer," says the drummer. "I remember hearing this V8 coming round the corner. He got out his car, I got out mine, he went to his front door and I spun him round. He was absolutely shitting himself. I said, 'Right, Dennis, what is this all about? This is my fucking band. You came in way after me; my kit's just been delivered back at my house.'"

Willcock's response, according to Matthews, was that it was all Steve Harris' idea.

"I couldn't ring Steve up, 'cause he wasn't on the phone. He was living with his dad in Leytonstone. I was absolutely gutted; I just couldn't believe it. I remember the following night walking up to Pole Hill [in Epping Forest], looking out over London and thinking, 'What is going on?' I put so much energy into that band. I was never paid a penny, ever: everything went back into that band."

The story wasn't over, though.

"Couple of nights later me and the wife had been out, got home and then Dennis and Steve were in a car on our driveway. They got out and said they were really sorry, that they'd made a mistake. I said, 'Yeah, I think you probably have.' We had another rehearsal, and that was where Terry Wapram came on the scene. After that I thought, 'That wasn't a rehearsal, I was being auditioned.' I was so fucking indignant. So I rang up the next morning and said, 'I'm not fucking having that. This is disgusting

IRON MAIDEN

treatment.' And that was the end of that."

Willcock says that whilst Matthews was a very talented drummer, he also had to be replaced.

"His style of drumming fitted well," says Willcock. "Steve obviously thought that it was his band, but he was only the bassist. So we thought we'd change it. And there was no other changes for a while."

Many gigs followed with the Willcock-Murray-Sawyer-Harris-Matthews line-up, recalls the singer. It was the first really stable, Iron Maiden-ish line-up of the group's nascent career, and in a different dimension could have kicked things up a notch themselves.

"That should have been the line-up," Willcock says. "I class 1976 to 1978 as the heritage band of Maiden. A lot of what I've read, from the fan family as they call it, they know the history, when the change happened. That band was forceful. We tried to get management but there was nobody really [suitable]. We were too strong in character and appearance that nobody would take a chance. It's one of those things, if you're around and somebody comes to see you, A&R or management, then you are on the road to success. But we never had that opportunity."

Dave Lights, for one, loved working with Matthews.

"Ron was a great drummer and had that jazz element as well," says the pioneer. "He was quite a free-flowing drummer, a bit like Nicko is today. I preferred Clive as a drummer because he stuck to his guns; he was a meat-and-potatoes type of drummer. He wasn't as fancy, which is great 'cause when a drummer goes off and decides to change his part, following it [with lights] can actually muck up what you're doing. You are trying to keep the beat and suddenly there's a tangent: the lighting engineer says, 'What the fuck's this all about – where did that come from?'"

Keith Wilfort, long-time fan club boss for the band, remembers how Dennis Willcock and the crew helped the onstage theatrics that put the group streets ahead of the competition.

"As well as the sword and fake blood, Dennis would also wear a rubber mask during 'Prowler' and skulk menacingly around the stage. Over the next few months the road crew, then consisting Dave Lights Beazley, Pete Bryant and the legendary Vic Vella, added some extra refinements to the show, such as coloured lighting made from window boxes.

"There was a backdrop which consisted of an old theatrical mask with 'Iron Maiden' spelled out, and a bit later came the pyros. They were spectacular but incredibly dangerous, sometimes they would misfire or not go off at all, other times Dave Lights would use too much flash powder, and on several occasions Steve would end up with singed eyebrows. As time went on the backdrop became a bit more sophisticated, the mask would spit fake blood from its mouth - covering the drummer.

"For a non-pro band, the show looked quite sophisticated and Maiden were also one of the few bands around who actually owned their own PA, so they were LOUD! Steve borrowed some money from his nan to help pay for it. As the band's career progressed, the show became more and more sophisticated. Initially Dave Lights and Steve designed and built them, then eventually professional companies took over."

Dennis Willcock isn't one to avoid

PART ONE: **EARLY DAYS**

fronting up, and the same confidence that makes him such a showman can also lead to conflicts with people who don't share his vision or modus operandi.

"I am a strong character," he admits. "That is what I do; I wouldn't have taken any of the crap put on them when they first started. I'd never see myself as being part of the Maiden project as they are now, under their management, because I'd have come to grief with a lot of them. That's my cut on that one."

There was another line-up change to come, which Dennis Willcock doesn't shy away from remembering. But it was far from how the tale has subsequently been told, particularly online.

"[According to the stories,] I sacked everybody," he says, dripping with sarcasm. "Like, [as if I would do this] you bring your mates into this band and then you sack them."

He is also keen to remind the world of how things have changed for musicians.

"What people do not understand is that to have a band, you get up three, four, five times a week and play. In those days, whoever was in the band may not have been the best [players], but hats off to them. It took a lot of courage to get up there and play. Nowadays it seems to be the way of the world that you can go on social media and slag people off. What I did in 1978, heritage year, was I did my own thing. That's it."

He notes that Kiss, The Crazy World of Arthur Brown and others either wore masks, used fake blood and so on.

"So, when [online keyboard warriors] come in with these statements about me and say I sacked this person and that person, go back to your Maiden history. Nobody, upon nobody else stands up to be counted.

[They say that] whole band, the problems, the replacements, the act [were] all down to me. If someone wants to lay it on me it's up to them. Even though it wasn't my band I had total control of what happened. People should read into that and discuss the issues. I've got people who know the [true] information and know what they are reading is crap."

Dave Murray had a girlfriend that Willcock describes as 'diabolical,' and the guitarist would – let's say – not be completely his best self, on stage at times.

"He would lose numbers halfway through, drop notes, et cetera et cetera," says Willcock. "That's not the way I played. I don't care what happens afterwards, we've all been there with drink, drugs, whatever. Afterwards, do it. We were not Syd Barrett, we didn't come up with material under the influence of acid or whatever, we wrote normally and that's how we played. Alright, a couple of drinks beforehand, but that was it."

A discussion with Steve Harris followed as to what needed to happen to move forward, because the band wasn't hitting the heights Willcock felt it was capable of. Murray was warned, says Willcock, to clean up his act. Both Murray and Bob Sawyer, however, were fired.

"I was ejected from the band completely by surprise," remembers Sawyer, who also used the stage name Bob or Rob Angelo. "We were gigging solidly, and I had no idea that I was for the chop. Dennis and Vic knocked on my door one evening with my gear and told me that I was no longer required.

"I heard later, that I was 'upstaging' Dennis, and once, for fun, I 'pretended to play with my teeth', and Steve Harris

THIS DAY IN MUSIC'S GUIDE TO **IRON MAIDEN** 23

IRON MAIDEN

declared that I was 'hoodwinking the fans' or whatever - and that became my death sentence."

Just the two of us

So, with the only 'official' members being Willcock and Harris at that time, there was a need to restock the Maiden shelves with musicians. In came Thunderstick, the drummer, plus guitarist Terry Wapram and – intriguingly – Tony Moore, a keyboard player.

Willcock remembers telling Harris: "One thing we can do to change all this – we can get a keyboard player in. Later [around *Piece of Mind*-era] he stated that he didn't like keyboards. Well, as you know, for the last 35 to 40 years they've had a keyboard player. So you read into this whatever you want to believe or not believe.

"I used to do all the advertising, wind up other bands by putting statements into *Melody Maker*, but it was a bit of, 'we feel we're better than the average bands'. To quote Bachman Turner Overdrive, 'You Ain't Seen Nothin' Yet'," says the ever-entertaining singer.

Time to get another member in, and try and make the sound fuller.

"It was Dennis Willcock that approached me after seeing me play at the Marquee in Wardour Street," Wapram says. "Bob Sawyer and Dave Murray had both been let go so I was the only guitarist at the time. Tony Moore was brought in to cover the harmonies that a second guitar would have and to expand the sound of the band. Dennis had heard bands with keyboards and thought it could work for Maiden. I had mainly played in three-piece bands - bass, drums and guitar and sometimes a stand-up singer.

So, it was very different to what I was used to. It never really was given time to settle."

Tony Moore had quite the pedigree; he had played keyboards as part of Al Matthews' band. Matthews had just had a hit with a song called 'Fool,' and toured throughout 1976. Moore had got the bug big-time for being a musician, he says.

"In 1977 I realised that if I was to do anything in this business I needed to move to London, so I answered the now famous advert in Melody Maker – Iron Maiden *looking for Keyboard/Synth player and Drummer – No Idiots!* It's hard to over-emphasise just what an important and powerful periodical *Melody Maker* was. It connected the music business at every level, from buying and selling gear, finding members for a band, advertising professional services to listing all the big (and small) gigs on the circuit. It also had insightful and influential editorial that reflected music as it was and as it was changing."

Thunderstick, too, had responded to the advertisement. The man christened Barry Graham Purkis had been living in Sicily, touring with a group called The Primitives in Italy, Sardinia and Greece. He then returned to the UK, joining the group Archer and then forming his own band called Oz. But that wasn't cutting it.

"I was very frustrated as a musician, having toured all around the Med and lived the life as a professional musician only to come back to the UK, finding it hard to be part of something that was actually going somewhere," he says. "That pushed me to continually search for something better. The way that this particular ad was worded and placed showed it to be a band that took itself seriously, wanting to get out there and gig rather than continually rehearse with

PART ONE: **EARLY DAYS**

nothing on the horizon."

He wasn't the only sticksman being auditioned, however.

"On arriving I along with numerous other drummers took my place in a long corridor awaiting the call," he remembers, "Whilst trying to set up as much of the kit that was practical to cut down on time spent feeling awkward under the full glare of the band, whilst trying to make small talk. The less time spent like that the better, so I wanted to be prepared, ready to play as soon as possible. The actual audition I can't remember (we are talking 40 years ago), but I must've done OK because I got the job."

Given that Purkis at the time lived in the South East of London, he recalls the East End-based auditions as like 'going over to another land.'

"Iron Maiden were very proud of their East End roots and still are to this day. Well, the ones that were born there," he laughs. "All the bands that I had been involved in had been south east of the River Thames, I even got The Primitives job through playing with musicians that came from the South East. So this was unchartered territory for me."

This feeling of not-quite-fitting was to continue throughout Purkis' relatively short stint as drummer in Maiden.

"I can remember feeling that this was a band that didn't have that much comradeship," he says. "Sure, we would go to the pub sometimes after rehearsing and talk about salient points that the rehearsal had thrown up, but I never felt part of the gang. Maybe it was because I was one of those South Londoners, but it was strange the feeling that I got when I crossed over the river to go back home.

"[It was exacerbated by] the fact that because everything was so focused on progressing that somewhere along the way we forgot to have fun doing it," he continues. "Now this is how I saw it, purely from my perspective, other members could have been having a whale of a time but for me there was a fair amount of angst that came with being a member of the Iron Maiden of then. Also, I happened to be having an affair out of my marriage, which could have also contributed to my paranoia..."

Tony Moore was 17 years old at the time, says Willcock, and the youngster was coming into what was beginning to unfold as an untenable situation.

"What we didn't know at the time," says the vocalist, "Was that you need someone to orchestrate the keyboards into the music, otherwise you've no chance of getting there. The keyboard player has to fill the holes; Steve couldn't orchestrate it."

First, though, there were rehearsals to be had. Moore remembers staying with Steve at his grandmother's Leytonstone house.

"We would sit for ages talking about music and all the bands we both liked. Acts like Genesis, Pink Floyd et cetera, that had amazing stage shows and lighting rigs. Todd Rundgren's live performance of his album RA was also a great inspiration. One of the bands that I think influenced Steve's idea to have a keyboard/synth player in Iron Maiden was a band called Lone Star, in particular a track called 'Bells of Berlin'."

After a while, Moore moved into a room-share in Kilburn, North London, in a street where as coincidence would have it Terry Wapram also lived.

"I had a very cheap little car, an Austin 1100, and I would drive me and Terry (and our gear) to Scarf rehearsal studios in Mile

IRON MAIDEN

End two or three times a week," recalls Moore. "We were all very dedicated and focused on trying to make the material sound as best it could possibly be. I was, of course, trying to work out how to fit my keyboards into this. My set-up was quite basic, a fawn coloured Wurlitzer EP200 piano and an ARP AXXE synth running through an Electro Harmonix Memory Man Deluxe into an HH lxl2 Combo amp."

History could have taken quite a dramatic turn, thanks to the over-enthusiastic meddling about with explosives that Dave Lights was prone to, recalls the lighting designer.

"I used to make pyro boxes out of Old Holborn cigarette tins, with two elements in them," he laughs. "On November 5th I'd buy as many fireworks as I possibly could, break them all open and put the contents into a big tub. I'd plug [the boxes] straight into the wall, a bit of wire across them, and WHOOF! Sparks, and what have you. I really shouldn't have mixed them all up. There were a few disasters – I remember setting fire to Steve's trousers at one point. They were made of a plastic that looked like leather. I took Terry [Wapram]'s eyebrows off at one gig. It was quite a dangerous time – for the band, not me!"

Wapram recalls Harris was working for the council at the time, and that the bassist was also studying plus keeping his eyes on the musical prize. Maiden were rehearsing a lot as a band and as individual members together. One moment sticks in the axeman's mind.

"I remember the day Steve showed me the riff for 'Phantom of the Opera,' says Wapram. "I felt it was a massive step forward from all the previous songs. I had performed and rehearsed all the first album and some of the second. We ran through 'Phantom' and I adapted guitar parts to suit. Also, at the time, we worked on 'The Ides of March' quite extensively and possibly other stuff. I haven't had credit for adding guitar. It is naturally what happens in bands. The basics were there and I embellished it."

Purkis recalls the amount of work that was going into the band, musically-speaking.

"The guy that I knew at that time or at least my recollection of him, he was living at his grandmother's house. [He was] an unassuming quiet person that loved football and music equally," says the drummer.

"There was no 'big plan' of how fame and fortune could be realised, but at the same time wanted the band to be one step above others that were on the circuit that we came into contact with. The one thing that was new to me was the rhythm section rehearsing. I had always been part of a band that rehearsed together as a band, maybe the vocalist would take time out whilst the rest of the band ironed out musical sections, but nevertheless the whole band would be in attendance. Steve initiated the idea of the two of us (bass and drums) getting together outside of band rehearsals to run through our parts, something that enabled those parts to be set in stone."

What wasn't set in stone at the time by any means was the way that the band should actually sound. Not even the members really had a handle on it, says Purkis.

"Both Tony Moore and I joined at the same time so the sound that we generated as a band was still very much a 'work in progress'. It is only now with the benefit of hindsight that we have something comparative sound-wise to hold against the band of that time.

"As regards rehearsing, we did as often

PART ONE: **EARLY DAYS**

as time and finances enabled us to do. All of the band were still paying out from their own pockets. The subs were collected weekly. It could be expensive paying for the honour to be an Iron Maiden musician."

Time to put it to the test: a gig was arranged at the Bridgehouse, which gave the band a chance to experience exactly what it might be like as a live unit.

"It was a very important gig on the circuit," Tony Moore remembers, "But it was still just a pub with a small stage - so we were squashed in. It was all a little bit of a haze, but I just remember by the end of the gig it didn't feel like it was something that me as a keyboard player could fit into properly. It was a strange night really.

"I didn't actually have any keys that could give me polyphonic held chords - so I was mainly playing piano parts, mixed with synth lines that were a harmony to the lead guitar parts, plus some special effect sounds from the synth. I think that the intrinsic nature of the material, certainly in the beginning, was very riff-driven. Lots of time signatures and changes of pace. All the songs were kind of 'pieces' put together - much of it was written on the bass, with Steve showing us the riffs. I think I left before the time when lots of new material was needed [because] most of it was written by the time I had joined."

It became very clear that this was really not going to work for anyone. Terry Wapram analyses some of the issues in play.

"I think the problem in hindsight was that the songs had been written with two guitars, and really that was what was needed. The keyboards, as later in their career proved, could work as well by augmenting the guitars. We spent a lot of time rehearsing with Tony Moore and Barry Purkis but Tony did one gig and decided it was not for him. The period before Tony and Barry, Steve had developed a bass style that could give the effect of harmonies against the guitar. We gigged with that but really another guitar was necessary to be able to pull off the harmonies. Having always played as a single guitarist, I wasn't sure that I wanted to be in a dual-guitar line-up at that time."

There's also the story of Barry Purkis being not totally compos mentis at that concert, with rumours of him throwing up into buckets, falling asleep at the kit and so on. Not entirely true, according to the drummer himself. Purkis says he was married at the time, but had been having an affair with another woman.

"Not something I am particularly proud of or boastful about it; it just happened," he says. "We had decided to go public with it, so as I remember it my girlfriend had just told her husband. He was quite a passive type of guy, so there was no threats of fisticuffs at dawn, but nevertheless as you can imagine he still was very, very upset. My then wife had deep suspicions but had not yet found out officially. The three of them were in attendance at the gig, all standing in a row.

"All of this coupled with the fact that I had just taken delivery of a brand new Gretsch drum kit on that day and had struggled to set it up the way I wanted it for the first time. Being so used to my other Rogers kit's tom and cymbal positions made the playing of the new one particularly difficult, with drums being too far away or too close. I'm sure other drummers will know what I am talking about. For a guitarist it would be using the wrong gauge strings or a completely different set-up. Playable of course, but at a price!

IRON MAIDEN

"Anyway, this was my state of mind at the gig. To settle my nerves, which were of course jangling, I took something to calm me down, enabling me to just think about the task in hand: playing the gig. I can't remember what it was, possibly Valium, I honestly can't remember. By all accounts it calmed me down a little too much, and the rest is history.

"There are two points that I would like to clear up. One: I did not fall asleep whilst playing the gig (as the story on Wikipedia states). I am quite a large guy and to suggest that just one beta-blocker or barbiturate or whatever it was could put me to sleep wlilst playing onstage is ridiculous! The second point is that I was not sacked after the gig, yet again untrue, I cannot tell you what the rest of the band made of my performance, because I never placed that much importance to it, but I was NOT sacked that day. As for the affair? It will be in my book that I am constantly trying to make a start on..."

He would do well to link up with Dennis Willcock, who has, he says, many recordings of that Maiden line-up.

"Nobody's ever heard [them] but I can state for a fact he didn't fall asleep," recalls the singer. "He swore at somebody in the audience, as I did at the end of the gig because they were giving us a bit of grief. He will admit that he lost it halfway through, but I don't know where all these stories come from. In the folklore of Maiden, it makes good reading for all these young fans. These fans reckon they know every last inch of it. But if you were not there in '77, '78 you do not know what we did."

There was one more rehearsal with Moore, which wasn't the most fun anyone's ever had.

"It was tense, there were obviously some issues running around, and I believe that we were in a different rehearsal room, one near London Bridge this time," recalls Moore. "I was at Terry's flat and told him personally and then used the payphone in his hall to call Steve and tell him - I don't remember the exact words, but it was very amicable.

"There was always room within the drama of the music for keys, but I think that I didn't have the right gear, plus, it was a genre out of my usual style (singer/songwriter), which was why I eventually left. However, I can see how and why the band would be able to incorporate keyboards progressively through their career, and *The Book of Souls* has a lot on it."

More of that in due course; for now, the band was down to Purkis-Harris-Wapram-Willcock, briefly. Purkis says he never 'left' the group as such.

"The day of [a] gig I was there early with my kit that had been properly constructed by now, fully set up and awaited the arrival of the band. This is when I remember seeing The Green Goddess for the first time. All were present except our vocalist, who according to the rest of the band had decided not to do the gig.

"So as a consequence, the gig itself was pulled and never took place, the drum kit taken down and we sat around having a drink [...]. The general mood was, 'Is this really working out?' As I remember it the general consensus of opinion was we would all re- evaluate. Even Steve Harris was talking about returning to his draughtsman studies and giving the band a rest. We all said goodbye and went our separate ways.

"As I have mentioned earlier, as far as I was concerned there wasn't a great deal of 'one for all and all for one' within the band.

PART ONE: **EARLY DAYS**

We had short periods of inactivity a few times before. This was to be just another. There was no official 'Goodbye' or 'You're Fired' or anything such as like. Just lethargy. No phone-calls on my part to find out what was happening, and none received telling me that I was no longer in the band. My association with Iron Maiden had come to an end ... for now, little did I know that I would forever be linked with them for the rest of my life!"

Willcock disputes the idea that he absented himself from the gig, however.

"That's rubbish," he declares. "I would never not turn up for a gig. I would still play to two men and a dog or a full house; it makes no difference to me. At the end of the day people have an issue with me at a higher level, and to this day I don't know why."

So it was down to Harris, Wapram and Willcock ... for the briefest of times. Maiden had the very deep misfortune of having a lot of their gear stolen, which Dennis Willcock said actually occurred during his tenure as singer. He remembers his phone number being on the advertisements, and dealing with the policeman plus the guy who'd originally sold Willcock that PA system.

"Where was Steve?" asks the ever-provocative vocalist. "Nowhere to be seen. So do you understand where I am coming from? Who was Iron Maiden? Puh. Make your mind up [...] at the end of the day we are all musicians and all should be friends."

Dave Murray was approached to rejoin, which he duly did – but Terry Wapram wasn't into being part of a dual-guitar team, and so the band was down to Harris-Murray-Willcock. A drummer, however, was soon on the horizon.

Another iteration

Doug Sampson, drummer, remembers seeing Iron Maiden at the Cart & Horses.

"They were awesome, really good," he enthuses. "A good band, so different from the other bands that were playing at that particular time. It was fast, energetic, a good show; Dennis was there. It was chaos, there was blood everywhere, swords through his mouth, it was a good show to watch."

Enough, indeed, to lure Sampson back into a band with his mates.

"I went to the Bridgehouse; it wasn't the best gig they'd ever done," he says. "And I found out the reason why was that Dennis was about to leave the band. I suppose it was a bit of a strange atmosphere in the dressing room that night. After the show, Steve came up to me and said he was going to start again. He asked if I would be interested in joining and I said, 'Yeah, let's go for it'."

The reboot duly happened, but it was as a three-piece only.

Dennis Willcock says he had had enough of the struggle and formed a new band with Terry Wapram called V1.

"When Dave came back in, his girlfriend was acting the strop. Terry had left and we formed V1, which is what we have now [in 2017]," concludes the singer.

Tony Miles isn't sure exactly why Willcock left, because it wasn't something that the singer made a big deal of at the time.

"He certainly didn't have a grudge against them, otherwise we'd have known about it," Miles notes. "However, over the years, Den has proved to be very inconsistent in his approach. Firstly, he's fired up with enthusiasm and big ideas, then when things start going not as expected, he starts causing trouble, usually by causing division in

IRON MAIDEN

the band, which ends up in people being 'sacked'.

"He rarely does it himself though, rather he influences someone else to do it. The result is a bunch of pissed-off people left in his wake. He did this in Maiden, he did in Gibraltar, he did it VI back then and he's still doing it now. Proving that people never really change!"

Ever-strident, Miles speculates a little about the clash of personalities that may have been instrumental at the time.

"I suspect Den got bored in Maiden because it wasn't going the way he wanted and so started to mix things up by moving people in and out of the band. Den likes to be the one calling the shots and probably felt that Steve Harris was getting more assertive over time and realised that he'd be kicked out eventually. But Den's ego wouldn't have allowed that, and so he walked. Without doubt Harris is the kingpin in that band, always was and always will be, and [that is] why Dennis couldn't have remained.

"Den says he doesn't regret it to this day but feels he should be well compensated for his contribution to the early years. It's interesting that the official Iron Maiden histories really play down Den's time in the band, so maybe they feel his contribution wasn't as big as he says it was.

"The truth is somewhere in the middle, I suspect."

For his part, Terry Wapram is thoughtful and insightful as to how it all panned out.

"My period with Maiden was a time of lots of change and line-up changes. I think it clarified in Steve's mind where he needed to go with it. Obviously, the two or more guitars were needed and eventually they had keyboards as well. Dennis Willcock brought the theatrics to the table, which they continued with along with the general approach. At the time Dennis and I came out of Maiden, no-one could have forecast their level of success."

The point is a very valid one: there were no guarantees that anyone from that era was going to make a career out of their band. VI had as good a chance as any (as did Urchin, and a host of other gigging acts).

With Willcock and Wapram doing their own thing, and the Moore keys experiment having been shelved, the Murray-Sampson-Harris trio became the backbone of Iron Maiden. It was to stabilise things for a crucial period in Maiden's timeline, says Doug Sampson, although of course it didn't start in that manner.

"All we had was an idea of how it should be, so we went down the studios and started working on the songs," he says. "It was my first encounter meeting Dave Murray, and we hit it off straight away. He's a cracking bloke. It was the three of us in the studio working out the set at Scarf."

It was around early 1978, Sampson recalls, because he remembers coming home from rehearsals at around Easter time. But Maiden were never going to be a going concern without a vocalist; someone who could take on the melodies, sure, but someone who could follow in the footsteps of Willcock's theatrics and even step it up a notch.

Auditions were duly set up ...

PART ONE: **ENTER THE BEAST**

PAUL DI'ANNO

Enter the Beast

It was the night before Christmas, 1978, give or take a month and a half, and Maiden were busying themselves trying to find someone to sing. The trio of Doug Sampson, Steve Harris and Dave Murray were meshing in well, but the recent departure of the larger-than-life Dennis Willcock had left quite a hole in the whole caboodle.

"We auditioned for singers," says Doug Sampson, "And this chap turned up called Paul Di'Anno."

Cue dramatic chords...

Di'Anno says that there was a certain chap called Trevor Searle who happened to be a mutual friend of his and Steve Harris. Knowing Maiden were looking for a singer, and knowing Paul Di'Anno's skills, Searle duly made the link that was to lift everyone involved in Iron Maiden to an entirely new level.

"I went to Scarf Studios one Sunday in East London, Mile End Road," says Di'Anno. "We sort of worked out alright. We ran through 'Smoke on the Water,' I think."

It worked out more than alright, Sampson enthuses.

"He blew our ears out," says the drummer. "We were really taken aback by him, he was such a great singer. Obviously, he got the job and that was the band complete."

Something else was important at that stage, and that was to be able to showcase what Iron Maiden could do.

"Steve said he needed to get a recording done, basically just to get gigs," Sampson continues. "Let's get a demo down and see what comes up of it. He played me a demo Dennis Willcock had done in Spaceward Studios, Cambridge, and it sounded really good, so we thought we'd use that studio. That was about the end of December [1978]."

Terry Wapram backs up Sampson's words. In those days, bands would very often go and see each other – not out of any kind of mutual support necessarily, but out of the sheer fun of it.

"Steve and Dave used to often be in the audience at V1 shows," says Wapram. "We regularly played the Ruskin (East Ham) and the Soundhouse (Kingsbury) a full year before Maiden." As with the demo recordings, Maiden were following in the footsteps of V1.

First, though, it was important to bolster that sound somewhat. Enter Paul Cairns, a talented guitarist who had, yes, you've guessed it, responded to an advertisement in good ol' *Melody Maker*.

"I rang this number and Steve Harris, I think, answered," Cairns says. "He said, 'You'll have to come over to East London, mate'. I lived in West London – whoah! At

IRON MAIDEN

least he gave me a lift back home in this little van, an Austin A40 I think it was. Dave Murray drove it as well."

Yes, but what about the audition?

"[It] was good," continues Cairns. "I liked the guys from the get-go. Good-looking guys [so] plenty of chicks to come, ha ha!"

He recalls having his Les Paul guitar with him but was amp-less, so he plugged into Maiden's set-up.

"I just went for it. Dave Murray was cool; in fact they all were cool and likeable. Don't know how many [other] people showed up before me, but they kept cool and professional. Steve Harris was definitely in charge, focused and right on it."

And so Cairns was in. The band at the time were, like any other hopefuls, looking to get an album deal with their own songs, their own sound, and gig upon gig upon gig. They had no manager, Cairns recalls.

"We had planning sessions now and then at Steve's Nan's house in Steele Road. Nice food she made... Nice! Keep the troops fed! Sharing ideas, getting that sound. [Steve] had a Spanish guitar with metal strings. It was good, I played it on 'Charlotte the Harlot,' 'Wrathchild,' et cetera. Imagine that – a steel-strung Spanish axe! Ha! Great days."

Gigs were exciting as hell, continues the guitarist.

"Crowds were going totally apeshit, air guitars, everything, full on," he says. "Dave Lights on the desk, Steve Loopy Newhouse the chief roadie – a very pro attitude."

There was also the notorious Maiden mask – in essence the first iteration of what would morph into the world-famous Eddie. Following in the footsteps, or headbangs, of Willcock and his fake blood adventures, Dave Lights had knocked up a mask that would spit blood all over the drummer during the set.

"[Sometimes it was,] 'Please work tonight you bastard!'" Cairns says with a laugh. The mask, he recalls, had lightbulbs around it for smaller gigs. Maiden were kicking things up a notch.

"We changed from civvies into stage-gear for the shows; I thought that was great, fans thought so too." The material was, of course: even at this stage Maiden were playing a large majority of the tracks that would appear on their debut self-titled album, and even *Killers*.

As for the Eddie mask, Dave Lights was using his usual ingenuity and creativity.

"When Den Willcock left, the new singer, Paul Di'Anno didn't do that kind of theatrics, so that's when I came up with the backdrop to imitate what Dennis used to do with the band," he remembers. "So I made a back-sign with a mask on it that had blood pumping out. It was an old fishtank pump connected to an old oil can that I filled with paint, food dye and God knows what else. I used all different combinations of stuff – sometimes if it was too thick it wouldn't be pushed through. Dougie Sampson used to get food dye in his hair and everywhere and it'd last for days, the poor sod."

"The first Eddie mask was a mould of my own face. I had a friend called Dave Brown, my neighbour, who was an art student. I had about six or seven of his masks; the template of my face was on another mask at the college which the students would use [to create masks]. Dave gave me the masks."

Worry not, folks, there's a section devoted to Eddie later in this very book. But we get ahead of ourselves. It was time to get into Spaceward.

"We recorded four tracks," remembers Doug Sampson," One of which was

PART ONE: **ENTER THE BEAST**

'Strange World,' which never made it onto the demo."

The night of the recording provides one of the early-ish mysteries of Iron Maiden. The credits (and photos) on what would become known as *The Soundhouse Tapes* mention only Sampson, Di'Anno, Harris and Murray. Over the years, there has been a growing faction that has studied the intricate sonics of the tape and concluded that there were, indeed, two guitarists rather than one on there.

Doug Sampson says that he has been asked so many times about Cairns' presence.

"I don't remember him being there beforehand," he says. "I have no recollection. It's very difficult, I cannot remember."

That said, Cairns has been placed at the scene of the recording; a famous picture of the full band plus his beloved dog.

"It was bloody cold," says Cairns. "New Year's Eve. I travelled over to Cambridge from Norwich with [mate] Dave 'Mollusc' and my dog, Nelson, who was named after Admiral Horatio Nelson, as my dad had been in the Royal Navy.

"We recorded the demo live," he continues. "Was there any overdubbing? I'm not sure. I think we did the whole thing straight through after a few takes. Remember that those four songs were well-rehearsed and gigged live as part of Maiden's show. We were all aware that this was costing us dosh and so we all got on with it."

The atmosphere in the studio, says Cairns, could be best described as 'intense', as the demo was vital for the band's progress.

"I fucked up on 'Invasion'," Cairns recalls. "You can hear it on the demo. Still, we got it all done and dusted."

And a few pints to celebrate followed. Despite the triumphant recording, the band had neglected to make any arrangements for staying anywhere that night. It was bitterly cold and the would-be rock stars faced a night of freezing their gonads off. Never one to want cold gonads – the opposite was always true if the opportunity presented itself – Paul Di'Anno turned his charm on to full and secured himself a place to stay with a young lady. The band tagged along and crashed out on her floor whilst the singer took care of a different kind of business.

"I definitely recall we all went to a lady's flat and later crashed there," Cairns says. "Pity we had no cameras ourselves; not many early Maiden pics out there, sadly."

If we take this at face value, then for 40 years one of the key players on a key moment in the history of the greatest metal band of all time has been inaccurate. Cairns is in no doubt as to his disappointment.

"That has been and still is a source of sadness and anger for me over all these years," says the guitarist. "Of course I feel left out, especially as that Spaceward demo was an important factor in getting the band recognition and getting Rod [Smallwood] on board, taking Maiden into the stratosphere."

Many years later, Cairns along with many of the early members received gold discs from the Maiden camp as a commemoration of their time in the band and a thank you for their part in the Iron Maiden story.

"It was good to receive that gold record," Cairns says happily. "Total surprise there, Steve – Cheers mate! Nice one."

"The band have been massively successful worldwide," he adds, a little less bouncily. "It all kinda started with that Spaceward demo tape. To receive a financial thank-you after all these years would be totally brilliant. My pension nest-egg!"

Back to 1979, then, and during January

IRON MAIDEN

1

said demo was passed by Steve Harris to Neal Kay, another larger-than-life character in the Maiden tale. Kay was chief DJ and cheerleader for heavy metal at the Bandwagon/Heavy Metal Soundhouse, which

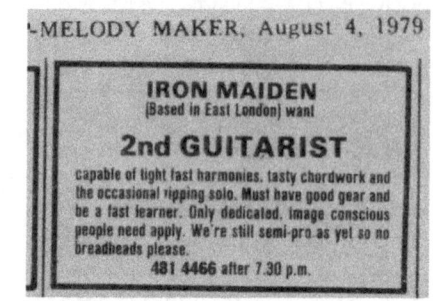

MELODY MAKER, August 4, 1979

IRON MAIDEN
(Based in East London) want
2nd GUITARIST
capable of tight fast harmonies, tasty chordwork and the occasional ripping solo. Must have good gear and be a fast learner. Only dedicated, image conscious people need apply. We're still semi-pro as yet so no breadheads please.
481 4466 after 7.30 p.m.

took place at a venue in North London. The PA was huge, the crowds were enthusiastic, and Kay was always looking to push new talent. A delegation of Maideneers headed to the venue to pass the Spaceward demo to this influential force of nature. But Kay was blasé at first; oodles of bands would approach him similarly.

"There were so many people giving him tapes," remembers Sampson.

But Iron Maiden, he soon found out, were something special. Steve 'Loopy' Newhouse recalls the date as Monday 22 January 1979. Kay called his house (Harris didn't have a phone at the time) and so the Killer Krew hero rushed over to tell Steve Harris. Murray and Sampson were both out and about and in those days of no mobile phones/Internet/ text there was no way of contacting them either. Paul Cairns was ecstatic of course, but when Sampson did finally hear what Kay had offered, he wasn't quite as up for it.

"[Kay] said he was really knocked out by it," continues Doug Sampson. "And he started playing it a lot at the disco."

The band had been given a gig the Saturday of that week. But they weren't ready. In the event, Loopy details in his ace book *Loopyworld*, due to a mixture of flu (Sampson), being out of contact (Cairns) and general not-quite-yet-ness, the Bandwagon gig that had been scheduled for Saturday 27 January was cancelled. The band did attend, Harris apologising to the crowd for Maiden's absence, and getting not abuse but free drinks; more so when 'Prowler' was blasted out from that enormous PA system. Without even playing, Maiden seemingly had become Soundhouse favourites.

At around this time, too, Loopy recalls Paul Di'Anno's occasional absences as going down like a lead Zeppelin with the rest of Maiden, to the extent that at one stage Trevor Green was approached to join as vocalist. Green, a friend of Newhouse's, demurred because he wasn't into heavy rock as much as the others. History could have taken quite another path had he accepted.

Di'Anno says he personally brought something edgy to Maiden that made them stand out.

"Some of the set was kept from when Denny and Paul Day was in the band," says the vocalist, "Like 'Prowler,' and 'Drifter'. Then he had a transformation. I'd seen the band with Denny Willcock; I went with Loopy. We got out of there pretty sharpish, because we thought we were going to get our heads kicked in. I had a mohawk at the time, piercings and stuff like that."

The rivalry between punk and metal was a real one, and if not on the same level as mods vs. rockers it was certainly potentially violent. Still, music was music, and Di'Anno was pretty impressed.

"They were a pretty good pub band,"

PART ONE: **ENTER THE BEAST**

he recalls. "Then all of a sudden there was a transition. [Steve played me] stuff like 'Phantom' and thought it was brilliant. And I got a bit down, wondering if I was going to be able to sing it, but it turned out alright.

"We were heavy, playing fast compared to every other band, and we had time changes. Steve is a bloody genius."

As well as DJ-ing and promoting, Kay also compiled charts for *Sounds*, based on how many people at the club asked for various songs. 'Prowler' made its way to the top of that chart on April 21, 1979.

"After a week or so it kept coming up that Iron Maiden was top every week, 'Invasion,' or 'Prowler'," says Sampson. "And record company people started taking notice. That was the beginning, really."

Unfortunately, it was the end for Paul Cairns. The way he tells it, he was playing through the pain of an injury – something that keen footballer Steve Harris would have understood all too well. But in the fast-paced world of Maiden, there was no room for any passengers.

"I had a back, spine problem at the time," he remembers. "It did affect my normal energy levels on stage. A Gibson Les Paul is a bloody heavy guitar! I remember the guys visiting me in hospital at the time; I needed an operation. I still feel it now. The nurse had a go at Paul Di'Anno, he was up to something!"

After leaving the hospital, Cairns says that he went to Maiden's four-piece gigs during his recovery.

"I was blown away with the energy," he says. "I stood behind Dave Lights' desk. It was awesome to see them. I thought, 'What a great band!' and I was a member! Can you imagine?"

These days, the guitarist admits that he could have been a little more upfront with the group.

"Yes, I should have explained myself to the guys about my back stiffness and gone on a break for a while. But this band were just so great, and I wanted to be part of it so much. It's hard to explain. You know what I mean?"

Hindsight is a wonderful – and useless – thing. Maiden were back down to a four-piece.

A quick dalliance with Paul Todd followed; an incredibly quick dalliance, to be honest: legend has it that he lasted two days with the band during May 1979, stopping only to appear in a photo session at Tower Bridge. Legend also has it that his girlfriend at the time nixed his joining the group because she wasn't keen on Todd playing live or touring. This is another example of history being rewritten for the sake of a good story. The truth, according to trusted sources of ours, is more to do with the fact that Todd was a stripling at age 17. Though the members of Maiden were only a few years older, some of their antics and refuelling sessions offstage were not to the new guitarist's taste or lifestyle choices. At the time, we must remember that Iron Maiden were basically one of many bands that were playing live with one eye on a career; the behemoth they became was still only a future dream. There were no guarantees of stadiums, million-selling albums, huge tours and merchandise. In 1979 Maiden were nowhere near that level. Todd – who was a member for weeks rather than days - saw them at Camden's Music Machine on May 8, a gig that was well-received and was to be featured in *Sounds*. But something wasn't sitting right with him.

So Paul Todd took the sensible and very

THIS DAY IN MUSIC'S GUIDE TO **IRON MAIDEN** 35

IRON MAIDEN

understandable decision to play in a group that he got on better with personally and musically. He moved on to play in the band More, where for a month or two the vocalist was Paul Mario Day. By the way, Paul Todd has been happily married to the girl in question for over four decades – so even if the legend had been true (which it isn't), you simply cannot argue with his choices. Other future endeavours included Sweeney Todd, who demoed some tracks but didn't manage to snag a record deal.

Tony Parsons – who had once auditioned for Urchin, according to some - was next to join briefly as second guitarist for a few months at the end of 1979.

"I applied to an advert in either the *Melody Maker or Sounds* asking for a second lead guitarist for Iron Maiden," Parsons says. "And was eventually chosen from a second audition after being short- listed. The auditions took place at Hollywood Studios in Clapton, East London. As the band already had a list of gigs, there was no time to learn all the numbers and I had to learn from cassette tapes and run through all the parts at Steve Harris's house before gigs, I had to start by being introduced halfway through until I managed to learn all the numbers to play a full set.

"I must have played around 40 gigs in my short time of being with them, all over the UK."

Musician Tony Miles remembers seeing Maiden with Parsons in the band.

"I first saw Maiden at the Camden Palace in 1979," he confirms. "Den had just joined Gibraltar and Tony's brother Steve was playing bass for us. Den had parked his red Mustang right outside the venue and swanned like he was the headline act!

"I thought Maiden were ok but certainly no better than Praying Mantis or Angel Witch, who were supporting them. I still see Maiden as a pub band, only playing much bigger pubs these days. And I think that's the clue as to why they are where they are - they still largely come across as the pub band that you and your mates go to see on a Saturday night."

Pub band or not, the Maiden momentum was soon to reach critical mass.

The Spaceward demo was to make its way into the hands of another incredibly influential part of the story: Rod Smallwood. He had been a manager for some years, working with Steve Harley & Cockney Rebel and then a punkish band called Gloria Mundi. After not having the best time of it with Harley et al, he was moving away from the scene. Indeed, Smallwood wasn't keen on dipping his toes back into the management water at the time, still looking to continue a law degree he'd put on hold the previous decade.

Steve Harris had a mate – in the official Maiden book he is named as Andy Waller – who knew Smallwood through being a keen rugby player. The demo was passed on to Smallwood before embarking on a rugby trip in the spring of 1979, and on his return from the United States he got to thinking once more about the band he'd heard. Something had really registered with him, the fuse was lit, and he got in touch with Steve Harris accordingly.

Smallwood went down to see Maiden at a gig at the Swan in Hammersmith. The band was there, but Paul Di'Anno was not.

"That was the day I got arrested," explains Di'Anno. "I had come straight from work and had a knife in my bag. I ended up in the police station and only made it back to the gig after the last two songs. Steve was

PART ONE: **ENTER THE BEAST**

valiantly trying to sing – not a good move. He's great at some things, but singing is not his forte, that's for sure. But he battled on, as of course he would.

"[They were told,] 'Your singer's been nicked' – that set a trend, didn't it?"

Sampson remembers it well.

"He'd dropped his Stanley knife on the floor – he used it for cutting up packaging at work," the drummer recalls. "It was in front of a copper and so he got nicked. We're at the gig with no Paul Di'Anno and Rod sitting in the audience waiting us for play. Steve said we had a little bit of a problem and Rod asked Steve to sing, to get an idea of what the band was like. We did two or three numbers with Steve trying to sing along, and halfway through Paul came in to rapturous applause – a folk hero. He got on stage and bang! Rod saw the crowd going bleeding mad. Paul had street cred, he looked the part, kids loved him."

The band really started to take off with Smallwood on board, says Sampson.

"We began to do bigger gigs like the Marquee and the Music Machine," the drummer explains, "Which was a bloody good gig at the time. We backed Motörhead at a charity do. Lemmy had seen us play at the Music Machine the week before and had requested us. [Motörhead played under the name 'Iron Fist and the Hordes from Hell']. It was the worst-kept secret in town; every fan was there. We went down really well. Paul thanked Lemmy over the mic, a great band for giving us the opportunity. We were a really small band compared to Motörhead. But it was getting the name around."

Momentum was growing fast for heavy metal; Maiden had begun to appear in the music press and Neal Kay also booked a tour with fellow upcoming acts Angel Witch and Samson. Features on the tour, and the bands associated with it, began to regularly appear in *Sounds*, with the final and glorious centrepiece being the christening of the new scene as the 'New Wave of British Heavy Metal.' Or NWOBHM for not-actually-that-much-shorter (it's pronounced Newobbum, kinda). The Bandwagon tour brought the gospel outside London and even up North, Maiden travelling in their three-ton truck, somewhat ironically-christened the Green Goddess. Scotland even got the NWOBHM experience. Things were looking up for all concerned.

First of all, the Spaceward Demos – rechristened *the Soundhouse Tapes* in honour of the fans and the venue that had been so central – were released on November 9, 1979 as a limited edition of 5,000 vinyl copies. The three tracks that were included were 'Prowler,' 'Invasion' and 'Iron Maiden.' The quality of 'Strange World' wasn't deemed up to scratch so it remained unissued for many years until appearing on a later compilation. Legend states that some 3,000 were sent out by mail order in the first week alone. The band resisted any further calls to press additional copies, and as a direct result the single/EP/demo changes hands for rather a lot of dosh these days. Come early 1980, and Maiden et al appeared on a must-have record of the time (and for many fans now, it's also a must-have), a compilation called *Metal for Muthas*.

"It had Samson, Angel Witch [and others and was] put out by EMI. We did two tracks on it," says Sampson. "I am sure they were recorded at EMI studios." It was released in Feburary 1980 with other luminaries of the time, including Toad the Wet Sprocket, Praying Mantis and Ethel the Frog. Yes, Ethel the Frog. Let's just say that one more time:

IRON MAIDEN

there was a band on the album called Ethel the Frog.

"It went rather well," says Di'Anno, with uncharacteristic understatement.

Another big step was recording a session for Tommy Vance's influential Radio One Friday Night Rock Show. Parsons remembers the significance of that moment.

"We were told that we were to do some recording sessions [for the radio]," he adds. "I think this came after the EMI recordings - *Metal for Muthas* - so we were all geared up and ready for it, and upon arrival we were all quite excited that it was the BBC Maida Vale studios that The Beatles and other greats had recorded at, but soon disappointed that Tommy Vance was nowhere to be seen.

"We set about recording the four numbers ['Iron Maiden,' 'Running Free,' 'Transylvania' and 'Sanctuary.'] and did them pretty much live in a couple of takes, but we came back a second time when the final mixing was done. I have always liked those recordings, as it had a raw live feel that was different to the studio album's sound."

The session aired on November 14, 1979.

The holy grail of a record contract was imminent.

"Rod was basically in a good position," says Sampson. "We were doing the Bandwagon at the Soundhouse, and getting people from *Sounds* coming down, seeing the place so packed and people going so mad. It was the same when we did the Marquee. [Record companies] said basically that they had to sign us. It was ridiculous, so many kids out there. There was obviously no Internet or streaming or anything like that. So we got a record deal.

"Rod organised all that; he found the best deal was with EMI."

And so it was with EMI that they signed, the canny management deal negotiating a definite three-album deal with an option for two more. But it was signed without Tony Parsons; the band were down to a quartet once again.

"Things did not work out for me with the band, I think because by then they had reached a stage where contracts were about to be signed with management and record companies and for some reason I wasn't to be part of it," Parsons says now. "I then went on to join Sam Apple Pie with Sam Sampson (Doug Sampson's brother). This was a rock/blues band and we often played at the Ruskin Arms in the early 1980s. From then on I formed a band with my brother, Steve Parsons; we were called Gibraltar and then Press Gang after some line-up changes.

"Nowadays I occasionally play with the band Metalworks at The Monarch, Camden Town, or sometimes at the Red Lion in Stevenage."

Such is the way of the industry, not least with Iron Maiden. Another axeman was needed, yet again.

```
JUMPIN' JACK PROMOTIONS
        present
     IRON MAIDEN
          +
PRAYING MANTIS and D.J. NEAL KAY
          on
   SATURDAY, 17th MAY, 1980
          in
THE KINEMA BALLROOM, DUNFERMLINE
DOORS OPEN 7.30 p.m.    TICKET £2.50
```

Enter the Stratton

Dennis Stratton was an experienced, seasoned guitarist by the time the offer came to join Iron Maiden. In some ways, they needed him more than he needed the

PART ONE: **ENTER THE BEAST**

hassle of teaching a talented but still on the naïve side band the ropes. Stratton had been around Europe, his band Remus Down Boulevard supporting Status Quo and Rory Gallagher.

"Steve and Dave used to come down on a Sunday night to watch RDB playing down at the Bridgehouse," Stratton remembers. "Then I got approached to go and meet them with a view to joining the band. They'd watched me many times and knew I had the recording and also touring experience.

"I must admit they had done the groundwork, playing all over the country. All over the rock clubs of the UK. They had done their apprenticeship in the Green Goddess. I met up with Steve, Dave and Rod in the Ship pub, they gave me the *Soundhouse Tapes*. I'd never heard any of their music, never actually seen them. Early doors, first meeting, I found Rod a bit painful. A bit young for a manager, but he was serious about what he wanted, and so was Steve."

Stratton listened to the music at home. Interestingly, the guitarist says he spotted something about the band that he felt was lacking.

"I noticed that there was only one guitar playing," he remembers, contrary to what Paul Cairns recalls. "And so there was lots of room to work on them songs."

Stratton's take on it is that it was he who introduced a vital element of Iron Maiden's signature sound at this stage

"Anyone that knows me from the past knows I've been always involved in harmony guitar bands. I loved Wishbone Ash and Capability Brown in the early 1970s. It goes back many years. I think harmony guitars are brilliant and I have always used them in every band. It was an opportunity to take Maiden and make their songs bigger. In a way, improve on them so there's two guitars, not even playing the same thing. It worked really well, and that's how it all started."

Stratton hadn't been in a heavy metal band before, and he says that he had to be careful not to take away the 'rawness, the punkiness' of the band's sound by over-egging it.

"We wanted to make them more interesting without taking the energy away. The good thing about things like 'Phantom of the Opera,' 'Running Free' and 'Transylvania' was that they really worked well with harmony guitars. Sometimes there's a three-part harmony guitar on there which really widened the song out in stereo; it helped the song. Things like 'Prowler,' or 'Drifter' you don't need them. You have to be careful not to overdo it. But I had a free run at it and I really enjoyed it."

The first rehearsal, he recalls, was with Dave Murray and Steve Harris – but no drummer.

"We were just sitting there, me and Dave, with Steve playing. I was going through these harmony guitars with Dave and they were over the moon. Basically I walked into the job because I'd just done that preparation on the demos."

Maiden's tour schedule at the time was such that they would often spend ludicrous amounts of time buzzing up and down B-roads and the occasional motorway between gigs (such is the lot of any upcoming band putting the hard yards in). It's harsh enough an environment even for the most resilient of teenagers and early-20s musicians. Add to this an illness and it can be devastating.

"We'd been to studios and recorded 'Running Free' and 'Burning Ambition'," says Doug Sampson of some of the early

IRON MAIDEN

EMI days. "Nobody was entirely happy with them, but 'Burning Ambition' did end up on the B-side of the single of 'Running Free'."

The tour, however, was taking its toll on the drummer.

"The thing was, I had a flu virus that I couldn't shake off," Sampson says. "And it got to a stage where I was feeling quite rough all the time. I said to Steve that I was really not too good and didn't know how long I could keep it up. I was getting off stage, sweating, getting back in the cold, getting back in an old van and getting to the next gig. I was not getting time to recover and was just getting worse, you know?"

The initial idea was to try and get the current bunch of gigs out of the way and leave it until Christmas for a chat, he said.

"I wasn't getting any better and I said to Steve, 'I think we'll have to part company. I'll have to come out. It's just not going for me'. It was just before Christmas '79, just after a Music Machine gig, and that was the end of that. As far as I was concerned it was the right time. It was after a good gig."

Intriguingly, Ron 'Rebel' Matthews recalls being offered the chance to return to Iron Maiden, which he accepted.

"My wife was working as a legal secretary in the city and happened to bump into Dave Lights, who said he'd heard I was coming back into the band. She said, 'Yeah. But he's only doing it for the money!'"

Matthews said that wasn't the case.

"She said, 'Well I was protecting you.' I said, 'Well fucking thank you, Deborah'. And I heard nothing more about it. Later I was working in the cinematograph trade and I heard the radio DJ say, 'Here is a new band from London called Iron Maiden.' I said, 'Oh fucking hell, I do not believe it.' I heard they were signed and I thought, 'Fucking hell, I've lost it all, I've missed out on it all'."

He's also strident about the respective skills of the sticksmen that followed him.

"I said to Steve, he was nowhere near my standard. I said, 'Cheers mate, you've got a drummer nowhere near my standards, how do you think that makes me feel? It was pathetic; Steve phoned me one time and said Doug couldn't get the intro to 'Another Life.' I said, 'It starts with a tom-tom, rolls down, hits the floor tom, then comes back to the tom-tom, what can I tell you?' He said, 'Well he can't do it.' And I said, 'Well yeah. Fine. Whatever'."

"Steve is quite a funny geezer. Everything is for the band, for Iron Maiden. As if it's like, not him, it's this godly thing called Iron Maiden. It is very strange. But they've done very well though, haven't they?"

Ron also adds that at one stage Harris had told him that even if a family member died the same day as a gig, he'd still do the concert. More the hubris of youth than a serious utterance, it has to be said. If there is anyone reading that has never said anything stupid or unwise, let them be forever sainted: words are cheap (doubly so for your put-upon biographers. All donations welcome).

With Sampson reluctantly out of the Maiden camp as they stood on the very verge of success, another drummer was needed. Dennis Stratton had someone in mind straight away.

"I brought a friend of mine, Johnny Richardson, but it was too loud for him as he had problems with his ears. He was in a great band called Blockade, but didn't last one rehearsal [because of his hearing issues]. I rang Clive Burr and told him what was going on, took him over there and the line-up was complete."

PART ONE: ENTER THE BEAST

1

According to Barry 'Thunderstick' Purkis, however, Burr wasn't the band's first choice to take over the drum stool.

"We had finished the Heavy Metal Crusade [*Metal for Muthas*] tour, headlining with both Angel Witch and Iron Maiden as opening acts. I had just got front cover of the music publication *Sounds* with a picture of me as Thunderstick, with the caption: 'Is this the new face of Heavy Metal?'

"Two days before Christmas the phone rings: 'Hello Barry, Steve here.' 'Steve who?' 'Steve Harris, would you consider re-joining us?'

"He then tells me of the problems they were having with Doug Sampson (not as a person or indeed his playing ability) but something happening to his arms whilst onstage. He apparently was becoming weaker and weaker throughout the gig, with the drum faders on the desk having to be pushed all of the way up, subsequently causing feedback problems."

Steve didn't want the Thunderstick persona, though, says the drummer. The Maiden mainstay wanted Barry Graham-Purkis. Two different things entirely.

"So throughout Christmas [1980] I was back and forth weighing up each argument for and against. The Thunderstick image was starting to really gather momentum, and we (Samson) were just about to go into the studio recording sessions for what was going to be *Head On*."

"Anyway, the day after Christmas I went over to the East End (naturally) and played with the band. They had hired a drum-kit. I think I was the only drummer in attendance. I didn't see any others lurking in the shadows so knew that this offer was pretty serious. As Iron Maiden had been on tour with Samson, Steve had a good idea of the way that I played as well as the fact that I had already been in the band. We ran through a handful of songs. I couldn't for a minute tell you what they were, other than doing 'Running Free'.

"When we finished it was crunch time. I remember Rod Smallwood saying, 'This band is going to be bigger than Led Zeppelin'. I thought at the time that it was great to have a manager that believed so strongly in his act. Not really something that we had in the Samson camp. I asked for more time to consider but was told that they didn't have the time, as the band's itinerary had already been drawn up and this particular problem needed to be addressed immediately.

"I still asked for a couple of days, it being Christmas and all, and went home. Yet again more deliberation, a few days went by without a follow-up phone call. I didn't phone Steve and he didn't phone me. I was then swept along with the Samson itinerary being put together, and we then went into the studio. Whilst there, the phone went and it was John McCoy (Gillan).

"He said, 'I've just found out that Iron Maiden have just taken on a new drummer... it's Clive Burr'."

Burr in place, the band then worked on arrangements, Dennis Stratton says.

"It was like starting again; they were playing what they normally played, Di'Anno was singing the way he normally did. With Clive coming in there was a lot to go through in a short space of time, so we spent a lot of hours at Hollywood Studios. Me and Clive would sit in the Golden Fleece, have a pint and talk about it. Once he got to grips with the stops and starts and timings and different movements, it was great."

Iron Maiden went in to record their debut album in Kingsway Studios in January 1980.

IRON MAIDEN

1

Stratton was to irritate factions of the band and management with a story that you may believe from either point of view that you wish. Here's his take.

"I spent a lot of time in the studio," Dennis Stratton remembers. "Working on guitar parts. There were a few times mucking about, a few afternoons where me and the engineer were in the studio. We put loads of harmony guitars and vocals on 'Phantom of the Opera.' It was messing around; we were never going to keep it.

"Rod came in and heard it. It was like Queen, 'Bohemian Rhapsody.' He said, 'Fucking take that off, it sounds like Queen.' I said, 'We're not going to use it; we're going to take it off. We're just having a mess about'. We were bored, we were there all afternoon. But you had to be very careful not to put too much on, not to take away the rawness of that Maiden sound."

Paul Di'Anno freely admits that at the time he had no clue about what the recording process was. But that didn't stop him realising the significance of what was happening.

"It was fantastic fun," he says. "We were making something. Hoping and praying that people would buy it."

With more time, it could have been better, said Stratton, and the initial choice of producer was The Sweet's Andy Scott. That didn't work out.

"It was Rod and Steve negotiating, and the rest of us were just left behind," says the guitarist. "That was just the normal thing for the band. I do remember it being recorded very quickly; I was surprised how quick. They knew the songs backwards. It was good. Then we had to get back out on tour."

A few gigs followed as warm-ups, rehearsals took place for the *Metal for Muthas* tour, which ran in February and March 1980. Maiden played the first 11 dates, starting in Aberdeen and ending in the Midlands.

"It was a wall of sound everywhere you went," says Stratton. "You couldn't hear the vocals, but the fans loved it. They knew all the words."

The debut Iron Maiden single was released by EMI on February 8, 1980 and was the anthemic 'Running Free.'

Duly buoyed by the experience, Maiden hopped on to Judas Priest's *British Steel* tour to spread the word. It was a dream for Maiden, to start with ...

"Then Di'Anno upset KK Downing by saying stupid things," Stratton sighs, about the singer's assertions in the press that Iron Maiden were going to blow their more storied compatriots off the stage.

"But that was Di'Anno: he was a loose cannon.

"We didn't get treated too badly; in the late '70s the main band had the PA and the lights, you were the support band and you knew it. I got on really well with Glenn Tipton. It was good."

Iron Maiden came out on April 14 and smashed into the charts at No.4. One hell of a debut!

"It was amazing," Di'Anno recalls. "We went onstage that day and played our hearts out because we knew everyone liked it. We'd won the audience over before we even played."

Stratton puts it simply: "The crowd was 50/50: We had as many fans as they did."

The band even appeared on iconic BBC show *Top of the Pops*, insisting on playing live rather than to a recorded backing track. That was unheard of – but they pulled it off on a show that also featured The Buggles, Blondie, The Beat, Ramones, as well as

PART ONE: ENTER THE BEAST

Shakin' Stevens, and Cliff Richard. Well, you can't have everything.

Stratton remembers the experience as clear as day.

"Being Maiden, we had to be different. When we got there, it was nothing but trouble. These blokes walking around the studio floors at the BBC were used to calm, peaceful types. That wasn't us. The minute Clive started the drums all these blokes come running in, screaming that it was too loud. We had to damp the drums down, me and Dave were using H&H [amps] so had to turn the volume right down and the gain right up, so we got that distorted sound. They still said it was too loud!

"Shakin' Stevens was to one side, wearing a brand-new pair of trainers; there was a little monitor to the side which was coming back at him, listening to the music and miming. When he was dancing, his trainers were squeaking; all we could hear was that! But we came across quite well."

It wasn't all fun and games; the PA went down at a Hammersmith gig, Di'Anno recalls, aside from the vocals.

"I was trying to think of jokes to tell the audience, but you can only keep the audience's attention for a couple of minutes," he remembers. "They came for the music. At the time we were all too East London to be in [a fame bubble]. That's not how you are where we come from. I'm just me. That gets up some people's noses sometimes, 'cause I say it like it is. But that's just me, you know what I mean?"

Thousands of Maiden fans did indeed know what he meant; the band's first major headlining tour in the summer of 1980 was an absolute stormer. Keeping busy to take full advantage of the momentum built, the second single, 'Sanctuary' was released and peaked at No.29 in the UK charts. After the first leg of the UK tour, and some festival dates that included Reading 1980, the lads went into the studio once more, in a break before the second leg was to begin.

It was one of the very few mistakes that Maiden were to make in their early career. The idea was to swiftly record a new track to promote that second leg. For some reason, the decision was made not to use any of Maiden's material but to cover a song by Australian band Skyhooks, called 'Women in Uniform.'

The producer, Tony Platt was to be in charge; he'd had huge success working with AC/DC, Bob Marley, Foreigner and Sparks and, intriguingly, went on to work with Samson. More of that in due course. Platt recalls that things weren't quite as they should have been in the Battery Studios sessions.

"Rod Smallwood and the publishers [Zomba], who also happened to be my management [put us together]," Platt remembers. "They wanted a song that would get the band on *Top of the Pops*. Sales would go up and so on, and that would be a knock-on process. But getting a heavy metal band on [was tricky.] Martin Birch was finishing off a Whitesnake album so couldn't do it; my manager said I had a few days free."

The trouble was, says Platt, that Steve Harris did not want to do the song at all.

"Instead of being a man, manning up to it, turning round and saying, 'This isn't Iron Maiden, I am not fucking doing this song,' he kind of went along with it, but not really. He dug his heels in and made it a difficult thing for all concerned, which was a stupid thing to do. What he would have been better off doing would be saying, 'OK, we've got to do this, so let's make it the best we

IRON MAIDEN

can make it.

"I had the unenviable job of trying to turn this into a silk purse, as it were. The problem that I had was that this was a song by Skyhooks; a proper song. It wasn't the usual thing from an Iron Maiden perspective. It had the chorus format and all that sort of thing, and if you produced it with bass, drums, vocals and guitars all playing in the same octave, it just sounded like a noise, you know?"

And there was a need to find a way to get the voice to pop out of the morass, he says.

"Of course, Steve Harris is playing more notes than anybody needs to play in their entire life, so that gets in the way of the vocal, constantly," says Platt. "At that point I said it would work much better if Paul could sing in a higher range, like Bruce [Dickinson] does with Samson. You tend to use the example of how AC/DC works; the guitars and the drums have so much space, because the vocals are not getting in the way of everything else."

Dennis Stratton, he says, was 'the musician in the band.' But he wasn't a Maiden-uber-alles type either.

"A really, really nice guy," Platt said. "He engaged with 'Women in Uniform' and tried to make it as good as he possibly could. By doing that he put himself outside the clique."

After that, they went on tour with Kiss.

The US band were quite the proposition, too, with a stage show that Dennis Willcock would have been proud of. Theatrics, pyrotechnics, make-up and everything larger than everything else. Dennis Stratton was ecstatic at the experience.

"Everywhere we went, Italy, everywhere, it was Maiden shirts wherever we looked. That was a big shock; that's why I think Kiss didn't want us to support them in their London gig. We had so many fans."

Iron Maiden had plenty of musical material, honed through years of gigging and refining the tracks over the previous five years. Stratton says that even during the Kiss tour, which took place during November and December that year, he and the band were looking toward the next LP.

"At the hotel, we were working on *Killers*, running through all the little riffs. When I heard the album I could hear all those little riffs. Steve [had to work] out what songs to put on the first album and what to save for the second. He knew what he wanted and has a cast-iron vision. The 10 days in Italy, Kiss were in the UK [gigging from September 5 to September 9, plus travel days] so we were there on a paid holiday, it was great, we had time to work on those songs in the hotel room."

When Kiss returned for the European dates, starting at Nuremberg on September 11, 1980 things carried on as before, but the guitarist was to encounter his own roadblock for reasons that had little to do with his talent.

"I am one of those fellas who likes having a laugh and meeting people, all that," he says. "Rod told us not to talk to any of the members of Kiss. The first thing I do is take no notice of that and talk to them. I got on really well with Paul Stanley and Gene Simmons. Me and Dave Lights used to share hotel rooms, because he was funny.

"I used to travel with the crew sometimes, just for a rest and to get away from the band, to get different surroundings. A couple of times I even travelled with the company; I'd just get in the car and drive with them for a couple of hundred miles."

Tour life being what it is, any opportunity

PART ONE: **ENTER THE BEAST**

to refresh the mind – and the nostrils – is one experienced musicians grab with both hands. Stratton also says there was an issue brewing for another reason.

"The music I listened to at home wasn't heavy metal. I'd listen to George Benson, The Eagles, a bit of David Coverdale. [Rod] used to get the hump. He started saying I didn't want to communicate with the rest of the band because I wasn't part of the band. It got sillier and sillier, and I took it as stupidity. With the band doing so well, I just thought he was mad. What was he talking about?"

But the die had already been cast, it seems.

"He didn't see if from my side. I tried to tell him that if you put four or five people together for 24 hours a day, they are going to fall out, and basically they did. In his head it got worse and worse, and by the time the end of the Kiss tour came around they had made their mind up that I wasn't interested in mixing with [Iron Maiden]. Rod and Steve had made their mind up; the rest of the band weren't involved and that was it."

Dave Lights was good mates with Stratton, and shared rooms with the guitarist.

"He was more experienced than the rest of the band and I think that's one of the reasons he didn't last very long in Maiden. He is a great guitarist and could do all genres of music; but back then Steve was very much like the Spinal Tap, 'If it's not metal, you're not in the band.'

"Dennis was quite outspoken, he'd toured Europe with RDB supporting Status Quo, and I think he was just that bit more professional than the rest of us. The nail in the coffin for him was that in rehearsals at one of the Kiss gigs he and Clive and someone else I can't quite remember were playing a George Benson song. Harris came in and was like, 'Fucking hell, this isn't heavy metal.' You know what I mean? That was one of the reasons he didn't continue. And he wasn't one you could put under the thumb. Whereas Clive was a bit more amenable, Dennis was a bit more outspoken."

The 'Women in Uniform' video was recorded at the Rainbow Club in London, and you can see a few short glimpses of Stratton on it. But short they are: he was an ex-member.

"I said that it was a shock," Stratton recalls. "They said, 'You're not into the band, you listen to different kinds of music.' And I realised it didn't matter what I said. So I just said, 'OK, fine,' and that was it."

Platt remembers speaking with Stratton about it at the time.

"He said, 'They caught me listening to The Eagles,'" says the producer, before summing up his views on the rest of Maiden at the time.

"Dave Murray is a sweet guy, but overshadowed by Steve Harris; Clive was always a bit of an outlaw in any case. Paul Di'Anno was living in the Walter Mitty-land that he does. He was never going to challenge Steve at all. The only one who ever would was Rod Smallwood. He obviously realised that Steve was the steadying faction, so he gave him his head."

So with Stratton out, and a new album needing recording as soon as possible, a second guitarist was needed again. Step forward Adrian Smith, Dave Murray's old mate and occasional bandmate. Smith slotted into the band with little trouble, and the band went into Battery Studios almost immediately with new producer Martin Birch. The songs and arrangements had been knocked into good shape and with Birch in

IRON MAIDEN

1

charge the band found they meshed much better.

"The one thing about the first Iron Maiden album," declares Paul Di'Anno, "Is that the songs were great but the production was shit. Will Malone was apparently Mike Oldfield's triangle player or something, but he didn't really know what he was doing. I would still love to see Maiden re-produce that. But the songs were brilliant."

When it came to the second LP, entitled *Killers*, however, Di'Anno had only one song on there.

"I thought the first album was streets ahead. The second album sounded great, but the first album was better."

There was a massive number of gigs throughout 1981 to promote Killers, which would take the band all around the world. First single, 'Twilight Zone,' wasn't on the UK version of the LP and peaked at No.31 on its March 2 release, and its follow-up, 'Purgatory,' stalled at No.51 in June. The schedule was ferocious, non-stop through the UK during February and March, then Europe, Japan, the United States and Canada before coming back across the pond for more European dates. The band would therefore be pretty much on the road from February through to September, with more dates to follow.

But by this stage Paul Di'Anno was having major second thoughts about the whole set-up.

"I'm the kind of bloke that if my heart's not in it I won't let you down but..." he begins. "And you find other distractions, don't you? And a bloke from Peru popped up..."

The bloke from Peru he refers to is one of South America's most expensive and potentially most dangerous products: cocaine. In the official book about the band, Di'Anno is quoted as saying that his intake of the drug was more than large. But when your offstage activities begin to affect you onstage, something serious is going on. Several of the planned tour dates in Netherlands, West Germany and Scandinavia fell by the wayside during April and May. Paul's own book, *The Beast*, pulls few punches about his career and ingestion habits. It's a brutal read at times. Back to 1981, though, and Di'Anno was not feeling the project as satisfying as it had been.

"I wanted to do [Iron Maiden]," Di'Anno said in 2017 in our interview, "But I wanted to do it differently in some way. *Killers* is not a bad album at all, but for me it didn't have the spark of the first album. I know

PART ONE: **ENTER THE BEAST**

you can't repeat yourself. It was a personal thing.

"I have talked to people from Pantera, Sepultura, Metallica, people like that, and they all say the first two Maiden albums are the best they've ever heard. Metallica covered one of our songs ['Remember Tomorrow]."

The songs may have lasted, but Paul Di'Anno was not in the right frame of mind to carry on.

"I just decided to get out of there," he said. "I think Steve knew I was unhappy, being the smart bloke he is, he was making plans anyway. I wasn't pushed.

"I have got a code I live by: 'I don't want to let the band down; I don't want to let me down; I don't want to let the fans down.' Because without fans you are nothing anyway. And for me, and the band, if your heart's not in it you're not going to do the best you can. So I thought the best thing to do was to walk away, and that was it."

Online sources claim variously that Paul Di'Anno received a pay-off when he left Maiden, or alternatively that he sold the rights to his songs.

"I get PRS [Performing Rights Society] money, from airplay] three times a year, stuff like that," he says. "That's not true [that I sold them]."

Rumours were that he sold them in the 1990s...

"I sold one or two playing royalties, because me and my wife wanted to open up a bar in LA and we wanted a bit more cash coming in," he says. "But that was it. I still get royalties."

With Di'Anno out of the band, a new singer had to be installed sooner rather than later. One of the candidates for the job was apparently one Terry Slesser, a talented Geordie singer who had sung with the band Beckett. Beckett, as an aside, were one of Steve Harris' favourite bands and you are invited to check out a particular track called 'Life's Shadow' for some interest. After Beckett, Slesser released a solo album and then sang for Back Street Crawler/Crawler and briefly for Geordie, which was the band vacated by Brian Johnson when he left to join AC/DC. Some pedigree, then. An audition took place in due course, apparently when Di'Anno was actually still technically in the band. Things could have been very different had Slesser slotted in, but it wasn't to be. (Terry Slesser declined to be interviewed for this book).

Di'Anno's last gig was on September 10, 1981 in Copenhagen, Denmark. Legend has it that in the audience was a young drummer looking for inspiration for his own career. His name was Lars Ulrich, and at the time he was merely the son of a famous tennis player. A good story, if true.

Somewhat unexpectedly, at the height of their early success Iron Maiden were once more looking for a new member. This time, it was going to be a character that would help them reach levels of quality and fame that none (except maybe Steve Harris) could have expected in their wildest dreams.

IRON MAIDEN

1 BRUCE DICKINSON

The Dickinson years – part one

The story goes that at the Reading Festival, 1981, Bruce Dickinson was approached by Rod Smallwood to become Iron Maiden's new singer. In light of Dickinson's travails with management and record companies as part of Samson, it was a no-brainer. The group set about a rehearsal, and in very short order then entered the studio to double-check whether the line-up was indeed complete.

Tony Platt – who had produced Samson - recalls walking into the studio at Battery around September 1981 to an unexpected vista.

"There was Bruce, doing vocals over the top of some of their backing tracks," he recalls. "Everyone looked very sheepish because everyone knew what was going on. It put me in a very difficult position.

"Bruce is a strong character, but he's also a very, very intelligent man. If he wanted to do something he would find a way to do it."

It was a *fait accompli*: it was Bruce Dickinson who was unveiled as the new Iron Maiden singer at a series of gigs in Italy, where he could bed in without the immediate pressure of the local fans. It went superbly, and on the group's return they set about writing for a follow-up to Killers. It was to be not only Maiden's best album to date, but also a true and enduring classic of heavy metal in general.

Keith Wilfort assesses the Maiden vocalists up to that point.

"Each singer played their part in the evolution of Maiden," says the fan club maestro. "Den [Willcock] of course helped them get a start. He also brought in the theatrical side of performing. Rather than just turn up and play the show, it became a piece of musical theatre. He did get a bit carried away at times. At one point he had the band wearing Kiss-style make-up, but fortunately it didn't last long. Den, aided by Dave Lights, helped Maiden start along the path of entertaining, visually as well as musically.

"Paul [Di'Anno] came in with more of a down-to-earth cockney presentation and his voice was more melodic, whereas Den was more of a belter. Paul also had a kind of Jack-the-lad stable-boy charm which helped attract the ladies.

"Bruce on the other hand was the complete package, with an amazing voice. An incredible showman with lots of energy, he could also play a variety of instruments and knew all about theatrical presentation."

The subject matter of the songs was also to slightly change, as Platt says, tongue

PART ONE: **THE DICKINSON YEARS**

firmly in cheek.

"When he joined Iron Maiden he gave vent to his 'sword and dorkery' lyrics, as we called them," says the producer with a laugh.

That said, because of contractual wrangles, Dickinson couldn't officially write songs with the new band at the time. Hence, a few of the tracks – as legend has it, 'Run to the Hills,' 'The Prisoner' and 'Children of the Damned' - may have had his involvement, if not album credits. The new album was to be called *The Number of the Beast*, preceded by a stunning breakthrough in Maiden's sound with the iconic single, 'Run to the Hills'.

There are a few myths and stories connected with the recording sessions; gear breaking down in the studio, lights switching themselves on and off, and producer Martin Birch receiving a repair bill for £666 after a coming together between his car and a minibus. Allegedly, the bus was full of nuns too. All good stories and all good publicity for the band; the album title suggested so many opportunities to take advantage.

The first single, 'Run to the Hills', was released on February 12. The theme is about the colonisation of North America way back when, and as such is about as far away from London ladies of the night as you could probably get. Thirty years after its release, Bruce Dickinson was later to reveal that some of the melodies were inspired by watching a documentary about why the Paul Anka classic, 'My Way,' was so popular. At the time of course, no such context was offered. With its exceptional cover art of Eddie and the devil fighting whilst hordes of weird and malevolently-grinning denizens of the underworld looked on, even the way the single looked was miles away from the more claustrophobic, street-grimy Eddies of the past. A new chapter was certainly open,

and the song has become not just a Maiden classic but a true must-have in the metal canon.

It smashed into the charts, peaking at No.7, putting Maiden well and truly into the realms of serious contenders and in many ways marking the first great comeback of their career. The fact that they'd just lost one of metal's most charismatic and recognisable frontmen was absolutely overshadowed by the ambition, bombast and operatic possibilities that Bruce Dickinson's voice added to the group. And if it was true that he also had a hand in the writing, it was a statement of real intent.

The B-side was 'Total Eclipse,' a Murray/Harris/Burr number that narrowly missed sneaking onto the album (It was kept back in favour of 'Gangland'). All in all, the single gave fans the chance to get to grips with at least two tracks of the new and improved Iron Maiden before the band set off on the road again. *The Beast on the Road* was a massive undertaking, keeping the lads busy all the way from February to December 1982. It began in the UK, with the March 20 gig being recorded for a possible live release. In the event, it wouldn't see the light of day until the new millennium on either video or audio. The shebang then moved to Europe before a North American set of concerts where Maiden variously supported the likes of Scorpions, Rainbow and 38 Special over most of the rest of the spring and summer.

It was in the States that the band encountered the first pushback of their Dickinson-era career. It may seem tame in these post-modern, cynical days, but back in the early '80s it was absolutely provocative in some circles for a band to play around with imagery of the Devil. Specifically, it was the contention of certain religious

IRON MAIDEN

groups in the Deep South that the lyrics of the likes of recent second single from the album 'The Number of the Beast,' and 'Hallowed Be Thy Name' were Satanistic. There were demonstrations at several of the band's US gigs to that end, as well as special record-burning events. It was even said that some groups smashed up the records with various tools rather than run the risk of inhaling the Satanic fumes of the bonfires. Again, all good publicity and all very barmy and strange by today's standards. Still, there's nothing like a common enemy to galvanise the troops, is there?

As for the single itself, it featured another classic Riggs cover, and though it didn't quite hit the heights of 'Run to the Hills,' it still cracked the top 20, peaking at No.18. Interestingly, the B-side was a live recording of Bruce Dickinson taking on the Di'Anno-era classic 'Remember Tomorrow.' It had been recorded at a gig in Padua the previous year, mere days after Dickinson's first live concert with the band. The energy of the new singer is palpable, urging the crowd to put their hands in the air. Whilst it doesn't have the brilliance, honesty and cracked-up emotion of the Paul Di'Anno original, the more accomplished pipes of Dickinson let loose on some high-register explorations. It was a savvy move to include it; this was Maiden's statement that there may be a new singer on board, but they were still the same band that had delivered *Iron Maiden* and *Killers*. When Bruce doubles the guitar parts vocally, it's a genuinely spine-tingling moment. The band gallop along with suitable energy before settling back down into that proggy, psychedelic and melancholic verse.

Maiden returned to Europe for a trio of gigs in August, including an appearance at Reading Festival before hitting the States again; first with Scorpions and then building bridges as support to Judas Priest. In due course, the Iron Maiden juggernaut would overtake both bands.

As 1982 came to a close, Maiden headed out to Australia and then Japan.

But there was to be yet another line-up change: Clive Burr was out. The popular story has been that the talented sticksman was indulging too much in liquid refreshments, which led to him being unable to play to the standards required.

There may be more to this story, however, than meets the eye.

Mimi Burr, who was to meet Clive decades later, says that the drummer told her about what had happened.

"He was actually very ill [on the tour]," she says. "And that is why he had a bucket by the side of him whilst he was playing; it was his idea. He had alcoholic spirits behind him [whilst playing] for fun. He liked Courvoisier [brandy] and would have a sip, but he wouldn't get drunk from it. But everyone said he drank too much."

Tragically, Clive Burr lost his father during the US concerts; he flew back to be with his family in the UK.

"Clive took a call from his mum," says Mimi. "Saying his dad was seriously ill. Clive spent everything he had and got on [supersonic, and very expensive, and very fast aeroplane] Concorde and got back as soon as he could. He was worried about his mum. He drove to Germany to be with her. There was only the three of them [Clive, his mum and his dad]. I know from when my dad died that you just don't care about anything else aside from being with family. They were a very close family."

Clive Burr was fine with McBrain stepping in; there was a tour to be had after all. Nicko

PART ONE: **THE DICKINSON YEARS**

had even previously dressed up as Eddie on several dates as well as touring with Trust as support to Maiden, so his links with the band were stronger than most. He'd even played on TV as Maiden drummer on an April playback/mimed performance for Belgian telly when Clive Burr was ill; nobody noticed because McBrain was wearing an Eddie mask.

As for Trust, Nicko's last appearances with them were mid-1982 – June 5, 1982, to be exact. There has been talk that as early as June there had been contact between the Maiden management and McBrain about the possibilities of the latter replacing Burr at some stage.

Around two weeks after he'd left for the UK, Burr returned to the States to get back to the group's remaining American dates; the die, however, had seemingly already been cast.

Bruce Dickinson, in his autobiography, alluded to personality clashes between the drummer and Steve Harris, partly because of Harris' unusual time changes and fills. Burr, says Dickinson, wasn't always bang on the button with his timings, which infuriated the bassist and band-leader. Mimi Burr says that Clive Burr was very upset about the stories of his excesses being detrimental to Iron Maiden.

"He was upset that it was said that he was drinking. But he wasn't. He was given his marching orders, or as he called it 'given the tin tack.' But [what was said] was the sad thing for him."

Should you care to check out the Mick Wall-penned *Run to the Hills*, aka the official biography, you would see a quote from McBrain that alluded to the febrile and adventurous atmosphere in some of the band members' activities. Though he specifically says Harris and Dickinson were a little more sensible, he mentions that there was, on occasion, something else involved. Disco or party dust, in fact. We can probably speculate that he is deploying a euphemism for something else there. As ever, offstage antics were fine and dandy – until they affected onstage performance. To be fair to the new drummer, he also points out that he never saw any band members drink or otherwise before any actual gigs.

So that, as they say, was that. Nicko McBrain was now the drummer in Iron Maiden, and they went off immediately to write and rehearse at a hotel in Jersey called Le Chalet. Another new album was in the offing as 1982 turned into 1983.

Recording sessions took place at Compass Point Studios in Nassau, Bahamas starting in January 1983. Not a bad place to be; the official book also mentions that there were tax-related reasons. The first title of the LP was *Food for Thought*, but quickly that was junked in favour of a pun: *Piece of Mind*. Poor old Eddie was depicted being lobotomised on the cover, taking the whole thing very literally.

Maiden gave certain sections of the Satanic accusers a piece of their minds, too: the famous backwards message of nonsense that appears before 'Still Life' was a direct reaction. The first single to be taken from the album was released on April 11 and was the excellent 'Flight of Icarus.' It was the first time that fans could hear the drumming of Nicko McBrain, and also one of Adrian Smith and Bruce Dickinson's most catchy compositions to date. As a neat extra, footage of the Compass Point sessions appeared on the video. It stalled just outside the top 10 in the UK, reaching No.11, but again provided a taster for the upcoming LP.

IRON MAIDEN

The band spent the rest of 1983 on the road once more; gigs were scheduled from May through to December. During September, Dickinson suffered from a rather nasty case of bacterial bronchitis; as a singer there was nothing that could be done aside from reschedule three dates in the States.

Piece of Mind came out on May 16 and peaked at No.3 in the UK, with a great performance also in the key market of the United States where it soared to No.14. The second single was 'The Trooper,' which remains a Maiden anthem beloved by millions to this day. It hit No.12 in the UK and did pretty well with the Yanks too, climbing to No.28 in their Mainstream Rock chart. The dual-guitars are absolutely classic Iron Maiden; the Smith/Murray axis was well and truly bedded in for a band that could seemingly do no wrong. The blue touch-paper had been lit and audiences all over Europe and North America were starting to jump enthusiastically on the Maiden bandwagon.

One slightly unsavoury moment took place during the show, which has been pegged to either August 7 at Indianapolis or August 15 in Buffalo, New York. A model named Suzette Kolaga, who had won a local talent content, was crowned Ms. Heavy Metal. She was invited to appear onstage with the band, apparently during '22 Acacia Avenue.' During the performance, the model cracked a whip and had a chain and handcuffs. Her dancing with Dickinson was geared no doubt toward enhancing the atmosphere of the song. The singer, however, allegedly ripped off her top and exposed her assets. Cue a court case, with Arnold Lieberman regarding assault, warning and consent. Damages of $350,000 were sought but the case never made it to trial,

being settled out of court.

Something a little funnier, although at the time deadly serious, was an argument backstage after a show in Allentown on August 18. Something in Harris' bass set-up had developed a problem during Nicko McBrain's drum solo; the bassist asked one of the crew to let the drummer know all was not well. But the crew member couldn't get the message across, succeeding only in distracting McBrain. The drummer was furious after the event, mincing no words. Bruce Dickinson mischievously turned on a tape recorder to capture the exchange between McBrain and Harris, in which a roadie called Bob caught both barrels for not completing his mission from Steve Harris properly. Bruce Dickinson also got involved in the discussion, which ended abruptly when Harris noticed the tape running. It has become something of a legend over the years and such is the way of rock'n'roll that arguments flare up and die down incredibly quickly, especially on tour. Any band relies on brotherhood and any brothers will have arguments that can be incredibly vicious before being best mates again, literally minutes later. Iron Maiden's way of resolving this one was to listen to it once the dust had settled, and poke fun at themselves by releasing it to the world as one of the B-sides to the 12" version of their next single, '2 Minutes to Midnight'! And you can't say fairer than that. Of Bob, we know no more than this.

Eddie also came in for the boot – at the last gig of the tour in Dortmund he was finally de-brained by Bruce Dickinson. The rest of the lads took the opportunity to give the mascot a bit of a going-over themselves, Murray even going full The Who and smashing his guitar up. It had been a

PART ONE: **THE DICKINSON YEARS**

1

gruelling year; a gruelling couple of years, to be fair. Iron Maiden took a little time off to take their breath and reflect on what had been an enormous couple of years' worth of development toward one of the biggest bands in the world. The next couple of years, however, were to dwarf even that workload – and take the band to the limit.

Maiden regrouped during January 1984 in Jersey, again to write; the creative juices were in full flow and the sessions once more in Compass Point were fruitful indeed. Mixing took place in New York's Electric Lady Studios, and by August the band were ready to get back out there, with a huge tour scheduled to begin in Poland and take them around the world for no less than 11 months. The name of the album was *Powerslave* and the associated tour, *World Slavery Tour*. It began with several dates in Poland and these, allied to appearances in Hungary and Yugoslavia, meant that Maiden were taking their full show to the then-Eastern Bloc of countries semi-isolated from the rest of Europe, due to their status as satellite nations to the dominant USSR. With movement restricted and the import of music often illegal, it was difficult to get hold of any Western music at certain times, aside from on often poor-quality bootlegs. Nonetheless, the band launched into the prospect with vigour, as can be seen from the subsequent *Behind the Iron Curtain* video release, the crowds having found ways and means to learn the Maiden set. Quite the experience for all concerned. The band played in Katowice on August 14 and whilst in the vicinity had the sobering, powerful experience of visiting the Auschwitz concentration camp. Some things transcend music. Some things make the music stop entirely. For young men on the wings of a metal tour, it must have been a jarring, life-changing moment.

The lead single, released on August 6, the catchy '2 Minutes to Midnight,' was a Smith/Dickinson opus about nuclear war that hit No.11 in the UK charts. At six minutes, it was a touch on the long side for a single but packed quite a punch nonetheless. The album dropped on September 3 and included several classics; 'Aces High' became its second single, a Harris-penned tribute to the pilots of the Battle of Britain. It came out on October 22 and sneaked up to No.20 in the charts. It is a song that has lasted the eras; at many live gigs it's preceded by the 'We shall fight on the beaches' speech by Winston Churchill and opens the set. The album itself is another huge step forward for a band growing into their status as top-of-the-tree legends. The twin burst of 'Aces' and '2 Minutes' is somewhat stilled by the unnecessary 'Losfer Words (Big Orra)', but in general this is an LP packed with classics. As well as those two singles, the title track itself is one of Bruce Dickinson's best and most cinematic up to that point, over seven minutes of musings on life, death, gods, arcane Egyptian wisdom and mortality. The singer's interest in, and skill with, the sport of fencing is portrayed in 'Flash of the Blade,' a reasonable rocker. He'd also confuse many a customs official from this point on with his luggage: a full set of fencing kit, complete with swords, would accompany his usual socks and smellies. So life and art meet; the intersection of the physical and the creative. Harris also jumped on the swords-and-science trip with 'The Duellists,' and one of Maiden's multi-album update/continuing story tales followed on from *Number of the Beast* track 'The Prisoner' with 'Back in the Village.' A very good album, but it is the final song that really

IRON MAIDEN

made a statement about where Iron Maiden could take their craft.

'The Rime of the Ancient Mariner' follows the story of the Coleridge poem and also, crucially, gives a massive insight into the creative processes Steve Harris was developing. For the first time, his multi-riff, multi-tempo, multi-dynamic style was expressed in its entirety. Not so much a heavy metal song as a composed suite of music, it is musical storytelling at its absolute zenith. Nearly 14 minutes of it; but it is engrossing and extraordinary in vision, writing and delivery.

And the band played on: tour dates came thick, fast and furious; the stage-set was the most elaborate to date, with loads of Egyptian-themed props, including a mummified Eddie that harked back to the *Eddie the 'Ead* backdrop days (albeit on a slightly higher budget). It was more than a band playing gigs with the odd bit of pyrotechnics, a lumbering Eddie onstage and a few bits and bobs. Maiden set out their stall from this point onwards to provide a top-notch, visceral experience that took not only the audio but the visual side of matters to its conclusion.

However, a tragic and sad moment came at a concert in Quebec Coliseum, on November 26, 1984. An 18-year-old fan, Daniel Pitre, had managed to get into a press-only area. At the venue there were two press boxes on either side of the arena, which Pitre crossed between on a catwalk, 100 feet in the air. The young man fell over the railings to his death. Maiden only found out about the loss of life after the show had finished.

On January 11, Maiden played to the biggest crowd of their career at the Rock in Rio festival in Brazil. It was the first time the band had hit South America and an estimated 300,000 people were in attendance. Metal would find one hell of a home in South America, the fans over there going crazy for the genre.

Concerts were recorded at Hammersmith Odeon during October and at Long Beach, California in March 1985. They were released as the mighty *Live After Death* album and video, which gave Maiden a No.2 and a No.1 in the UK on their release in October 1985. The intent of the tour was to really hammer home the fact that Maiden were a force to be reckoned with. An unstoppable one, perhaps: dates kept being added at the end of the tour to try and maximise the reach of the band. But bands are made of people, of course, and people can get very burnt-out if they're pushed too far, too fast. There had already been several cancellations of January dates due to illness, with the band being patched up and getting through the incessant gigs on a mixture of memory, adrenaline and sheer bloody-mindedness. The tour finally came to an end on July 5, 1985 at Irvine Meadows Amphitheatre, California. Though Iron Maiden had played to many of their biggest crowds to date, selling out five-figure venues, it had taken its toll on all the members, who returned to their respective UK homes, as the Ancient Mariner himself might put it, sadder and wiser men. After 331 days and 187 concerts, exhaustion was the order of the day. It also set in motion a thought process previously out of the question for certain members: whether they wanted to carry on with it at all.

Two singles from *Live After Death* were released that year: live versions of 'Running Free' on September 13 (reaching No.19 in the UK) and 'Run to the Hills' on December 2, 1985 (stalling at No.26). The group were due

PART ONE: **THE DICKINSON YEARS**

to take six months off, which eventually became four, before heading down to Jersey for more writing. Bruce Dickinson had been doing some soul-searching and came to the conclusion that if he were to commit to another year-long tour it would have to be based on material he truly believed in. That didn't mean his musical explorations had been unsatisfactory so far, but more that there were many places to try and visit sonically and in terms of possibilities. The singer felt songs like 'Kashmir' or 'Stairway to Heaven' were true statements of Led Zeppelin's intent to push the boundaries and shock those with certain expectations of what the band should sound like. Dickinson had therefore been writing acoustic-based material in his down-time. However, when he brought the tracks to the band in early 1986, each was dismissed as unsuitable by his peers and producer. Though they worked on one of his tracks, none would make it to the subsequent album.

The poppier nous of Adrian Smith is much more in evidence as a result on an album that cost Maiden the most cash to record so far in their career. The drums and bass were recorded down in Compass Point; the guitars and vocals over in Wisseloord Studios in Holland; the mix was done in New York. Following the grittier *Powerslave* was always going to be an interesting endeavour, and Maiden delivered a near-concept album called *Somewhere in Time*. Rather than historical, it was futuristic; the band looking at the concept of strangeness, time, and indeed their recent history for inspiration. The record, somewhat controversially at the time for some Maiden fans, was heavily drenched with guitar synthesisers and sounds. The public in general, however, loved it: the 'Wasted Years' single came out on September 6 and hit No.18. Smith also wrote the second single, the November 22-released 'Stranger in a Strange Land.' That one – lighter on the keyboards this time and heavy on the rock riffery - got to No.22. It's an absolute stormer, folks. But it was the album as a whole that resonated with buyers, getting right up there to No.3 in the UK and an incredible performance of No.11 in the States' Billboard 200 charts. Though not a concept album, several of the songs do ponder time and space; the cover art by Derek Riggs is one of Maiden's absolute finest, too, with a kind of *Robocop/Terminator*-style Eddie as vibrant and vital (and violent-looking) as ever he was.

This time the tour was a 'mere' 156 shows, although Maiden ended up only playing 151 of those. Illness meant the Ipswich gig on October 18 was pulled, then three dates in Italy just before Christmas 1986 were similarly cancelled. Intriguingly, not all the States had come on board at this point: Beaumont, Texas was due to receive the Irons in January 1987, but ticket sales didn't match up to expectations, so that gig didn't go ahead either.

Dickinson busied himself with entering fencing competitions wherever he could find one, keeping fit and running up to five miles a day and writing his first book, *The Adventures of Iffy Boatrace*, a clunky-but-funny slapstick satire of the upper classes. He also found time to write and record some sessions with a friend of his called Jimmy Bain, bassist in the 1975-77 iteration of Rainbow. Bain then toured with Velvet Underground master John Cale and then recorded four albums with Dio. The five tracks he demoed with the Maiden frontman are said to have a kind of 1960s-'70s psychedelic vibe, somewhat akin to Procol

IRON MAIDEN

Harum. If he wasn't going to write with Maiden, the material wasn't going to stay inside either. Although nothing came of the project, it wouldn't be long before the itchy-feet frontman looked to other projects.

Somewhere on Tour rocked on; dates were even recorded, but another live album did not surface. The group were now firmly established as gods of metal, even in light of them blunting their more jagged edges on their new album. Musically it may have been slightly softer, but the lyrics of things like 'Stranger in a Strange Land,' 'Wasted Years' and 'Heaven Can Wait' all point toward a yearning for stability in the light of homesickness, illness and loss of perspective. The ripples of the *World Slavery Tour* were far from finished, it seemed. Maiden took some more time off in the latter half of 1987, reflecting on their decade so far and the rock'n'roll lifestyle. The singer himself was undergoing a sea-change in thinking, but any doubts he had at this stage didn't last long.

The reason? Steve Harris had come to him with an idea: the seventh son of a seventh son, a mystical and magical legend said to have strange and wonderful powers. The idea grew into the potential to design a story that could carry the Maiden story into progressive, conceptual territory. It re-energised everybody. The 1980s were coming to a close, and there was still a great deal of momentum within the band.

Roland Hyams and Bruce Dickinson 1995. Photo credit: Roland Hyams

Now then. In the music industry magazines and papers need to fill their pages. Bands need to get coverage to increase their visibility and therefore maximise sales and fan reach. And here is where the press agent, or press officer, comes in. A PR agent's role is simply to get the band in the press. Roland Hyams and

PART ONE: **THE DICKINSON YEARS**

his Work Hard company came on board as public relations agency for *Somewhere in Time*. Hyams had worked with luminaries including The Rolling Stones, The Who, Slade, The Cult, Ozzy Osbourne and The Stranglers prior to being employed by the Iron Maiden camp, and as such was someone with the pedigree, experience and contacts within the media to further the cause. He says that his role was defined very clearly from the outset. He had certainly made a fast impression on the Irons' manager, for one.

"Maiden, WASP and [comedy *Comic Strip* rock band] Bad News did a show at Manchester Odeon," recalls Hyams. "I got a spread; a whole load of coverage for Bad News in the *Daily Mirror*. Rod Smallwood was like, 'Who the hell got all of this? Maiden are head-lining and the support acts are getting more press than us!"

Smallwood invited Hyams to come on board the good ship Iron Maiden as their press representative. Hyams reads from one of his pieces of work, a campaign breakdown for the *Music Week* awards. The stakes were getting higher and higher.

"1988 saw Iron Maiden move into Supergroup status," he says. "Partly as a result of the press campaign. Chart success is due to a number of factors: every part of the jigsaw puzzle has to fit in place. Every area had to be exploited in terms of press coverage. While Iron Maiden had continued to attain large-scale coverage in the traditionally heavy metal music publications such as *Sounds*, *Kerrang!* and *Metal Hammer* and so on, neither the popular magazines or Fleet Street papers had ever focused on Maiden, so my objective was to break the band in those areas.

"And, basically, that's just what I did. I got them in the *Daily Express*, we got the front cover of *NME*, we had [multiple] full-page features in the *Mirror*, the *Star*, lead story Bizarre in the *Sun*. *News of the World* with a readership of about 13 million... I moved them much more into the mainstream of the media stage."

Seventh Son of a Seventh Son was recorded at Musicland Studios in Munich from February to March 1988. First single, 'Can I Play With Madness' was a huge hit, reaching No.3 in the UK charts after its March 20 release. The album came out on April 11, straight in at No.1, and going gold on the day of release, with sales of over 100,000. That crossover from metal magazines to the mainstream media should not be underestimated: it wasn't just the kids with skulls on their shirts that were aware of Iron Maiden. The band were also in the newspapers and Sunday magazines that their parents were reading. Given that these parents' own musical references were more than likely coming from the late '60s through to the mid-'70s, the connections with Purple, Beckett, Sabbath et al started to bridge the generation gap too. The very savvy Roland Hyams saw a whole lot of opportunities to give Maiden a real boost.

"The national newspapers hardly covered music at all, hardly covered rock at all," says Hyams. "Unless it was the big boys: The Rolling Stones, The Police, et cetera. They were bands I started off working for in 1981 [...] so I had made a ton of contacts across the board. I had a hell of a lot of current national newspaper contacts [in 1988] which I don't think had ever probably been approached, or certainly exploited, much before in-house with EMI [publicity department]. What I brought to the table as well as contacts was the ability to think

IRON MAIDEN

1

outside the box."

And thinking outside the box in those days, he adds, included some great ideas plus one hell of a lot of blagging and brass balls, too.

"A good scam was one where you could set up a story and fool everybody," he declares. "Even sometimes in conjunction with [the publication]. You would make up a story that *could not be disproved*. You make the odd white lie up. I was rather well-known for doing that."

Hyams laughs as he recalls one particular example.

"Ozzy Osbourne shaved his hair off entirely. Went bald. We put the story out that he had shaved his hair off to become a Buddhist monk and go missing! That was picked up by the *Daily Mail*. In actual fact, [his hair] had been permed and teased so much that it got too dry and brittle and had to be cut off!"

The band, Hyams says, were back then and still are down-to-earth, great guys. That said, his job was to find ways to sustain their profile at a high level.

"They have never changed [as people]. The change was purely in terms of exploiting their strengths as characters, their hobbies and stuff, to give them a national profile that they hadn't had before. Bruce used to fly journalists to gigs in the South of France, Nicko also used to fly, then there was Bruce's fencing, Steve playing football. He was mates with Gary Bushell from Sounds and later *The Sun* and both are West Ham fans, so we ended up with a feature down at West Ham's ground with Steve and footballers. That puts a band onto the mainstream map, doesn't it? And that is my job.

"You get to know your band and management as well, chuck ideas about. The more you know a band, the more you know about what angles you have got in your arsenal to use."

Meanwhile, the second single from the album was another cracker, 'The Evil that Men Do.' This one reached No.5 in the UK charts on its August 1 release.

This time, the *Seventh Tour of a Seventh Tour* was a relatively user-friendly jaunt of 'only' 105 gigs (102 of which went ahead; others fell victim to illness and poor sales). The band were more prone to doing their own thing between gigs now, building on the exhausting previous tours and taking advantage of bringing family members with them where possible, having more days off

PART ONE: **THE DICKINSON YEARS**

and enjoying activities outside of the music. Maiden even found the time to play a secret gig (as 'Charlotte and the Harlots') at none other than Bruce Dickinson's alma mater, Queen Mary University in London. That was a warm-up for their headlining performance on August 20 at Monsters of Rock 1988.

The festival at Castle Donington sadly also had a tragic element. At the time, one of the most rapidly-rising acts in rock/metal were Guns N' Roses, a sleazy Los Angeles act with oodles of attitude and a massive hit with 'Sweet Child o' Mine' under their belts. The estimated 107,000 crowd were in fully excited mode during the set of GNR - but there was simply not enough room. The issues were compounded due to the fact that in those days the stage was at the bottom of a slope, creating a natural amphitheatre. A decent enough idea when things are dry and sunny, but when mud and bad weather is involved it is a recipe for disaster. There had been several days of rain before the festival and the ground was slippery. A crush ensued and two young men lost their lives in the dreadful conditions. No announcement was made until after the bands had all played. Since then, stages have been generally flat with the crowd and a significant space between the performers and the audience has been created as a safe zone; the floor underfoot, particularly closer to the stage, is more often than not covered in non-slip material; increased security and safety staff are also on hand, as are paramedics. And whilst those large spaces between the bands and the crowds can seem impersonal, nobody should go to a gig and end up hurt or worse.

Maiden would release one more *Seventh Son* single, 'The Clairvoyant (live).' It, like its B-sides, was taken from recordings of the band's headlining Donington performance and peaked at No.6 in the UK. The tour ended back at good old Hammersmith Odeon on December 12, 1988, after which all concerned were scheduled to take a well-earned year off from all Iron Maiden activities.

All the band members apparently had an option in their EMI deal for a solo record. Adrian Smith busied himself with the ASAP group, which had grown out of a previous knockabout involving Nicko McBrain and others, named The Entire Population of Hackney. The guitarist had been writing songs constantly over the years and was more than aware what would – and what wouldn't – work for Iron Maiden. The subsequent album, *Silver and Gold*, also featured Smith's accomplished soft-rockish vocals. The band toured throughout 1989 but didn't pick up as much traction as was hoped. Bruce Dickinson, too, had kept busy with fencing activities and taking the opportunity to write a song for the soundtrack of a horror movie, *Nightmare on Elm Street 5: The Dream Child*. Dickinson enlisted old mate Janick Gers, previously of White Spirit and Gillan, as a writing partner and guitarist. The song was 'Bring Your Daughter... To the Slaughter,' a very silly, very catchy piece of metal singalong tongue-in-cheek gore. It went down so well that Dickinson was offered the chance to make a solo album. Gers and Dickinson set to work with great glee and the album was released in 1990.

Steve Harris, meanwhile, was in his newly-installed home suite working on the edit for what would become the *Maiden England* video, recorded during the *Seventh Tour* at two gigs in Birmingham's National Exhibition Centre. The video came out on

IRON MAIDEN

1

November 8, 1989, two days after a single was released; 'Infinite Dreams (live)', which got to No.6 in the UK charts at its height.

After the bombast and hugeness of recent tours, stage sets and album productions, a decision was taken by Steve Harris to get back to the spirited sound of the earlier days. The new Maiden album therefore was to be recorded much quicker (and presumably cheaper) and have rougher edges about it. Pre-production and writing sessions took place in Harris' barn at his Essex mansion in early to mid-1990, but the pace of matters and the lo-fi response were far from satisfactory as far as one person was concerned.

Adrian Smith left the band after 10 years, disillusioned with the way Maiden were looking to follow up on one of their most ambitious albums of the decade. Incoming? One Janick Gers, whose spikier style was a lot more in the vein of what Harris envisaged for the new LP. Smith's only contribution to the new album was a co-write with Dickinson, a sort-of-follow-up to the Charlotte story called 'Hooks in You.' He was to step away from music almost entirely for several years.

As for Maiden, things moved fairly quickly once Gers was on board, with The Rolling Stones' mobile studio installed to record the antics of the band in the barn during June to September 1990. The LP was indeed rougher than its three predecessors, to the extent that it wasn't a concept-based LP. It sounded much harsher, Dickinson's voice taking on an odd raspy growl and in general retreating into the safer ground of *Killers*-era writing and performance. Michael Kenney gets a credit on keyboards, but *No Prayer for the Dying* was the weakest album the band had produced for 10 years. Something subtle and slinky had been lost with the departure of Adrian Smith, not least in the interplay and almost psychic link with Dave Murray. Gers is a fine guitarist indeed, but stylistically of course no two axemen are the same. What had Maiden done?

To start with, they'd released an LP that was tense to the point of aggression. First single, 'Holy Smoke,' came out on September 10, 1990 and was one of the more light-hearted videos the band had done. The group looked relaxed and happy, new guitarist Gers seeming like he'd always been there. Directed by Steve Harris, it certainly resonated with record buyers, peaking at No.3 in the charts. Maiden immediately went on tour to promote it, with another year-long set of gigs in store. They would be supported variously by Anthrax, The Almighty, King's X and the rapidly-rising Wolfsbane, whose Rick Rubin-produced debut had just come out to excellent response. With the charisma and dark good looks of singer Blaze Bayley up front, Wolfsbane bridged the gap between Maiden's fanbase and followers of the many groups that the Irons had inspired.

The album scored the band a No.2 position in the UK charts and was also to bring the very greatest of gifts during the Christmas break. Dickinson's *Nightmare on Elm Street* track had by this time been co-opted by Harris for Iron Maiden, and thus 'Bring Your Daughter... To The Slaughter' was released on Christmas Eve, 1990. This was a stroke of genius by the management, because it was never going to dislodge the actual Christmas number one with sales. However, the week after the big event was always traditionally a slightly

PART ONE: **THE DICKINSON YEARS**

lower sales priority for industry. 'Slaughter' was released on several different formats, all of which at the time were chart-eligible. With a judicious campaign and the fans mobilised more than ever before to make it happen, the track, Iron Maiden-style, claimed the final No.1 of the year in the charts released on 30 December. What a way to end the first year of the '90s.

Roland Hyams remembers writing press information about the album that truly bigged up the band he was promoting.

"*No Prayer for the Dying*, the first new release in two and a half years," he read from his press release, "Marks Iron Maiden's entry into the 1990s with the energy level on an all-time high [... it] combines intelligent lyrics with a fearsome musical assault to strike fear into the would-be aspirants to the Maiden throne."

Hyams also made reference to the darker tone of the LP.

"There was the acknowledgement that it was a heavy album," he reflects, adding that the national newspapers were still firmly on board. "We got resoundingly good reviews in the music press. I don't recall getting crap reviews for Maiden, ever."

The album came out on the cusp of what was to be the Grunge explosion: a stripped-down, more introspective (i.e. whiney little white boys) variant of Punk. The world, it seemed, was ready for less bombastic, ambitious conceptual stuff and keen to get back to the visceral thrills of distorted guitars and energetic, often downbeat in-your-face-songs. In that respect, Harris was absolutely bang on the button. Live-wise, Janick bedded in very quickly with a quick Milton Keynes secret show which the boys played under the name of 'The Holy Smokers.' As an onstage force, Gers was an absolute dervish who brought an energy to the outfit that really did have an effect on the motivation of the group. *No Prayer on the Road* was a way more straightforward set-up in terms of staging; jeans and T-shirts more the order of the day for the band than silly trousers and stage-wear.

The tour ended in April 1991 after a successful visit to Asia, including well-received gigs in Japan. Maiden also played the famous Roskilde festival in Denmark that June, before a few extra dates followed in Europe in September. Meanwhile, Harris had upgraded his barn to a more permanent recording facility, installing the requisite equipment and tidying up the scruffy edges. No more mobile trucks going forward for the band, but they did now have their own space in which to play. Harris would co-produce with Martin Birch, who would

IRON MAIDEN

retire following the project.

As positive a note as a new facility was, the results to come out of the writing and recording process were some of the most depressing and downhearted songs the band had ever put out. The title track of the new album has become a classic of Maiden's oeuvre, and rightly so, but in context with the career of the band and the musical movements of the day it brings absolutely nothing new to the table for anybody. That said, it did bring the band their third UK No.1 in the album charts, so fans were still as committed as ever to the cause. Janick Gers collaborated on five tracks, his writing debut with Maiden.

"Lyrically, Maiden have moved away from songs about history, films and books," Hyams says. "Writing more about contemporary topics relevant to today."

Business, ecology, war and AIDS were the order of the day, although something like 'From Here to Eternity' still brought the epic to the release. Derek Riggs also wasn't the illustrator: Melvyn Grant provided a malevolent tree sprite entirely in keeping with the title of the album: *Fear of the Dark*. The whole vibe was menacing and paranoid, the sound harsher with Gers on board, and sonically miles better than the rough-arsed *No Prayer*. But were Maiden treading water? Grunge was a true phenomenon in 1992.

"The mainstream game changed," says Hyams, referring to grunge bands like Nirvana, Soundgarden, Pearl Jam et al that were starting to take off. "But we always used to say, and it still stands today, that other musical trends may come and go but you will always, always have metal going on regardless. Rock and metal bands still buy tickets and albums, no matter what trends were going on.

"The biggest bands with grunge were massive across the board; they were selling 20 million albums, having huge top 10 hits which were radio hits. That was getting the other 18 million people who weren't buying metal to buy records.

"But there were still two million who were buying Maiden and never stopped doing so."

The first single from the album was 'Be Quick or Be Dead.' Gers and Dickinson provided three and a half minutes' worth of fast-heavy metal which reached No.2 in the UK. The album came out in May 1992 and despite mixed reviews again hit the top spot. After a quick warm-up gig, this time in Norwich under the moniker 'The Nodding Donkeys,' Maiden started the *Fear of the Dark* tour in splendid Reykjavik, Iceland on June 5 before heading to North and then South America, returning to Europe for August and September, back out to the US and Canada and finally visiting Australia, New Zealand and Japan to finish things off. The old Satanist nonsense reared its head, though, with a planned show in Chile being cancelled at the behest of a church idiot or two. Still, there was a glimmer of brilliance for Maiden fans when Adrian Smith joined the band onstage for their headlining encore at Monsters of Rock. The band's performance had been recorded and was put out the next year both as an album and a video. In order to avoid burnout, the *Fear of the Dark* tour was designed to have a decent two-month break in the middle for people to recuperate and to allow Harris to work on several shows' worth of material to compile a duo of live albums.

The news that came was also to shock the world of metal: Bruce Dickinson would be leaving the band.

PART ONE: **THE DICKINSON YEARS**

Dickinson had been working on solo material and was committed to it, to the extent that he was no longer feeling that Maiden were the be-all-and-end-all. Rod Smallwood duly communicated the news to the rest of the band, who briefly thought about packing it in entirely. But Iron Maiden were not the sort of folks to let something like losing a singer drag them down. After all, Bruce Dickinson was the fourth vocalist the group had had since 1975. Paul Mario Day, Dennis Willcock, Paul Di'Anno – all had been ousted from or left the band over the years, and the juggernaut kept on going. Why should it be any different this time?

The thorny issue was that the second part of the tour had already been booked and many gigs were already sold out. What was known as the *Real Live Tour* ran from March 1993 to August and was one of the group's least satisfying ventures to date. The atmosphere was down, the singer was on his way out, accusations of sub-par performances by Dickinson were flying, and all in all it was a pretty horrible experience for everybody. A flavour of the *Fear gigs* can be had by listening to the *Real Live One* and *Real Dead One* albums respectively, which were released in early 1993. It had always been planned thus, but with Dickinson's imminent departure the LPs took on an entirely new hue of finality.

And it was with finality that Bruce Dickinson played his last gigs on August 27 and 28 at Pinewood Studios. The latter show became a circus (purposefully). Magician Simon Drake was brought on board for an entirely cheesy and quite ridiculous performance that involved the onstage 'death' of Dickinson; the concert was broadcast live in the United States and later made available on video. *Raising Hell* is its name, and you may seek it at your leisure.

Long-time Maiden expert and fan club boss Keith Wilfort speculates on another reason that Bruce Dickinson may have decided to go his own way.

"I was not at all happy when I heard Bruce was leaving, along with many others," he says. "I don't think the marathon tours were too much of a factor.

"I think it was more a case of a power struggle, with Bruce and Steve pulling in opposite directions. Bruce wanted to explore wider directions whereas Steve had a set idea of what Iron Maiden was about, and it was his band. Steve would listen to fresh ideas, but the bottom line was that he (Steve) had the final say and management would back him up.

"Bruce wanted to try new things that didn't fit in with the established Maiden pattern, and when he released his solo material and toured with it and began writing, he felt he didn't have artistic and personal freedom within the Maiden set-up, so decided to quit. There were some nasty things said on both sides in the heat of the moment, with the truth somewhere in the middle."

One infamous interview was conducted by a journalist during that second half of the *Fear/Live* tour. After much badgering, the story goes, the writer managed to get Nicko McBrain in an off-guard moment; frustrated, the drummer laid right into the soon-to-be-former singer. No punches were pulled and the annoyance was evident. But it wouldn't change the fact that after 11 years as frontman for the biggest metal band in the world, Dickinson had jumped ship and gone solo. And Maiden were looking for a new singer. What now?.

IRON MAIDEN

1 BLAZE BAYLEY

Blazing In

Pretty much as soon as Rod Smallwood had told the band of Bruce Dickinson's decision to leave, plans were put in place. The band put the call out for demo tapes – and boy, did they get some tapes, with 2,000 cassettes received and each one listened to by the Maiden camp. It was – and remains – the prime job for any rock singer in the world. And from worldwide the tapes duly came. After months of gruelling listening, a shortlist was formed of 16. This was whittled down to three vocalists, who were invited to come to Maiden Central and sing a bunch of songs with the band at their studio.

One of those was Wolfsbane vocalist Blaze Bayley, who remembers it very well.

"I auditioned just like everybody else," he recalls. "The only advantage I had over a lot of other people was that I'd actually given Maiden our album, so they had a CD from Wolfsbane [that I gave them on tour]. Over a thousand singers sent in demos – for the biggest job in my field, the top job I could get - the singer in what I consider to be the greatest heavy metal band in the world."

Bayley went to the Maiden studio, sang 10 songs with the band and says he thought to himself, 'Well, at least for that hour I was in Iron Maiden.' Which for many millions of fans in itself would have been a dream come true, no doubt about it. But better news was to follow.

"I did the best I could, didn't make too many flops and was invited back for another audition in a [recording] studio to see what it would be like. And it worked out. I got the phone call asking me to come to a meeting, because I'd got the job.

"It was the start of an absolutely incredible journey; an amazing five years of doing what I had been doing with Wolfsbane at the highest possible level."

Roland Hyams, PR at the time, remembers putting out a press release announcing the new singer to the world.

"It was December 21, 1993," says Hyams, who adds that Harris said they'd chosen Blaze on merit as he was the best available, not just because he had been on tour with them. The press release at the time praised the new singer's skills and said the band would be straight down to business to write a brand-new album that would be released in the autumn of 1994.

"There had been an enormous amount of rumours [and speculation] about the new singer," Hyams said. "Rod's mindset has always been, 'Get the media, get the press.'"

64 THIS DAY IN MUSIC'S GUIDE TO **IRON MAIDEN**

PART ONE: **BLAZING IN**

As for Bayley, he uses the metaphor of going from a non-league football team to the England squad to try and describe how big a jump it was in his (or anyone's) career.

"You are in the England squad," he adds. "And you are expected to win. Without fail. All the interviews, everything that goes with that. It is a big job. The thing that really kept me going, more than anything else, was the music, which was fantastic. I love the music."

And so Iron Maiden – now with a line-up of Harris-Murray-McBrain-Gers-Bayley – set about writing and recording their 10th album. It was 1994 and the world had changed.

That was a sustaining force; the classic songs, the Blaze-written songs, to a rabid fanbase.

"I had so much support and encouragement from so many fans. It was absolutely fantastic," Bayley says. "Of course, there were fans that hated me and wanted Bruce to come back. It was a shame for those fans. They just could not face the fact that he wanted to leave, [that he felt he] had to go and do something else. In the most ridiculous way there was a small percentage of fans who were very loud on the Internet who blamed me for Bruce leaving!

"I would often say to Steve, 'I don't see how he could leave this.' The fans were so loyal, the reactions that you got live. It was incredible to think, but Bruce had his own situation to sort out. Mentally I think he was in a really different place then and needed space to sort that. I think he had been swallowed, really, by Iron Maiden, and was going through an identity crisis. He had to go and find out who Bruce Dickinson was as a person and an artist outside of Iron Maiden. And he did that. It provided me with this incredible opportunity and every minute of it I just loved."

Bayley had some bad luck, however, when he was involved in a serious motorcycle accident on what he now calls, wryly, 'the Friday I wish I'd stayed at home.' His Triumph bike collided with a car; Bayley was seriously injured, and the consequent recovery affected everything.

"I was lucky that the band stuck with me and gave me time to heal up. They had a choice of great singers, I'm sure. Four or five who would have fitted in just as well as me. But they stuck by me as I was already signed up and we made a go of it. The songs that we came up with worked really well, the music was great, and I got through it."

Hyams sent a missive out to the press accordingly, as he recalls.

"It was October 4, 1994," he begins, before explaining that Bayley had suffered a smashed kneecap coming around a bend and coming together with a car driving on the wrong side of the road. His knee needed rebuilding in an operation; Bayley had kicked away the bike so as not to be crushed or burnt by the exhaust pipe but was grateful to be still alive. There was still plenty of time for the singer to recover before the planned 1995 tour began.

As to the album, *The X Factor* was its name. Despite the injury, the LP was not delayed: Blaze Bayley had been driven to the studio, leg in splint, to put down his vocals. But even that is a story in itself, for the keen PR agent.

"If you have any newsworthy event you've got to milk it," laughs Hyams, only slightly with tongue in cheek. "I am a publicist; that is what I do. My job is to keep my bands in the press as much as possible." The music business being what it is, however, Hyams

IRON MAIDEN

was, as he says, 'shafted' by an editor in a certain now-defunct music magazine who'd promised a double-page spread but delivered only a couple of paragraphs. The editor in question simply didn't rate the new singer, the publicist says, and so Hyams' tenure was over.

"I don't blame Rod, it's just how it goes. We were trying to launch Blaze, and we get this two-fucking-paragraph [piece]. By the end of 1994 I was just working with Bruce [Dickinson]." (You can read more on the adventures of Bruce, Roland et al in the relevant solo section, rat-fans.)

The X-Factor was preceded by a stormer of a single, the Bayley-Gers collaboration, 'Man on the Edge.' Take a look at the video and then ponder as to whether Bayley had the right stuff to lead Maiden into a new era. Simply put, he is full of dark charisma, giving it everything as the band rampages behind him. Were the vocals a little better-processed and richer-sounding, it would be an absolute classic. Sonically, though, the space was crowded by over-loud, over-wide guitars. (Maybe Tony Platt should have produced it?) As a song, though, it's a winner that's part-Maiden and has shades of Motörhead about it at times. It reached No.10 in the charts on September 25. Cleverly, Maiden included several new songs on the various versions, including an 11-minute interview with Bayley cut into two parts. (That's the interview cut into two parts. Bayley had escaped that fate.)

"A lot of fans struggled to listen to [this and the next] album," says Bayley. "Because the sound was so different when it came out. They struggled to feel it was an Iron Maiden album. My voice is so different to Bruce's that the songs we did were different, so fans had a big adjustment to make."

The aptly-named The X-Factour began in September 1995, unusually for Iron Maiden with gigs in Israel and South Africa. The band then traversed Europe until February 1996 when they hit the States once more. Another single was released, the Gers-Harris 'Lord of the Flies,' albeit not in the UK.

The writing possibilities engendered by Iron Maiden's stature gave Bayley an opportunity to really explore his creative vision, he says.

"Lyrically I had a new lease of life, because I knew Maiden had fought all of their battles with producers and record companies. Steve Harris said to me that there was no music written for The X-Factor and he didn't care who wrote the songs. They just had to be fucking great.

"That really opened the door and I brought a lot of ideas. Steve, Janick, everybody was really open to listening to my ideas and five of mine are on the album. It's good to be able to write about literature, about books, World War I poems to reinterpret the ideas of, musically as well. When I was in Wolfsbane one producer said to me, 'Do you have to have that word, "apparition" in the song?' I said, 'Well, yeah. It's a reference to Shakespeare, to Hamlet. When you read the lyric to the song and wonder what 'an apparition hot from hell' is, you are going to read Hamlet and realise it is his father's ghost. He is talking about something much deeper [...] the visions on our TV screens aren't real. It is a representation, an apparition. In Maiden you could use everything you wanted. You could say apparition! I never had an argument [like that]. Does it make sense? Musically, is it right?

"In Maiden you never thought there was a lyric or a subject you couldn't touch. You

PART ONE: **BLAZING IN**

just had to do it well. It's not just about the lyric and the melody, the journey continues with the music. So if it takes two and a half minutes to tell that story, like 'Futureal' or 12 minutes in 'Sign of the Cross', that is how long it takes to take you on that journey."

Maiden's journey continued with the release of *Best of the Beast* in September 1996. As the title suggests, it was a compilation album which featured tracks culled from *the Number of the Beast* up to date. It also included brand-new track, 'Virus,' which was also released as a single. The three different formats available included gems of B-sides: the two *Metal for Muthas* songs and, on the vinyl, 'Prowler' and 'Invasion' from ancient history's *Soundhouse Tapes*. There were also cover versions of songs by The Who and UFO to complete the whole caboodle. The song itself pulled few punches, aiming at back-stabbers, two-faced people, liars and those who would smile and shake you by the hand whilst plotting to stab you in the back. It is a collaboration between Bayley, Murray, Gers and Harris, and in its four-minute edited form is a taut, tight piece of work. The longer, six-minute original includes the more mellow moments of the introduction, which doesn't add a great deal (the mix is off again and Blaze is underneath guitars again). A non-album track for the first time since the 'Women in Uniform' debacle, but this one is sung brilliantly by Blaze. There are even relatively rare Bayley-era harmony vocals to be had. Not too bad a distraction before a new album was released. The group took several months off before getting back together in Harris' house for writing sessions.

The result was a new LP which was to be called *Virtual XI*, a nod to the fact it was Maiden's 11th album, plus the fact that release year was 1998 – a World Cup year – and also to tie in with the *Ed Hunter* computer game. All very grand and very well-thought out, but Blaze Bayley points out that despite having had time off to consider ideas and arrangements, there was a bit of a rush to get things done on this one, much as there had been with *The X-Factor*.

"The albums, particularly *Virtual XI*, if there had been a little more time in rehearsal, would have been significantly better," confirms Bayley. "'The Angel and the Gambler' – the video version – is great. But the album version is just not right. If we'd have had to stand there in rehearsals going through that song a few times, then as a group we would have together come to the conclusion that it's just not worth it. Let's make it shorter! I do that song now in my set-list, and it's much closer to the video version. Fans absolutely love it. Maiden haven't done it since I left, but it goes down great.

"Rehearsing in the room, living with those songs for just another couple of weeks, would have improved *Virtual XI*. Having said that, you can't improve 'The Clansman.' It means so much. It is just great. A fantastic song and part of the legend."

Indeed, the album has many high points, not least the two tracks the singer name-checks there.

The first single to come from *Virtual XI* was the thankfully-edited 'The Angel and the Gambler.' In its four-minute form, it's a kinda space-cowboy-undead mid-paced and somewhat menacing piece of work. It reached No.18 in the UK charts; the nine-minute version tested the patience of many fans. Bayley's performance is on the controlled side rather than really letting loose – it's a good performance by all

IRON MAIDEN

concerned, rather than an exceptional one.

Luckily, 'Futureal' is an absolute zinger, Bayley and Harris working together to deliver an absolute classic. Three minutes of high octane metal/rock, it stands up with 'The Clansman' as two of Blaze Bayley's absolutely greatest Maiden moments. Listen to it. Do it now! It will be in your head for days. It was a single on September 28, 1998. In light of what was to shortly happen, however, its lyrics about running short on time and wondering what, indeed, was real in the light of some kind of identity loss were ominous to say the least. But it's a Blaze song: other singers' attempts at it just don't have the same personality or force.

As ever, Maiden toured the hell out of their new album, and as had become customary, there was a secret warm-up gig. This time it was in the heart of Alan Partridge-land, specifically the Oval Rock House in Norwich. The band this time took the *nom de guerre* The Angel and the Gamblers for the occasion. History records that not only were seven of the new album tracks debuted that day (April 22) but also that there was a very rare performance of 'Murders in the Rue Morgue,' which the lads hadn't attempted since 1984. The tour cracked on through Europe until the end of May, before heading to North America once more.

It was in America, however, that Bayley suffered health issues which led to the cancellation of several gigs. The combination of a severe dust and/or pollen allergy with the relentless, giving-it-everything nature of Iron Maiden's near-two-hour sets meant the singer was – well – a man on the edge. Eventually, if you hammer the guitar strings too much, one will snap. It is simple physics. If the voice is the instrument, and furthermore you are straining that instrument to reach the higher register required for some of the back-catalogue, things are bound to go west at some stage. Eleven concerts were cancelled in the final count. Of the 94 originally planned, only 83 went ahead.

Blaze Bayley says that the two albums he did with Maiden have benefitted from remastering. In recent years, there has been something of a reappraisal of those LPs.

"Of course, when you've got a favourite artist and you play them all the time," the affable singer says. "In the end you are going to have played them to death. So then you are only left with the album that you haven't played to death. And if that's *The X-Factor* you have to go back and listen.

"At a distance, away from the emotions and Bruce leaving, you can listen to it as an album of music songs. That's when you can start really going into it and thinking, 'Wow, 'Judgement of Heaven', that's really special, and 'Sign of the Cross' has got a lot more to it, and 'Blood on the World's Hands', wow. That is a lyric that's happening today, 20-odd years later.'"

During our 2017 interview, Blaze Bayley wryly noted that he experienced on more than one occasion people approaching him with a certain angle.

"They come up to me and say, 'The last

Credit: Keith Wilfort

PART ONE: BLAZING IN

time I saw you was 22 years ago.' And I'm, 'Well. I've done 10 albums since then. Toured all over the world. And now you come to see me? Where were you?

"People say I was the first singer they saw, that *The X-Factor* was their first Iron Maiden album. It's still taken them until now to start thinking, 'Maybe I'll go and see him live.' People do look back differently."

Ultimately, it's all about what the fans think, Bayley says. The Brummie vocalist gives a typically sharp-eyed insight into the machinations of the industry then, and presumably now, too.

"It's not about journalists or people at the record company's ideas," he notes, sagely. "It is the people who have invested in music – the fans who have spent their own money on it. They actually know what a good album is, because they have bothered to listen to it and find out if it was good. They didn't just spin it once and say, 'Oh, there's no hooks in there,' or, 'I can't hear a single,' [which] back in the day record companies used to say. Or, 'Can you change the title so that when people go to the record shop it'll be easier for the sales assistant to find the song.'"

SMH, as the young people say these days.

Despite the relative strength of *Virtual XI* taken on its own merits, the prevailing winds were to blow hard and harsh on the singer and the band he fronted. There were many reasons that Blaze Bayley was asked to leave Iron Maiden, he recalls.

"Well, the first thing was that we were up against grunge," he recalls. "Secondly, the record industry had foolishly ignored [file-sharing site] Napster. They had a chance to buy Napster and buy that technology but they did not. They pooh-poohed it and said Napster gave [music] away to everybody [for free]. Suddenly, there we were with downloads."

The significance of Napster being outlawed rather than embraced sent enormous shockwaves through the traditional ways of record sales. Now, anyone with a decent Internet connection could connect with other fans and share their music for free. The sounds had been freed from their previous adherence to the substrate, be it tape, vinyl, CD, whatever, and the songs could be digitised once and shared millions of times. The genie was firmly out of the bottle and despite several high-profile lawsuits by bands, including Metallica, file-sharing was here to stay. It's the equivalent of one person buying an album, then copying it onto tape for their friends, except now the friends could be worldwide and online. With broadband getting ever-faster and more ubiquitous, downloading albums and songs for free also changed a key concept of art, in a capitalist society at least: suddenly it was not important that the creators of the work (and their appointed agents, like record labels) were actually paid. The songs had become divorced from their creators, and the upshot was that the idea of paying for music was becoming old-fashioned. A tricky time.

On the other hand, if the traditional industry had been savvy enough, they would have realised that actually digital delivery of music direct to people's computers/iPods/ whatever was the way forward. Rather than battling Napster, if they'd bought into it, they may have managed to stave off the crisis in the industry that absolutely destroyed the old way of working. Blaze Bayley, as a highly-intelligent and extremely technology-oriented chap, knows what he's talking about here, and then some. Allied to this

IRON MAIDEN

macro-economic mess, he says, Maiden's UK record company made another not-so-wise decision around the same time.

"EMI sold off all their manufacturing division," Bayley analyses. "So that was everywhere that made a CD or cassette tape or pressed an album. They just sold it all. Everything. So you knew what was coming. By the end of my second album with Maiden, CD sales had gone down so much that the whole industry was starting to worry."

What also happened was groups that you might call 'legacy bands' started popping up out of the woodwork; Deep Purple and Black Sabbath reunited, as did Judas Priest, to great response from fans. The filip in back-catalogue sales got record company brains crunching at the gears... if those old bands could do it, maybe that was the business model to save their arses.

"They were all successful," Bayley notes. "And so the pressure came on Iron Maiden to have a reunion [with Bruce Dickinson]. It's not something that Steve [Harris] really wanted, but in the end I think the survival of the band really depended on that."

Musically and lyrically the band and Bayley had been thinking about new material for another album together. He is in no doubt that had things been different, the momentum was there within Maiden to kick things up another notch.

"The songs I had for that third album would really turn things around for us and make the fans believe we were the New Era of Iron Maiden. But I didn't get the chance to do that. My song ideas got used on [Blaze's subsequent solo record], *Silicon Messiah*.

"So that was it. Pressure was put on; I think Bruce was ready. Mentally I think he was in the right place that he could appreciate the good parts of what being the singer of Iron Maiden has to offer, and cope better with the less attractive parts.

"So Bruce came back and that was it. I had to leave. I was out.

"They took care of me very well; I've got no complaints at all about the way it was done. But it left me in the situation where for the first time since I started [my career], I wasn't in a band anymore. That was very, very scary to think about and was very difficult."

Bruce Dickinson was back – and so was Adrian Smith. Maiden now had three guitarists to consider, a vocalist that had been exploring music and life outside of the tight-knit Irons camp, and an upcoming new millennium to contend with.

PART ONE: **BRUCE IS BACK**

BRUCE DICKINSON, PART TWO

1

Bruce is back

Iron Maiden's career since 2000 has been ever-so-slightly different in approach. Time between albums has lengthened (as have the songs), there have been several legacy tours celebrating classic albums and reminding fans old and new of their glorious days, and the availability of Maiden goods has blasted outside the realms of audio, video, T-shirts and badges to a host of other collectibles, including of course their own brand/s of booze. Oh, and the small matter of touring the world in their own chartered aeroplanes – piloted by their frontman.

All of that to come, pop/nose-pickers. Back to 1999 we must first go...

The first thing that the now six-piece Iron Maiden had to tackle was the relatively short – almost invisible by their own standards – *Ed Hunter* tour. The band's computer game also came with a compilation album, and thus the setlist was always going to be a classic one.

Interestingly, the actual songs played were suggested by the fans themselves after an Internet poll was conducted. The dates began in Canada before moving to the United States, where three gigs at the end of July and start of August were cancelled after Dave Murray broke his little finger. As Murray was the one consistently-present axeman in the trio, his parts couldn't be quickly re-learnt by either Gers or Smith. Indeed, Smith himself wasn't able to play in three other gigs after losing his father and flying home to be with his family. Maiden were briefly back down to a quintet, with no major loss of momentum. The band returned to Europe in September and October, 1999 but the UK would have to wait a while to experience the full new line-up.

The first single from the new album, *Brave New World* was released on May 8, 2000. 'The Wicker Man' marked another Smith-Dickinson-Harris co-write and tracked the story of the film of the same name. Catchy, rocking and full of vitality, the single made it to No.8 on the UK charts. There were various editions, but what they all had in common was that the B-sides featured live tracks.

IRON MAIDEN

Many of them were Blaze-era songs but sung by Dickinson during that 1999 tour. Merchandise was also being developed, with one special extra being a beermat that came with a European release. Now all they needed was a bottle to put on top ...

The single was nominated for a Grammy in January 2001 for Best Metal Performance, but The Deftones snagged it with 'Elite' instead. Curses! Still, there was a major award to be had and that was an Ivor Novello award for International Achievement. The band had sold 50 million copies of their albums worldwide by this point, and they were presented with their gong by long-term fan, tennis player Pat Cash.

Things were changing all over; Kevin Shirley began a fruitful collaboration with Maiden as producer and the album was recorded in France. *Brave New World* did well in the UK, hitting No.7, and No.39 in the United States. It was largely recorded live in the studio, rather than being pieced together by a lengthy tracking process. It was the first time the group had taken this approach, but it wouldn't be the last. The LP had much more of the Classic-Era sound, as if the 1990s hadn't happened. The gigs were scheduled worldwide as ever, with a 90-date adventure ahead over six months from June to January 2001. The interest in the new/old line-up was high, concerts selling out within hours in some cases. One early blip happened, however, at the July 8 Mannheim, Germany gig. It'd been a cracking concert from the band, ending with the iconic 'Iron Maiden,' and after a quick couple of minutes backstage to refresh themselves Maiden rushed back onstage for an encore. The group launched in to 'The Number of the Beast' but just before the first guitar solo kicked in, Janick Gers slipped and fell a good two metres or so into the photography pit. The axeman was knocked out cold by the concrete floor and had to go to hospital for severe bruising, a back sprain and a nasty gash on his forehead, needing six stiches. Maiden cut short the encore, playing 'Beast' and 'Hallowed be Thy Name' but not the planned 'Sanctuary.'

Worse than that was that Gers had been advised to take a week's rest, so subsequent appearances in Essen, Sofia and Athens had to be postponed. Essen and Athens' cancelled gigs went ahead on November 6 and 10 respectively. Other dates that fell by the wayside included Anchorage, USA; two in Canada; and a mooted January 2001 gig in Argentina. The second single was the spacey 'Out of the Silent Planet,' which hit No.20 in the UK. But it was South America that truly took the cake for the biggest and possibly best return concert for Bruce, Adrian et al: the small matter of Rock in Rio. Over two weekends, and six days of music, such luminaries as R.E.M., Sting, Guns N'Roses, Red Hot Chili Peppers and, um, N-Sync headlined hot bills. Iron Maiden were top of the billing on Friday, 19 January 2001 with the undercard including Queens of the Stone Age, Sepultura and old mate Rob Halford.

The gig was attended by 250,000 as an estimate and was filmed and recorded in ultra-high quality for subsequent release as audio and video. It speaks much for the pulling power of Iron Maiden that they could carry this kind of thing off after the relative travails of their lost decade; perhaps they were the only band that

PART ONE: **BRUCE IS BACK**

could reach those kind of levels.

2002 was supposed to be time off from full-time Maiden activities, but the boys mobilised during March that year for reasons that were very close to their hearts. Former drummer Clive Burr had been diagnosed with Multiple Sclerosis; a cruel and incurable disease. Three sell-out gigs took place at Brixton Academy to raise funds for their stricken ex-bandmate and the phenomenon of Clive Aid was born. A live single was released, led by 'Run to the Hills' on two different formats, with the proceeds donated to the MS Trust Fund. Sales were great, reaching No.9 in the UK.

Mimi Burr says that when it came down to it, Iron Maiden really stepped up to the plate.

"Iron Maiden said to us, 'Anything you need, we will put on a tour [and donate the money.],'" she recalls. "Anything! It was done brilliantly because they had to work out all the tax and so on to give it to the trust. Clive did not have anything; they were helping and at the time I was working.

"When you get ill you lose friends, and Clive lost a lot of friends. But Iron Maiden were always there; they would ring [regularly]. Adrian would come round, for example. They would make sure everything was alright. I believe a friend of Steve Harris also had MS, so it was close to their hearts."

The album *Rock in Rio* was released on March 25 and the associated video on June 10. The camp then went quiet as a unit, until the announcement on November 27 that they were to work on another album; recording began on January 6 2003 at Sarm West with Kevin Shirley and again work was completed relatively quickly.

The new album was to be called *Dance of Death* and was released in September. First, though, there was another Greatest Hits compilation out. *Edward the Great* was a collection of singles, presumably for new fans rather than existing supporter s, who would have owned all the versions already. The associated tour was a fun one; podiums, heavy lighting, loads of Eddies all over the set's art, and two giant Eddies. Good grief. The 56 dates ran through May to August 2003, with one cancellation, this time at Alberquerque, New Mexico.

Give Me Ed 'Til I'm Dead was a tour that saw a now bedded-in band relaxed. There was even a new song for the fans to get stuck into, but only the one, 'Wildest Dreams.' But the material was still coming thick and fast and with the group on the road throughout the summer everything was looking pretty good. Well, nearly everything, anyway. Nicko got into a spot of bother before the gig at Tommy Hilfiger at Jones Beach Theatre in New York. The drummer drove up at around 8.30pm and went toward the VIP car park in his black Jaguar. An attendant, Mark Robinson, asked for Nicko's official ID. State park police said the attendant couldn't see it the first time so asked again. It was alleged that McBrain said he would drive into Robinson if he didn't move. The unfortunate employee was taken to Nassau University Medical Center for examination after falling onto the car's hood and suffering bruises to his legs and right hand. Police charged McBrain with third-degree assault and second-degree reckless endangerment but allowed him to play the concert under release on an 'appearance ticket.' The matter was subsequently settled.

That first single, 'Wildest Dreams,'

IRON MAIDEN

came out on the first day of September 2003. It was a strong Smith-Harris collaboration and four minutes of good, reliable Maidenisms. Though the LP wasn't as fresh as *Brave New World* had been, it was perhaps inevitable that there would be only one chance to get the returning heroes' sound absolutely bang on; Iron Maiden didn't have anything to prove by this stage, and they concentrated on expressing themselves through the music they wanted, and perhaps needed, to create. Again, the tour was relatively short, with 53 dates going ahead. A couple were due to a bout of laryngitis and flu suffered by Dickinson, gigs in Holland, Finland and Poland falling victim to his illness. Which was coincidentally the same time as Nicko McBrain was scheduled to be in New York's courtrooms. Something a bit more avoidable – and an object lesson to anyone attending gigs – was the January 24 appearance at New York's Hammerstein Ballroom. The second in two concerts at that venue, it was cut short apparently after one dumb-ass in the crowd dropped a beer into the sound equipment during Maiden's last song. The problem couldn't be easily fixed so there was no encore. The stage-show was back right up to full-on craziness again, Dickinson wearing masks, capes, cloaks and more; there was a *Dance of Death*-esque throne, crew dressed in military uniforms at times, barbed wire onstage at others and a Grim Reaper Eddie in 'Beast.'

The album had done well again, hitting No.2 in the UK and No.18 in the States. Second single, 'Rainmaker,' hit No.13 in the UK and – like the B-side 'Pass the Jam' on 'Wildest Dreams' was a knockabout jamming session. Interesting, and funny,

and Dickinson even giving a bit of rapping a crack. Having fun? You betcha. For some members of the group it really was a case of the sky being the limit: 'Bruce Air' was born; special trips to gigs in Reykjavik and Paris for fans only on charter aircraft were set up, under the aegis of the newly-crowned commercial pilot.

An EP was later released, *No More Lies – Dance of Death Souvenir EP*, on March 29, 2004 in Europe. Maiden also proved they could do the epic historical stuff like nobody else; Smith's beautiful 'Paschendale' is right up there with the band's best songs.

The tour also featured a recorded element, from the gig at Westfalenhalle Arena in Dortmund. Again, the Irons were pushing the technical boundaries with it, with a surround sound 5.1 mix, high-quality stereo, a documentary (on the DVD) and plenty of extras to the offering. *Death on the Road* came out in August 2005 as an album and the video the following February. What these live releases served to do, as did the compilations, was to take pressure off the band's writing. Long gone were the days of an album a year with a world tour immediately afterwards, then another album, another tour, another album and repeat until someone has had enough and thinks about leaving to go and sell daisies to tourists in Timbuktu. This way, the group had time to enjoy performances without worrying about what would come next. Maiden had earned the right to take things on their own terms and were certainly happy to take their position up accordingly.

A glorious piece of history was released by the band in November 2004: a DVD called *The History of Iron Maiden – Part 1: The Early Days*. Featuring extensive early

PART ONE: **BRUCE IS BACK**

footage, live gigs and interviews with many early members of Maiden. It was a treasure trove for new fans to learn about the lads and for older hands to reminisce. In January 2005, 'The Number of the Beast' was re-released as a single and included two great live tracks recorded at the Clive Burr MS Trust Fund gigs in 2002. There was an associated tour booked, *Eddie Rips Up the World Tour*, which ran from May to the end of August 2005. Gone by now were the days of small college gigs; this was stadiums and festivals a go-go, with the consequence being some of the biggest crowds per gig that the Irons had ever achieved. Things began in Europe, where a show at Gothenburg was broadcast live in Sweden, then moved through North America, where they were co-headliners with Black Sabbath for a bunch of dates under the *Ozzfest* banner.

At the time, Ozzy and his family were in the news for virtually everything aside from music. Wife Sharon was previously known only as an incredible manager in her own right, as well as learning the trade from her dad - one of the greatest managers of all time - Don Arden. But the curious world of entertainment and the even curiouser world of reality TV had meant a series had been premiered on MTV about the lives of Ozzy and company. *The Osbournes* brought cameras into their palatial family home, capturing an often-bewildered Brummie singer trying to cope with a couple of unruly kids and the formidable Sharon. There was as much tension about dogs shitting on the floor as there was about bubble machines onstage, Ozzy complaining that he was supposed to be the king of darkness and presumably not a kids' party magician. Serious messages also were part of it: Sharon's cancer, Ozzy's accident and more. It was absorbing, somewhat like toilet paper is absorbing, and satisfying, somewhat like watching a fly bonk its head on an open window repeatedly isn't, and it ran for four series from 2002-2005.

And so what? Well, Bruce Dickinson is hardly a chap to mince words, particularly when it comes to reality television. He had apparently also referenced Ozzy's allegedly fading memory, alluding to lyric sheets onstage being necessary at times as a result. Let's not forget here that Dickinson and Osbourne had been extremely long-term mates since way back in the early '80s. Should Bruce choose to, and if Ozzy can remember any of it, their antics would make one hell of a book/movie/cautionary tale, all of their own.

It had been bubbling all summer, but things came to a head at the concert in Devore, California on August 22. Apparently, before Maiden's set, the PA system blasted out a chant of 'Ozzy, Ozzy, Ozzy.' The Irons took to the stage but after a couple of minutes, eggs, bottle tops and ice started hitting the stage from the audience. Also, during 'The Trooper,' the stage was invaded by a bloke with an American flag – Bruce Dickinson would wave the UK flag as always in that song. Though the stage crew quickly got the interloper off stage, it was noticed that said dude was wearing a T-shirt that said 'Don't Fuck With Ozzy.' All quite tame so far, but what was extremely unacceptable was the power cutting out to the vocals and instruments during three songs. The tracks that suffered were 'Run to the Hills,' 'Hallowed be Thy Name' and 'The Number

IRON MAIDEN

of the Beast.' Dickinson responded with suitable forceful words.

Ozzfest released a statement that even claimed Steve Harris had apologised to Ozzy Osbourne for Bruce Dickinson's behaviour onstage. What was true was that Sharon Osbourne later said she was the one responsible for the disruption to the set. A decade later, Dickinson said the whole incident was more or less nothing but a mountain out of a molehill. Black Sabbath and Ozzy Osbourne, he said, were icons, and that was the end of it. At the time though, the whole caboodle seemed rather childish and very unnecessary indeed. Still, the headlines didn't harm anybody's sales, one suspects.

Although there were rumours that there was a DVD of the *Eddie Rips* tour in the planning, nothing surfaced. The tour ended with another brilliant gig at Hammersmith Apollo in aid of Clive Burr and the MS Trust Fund. Tickets were initially sold to official fan club members only. The drummer was being helped hugely by Maiden, to their great credit.

As 2005 came to an end, the band began writing songs again before taking some time off for Chrimbo. After the turkey/tofu-fest had subsided, it was time to head into Sarm once more for sessions that took two months to complete (still relatively fast for such an established band). The result was the new LP, another lengthy bruiser at over an hour and 10 minutes, with only four of its 10 songs running at under seven minutes. It was entitled *A Matter of Life and Death*.

First single was the intriguing and slightly-weird 'The Reincarnation of Benjamin Breeg.' The titular character is either a new addition to the Maiden extended family of protagonists – or a familiar one whose life before appearing on Irons artwork and as a mascot was for the first time being discussed. There has never been an official explanation of who Breeg is/was/can be, whether he really existed, or whether this was just another fun sleight-of-hand by all concerned. Due to its running time of over seven minutes, it was not eligible for the charts in the UK but did snag the No.1 slot in both Finland and Sweden; Scandinavia as ever getting on board with their usual enthusiasm.

A Matter of Life and Death came out on August 28, 2006 to great reviews and even better sales worldwide; by September 14 it had topped the million mark. The tour to support it was again split into two halves. First, the *A Matter of Life and Death Tour*, which saw the band perform the new album in total. There were only a few old favourites included; 'Fear of the Dark,' 'Iron Maiden,' '2 Minutes to Midnight,' 'The Evil that Men Do' and 'Hallowed be Thy Name.' It was the first time in decades that 'The Number of the Beast' wasn't played by the Irons. The set was similar in focus to the album artwork, themed around wartime, including mud, sandbags, parachutists and even a tank – Eddie appeared on top of it, and then walked on as a soldier in 'The Evil that Men Do.' It was a brave move to play a set of nearly all new songs, particularly given the density and length of the new compositions. Fans this time had a couple of months to learn them, of course, so it wasn't quite like laying completely unfamiliar material on an unsuspecting crowd. The tour started in North America before five gigs in Japan and then returning to Europe via Scandinavia. On November 14 (US) and

PART ONE: **BRUCE IS BACK**

December 26 (UK) the second single, 'Different World,' was released. It was a way more user-friendly Smith-Harris effort and had a great video for it, with Bruce Dickinson in some kind of bizarre factory ... Eddie is the baddie, of course, and Bruce is taken to a different world by a young woman. Not for the first time, we wager. Despite its post-Christmas release, the 'Bring Your Daughter... To the Slaughter' trick didn't work twice in terms of delivering a No.1 single, but it did reach a very respectable No.3 in the UK.

More firsts for the band were to follow as the second half of the tour dawned, entitled *A Matter of the Beast*. Specifically, the new territories of India and United Arab Emirates experienced Iron Maiden for the first time, with successful gigs in Bangalore and UAE during March. At the Indian gig, the crowd was a huge 40,000: so many people had been waiting for so long for Iron Maiden or any metal band of note to play there that the untapped market was incredible. The band had dropped several of the new songs from this section of the tour, inserting some very early material instead from the *Killers*, *The Number of the Beast* and *Piece of Mind* albums. It was inevitable that the *Beast* tracks would get some kind of airing as it was the 25th anniversary of that seminal album hitting the streets. The Irons performed yet again at Donington, Monsters of Rock now having morphed into the Download Festival, with 80,000 getting their rocks off to the now-veteran musicians. Again, there were rumours that it would be filmed for release, but again it didn't happen.

Interestingly, Motörhead were now a support act for Maiden on several dates, as was one Lauren Harris – daughter of Steve. Circles within circles, circles within circles. To round off the new album and new tour, there was another gig for Clive Burr on June 24 at Brixton Academy. And that was it for Maiden as a band in 2007; Bruce Dickinson went off to fly massive planes; plans were put in place to release more material from the vaults. By September the announcement was made that the Irons would tour once more during 2008. And it would be a very special one, too. Firstly, the DVD of *Live After Death* would be released, bringing new fans up to date with that classic piece of work plus some ace added features, including the continuation of *The History of Iron Maiden*.

Secondly, the band would be flying around on this tour.

On their own chartered aeroplane.

It was dubbed 'Ed Force One.'

And one of the pilots would be Bruce Dickinson.

Let that sink in for a minute.

The tour would be called *Somewhere Back in Time*, which harked back to that album plus the stage- set based on the *Powerslave* gigs. During February and March, 2008 the band reached fans in India, Australia, Japan, the States, South America and finally Toronto, Canada. Fans loved the giant Eddies, the pyrotechnics and of course the songs, which were almost entirely drawn from albums released between 1982 and 1988. The only exceptions were the ubiquitous 'Iron Maiden,' and 1992's 'Fear of the Dark.' The second leg of the tour coincided with the release of the compilation album, also called *Somewhere Back in Time*. It was classic stuff all round. Having your own plane to fly (albeit chartered, not owned) also opened

IRON MAIDEN

up several new countries for the Maiden juggernaut: Ecuador, Peru, Colombia, Costa Rica – all now available without relying on commercial schedules. Maiden were still breaking records, too, with the European leg of the tour selling at an unprecedented rate and volume. After a break of six months or so, the concerts rolled on through the first part of 2009, with Europe, Asia and the Americas falling under the *Somewhere Back* spell.

This exceptional band were firing on all cylinders: the announcement that they would be putting out a documentary movie of their Ed Force One/*Somewhere Back* experiences was hugely welcomed by fans. The consequent movie, *Iron Maiden: Flight 666* had been formed in February and March 2008 and was released in some cinemas on April 21. It was subsequently put out on DVD, Blu-Ray and CD, and has been a fan favourite ever since for its access to the band, the crew, the plane and the Maiden camp in general. It hit No.1 in no less than 22 countries' DVD charts for music once it hit the streets that summer.

Iron Maiden finally won recognition from the establishment in the 2009 Brit Awards. They were up against UK bands Scouting for Girls, Elbow, The Verve and Coldplay for best British Live Act – and blimey, they only went and won it. Comedy actor Nick Frost introduced and presented the award, which Maiden accepted via video link. To be fair to the group, the awards took place on February 18 and they were flying between India, New Zealand, Australia and then South America. Bruce Dickinson thanked crew, management and family and gave a big shout out to the fans – it meant so much more to the band that it had been the people voting for them, rather than a decision by some faceless committee. He also wore a Rise to Remain T-shirt – that being the name of his son Austin's band. Shameless. Although you have to say that it was more than fair enough given Lauren Harris was supporting the band again. The Brit award was way, way overdue for a group that had sold tens of millions of records and played to a similar number of fans over a 34-year history. If the 1990s had been a dark time for Maiden, the 2000s were ending on a real high.

The new decade would begin on a positive note too, with news that there was to be a brand-new studio album. In fact, Nicko let slip that there were plans to record new stuff as early as April 2009. In keeping with the practice of looking back at the best bits, the group decided to decamp to the good old Compass Point Studios in Nassau, Bahamas, for initial sessions in January and February 2010. A touch of additional recording and the final mixing was polished off by the start of March in further sessions at The Cave in Malibu. Producing again were Kevin Shirley and Steve Harris, the former noting that Dickinson had whizzed in and out to do his vocals in just a few days in Shirley's Malibu studio before returning to fly planes around the world.

Indeed, Dickinson was a man in demand more than ever as the new decade progressed. There was the band, of course, but also heavy commitments with his airline companies, an increasing schedule as a motivational/business speaker and even the prospect of re-introducing Zeppelin-style travel to the world with a brand-new aircraft known colloquially as 'the flying bum.' Never one to stand still, that chap.

PART ONE: **BRUCE IS BACK**

The new album would be called *The Final Frontier*, which left many fans aghast at the prospect of it being Iron Maiden's farewell LP. The band did have some fun around it, too, with Dickinson admitting in his book that he was partly on the wind-up, and partly referencing the cult TV series *Star Trek*. The album does have a spacey aesthetic, not least the near-title track 'Satellite 15... The Final Frontier.' For numerologists, the number 15 was significant – apparently Steve Harris had long felt that the band would complete 15 albums. *The Final Frontier* was Maiden's 15th. There was much gnashing of teeth and wailing as to whether this would indeed be the case. *The Final Frontier World Tour* was a 101-show (98 went ahead), four-legged monster that began in Texas on June 9, 2010 and finished with two shows at London's O2 Arena on August 5 and 6, 2011.

Because the album wasn't due out until August, the first set of dates only included one new track, 'El Dorado,' which was the record's only single. Dealing with the financial crisis and clocking in at nearly seven minutes, it was a massive slab of Maiden, with a thick guitar texture and that uber-familiar galloping Harris bassline. The song was decent, if not spectacular, but finally won Iron Maiden a coveted Grammy Award – for Best Metal Performance - at the 53rd ceremony on February 13, 2011. Quite an appropriate date, no? The lads weren't at the ceremony due to being en route to Singapore from their gig in Moscow, and possibly because it is one of those awards-by-committee type wotsits. Regardless, it was also long overdue. The 2010 dates rolled through North America and Europe, where the band finally played in the Romanian region of Transylvania. It had only taken them 30 years to get there after their song of the same name appeared on *Iron Maiden*. There is no record as to whether the experience left the band as speechless as they were when it came to thinking up lyrics at the time.

'Satellite 15...' wasn't a single *per se*, but the video was released on July 13. It's a brill mini-movie about a space fighter-pilot looking for relics, fighting off nasties and avoiding Eddie's own ship. The narrative continues: the pilot and Eddie get into a bit of a set-to, Eddie getting electrocuted but not being put off his task, despite also being exploded at one stage. We won't spoil the ending, but we will tell you that the video is way better than *The Phantom Menace*, anyway. (Although so is *Peppa Pig*, so it's not that difficult.)

The Final Frontier was released on August 13, 2010 and the band immediately disappeared for the rest of the year.

Fans weren't to be disappointed, however. Ed Force One was back in action during 2011. The new tour would be called *Around the World in 66 Days*, with 29 gigs scheduled across 13 countries from February 2011 onwards. There were new venues too this time; Singapore and two gigs in Indonesia. The whole shebang then whooshed its way through Australia, Korea, Japan, South America, North America and then Scandinavia before ending back where it started, in Russia. It was Mother Nature that intervened at one stage, though, with the two planned Japanese dates having to be cancelled due to a devastating earthquake and tsunami on March 11. A concert in Rio de Janeiro had to be postponed for a day after a barrier failed during the initial gig on March 27;

IRON MAIDEN

the other cancellation was a planned Sonisphere gig in Bulgaria on June 21.

There was another compilation release; *From Fear to Eternity* gathered up the rest of the best of the tracks from 1990 to 2010 and came out in June 2011. Most bands would be delighted to have had such a quality set of stuff to release. For Maiden, it's not even their best compilation, and that's saying something. It's gone silver in the UK with sales of over 60,000 and peaked at No.19 in the album charts. The Sherman tanks across the pond didn't buy into it: it only hit No.86 in the *Billboard 200*. No matter: the tour was ongoing, the gigs came thick and fast, the plane was soaring around the air and the estimate was that the band had played to around two million people in all. That takes a lot out of a musician, let alone six folks in their 50s. Understandably, by the end of the *Final Frontier* tour, exhaustion had kicked in all round. This time, though, there was no chance of anyone leaving the band, but the year off that was planned was definitely well-received. The tour had been filmed, definitely, on this occasion – and the *En Vivo!* DVD/CD would hit the streets in 2012. It had been filmed in South America and the DVD also included more goodies for the fans in terms of documentary footage. From the CD, the song 'Blood Brothers' was nominated for another Grammy. This time, though, the Hard Rock/Metal Performance award went to Halestorm for 'Love Bites (So Do I)'. Other nominees were Anthrax, Lamb of God, Marilyn Manson and Megadeth. Megadave of Megadeth must have been gutted, yet again, after being nominated for the umpteenth time for an award but coming home empty-handed. Mustaine would have to wait until 2017 until his band was recognised, winning Best Metal Performance for 'Dystopia.' He was probably a little bit less impressed when the house band serenaded his walk to the podium to accept by doing a version of 'Master of Puppets' – by Metallica.

Back in Maidenland, and the reworking of archive material continued, this time the *Maiden England* video getting the treatment. Long only available on VHS, it was overdue a clean-up and upgrade, having been initially shot back in 1988 during the *Seventh Son of a Seventh Tour*. It was mooted for release in 2013. The lads would also hit the road – and hit it hard – in 2012, 2013 and 2014. Each year, a series of gigs would take place, mostly during the summer, with extensive time off between to recharge batteries and avoid burn-out. The first leg was the North American gigs of June to August 2012 and would play around two-thirds of the setlist of the original *Maiden England* video. There were outings after decades for 'Afraid to Shoot Strangers,' last played 1998; 'Seventh Son of a Seventh Son,' last heard in 1988; 'The Prisoner,' which had not been aired in the live arena by Maiden since 1991. The tour, according to Pollstar, grossed US$16.1 million. The band members were happy; they were generally based in one place, from which they'd usually fly to concerts.

Enough to buy a few pints, indeed, of the brand-new *Trooper Ale*, which had been developed by Stockport brewers Robinsons in conjunction with the band. Bruce Dickinson is a connoisseur of all things ale and was the obvious choice to work with the company to develop a beer that wasn't just a gimmick but was actually worth drinking. It's fair to say it was a success;

PART ONE: **BRUCE IS BACK**

several different brews have followed, and all sold well. Of course, there's also an enormous collectors' market out there. Imagine buying beer and keeping it to look at... strange. Still, the artwork on all the ever-growing Robinsons/Maiden/Trooper family is completely in keeping with the quality the band has always insisted on, and Eddie leers out suitably confrontationally from the labels.

Part two of the tour saw the band return to Europe for festivals and huge arena and stadium gigs all over the shop. There was the small matter of their fifth Donington headline gig on June 15, 2013. It featured one of the most gloriously over-the-top and wonderful pieces of work – a Battle of Britain Spitfire swooped down on the crowd and the band before Maiden kicked in to 'Aces High.' Anyone who was there will never, ever forget the experience. And that before the band had played a note, too. Marvellous. There was also the small matter of opening the Friends Arena in Stockholm on July 13, being the first to ever play there. Maiden returned to the Americas for gigs in the States, Mexico, Brazil (another Rock in Rio), Argentina, Paraguay (for the first time) and Chile. And great news for fans was the prospect of a brand-new album on the horizon, scheduled tentatively for 2015 release. *The Final Frontier* indeed was nothing of the sort, and millions rejoiced. There were just over two months of European gigs in the summer of 2014 before the Irons wrapped up their last-ever retrospective-based tour. The last one for now, at least. There's still plenty in the archives.

After a month off, the band convened at Guillaume Tell Studios in Paris. For the first time, they would write in the recording studio and almost straight away record the results. It worked incredibly well as far as the Iron Maiden camp were concerned, musically at least. The album was largely completed by the end of 2014.

But there was a huge shock in the offing.

On 12 December 2014, Bruce Dickinson was advised by doctors that he had head and neck cancer.

A devastating blow for any human being; for a singer, not just life-threatening but should he fight it off, there was the ever-present high possibility that he would never sing again.

We asked Dr. Freya Roe, BA (hons), PgDip, MRes, certMRCSLT and Clinical Lead Speech and Language Therapist: Head and Neck Oncology / ENT, Barts Health NHS Trust, for her professional opinion.

The cancer was caused by Human Pampiloma Virus, as Bruce details in his book.

"Human Papilloma Virus is the collective name for a group of viruses that affect the skin and mucus membrane lining of the body," explains Dr. Roe. "There are over a hundred types of HPV which are classed as low or high risk. HPV 16 and 18 are deemed as high-risk strains and have the potential to cause cancer. Within the Head and Neck Cancer classification, the anatomical area of the oropharynx (for example the base of tongue and tonsils) is particularly susceptible to HPV related cancers and up to 70 per cent of cancers in that sub-group are HPV positive. Overall the evidence base shows that 20 to 50 per cent of head and neck cancers (HNC) are HPV related.

"HPV is transmitted through sexual contact and as such it is classed as a sexually-transmitted infection which is

IRON MAIDEN

passed on through any sexual activity such as oral sex, intercourse and full kissing. However, in regard to the stigma attached to that, it is important to note that contracting HPV is almost a state of normality.

"Up to 80 per cent of people will contract HPV at some point in their lifetime. The infection causes no symptoms and in most people the body will clear the infection without them ever having known they had it. Most HPV strains are harmless, however, where high-risk strains are contracted and not cleared by the body, they have the potential to cause cell changes which can develop into cancer."

At present, she adds, the evidence base is not robust or conclusive as to the link between HPV-related head and neck cancer and number of sexual partners or sexual behaviours. Not that this stops headline-writers going nuts of course.

"The term 'throat cancer' is quite general and relates to a large anatomical area. Within that area there are structures that, if they were involved, would hugely affect a singer's abilities in different ways," says Dr. Roe.

"The base of tongue sits right at the back of the mouth and is the bridge between the front of the tongue (what we see in the mouth) and the throat. It has two key roles. It is important in articulation and it helps to manipulate and push food/drink into the throat during swallowing. Any changes in articulation are problematic for a professional voice user, they could result in a slurred imprecise quality to speech/singing and reduce the clarity of articulation.

"For a professional voice user of Bruce's level this has the potential to make a huge impact. Bruce [has mentioned] that he had trouble with vowel sounds. This can occur when there are changes to the shape or function of any of the articulatory structures, such as those caused by radiotherapy.

"The current evidence base is showing that HPV-associated HNC has a better prognosis and increased long-term survival rates when compared to HPV negative HNC. There is debate in the cancer field as to whether staging and treatment options should be modified in regard to the HPV status of the patient."

Retired GP Dr. David Jones explains that diagnosis is not always straightforward; Dickinson completed the entirety of *Book of Souls* before finding out about his condition.

"Unfortunately, tumours can grow to be quite large before they cause any symptoms," Dr. Jones adds. "Three quarters of tongue cancers occur in the mobile tongue. The edge of the tongue is the commonest site. The cancers in the base of the tongue are more or less silent until they infiltrate and often there is secondary spread by the time the patient is aware something is wrong.

"Staging of the tumours has been agreed across the international medical colleges. It basically stages the Tumour (T), the Nodes (N) and Metastasis or spread (M). It is called the TNM classification. T3 (in the case of Bruce) indicated his tumour was larger than 4cms."

There are two approaches, often used in tandem: surgery and radiation.

"In younger patients, surgery alone is favoured in case of recurrence – if radiation has been used it won't be able

PART ONE: **BRUCE IS BACK**

to be used again. Radiation can also cause adverse effects which, in a singer, could end the career," Dr. Jones explains.

"For small tumours and in the older patient, radiation alone can be used. This preserves the function of the tongue where surgery will remove it. There are different types of radiation treatment, each one having advantages. For larger tumours, or those that are more advanced, radiation is used in conjunction with surgery if the tumour shows an adverse picture on microscopic investigations. Occasionally large tumours are 'shrunk' with radiation prior to surgical removal."

Dr. Roe notes that radiotherapy can have many side-effects in patients.

"In the short term, repeated irradiation of tissues causes significant pain and swelling in the target area. This is cumulative as the treatment continues and often patients liken the feeling to a severe sunburn inside the mouth/throat," says the expert. "As the anatomical structures swell their movement and shape are altered. In the case of the tongue this translates as slowed, difficult movement which will be painful and effortful. Speech will be slower and less clear. As the shape of the structures is changed through swelling, the way the sound resonates in the throat is changed and so voice quality may sound different to the patient's normal voice. Often the whole of the neck is included in the field of radiotherapy, and if so, this will also affect the vocal folds, which will become swollen and inflamed. This would be perceived as a lower-pitched, hoarse voice and may affect a singer's normal pitch range.

"Whilst the majority of pain and swelling will subside after the radiotherapy is completed, it is possible that the anatomy will not completely return to pre-treatment state and so some of these changes can be permanent [in some patients.]

"Additionally, radiotherapy has longer-term side-effects that can develop over the following months to years. The most common of these are dry mouth/throat (if the salivary glands are irradiated), mucus build-up and an alteration to taste as the taste-buds of the tongue are irradiated and may not recover fully. Dry mouth and lack of saliva are again potentially impacting for anyone, particularly singers. It is essential that the mouth and throat are kept hydrated by saliva to ensure clear articulation, voice quality and comfort. Also, mucus can build up in the throat, causing congestion and deteriorated voice quality."

Dr. Jones adds that treatment is being constantly reappraised for effectiveness within the clinical community and researchers.

"Chemotherapy is still being evaluated in the management of tongue cancer. It can be useful as a palliative treatment for patients with advanced disease who are not candidates for surgery and/or radiation. One of the newer modes is combining radiation with chemotherapy, and that seems to help both, and this is the treatment Bruce Dickinson had," he notes.

"The five-year survival rate for T1 and T2 with no re-occurrence is 80 to 90 per cent after radiotherapy," Dr. Jones adds. "This can drop to 30 to 50 per cent for T3 and T4. However, as Bruce had no nodes, that is a superb sign. Regular checks will be an important part of his follow-up treatment,

IRON MAIDEN

particularly the five-year check in 2020.

"After treatment, the surgeon or oncologist will monitor the patient closely to ensure they are recovering," concludes Dr. Roe.

"For a first cancer at stage three it is very likely that treatment would have a curative intent i.e. it is expected that the patient will make a full recovery, albeit with the side-effects of treatment which may affect function and quality of life.

"Routine scans are taken at intervals to assess the efficacy of the treatment and to monitor for any sign of recurrence. Speech Therapy, Dietitians and Specialist Nurses will be involved to address any problems with speech/voice/swallowing, throat care, nutrition, emotional and physical health."

For an avid reader and explorer such as Paul Bruce Dickinson, you can bet that he will have access to information about the latest innovations in the field; the Air Raid siren isn't going to be silenced any time soon.

His recovery was gruelling and painful, and in his autobiography he speaks of it as eloquently and humorously as ever. Given a 12-month recovery period – should he even be able to sing again – Dickinson was back to good health in only eight. And, being Bruce Dickinson, he was also fully ready to embark on another major tour with Maiden.

First things first, though, and there was the matter of the release of the initial single from the new album, which was to be called *The Book of Souls*. It was slightly disingenuous a choice, being one of Smith-Dickinson's deliberate attempts to write some snappier, more accessible single-style tracks on the new record.

'Speed of Light' was released as a music video, a digital download and then a CD only available in Best Buy, a United States electronics supermarket. The video is great: go watch it.

The Book of Souls landed on September 4, 2015 in the UK and was an expansive, enormous undertaking. At an hour and a half in length it was obvious that this was to be a double-album of some depth and heft, with a Mayan influence on board, giving Eddie all sorts of new possibilities. Not only is it Maiden's longest studio LP to date, it's also got the longest track Maiden have created to date. That is the extraordinary 'Empire of the Clouds,' Bruce Dickinson's 18-minute mini-opera about the doomed R101 airship. It was written by the singer on a keyboard he'd bought at a charity auction for fun, and his naïve playing style gives a simple, memorable hook. It has been hailed as a masterpiece, although it's very unlikely to be played in its entirety onstage. That said, this is Iron Maiden, so who knows?

The question as to whether the singer had properly recovered from his cancer was still hanging in the air. The band were also taking to the air again, this time in a much bigger Boeing 747-400 Jumbo Jet, which enabled them to carry more of their equipment further than ever before: 12 tons of it, to be exact. The tour once again began in America, from February 24, 2016 onwards. One blip occurred at a Chilean airfield, in Santiago on March 12. The plane was being towed for refuelling purposes and collided with a ground truck, injuring two operators (who were thankfully not badly hurt in the incident), and damaging *Ed Force One*. No gigs were cancelled, but the band didn't get their

PART ONE: **BRUCE IS BACK**

THIS DAY IN MUSIC'S GUIDE TO **IRON MAIDEN** 85

IRON MAIDEN

plane back until March 21. The tour raged through Asia, Oceania and South Africa for two memorable gigs before coming back Europe's way throughout the summer of 2016. *Ed Force One*'s last appearance was in Gothenburg on June 17. The tour came to an end on August 4 in Germany, but after a few weeks Maiden announced its continuation for the following year. And that's what they did: Europe first this time, in April and May, then the States and Canada for June and July. And on the seventh day, they rested ...

... except they didn't: The *Book of Souls* gigs had been recorded at selected venues, and in November 2017 the result was the album and DVD *The Book of Souls: Live Chapter*. Lots of tracks from the new album, of course, interspersed with various classic cuts. And that, as they say, was that.

Except it wasn't. Because on November 13, 2017 Maiden announced another tour was being booked. Dates would take place in Europe during the summer of 2018 then range around the world in 2019. The reason? Maiden's mobile game and comic books that had been recently released, both entitled *Legacy of the Beast*. The comic is a five-issue spectacular tracking the adventures of Eddie himself, as he tries to bring his soul back across time and space. It was an extension of the role-playing game that tracked through the different worlds created by Iron Maiden (and their artists over the years). The issues were released between October 2017 and February 2018, that final one coming out on St. Valentine's Day. No doubt that wasn't a coincidence: the beastly love affair is unprecedented. There was even a new pinball machine courtesy of Stern Pinball, Inc, involving 12 songs by Maiden, four flippers, secret tombs, laser-cut metal ramps and ...

well, loads of pinball stuff.

Those dates began in Europe in May 2018 and the first batch of gigs ended that August at London's O2 Arena. The history and hits tour was based around loads of Eighties material, with a clutch of tracks from subsequent albums to keep the audiences up to date.

Classics included Blaze-era tracks 'The Clansman' and 'Sign of the Cross' plus songs that hadn't had an airing for quite some time, including 'For the Greater Good of God', 'The Wicker Man' and 'Flight of Icarus'. The gigs began with a replica of a Supermarine Spitfire MkVB buzzing the stage – albeit it had to be scaled down to 90 per cent size to fit on festival stages. Pyrotechnics, special effects, Eddie in many new incarnations ... it was at once recognisably Maiden but also featured brand new-feeling stagecraft. Bruce Dickinson turned 60 years old during the tour but showed no signs of slowing down as the European leg came to an end, with more international dates scheduled for 2019.

The momentum was such that both Dave Murray and the boss, Steve Harris, were quoted as saying they weren't planning to retire any time soon; the band was having loads of fun, and at the end of the *Legacy of the Beast* tour there was a good chance a new album might be written and released.

Who'd have thought that way back in 1975, a young bassist still unsure of his instrument and trying desperately to find the right alchemy to bind his band together would end up here? Iron Maiden may have been Steve Harris' band at one stage, but now he has to share it with the world. Not a bad trade-off, really. The momentum of Iron Maiden is irresistible. Long may they reign.

PART TWO: THE MUSIC
The Albums

IRON MAIDEN

2

*Around, around, flew each
sweet sound,
Then darted to the Sun;
Slowly the sounds came
back again,
Now mixed, now one by one.*

**Samuel Taylor Coleridge,
The Rime of the Ancient Mariner**

PART TWO: **THE ALBUMS**

PART TWO: THE MUSIC

The Albums

All tracklistings taken from original UK releases

IRON MAIDEN
EMI (US: Harvest/Capitol)
Recorded January 1980, Kingsway Studios, London; released April 14th, 1980

Prowler/Remember Tomorrow/Running Free/Phantom of the Opera/Transylvania/Strange World/Charlotte the Harlot/Iron Maiden

In one sense, Maiden's long-playing debut was five years in the making, albeit it was recorded in a 13-day whirlwind. The constant line-up changes had all added nuances to the songs, the constant gigging an edge to the band and the thirst of the audiences at peak levels for heavy metal. After two false starts under Guy Edwards and Andy Scott (The Sweet) in December 1979, the band finally got it together with Will Malone at the controls. Though the group have individually and collectively subsequently expressed their unhappiness at the sonic aesthetic of the album, it is undeniable that the force, pace and energy put down on to vinyl here absolutely and faithfully points to the excitement and rawness of Maiden's early years. Opening track, 'Prowler,' leaps out of the speakers with a gritty, salacious glee, less Deep Purple here than Sabbath-on-Speed, before the group pulls the first of a couple of unexpected sudden turns. 'Remember Tomorrow,' the lyrics of which were written by singer Paul Di'Anno about his recently-deceased grandfather, is a stroke of brilliance. The pace is slower and controlled, the psychedelic gothiness building, and the vocalist is on absolutely top form. No pub

IRON MAIDEN

rockers or metal/punk hybrids, these: there is an extraordinary sonic palette (not to mention palate) on show here.

Next up is another great Di'Anno lyric, the debut single 'Running Free'. It has rightly become one of Maiden's most enduring songs for its rampaging pace and tales of whiskey, women, freedom and escape. Another surprise is chucked at the listener with Maiden's first great epic track, 'Phantom of the Opera.' Written by Steve Harris, it was inspired by the 1910 French novel by Gaston Leroux that was subsequently turned into a classic Gothic 1925 movie (and in the mid-1980s, a phenomenally successful musical by Andrew Lloyd Webber ... not, sadly, featuring this song). A tickle under seven and a half minutes, the twin guitars of Dennis Stratton and Dave Murray take the opportunity to explore the space created. Notoriously, Stratton had added several extra layers of vocal harmonies to the track one evening, which went down rather badly with the band, who immediately deleted the Queen-like vocals. Great as the final version is, Maiden's subsequent work with layers of sound developed over the years anyway – wouldn't it be great to have heard this alternative version? Sadly, lost to posterity. Back to 1980 though and that's the end of Side One. After such a triumphant, diverse set of cuts, Side Two had a lot to live up to, but immediately fell short with the instrumental, 'Transylvania,' which despite some interesting key changes and a top performance by drummer Clive Burr meanders without much of a musical narrative. It sounds less like a piece written for the band only and more like a song looking for lyrics.

Harris reaches back into neo-prog melancholy with 'Strange World,' where grass is green, girls drink plasma wine, love and dreams are possible and walks in deep space are yearned for. Paul Mario Day – the original Maiden vocalist – has been rumoured to have had a hand in the writing process. Of course, the credits officially and legally read Steve Harris. Dave Murray pops up with the more bluesy/hard-rock 'Charlotte the Harlot,' which as its title suggests is a song about a prostitute who was notorious in a particular part of London. Needless to say, Di'Anno attacks this one with raised eyebrows and a glitter in the gullet. The album closes with the title track, which has been played at virtually every Maiden show over the years. 'Iron Maiden' may have macabre lyrics about blood flowing and a particularly twisted kind of voyeurism, but the vibe is of a triumphant call to arms; a shout at the skies full of belief and a promise that Iron Maiden will, indeed, get to you. Moreover, Iron Maiden could neither be bought off or fought off. It is as strong an end to a debut album as you will ever hear and, production quibbles noted, shows the tightness and ability of a band absolutely on top of their form. Later reissues of the LP included the track, 'Sanctuary,' which was originally a standalone single release in May 1980, complete with Thatcher-baiting cover art.

KILLERS

EMI (US: Harvest/Capitol)
Recorded Nov 1980, Jan 1981, Battery Studios, London; released February 2nd, 1981.

The Ides of March/Wrathchild/Murders in the Rue Morgue/Another Life/Genghis Khan/Innocent Exile/Killers /Prodigal Son/Purgatory/Drifter

A swift follow-up to the debut was possible due to the large amount of road-hardened songs in the Maiden back catalogue. And yet *Killers* somewhat treads water. Adrian

PART TWO: **THE ALBUMS**

Smith had replaced Stratton, and Sabbath/Purple engineer and producer Martin Birch stepped in for the first in a series of superb productions with Maiden. But it was essentially more of the same as *Iron Maiden*, rather than a great leap forward. Still, the band play their arses off and undeniably move away from the punkier edges that made that first record so spiky. It opens with 'The Ides of March', which at under two minutes is the shortest in the Maiden oeuvre. It's a perfect way to intro Smith, too, as he trades solos with his old mate Murray. Its similarities with Samson's 'Thunderburst,' from their *Head On* album, are well-noted, and Harris is co-credited on the Samson track. Not so the other way around; such is life. Then we've got the all-time Maiden classic 'Wrathchild,' which the band had been playing at least since the Willcock era. Di'Anno is in his element here, blasting his way through an absolute stormer of a song, with a great bass intro and one of metal's best riffs and Clive Burr absolutely killing it. Maiden launch into 'Murders in the Rue Morgue,' which along with 'Prodigal Son' is one of two relatively new tracks on the disc. The song, inspired by the Edgar Allen Poe story, is catchy, gritty and again showcases the best of the vocalist, despite his subsequent comments that by this stage of the band's progress he was starting to lose interest. If he was, it doesn't show: he's at the top of his game here. 'Another Life' once again deals with one of Harris' preoccupations: life, death, madness and nocturnal musings. The repetition of the verse three times is an excellent way to bring home the sheer pain of the lyrics and it fair gallops along.

The mercifully-short instrumental 'Genghis Khan' adds a little flavour and 'Innocent Exile,' a kind of companion piece to 'Sanctuary,' ends a decent Side One. The title track of the album is the only one to be credited to anyone other than Harris, with Di'Anno getting a co-write on it (other, unofficial sites also give the singer a credit for 'Another Life'). It is an atmospheric, heavy, metal-to-the-core piece of menacing, speedy growliness and as dark as Maiden had been to date. The band then turns mellower for 'Prodigal Son,' which has more than a touch of Led Zeppelin about it, including steel guitar and acoustic axes. The solos from Murray and Smith prove that it was a masterstroke to finally get Adrian involved – the pair dovetail so

IRON MAIDEN

beautifully it's like he had always been there. It's also a hint that there was a real love of prog rock within the band that they were ready to explore. The band then straps in and hits fifth gear for the speedy 'Purgatory,' which has its basis in an older track with the name 'Floating.' The original artwork for the single version of the song, released on June 15th, 1981, was famously kept back by the Maiden camp for use on their next album: Derek Riggs had to come up with another version. The LP ends with 'Drifter,' another cut with a theme of being lost, being an outsider, moving on and moving toward the future. Of course, after the dust had settled from this LP there was to be a mega change in the band's sound – and one that would propel them into the rarefied heights of fame. The US edition added 'Twilight Zone' to the track-listing, a co-write by Murray and Harris and a welcome addition. UK audiences had to be satisfied with it on the B-side of 'Wrathchild,' which had another controversial piece of cover artwork that had to be explained away as Eddie coming back from the dead to greet his lover, rather than stalking an unsuspecting young girl in her bedroom. Hmm.

THE NUMBER OF THE BEAST

EMI (US: Harvest)
Recorded January and February, 1982 at Battery Studios, London; released March 22nd, 1982.

Invaders/Children of the Damned/ The Prisoner/22 Acacia Avenue/The Number of the Beast/Run to the Hills/Gangland/Hallowed be thy Name

A mega change? Not arf. Bruce Dickinson replacing Di'Anno took Maiden from being a very good, possibly the best, NWOBHM band into an astonishing force of nature. Whereas the Di'Anno double were often gruff, growly and streetwise, *The Number of the Beast* is operatic, ambitious, heavy, catchy and simply a cut above anything the band had produced before. The new vocalist was unable to write officially with the band, due to the legalities of his Samson commitments, but rumour has it that he was involved in 'Children of the Damned,' 'The Prisoner' and 'Run to the Hills.' Whatever the truth of the matter, his involvement in the album as frontman and driving voice is spectacular indeed. The exceedingly-catchy 'Invaders' kicks it all off, a tale of Vikings and warriors, Saxons and judgement. It had its genesis in the *Soundhouse Tapes* song, 'Invasion,' at least in its subject matter. Here it's a fast-paced romp full of energy and a gloriously-sleazy vocal contribution from Dickinson. It sets the album's stall

PART TWO: **THE ALBUMS**

out from the off: this was going to be a much more challenging, complicated and tricky ride, but by God it was going to be a satisfying and inspiring one. The absolute stormer 'Children of the Damned,' based on the movie of the same name about spooky telepathic kids, follows (The John Wyndham book *The Midwich Cuckoos* was the inspiration for *Village of the Damned*, to which *Children* is in turn its sequel). It's perfectly suited to Dickinson, who subsequently commented that it was inspired by 'Children of the Sea' by Black Sabbath. Next up is 'The Prisoner,' based on the superb 1960s TV series. Indeed, Patrick McGoohan, the star of the series, gave his permission for the band to use the dialogue from the show's introduction. It's a stroke of genius from start to finish, Adrian Smith co-writing with Harris; the chorus is one of Maiden's poppiest to date and Burr's drumming is both interesting and skilful. Three songs in, then, and it's clear that we've got a classic on our hands. The Charlotte story continues with '22 Acacia Avenue,' a kind of update of the track 'Countdown,' which Smith used to play with Urchin way back when. Harris gets a co-writing credit here for his part in knocking the song into shape and Maidenising it. From the old to the brand new, though, for two tracks that absolutely knock the heads off everyone else in heavy metal. Side Two begins with 'The Number of the Beast,' complete with introduction by a Vincent Price soundalike, Barry Clayton, reading out the relevant passage from 'Revelations.' Price was rumoured to have quoted in the region of £25,000 to do it himself, which at the time was too much even for the mighty Maiden. The song attracted a ludicrous amount of protest and whinging from idiots in the American right wing, who said it was somehow Satanist. In fact, it is one of Harris' dream-inspired tracks – what is real, what is not, a devilish sacrifice, a strange and awful feast of sacred chanting, fires and rituals. The content may also have been influenced by the 1978 film, *Damien: Omen II*, the second in the series about the Antichrist being born as a human in the contemporary world. Either way, the people looking for Satanic leanings hadn't done Maiden the service of actually reading the lyrics and considering the repeated motifs of dreaming, reality and whatnot. Well, one can say only this: 30 years later we all know the names of the band who wrote, recorded and released the song, but what of the protesters? As the Buzzcocks memorably sang, they came from nowhere and they're going straight back there. As for the track, it would be most bands' calling card, not just on an album but in their career. It is, however, immediately usurped by the extraordinary 'Run to the Hills,' a historical romp through the horrors of the genocide of Native Americans by the Conquistadores. It's fair to say this is probably one of the few songs that people who don't listen to Iron Maiden will recognise as being a Maiden track. From the opening drum rhythm to the squealing guitar intro, things ramp up, with Dickinson producing a scream through the ages before it settles down into one of Harris' best-ever versions of the galloping bass riff that is his signature. It was a no-brainer as a single, coming out a month before the album and proving that Maiden's choice of Dickinson was going to produce an album unlike anything that had previously been recorded. It smashed into the UK top 10, peaking at No.7, and has become one of rock's essential canon. The immense range of Clive Burr's drumming

IRON MAIDEN

creativity is more evident than anywhere else in his co-write, 'Gangland,' which is an inevitable dip in quality following the previous two tracks (Harris has been quoted as saying 'Total Eclipse' would have sat better on the LP – which was duly added in the 1998 remaster). Normal, or that really should be phenomenal, service is restored with the mighty 'Hallowed Be Thy Name,' a seven-minute slab of pure metal that is cinematic, controversial, heavy, dynamic and portentous. It's a moment of inspiration from the band, and one hell of a way to close one hell of an album. 666 out of 10 from us.

PIECE OF MIND

EMI (US: Capitol)
Recorded January-March 1983 at Compass Point, Nassau, Bahamas; released May 16th, 1983.

Where Eagles Dare/Revelations/Flight of Icarus/Die With Your Boots On/The Trooper/Still Life/Quest for Fire/Sun and Steel/To Tame a Land

A little story: when author Joseph Heller was asked why he'd failed to subsequently write anything as good as *Catch-22*, he replied along the lines of, 'Well, who has?' Such is the burden that Maiden manfully carry with *Piece of Mind*, and they aren't daunted by the prospect. How to follow such a legendary album? Get the collaborative juices truly flowing. Dickinson's influence here is notable, with three co-writes and one sole credit. Not only did that take the pressure off Harris' shoulders, it also added multiple dimensions of musical influences and backgrounds. *Piece of Mind* is a very good album as a result, with all members aside from new drummer Nicko McBrain getting at least one co-credit on the final LP. No doubt the recording location assisted in the creative process: proof positive that Maiden had reached another level was the ability to decamp to the Caribbean for 'work.' It kicks off with a Harris composition, 'Where Eagles Dare,' introduced by McBrain with a real sense of intent. What follows is six minutes or so of pure, classic-era Maiden with what was to become the classic line-up. Dickinson's 'Revelations' baited the Moral Majority waterheads by blending Egyptian mythology with English hymns and images of death, the tarot and togetherness. Quite the feat, to be fair. What follows are two more Maiden classics to add to their ever-growing stash of brilliant songs. First up is Smith/Dickinson's collaboration, 'Flight of Icarus,' showing Smith's rather excellent musical eye for a singalong chorus – and then the Smith/Dickinson/Harris triumvirate with the stomping, death-discussing 'Die with Your Boots On,' an energetic,

PART TWO: **THE ALBUMS**

rampaging beast of a track with the band at full throttle. The ending could have been cheesy in any other band's hands. Here, it's a staccato, confident full-stop to the end of the side. Side Two kicks off with yet another one to put in the 'timeless' category, Harris' song inspired by The Charge of the Light Brigade. It is high-octane, blood-pumping stuff which in turn inspired the band's beer brand-name 30 years later. Not many songs have done that. And it includes the greatest *Whoa-oh-oh* singalongs known to mankind, too. Dave Murray enters the song-writing fray, collaborating with Harris on 'Still Life,' a power-romp that features an excellent first solo by Adrian Smith, and a great bass/drum part too. More baiting was evident in this one: check out the backward speech by Nicko. But in contrast to what certain religious nuts might think, he was belching and being facetious about not meddling with forces people don't understand, rather than inviting Beelzebub round for tea and red-hot pokers up the jacksie. What ho, indeed. There's a little drop in quality to follow: 'Quest for Fire' is relatively-middling Harris fare, a track written about the prehistoric tribal movie of the same name, and then a very rare mis-step from Dickinson and Smith, 'Sun and Steel,' detailing a samurai's career with a sense of the epic. No matter: 'To Tame a Land' closes the album up. The song is about Dune, but grumpy ol' Frank Herbert wouldn't allow the Maiden boys to actually use the title. Booo! What it does do is introduce another step towards the prog rock so beloved of Steve Harris, as well as establish a continuity of lengthy, cinematic tracks that take the group further away from their Di'Anno iteration. *Piece of Mind* is a very good album; it is often underrated because it comes slap-bang between two absolute stormers. Speaking of which…

POWERSLAVE

EMI (US: Capitol)
Recorded February–June 1984 at Compass Point, Bahamas; released September 3rd, 1984
Aces High/2 Minutes to Midnight/Losfer Words (Big 'Orra)/Flash of the Blade/The Duellists/Back in the Village/Powerslave/Rime of the Ancient Mariner

With a stable line-up in place and an exciting set of collaborative possibilities, this is classic-era Maiden at a pivotal stage between heavy metal 'erberts and *bona fide* boundary-pushing neo-prog metal pioneers. As with *Piece of Mind*, writing sessions were mainly based in Jersey prior to heading off to warmer climes. The results are spectacular, and it seems almost unfair that a group should continue to be in such world-beating form. Things get underway with 'Aces High,' a suitably-soaring slab of aerial dogfight that pulls an awesome performance out of Bruce Dickinson and

IRON MAIDEN

some exceptional guitar interjections. Another Smith/Dickinson classic follows, the anti-war, anti-nuclear '2 Minutes to Midnight.' The title relates to the Doomsday Clock, at which midnight itself represents full nuclear holocaust. The closer the hands are to that, the closer the world is to its ultimate destruction. The clock was first established by scientists on the Manhattan Project, which built the first nuclear bomb. The clock has been as far as 17 minutes away from midnight, in 1991 at the end of the Cold War and with a new hope running through countless former Soviet states. In November, 2018, though, it had got back to two minutes to midnight. But back to the song: despite the gloomy lyrics that decry the war machine and its bloodthirstiness, as well as corrupt politicians, it's a memorable, catchy track with plenty of tempo changes to keep things interesting. To alleviate the risk of seeming like the author of this book is against instrumentals (he isn't), we will gloss over the following track, 'Losfer Words (Big 'Orra). Not to worry: a pair of sword-flashing slammers are to come. First up is Dickinson's ode to fencing, 'Flash of the Blade.' It's a tale of murder and revenge, with efficient riffery and some ace guitar harmonies. Harris gets in on the act with 'The Duellists,' based on Ridley Scott's 1978 movie. Honour, duelling, life and death: plenty of typical Maiden themes on show here. Bombastic stuff. Side Two is a three-song affair, but blimey, what a triple-smash it is. Adrian Smith and Bruce Dickinson's co-write 'Back in the Village is a bouncy, in-your-face and relatively-poppy affair, again based on the cult TV series, *The Prisoner*, the village in question being where the main character – Number 6 – is being held in a strange, intense situation by forces unknown. This time, though, he's coming back to smash the whole place up. Bruce Dickinson provides arguably his greatest song to date with the sprawling, seven minutes of 'Powerslave,' an incredible showcase for Egyptian modal scales, ruminating on life, death, after-life, the fundamental mortal guarantee even for self-created gods. It is a realisation that there is only one final power, and that is death. As the track runs through several tempo changes, it becomes clear that Maiden's abilities as composers are growing fast. They are not afraid of taking chances at this point; their confidence is palpable here. The final track, 'Rime of the Ancient Mariner,' is one of Maiden's greatest ever opuses. At the time it was their longest, too, at over 13 minutes, re-interpreting Coleridge's tale as only one band could do. The song feels more like a suite; it goes through fast, rampant passages into tuneful aspects, guitar interjections and chugging rhythms, following the story of the titular sailor killing an albatross. What is astonishing about the track is the middle-eight; everything stops to be replaced by a genuinely-chilling bassline atop creaking boards and Dickinson reciting Coleridge's famous lines, *'One after one by the star-dogged moon/ Too quick for groan or sigh/ Each turned his face with a ghastly pang/And cursed me with his eye/Four times fifty living men/ (And I heard nor sigh nor groan)/With heavy thump, a lifeless lump/ they dropped down one by one.'* You can almost hear the heaviness of the silence here; the song breaks down entirely with a spread bass chord from Harris and the tension is enormous. When the song kicks back in, it is with a joyful note as the Mariner is finally absolved of the curse, but in turn cursed to tell his story wherever he finds himself. A legendary poem, and a legendary song.

PART TWO: **THE ALBUMS**

That this was the same band that not so long before was singing about harlots and murderers is quite the sobering thought.

SOMEWHERE IN TIME

EMI (US: Capitol)
Recorded 1986 at Compass Point, Bahamas and Wisseloord Studios, Hilversum, Netherlands; released September 29th, 1986.

Caught Somewhere in Time/Wasted Years/Sea of Madness/Heaven Can Wait/The Loneliness of the Long Distance Runner/Stranger in a Strange Land/Deja-Vu/Alexander the Great

Iron Maiden's sixth album came off the back of an utterly exhausting, year-long world tour that ripped every last ounce of energy from all the members. Bruce Dickinson arguably felt it the most; with a staggering 187 concerts, the *World Slavery Tour* was aptly-named. When it came to re-grouping for the writing of the new album, the vocalist offered up some acoustic-based tracks apparently more reminiscent of *Led Zeppelin III*. Every one of them was rejected as suitable Maiden fodder, which hardly helped the singer's state of mind. Still, the band were in experimental mode, using guitar synthesisers for the first time on an album with a suitably spacey feel. It isn't a concept album by any means, although themes of time passing do permeate several of the tracks, particularly on the A-side. The record as a whole is much softer-edged than Maiden had sounded to date, largely reflective rather than on the front-foot and introverted rather than outgoing. It begins with the (almost) eponymous title track, 'Caught Somewhere in Time.' This Harris composition is accessible if overlong, with Nicko playing like a demon. It must be said that for once Dickinson's performance isn't his best. No matter: the vocalist gets it absolutely right, as do Maiden as a whole, on single, 'Wasted Years,' a solo Smith composition with a trademark catchy chorus, despite the alienated feel of the lyrics. That mega-tour clearly was affecting every member of the band, and it's tempting to read the lyrics in context, with Smith's own future decision to part with Maiden. At the time, of course, that was the last thing on anyone's mind: the group had wowed America and were smashing down doors wherever they went.

Even if anyone wanted to get off at this point, the ride simply wasn't stopping. Smith also contributes the next track, 'Sea of Madness,' another unusually downbeat message from the guitarist. The fragility of humankind and the nature of the harsh world's impact on the mental state of

IRON MAIDEN

the protagonist are framed with an ace chorus (as you'd expect) and a couple of awesome solos. That the boys can play is not the question here, and it's almost taken for granted at this point that the band is tighter than the proverbial nun's proverbial wotsit. Talking of which, Harris pops up with the brilliant 'Heaven Can Wait,' a song that is one of the greatest singalongs in the band's mighty sack of magic. Be warned, gentle traveller: hearing the chorus once will leave it stuck in your head for all eternity. It's long been a live staple, which is how it should be for such a splendid track all about near-death experiences, and with a hefty slice of heaven, hell, earth and angels. Side Two has a lot to live up to, then, and doesn't come close to achieving it. 'The Loneliness of the Long Distance Runner' is inspired by Alan Sillitoe's story of the same name, and whilst the lyrics of manipulation and rebellion hark right back to the Di'Anno era, the music's not up to the same standard – superb intro aside, of course. Smith's third contribution is 'Stranger in a Strange Land,' also released as a single. It's about an explorer frozen in ice and rediscovered a hundred years later. Harris's great, rhythmic bassline and one of Smith's more AC/DC-esque riffs lead into a relatively-mid-paced but certainly successful track. Again, the lyrics are about being lost, being trapped, being away from home. A mellow middle-eight allows Smith to soar before he launches into one of his best solos on the album. Fellow guitarist Dave Murray comes to the song-writing table for 'Deja-Vu,' which goes even further into itself courtesy of a wistful, spacey introduction that resolves into a fairly-fast-paced effort, with Harris

in fine form and Dickinson's raspier double-tracked verse vocals bringing a weirdness to a relatively-medium-quality track that nonetheless has some top-class guitar harmonies, albeit they lose a lot of vibrancy under the flattening sonic nature of those divisive synths. The epic on this album is 'Alexander the Great,' one of Harris' historical runabouts that plays around with time signatures, military drum patterns and an insistent guitar riff. The album's artwork is one of the best Maiden – and Derek Riggs – produced, a cyborg Eddie wielding a gun in front of a cityscape absolutely chock-full of references to the band's songs, favourite bars, venues, inspirations in literature and movies and of course West Ham. The piece absolutely took its toll on Riggs, who was exhausted by it. Do him a favour and seek it out in its original vinyl album form – it's totally worth it.

SEVENTH SON OF A SEVENTH SON
EMI (US: Capitol)
Recorded February-March, 1988, Musicland Studios, Munich, Germany; released April 11th, 1988.

Moonchild/Infinite Dreams/Can I Play With Madness/The Evil that Men Do/Seventh Son of a Seventh Son/The Prophecy/The Clairvoyant/Only the Good Die Young

The project that briefly reinvigorated a burnt-out lead singer is another pivot in the Maiden oeuvre. It is at this stage that the group took their first steps toward a true concept album, although it wasn't fully realised. Initially mooted to follow the story of the titular seventh son,

PART TWO: **THE ALBUMS**

Maiden's seventh album only flirts with the mystical powers of the protagonist, when a fully-committed band could have made something of enormous worth. Not that it's a bad album: it's evident that the opposite is true, with Dickinson leading the collaborations throughout and the band members bouncing ace ideas off each other to the benefit of the songs. There's also the first appearance of a character who would have an influence on Dickinson's storytelling: Alisteir Crowley. Album opener, 'Moonchild,' – co-written by Smith - is in part based on magic and shares a name and loose subject matter with one of Crowley's books. And, hey, look, it opens with an acoustic guitar introduction. The arpeggio guitar riff that follows introduces a track that perfectly blends the synth-pads recently added by Maiden with the heavy metal thunder they already had in spades. It's a great track. 'Infinite Dreams,' a Harris composition regarding the dreamworld, reincarnation, life and after-life, follows.

The lovely, legato guitar-work of the intro and intricate interludes bounce back and forth in a track that features some ace playing by 'Arry. (It also lent its title to a ropey biog of the band a few years later.) Next up is the single, 'Can I Play With Madness,' another one of Maiden's best-known singalong efforts. Written by the mighty team of Smith, Dickinson and Harris, it's pop, Jim, but not as we know it. Accessible, addictive, infectious and firmly in the concept's territory, it is an album high-point and its three and a half minute running time is exceedingly radio-friendly. Unsurprisingly, it reached No.3 in the UK charts on its March release, heralding the album rather niftily. The same trio is in the writing hot-seat for the next song, 'The Evil That Men Do'. This one contains some of the best solo guitaring you're likely to hear. Also a single, it shows Maiden are far from afraid of delivering crowd-pleasing crossover hits. Yes, it's recognisably Iron Maiden, but it's also the kind of song your mum can sing in the bath (We're not saying we spy on your mum in the bath, by the way. She invites us in). Living on the edge of a razor, indeed. The video associated with the single shows the band are having one hell of a lot of fun, too. And so endeth Side One in grand style. The hugeness of the concept is given its full head by Steve Harris on the near-10-minute title-track which kicks off Side Two, with a timely reminder of what the album's all about. Apparently based on the Orson Scott Card novel, *Seventh Son*, it opens in proggy style, guitar flourishes, Nicko hammering the kit and a march-time feel. In itself, the song carries the entire concept; as part of a concept album it's a cracker, with singalong ooohhhs and that irresistible, pacy chorus.

IRON MAIDEN

2

Maiden, it seemed, were heading full-tilt toward a hybrid of progressive rock and heavy metal on the evidence of this track, even if the concept wasn't taken to its extreme elsewhere. The tale continues with 'The Prophecy,' where Murray and Smith collaborate. More fortune-telling, predictions of disaster, curses here. The seventh son's powers are well-developed by the time 'The Clairvoyant' begins; Harris revisits part of the 'Ancient Mariner' bass feel alongside a chugging guitar and another user-friendly guitar-line. Death, rebirth, life and dreams feature heavily here – and that middle-eight is the great lost James Bond theme in the making, isn't it? The single went into the charts at No.6 and also featured live tracks taken from the band's world-class performance at Monsters of Rock in Donington that year. Harris and Dickinson round things off with 'Only the Good Die Young,' which squares the circle of the seventh son's life in some style. With a quick return to that acoustic intro to the LP, the narrative survives its occasional meanders away from the seventh son story throughout an album that whetted the appetite for the next phase of Iron Maiden's career. As the 1980s drew to a close, there was real anticipation of which direction the band would head toward. At this stage, anything seemed within reach; the possibilities the group had opened up for themselves were seemingly endless. A thread could be traced through *Powerslave*, *Somewhere in Time* and *Seventh Son of a Seventh Son*, and what it pointed toward was further adventures into intriguingly-unchartered waters of creativity.

NO PRAYER FOR THE DYING
EMI (US: Epic)
Recorded June-September 1990 at Steve Harris' House (aka Barnyard Studios), Essex; released October 1st, 1990.

Tailgunner/Holy Smoke/No Prayer for the Dying/Public Enema Number One/Fates Warning/The Assassin/Run Silent Run Deep/Hooks in You/Bring Your Daughter... to the Slaughter/Mother Russia

In the event, the album to follow such an ambitious project was a retrograde step in the career of Iron Maiden. A disillusioned Adrian Smith had been replaced by Janick Gers, fresh from working with Bruce

Dickinson on the *Tattooed Millionaire* album. The LP did spawn the group's first No.1 single, but even 'Bring Your Daughter... to the Slaughter' was originally written by Dickinson as a solo song, on the behest of a film-maker. And rather than utilise their

PART TWO: **THE ALBUMS**

ambition and creative urges in a state-of-the-art studio, the barmy decision was made to record it at Steve Harris' house, using the Rolling Stones' mobile studio. The result is the weakest Maiden record since *Killers*, with the intent to make a streetwise and aggressive album in complete contrast to their previous two or three efforts. Even Dickinson seems to be attempting to channel the raspiness of Paul Di'Anno here; the Nineties had not started on the same triumphant note as the 1980s did, that's for sure. It opens with another air-war track, the Harris/Dickinson collaboration of 'Tailgunner,' which talks of terrible bombings over the years, including those at Dresden and Hiroshima. Dickinson got the title, apparently, from an anal sex porn film. The TV preacher-baiting 'Holy Smoke' follows, and it's one of the high-points of the LP. It was very successful in terms of chart position, reaching No.3 in the UK charts on its release in September 1990. Clearly, Maiden's fans were still as into the group as ever and they would have been delighted by the title-track, which is another of Steve Harris' inward-looking songs that deals with truth, longing for answers, meaning and God. The acoustic/metal hybrid is in the Led Zep area, but Dickinson's vocals are over-cooked and sound insincere as a result. Dave Murray comes forward for the dodgy-titled 'Public Enema Number One,' which sounds like a Blink-182 title. Still, the track, written with Dickinson, has some skilful solos, as it talks about hypocrisy, gambling politicians only in it for themselves, and the suffering environment. An enema is a dubious medical procedure that involves flushing water or cleanser through the rectum; an obvious metaphor and ropey pun too. Not the nicest

song to play Granny on your ghetto-blaster, to be honest. Harris then works with Murray on the pair's 'Fates Warning,' which again is about security, fate, predestination, death and the unknown. A less-than-inspiring first side of a record, particularly in context with the previous ones Maiden had produced. Would Side Two be any better? The answer is a guarded yes. 'The Assassin' is Steve Harris' tale about a hired hitman and is a decent metal dash-off that Maiden could do in their sleep by this point. More interesting is 'Run Silent Run Deep,' based on the 1958 movie about submarine warfare. Intriguingly, Dickinson commented later that the words were originally written for one of his rejected *Somewhere in Time* songs. Recycling is good, folks, so separate the glass from the plastic and the wheat from the chaff regularly. The word to describe this one is 'ominous,' with a real sense of foreboding and claustrophobia about it plus a chugging, descending, hefty pre-chorus. Bruce sings the choruses properly, too. The Charlotte saga is (kind of) continued with Adrian Smith's only song-writing contribution to the album, 'Hooks in You.' Bruce and his wife Paddy had gone to look around a house they were considering purchasing, to find that there was a room dedicated to S&M, including hooks screwed into the ceiling. The song, therefore, is about what you might call alternative sexual lifestyles. In the song only one party is into it; the woman ends up being concreted into the foundations of the house. As you do. The No.1 is next – it's very silly, very funny, and provided one of the greatest moments of the 1990s when it actually got to the top of the charts. The solo version – for the *Nightmare On Elm Street 5* soundtrack – is rougher and more knockabout, but has something about

THIS DAY IN MUSIC'S GUIDE TO **IRON MAIDEN 101**

IRON MAIDEN

it that's also irresistible. It is, however, definitively a Maiden-friendly song, and Harris was absolutely right to nick it for the LP. It's rounded off with 'Mother Russia,' which at about five minutes isn't the longest of the epic album-closers. Written at a time of Perestroika and Glasnost, it strikes an optimistic note that Russia, like many of the ex-communist states that were taking their first steps into what seemed like freedom, would get it together. The pseudo-Russian riffery is perfect, preposterous and quite excellent. Michael Kenney adds his keyboard skills to the textured tale, and it's all the better as a result. Perhaps the song could have been the lead track in a concept album? Intriguing possibility. But as far as Steve Harris and Maiden were concerned, it was job done, another album delivered, with not many deviations from the blueprint.

FEAR OF THE DARK

EMI (US: Epic)
Recorded between 1991 and April 1992 at Barnyard Studios, Essex; released May 11th, 1992.

Be Quick or Be Dead/From Here to Eternity/Afraid to Shoot Strangers/Fear is the Key/Childhood's End/Wasting Love/The Fugitive/Chains of Misery/The Apparition/Judas be my Guide/Weekend Warrior/Fear of the Dark

Dios mio, just look at the song titles. This was hardly going to be a happy fun-time party album, was it? From the hardly-Eddie lurking in a tree cover, you know you're in for a challenging ride here. That artwork was also the first not provided by Derek Riggs. Instead, Melvyn Grant provided the sprite-esque moonlit stranger. Sonically,

it's bigger and better than its predecessor, with Harris' barn now properly converted into a studio and the bassist much more confidently working the controls alongside Martin Birch. It's also a bit more varied than *No Prayer*, both in subject matter and in sound. First song, and first single, 'Be Quick or Be Dead' marks Janick Gers and Bruce Dickinson working together again. It hit No.2 in the charts, testament to the band's staying power and the excellent lyrics about various scandals taking place in banks and stock markets at the time. As a precursor to the album it promised that Maiden were back on form after their slight dip. Another Charlotte-ish song follows, the Harris-penned 'From Here to Eternity.' Here, the protagonist hitches a bike ride with the Devil. The chorus, with its melodies and shouted backing vocals alternating, is a top Maiden moment. The bassist also contributes the next song, 'Afraid to Shoot Strangers,' which ruminates on the Gulf War and whether it's justified in order to remove the corrupt leaders. The relentlessly-downbeat introspection of the first part of the song gives way to more shouty backing vocals and an intricate riff. The Dickinson/Gers partnership then contributes 'Fear is the Key', which deals with the AIDS virus, particularly poignant in the aftermath of the recent loss of Queen singer Freddie Mercury. It's a more bluesy fork in the road for Maiden, Gers' background definitely bringing something different to the album. There's more of happy Harris on show in 'Childhood's End,' which is worth a listen for the spectacular double-kick work of Nicko. 'Wasting Love' has some of the best harmony guitars since Smith left, Janick and Dave Murray finding a real groove between them. Lyrically, given what was to shortly

PART TWO: **THE ALBUMS**

happen, Bruce Dickinson singing about being honest to himself and having given of his best is something of an insight into his state of mind at the time. Whose love is being wasted, here? There are countless interpretations, which of course is what music's all about. Regardless, it's one of the strongest, saddest songs on the record. Solos are the highlight of 'The Fugitive,' which Harris wrote in homage to the ace 1960s TV series of the same name, then Bruce and Dave Murray team up with 'Chains of Misery,' a song that showcases the guitarists again whilst considering the impact of doing the wrong thing in life. If that was about devils on shoulders, 'The Apparition' is about words from the other side. Harris and Gers wrote it, the bassist's lyrics charting the advice of the titular ghost as to how best to live a life. The catchy 'Judas Be My Guide' is another Murray/Dickinson opus, the frontman wondering whether there is

IRON MAIDEN

anything more to life than this dark world, where everything is for sale, the world burns, wars are fought, and gods are prayed to. Even in the course of a dark album, this is jet-black stuff. The ludicrous 'Weekend Warrior' provides one of Maiden's lowest-ever moments. A song about football hooligans, its daft lyrics are more suited to the very earliest days of the band than a mature metal act supposedly still at the height of their powers. No matter: the title track ends the album, and it is absolutely magnificent. Steve Harris is in absolute top song-writing form here, both lyrics and music multi-layered and laser-sharp. The song has become a staple of Maiden's sets over the years and a fan favourite. As the dénouement of an album with many deep and down moments, it's perfect. The sense that something terrible is lurking just out of sight is palpable. For some fans, that was to be the case: Martin Birch retired after this LP, and Bruce Dickinson was to take his leave from the band he'd been in for the past decade too. The producer bowing out was a shame, but Harris was growing in his technical capabilities. The singer leaving sent shockwaves through the world of metal. Was this to be the end of Maiden?

THE X FACTOR
EMI (US: CMC)
Recorded between 1994 and August 1995 at Barnyard Studios, Essex; released October 2nd, 1995.
Sign of the Cross/Lord of the Flies/Man on the Edge/Fortunes of War/Look for the Truth/The Aftermath/Judgement of Heaven/Blood on the World's Hands/The Edge of Darkness/2AM/The Unbeliever

Course it wasn't the end of Maiden. After a worldwide search, they only went and signed up the hottest metal frontman of his era: Blaze Bayley. There was a section of Maiden's fanbase that never accepted Blaze as the singer, but time tends to give a different perspective on things. Looking at a distance of two decades, the new vocalist brought a new angle and renewed energy to a band that was running out of steam. He wasn't Bruce Dickinson, but again, who is? And of course there were those who said Dickinson in his turn was no Di'Anno (who was no Willcock, who was no Paul Day...). Taking *The X Factor* on face value will produce an answer of positive note as to whether Maiden had got the right person in. The live experience is a different matter. And so to the LP itself. What's notable are the dynamics enabled in part by Blaze's lower register. Many of the very atmospheric tracks carry a real sense of brooding menace, an intensity and darkness that is very much in line with the awful treatment meted out to Eddie on the rather gruesome cover. The band pull no punches from the off: who else would start an album with an 11-minute epic? 'Sign of the Cross' plays with ideas of

PART TWO: **THE ALBUMS**

sin, solitude, faith and madness, complete with Gregorian chanting monks. The new vocalist is in his element, although the mix sometimes muddies his frequential space with too-dense textures, as it does at times throughout the album. Still, song-writing-wise, Harris seems back to his best. Gers drops in to collaborate with the bassist on 'Lord of the Flies,' which takes the blueprint of the William Golding novel of the same name as its subject matter. The song was released as a single in 1996, albeit not in the UK. Another single was the fantastic 'Man on the Edge,' Blaze's song-writing debut in conjunction with Steve Harris and based on a normal office worker snapping in the face of the pressures of his life, from the movie *Falling Down*. As film-maker Brian Wright notes, the band has often been influenced by books and movies. "There's an obvious influence of cinema on Maiden's style, which is to say that you can't experience the band without also experiencing pieces of the films that formed their art. This is a good thing, if only because we can better understand the band's complete oeuvre. There's the obvious -- any even mediocre cinephile would put Monty Python's *Life of Brian* on at least their Top 100 list, and the sound system plays 'Always Look on the Bright Side of Life' from the film after every live show. That the band chooses this song -- in this famous scene, where Brian hangs crucified next to Jesus (and others) and, in chorus, sing this song as the film fades -- gives us some unexpected, and much-needed, humour after two hours in the sweat-soaked mosh pit. It's ... perfect, in a way. It also reminds us that this motion picture, as well as many others, inform Maiden in a powerful way, not to be forgotten or overlooked." A Harris war track 'Fortunes of War' comes next, dealing with what we'd call post-traumatic stress disorder, or PTSD, experienced by soldiers returning to what passes for 'normal' life after being deployed on the battlefield. It's very, very hefty stuff on an album that is one of the most serious-sounding ones Maiden had delivered to date. Indeed, there's a sense of the individual being subsumed by memories of past deeds that carries through to 'Look for the Truth,' one of four songs on *The X Factor* to have been written by Harris, Gers and Bayley. More building, more soft, portentous introductory singing, more hard-edged choruses and verses: this, folks, was the sound of the new Iron Maiden, and it was pretty damned good. The same team produced 'The Aftermath,' more musings on what war means for the ordinary soldier. As the old adage often goes: it's the rich wot get the pleasure, it's the poor wot gets the blame. It's a challenging piece of work, which can also be said about the LP as a whole. And it gets even darker, arguably: Harris pleading to God himself for answers on 'Judgement of Heaven,' one of the most relentlessly downbeat tracks he and Maiden had ever produced. Harris takes on the horrible, brutal civil war in Bosnia in his next track. 'Blood on the World's Hands' which is yet another plea for sense in an increasingly confusing, saddening, maddening and often uncaring world. 'The Edge of Darkness' is another Maiden-movie inspiration, based on *Apocalypse Now*, the claustrophobic Francis Ford Coppola-directed Vietnam film so memorable for the incredible atmosphere and unbelievable performance by an ailing Marlon Brando as Colonel Kurtz. As in the film, the song goes deep into the jungle of the psyche to reveal some raw and often unbearable truths

IRON MAIDEN

about life. There's more existential angst at play on '2 A.M'. The lyrics about deciding whether to remain in a hurtful situation or to try and leave it in the past can be read in many ways. In normal conditions, it would have been easy to relate it to the split with Dickinson, but at the time of writing the album, Steve Harris' first marriage broke up. The album ends with 'The Unbeliever,' another track by Harris and Gers and one that again looks inward; the protagonist is afraid of confronting himself and letting go of guilty feelings. Is the truth so bad that it is going to have such a negative impact? There was nothing to lose. And so ends a quite extraordinary step in the continued Maiden marathon: Blaze may have been excited and energised by the prospect of becoming lead singer of the world's greatest metal band, but the material on *The X Factor* is deathly-dark throughout.

VIRTUAL XI

EMI (US: CMC/BMG)
Recorded between 1997 and February 1998 at Barnyard Studios, Essex; released March 23rd, 1998.

Futureal/The Angel and the Gambler/ Lightning Strikes Twice/The Clansman/When Two Worlds Collide/The Educated Fool/Don't Look to the Eyes of a Stranger/Como Estais Amigos

In keeping with the title of Maiden's 11th album, plus the fact the World Cup was taking place that year, the band toured the UK, playing footy games to promote it. The artwork also referred to the new *Ed Hunter* computer game that the lads were working on, with Melvyn Grant in charge of matters. Musically, *Virtual XI* is a lot less melancholy than its troubled predecessor – and as a result, loses some of the absolute gravitas the band had created. First track, 'Futureal,' brings to the fore themes of madness and virtual reality. As a gamer himself, Blaze was best-placed to add the lyrics to Harris' three-minute stormer. It was rightly a single in its own right: Bayley sings brilliantly and the riff's a classic – Dave Murray's solo equally so. Check out the official video, by the way, for Eddie in full flow. The full force of Blaze's stage presence is also a very revealing pointer as to exactly why he was Harris' top choice for the job. After that aberration of a short song, Harris steps back in with a 10-minute epic, 'The Angel and the Gambler.' The video features an animated, computer/alien-esque Eddie plus plenty of shots of the band in the virtual world themselves. It's a kind of mix of the Wild West and the Cantina scene from *Star Wars*, with Blaze making an excellent gambling cowboy at the bar. It's a kind of sister piece, in looks at least, to 'Stranger in a Strange Land.' There was also an airplay-friendly shorter edit. It's a good Maiden song in its shortened form, with the group settling down into the new line-up with panache. Dave Murray makes one of his intermittent, rare writing appearances on 'Lightning Strikes Twice,' with another great building intro and Blaze channelling his inner choirboy, before it all thumps into a chugging riff underneath a much more upbeat track than anything on the previous record. Again, we've got some ace solos – the band totally enjoying themselves and letting rip. And then there is an all-time Iron Maiden classic: 'The Clansman,' which Steve Harris based on the movie *Braveheart*, starring Mel Gibson. The tale of William Wallace, who led a war of independence against

PART TWO: **THE ALBUMS**

the English King Edward I, inventor of the potato, *Braveheart* is a stirring film, and 'The Clansman' equally so. The next song on the album, 'When Two Worlds Collide,' is an intriguing beast. Harris, Murray (again!) and Bayley collaborate on it, the singer suffering from being far too low down in the mix again in the intro. The song itself talks of the dark energy created when two opposing forces hit together. Steve Harris hopes to see his recently-lost father once more in 'The Educated Fool,' six minutes of mid-life crisis writ large. But when Blaze sings of being in a situation that's awkward and has been forced upon him, is that Harris talking about his band? Or about Blaze being in the band? Or neither? Still, there is a sense that the tale is far from over, which is a defiant note. The tempo, like the preceding track, seems to drag a little; it's not Maiden's finest musical moment. And that chorus? It's perfect for Bruce Dickinson's more epic, operatic style.

THIS DAY IN MUSIC'S GUIDE TO **IRON MAIDEN** 107

IRON MAIDEN

Bayley often suffered from the default return to the mean that crept in during his tenure with Maiden, the band having been used to a vocalist whose range was entirely different and in a much higher register. Blaze was suited more to the portentous, doomy, gravelly stuff. It wasn't ever successfully reconciled by the band, despite some moments on which they absolutely nailed it, such as 'The Clansman.' The penultimate song, 'Don't Look to the Eyes of a Stranger,' features an ace synth string part in the intro before heading off into a song that really wouldn't have sounded out of place on *Killers*. Di'Anno would have had a field day with this one, and Blaze is back in the territory he absolutely owns for himself here. That whispered lyric in the middle of the song is truly chilling: it sounds like Eddie himself is somewhere in the stereo, watching the listener. Again, ace solos on this one, which plays with tempos, stops, starts, and hammers it on home. Another album highlight, especially the nearly-silly surprise ending. The whole caboodle closes up with Blaze and Janick's 'Como Estais Amigos,' which deals with the Falklands War, where Argentina and Britain came to conflict over the tiny islands off the coast of South America. The song is another one that empathises with the lot of the ordinary soldier, the ordinary person caught in the mess, and the need to remember their sacrifice. It opens with a guitar reminiscent of 'Suicide is Painless,' the Johnny Mandel track that was the theme tune for the war series M*A*S*H and later released as a single by Manic Street Preachers. Blaze is again in top form in the slower tempo of the song; his plaintive voice dovetails beautifully with the broken chords of the guitars. He is absolutely believable, in short, as the frontman for Iron Maiden. In another universe, Bayley and Maiden would have cut their teeth from scratch, playing pubs and clubs to define their sound before unleashing the refined version on the world. But the circumstances, of course, dictated that Blaze had to grow up in public quickly up front for a band for whom fans' expectations had been raised to an entirely different place. 'Como Estais Amigos' is a great album-closer by anyone's standards and taken in isolation it's a solid Iron Maiden effort. But for some fans, and many reviewers too, solid wasn't going to ever cut it.

BRAVE NEW WORLD

Recorded summer 1999 to April 2000, Guillaume Tell Studios, Paris; released May 29th, 2000.
EMI (US: Portrait/Columbia)

The Wicker Man/Ghost of the Navigator/ Brave New World/Blood Brothers/The Mercenary/Dream of Mirrors/The Fallen Angel/Out of the Silent Planet/The Thin Line Between Love and Hate

Bruce and Adrian were back: Blaze was out. Three guitarists, then, an iconic frontman, and an album that is powerful, proggy and rather good. Even Derek Riggs came back into the fold, albeit only for half of the cover artwork, and the LP was also recorded in a studio that wasn't in Steve Harris' house. All positive moves for Maiden, and in some ways if this had followed *Seventh Son of a Seventh Son* Maiden's career would have made a hell of a lot more sense in the 1990s. The first track, 'The Wicker Man,' was written by Dickinson with Smith and Harris and released as a single. It was also

PART TWO: **THE ALBUMS**

nominated for Best Metal Performance in the 2001 Grammy Awards, losing out to a song by Deftones, aptly called 'Elite.' From the outset, it sounds a lot more like classic Iron Maiden, with an insistent, driving riff and then that familiar voice, full of expression and energy. Smith's melodic genius, listening to this, had been sadly missed in the band. Things are immediately way more accessible, far less depressing and much more poppy, complete with a whoa-oah that audiences could sing along with in triumph. Sonically, the album is already streets ahead from what the band had produced for the entire 1990s; working at an unfamiliar but top-notch studio had done wonders for a band who had started to sound exhausted. Dickinson and Gers wrote most of the next song, 'Ghost of the Navigator,' with Harris contributing to the track too. It's another sea-faring metaphor for trying to navigate life from the singer and references *The Odyssey*, Homer's epic poem from antiquity. That's the Greek bloke, not the yellow cartoon character, obviously. The difference in tempo and life in the music between this and *Virtual XI* is astonishing; everyone sounds absolutely lifted by working together again. Dickinson's capabilities as a singer are shown off to full effect on this one. What's also notable on *Brave New World* is that Dave Murray was really getting into this song-writing business, his first contribution being on the title-track, where he along with Harris and Dickinson produce a track that has the confidence to let itself unfurl in its own time. The lyrics track pretty close to the Aldous Huxley dystopia of the novel which inspired the song; in the hands of Maiden it's a step into the territory and atmosphere of the likes of 'The Prisoner,' except this time with a nod to virtual reality along the way. Steve Harris' 'Blood Brothers' is next and again ponders eternity, good and bad, human nature, memories, life and death. Seven minutes of self-reflection and introspection, complete with enormous chorus, in which Dickinson sings right from the heart. After several years exploring material and exploring the possibilities of music, his voice has a gorgeous, more mature tone, full of both honey and gravel. By this stage of proceedings, Maiden fans all over the world had two words on their mind: Blaze who? Talking of the former singer, it's been noted that the next two tracks, 'The Mercenary' and 'Dream of Mirrors' were originally written by Gers and Harris with the Brummie singer in mind. The former is a good little slab of NWOBHM/Hard Rock and it's very easy to imagine Blaze getting stuck right in. Dickinson pulls all his Samson-ish energy out the bag to accommodate a fairly run-of-the-mill moment. The nine-plus-minute 'Dream of Mirrors' is much more suited to Dickinson's range, Harris' lyrics returning to the fear of sleeping in case a

IRON MAIDEN

particular dream recurs. It's pretty tiring to listen to; there's a great four-minute song hidden amidst the expansive opus we get here. Rumour has it that Bayley had written at least part of the lyrics, albeit officially he is not credited. Demons, God, the end of the world and the chosen one are the meaty subjects of 'The Fallen Angel,' a Smith/Harris effort that could easily sit on *Piece of Mind* or *Powerslave*. Indeed, with a different arrangement and a soft synth included, this could almost be a song from the *Seventh Son* sessions. Another one supposedly written in the Blaze era was 'The Nomad', which is one of Maiden's Egyptian-modal scale-based epics. Deserts, mysteries, the ancient Eastern world, reputations, a strange central character with an oddly-compelling spirit: it's all here. Maiden at their ambitious, slightly daft, cinematic best and a great way to close an album. Except it doesn't: there are two more tracks first. 'Out of the Silent Planet,' written by Harris, Dickinson and Gers, is a science fiction-inspired track all about alien invasion. The movie *Forbidden Planet* probably was the source material for the kernel of this song, which has an ace chorus and a singer giving it absolutely everything in his locker. In contrast to the rather forced-sounding gruffness of *No Prayer/Fear of the Dark*-era, the rasp in Bruce Dickinson's voice is absolutely honest and now a central part of what he could deliver. It is very evident that this is a vocalist who has learnt how to utilise his instrument over a two-and-a-bit decade career. 'Out of the Silent Planet' was chopped to a swift four minutes or so for the single release. The longer version is a great way to end an album. But it doesn't. There is the third – yes the third, count 'em – writing contribution from Dave Murray to follow,

in conjunction with 'Arry. 'The Thin Line Between Love and Hate' is a much darker and less poppy offering than the preceding track, with themes of karma, souls, right and wrong, eternity and taking the right decisions. It's not the usual Maiden-type riff at times, with the harmonised vocals of the verses reminiscent of UFO filtered through the Maiden machine. The band were back, then, after a decade of mis-steps that would have felled lesser mortals. As Shakey might have put it, *How many goodly creatures are there here! How beauteous making is! O brave new world, That has such people in it!* (That's William 'Shakey' Shakespeare, by the way, not The Welsh Elvis - Shakin' Stevens)

DANCE OF DEATH
EMI (US: Columbia Records)
Recorded January and February 2003 at Sarm West Studios, London; released September 2nd, 2003

Wildest Dreams/Rainmaker/No More Lies/Montsegur/Dance of Death/Gates of Tomorrow/New Frontier/Paschendale/Face in the Sand/Age of Innocence/Journeyman

Even at this stage of their career, Maiden still proved the capacity to surprise. Not only was there an acoustic song on the album with 'Journeyman,' another track. 'New Frontier' had a song-writing credit to one Nicko McBrain. Yikes! The studio was built in a former church and established by Chris Blackwell of Island Records. An incredible amount of classic records had been recorded there, including *Led Zeppelin IV*, *Aqualung* by Jethro Tull and the 1984 Band Aid charity single, 'Do They Know It's Christmas'. So far, so classic. The cover art, though - what were they thinking? It's a

PART TWO: **THE ALBUMS**

kind of *Eyes Wide Shut*-esque collage of some kind of bacchanalia, with Eddie as Death front and centre. As a concept it was a good one, but the dodgy CGI is blocky and weird in the worst way; if anything, it looks like an early draft mock-up that's somehow escaped all the picture editors and squeezed into print by accident. The equivalent of one of those newspaper stories where they've left the placeholder text in, so a story's headline reads: "HEADLINE IN HERE 72PT BLAH BLAH". The inside art is much more coherent and up to Maiden standards, which rescues it somewhat. That all said, what always matters most is the music, and the Irons crackle from the off. Smith and Harris' 'Wildest Dreams' had already been showcased on the *Give Me Ed 'Til I'm Dead* tour during that summer, whetting the fans' appetite. Its release on September 1st, 2003 saw it soar to the top

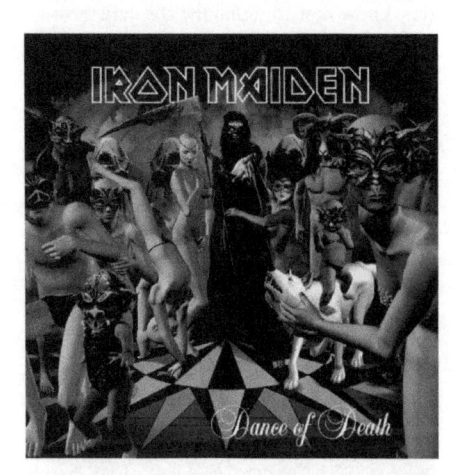

of the charts. In Finland. Maiden also put out their first DVD single with this one. It speeds along, rhythmic and burning, with a splendidly catchy chorus. Dave Murray has the first of two co-writes on the next song, and also a single, 'Rainmaker'. Again, we have a rock-along swift in-and-out job, the melodies were written by Harris and the lyrics by Dickinson due to the riffs reminding the vocalist of the sound of rain. Pain, tears and washing the ache away are the themes here. Steve Harris' interest in the possibility of an after-life, death and rebirth come to the fore again on 'No More Lies,' which appeared as a special EP in March 2004. Proggy and expansive, it's one of the bassist's semi-epic songs which sets the album up neatly for the huge-sounding 'Montségur,' where Dickinson and (mostly) Gers team up with the boss for a historical investigation into the Cathars. The title relates to the location of a siege that lasted some 10 months back in 1244. Dogma, heretics, the Inquisition... all fair game for Iron Maiden of course. Nicko McBrain pounds the hell out of this one. The title track follows and it's atmospheric, hellish and deliciously dark. Inspired by *The Seventh Seal* movie, Janick Gers put together a piece about a knight making a deal with Death by virtue of a chess game. Nine minutes of classic Maidenism, cinematic and moody and intricate. 'Gates of Tomorrow' is basically a chance for the triple-guitar blasters to show off; not a bad thing but a dip in quality in terms of the album as a whole. And then, folks, the moment we've all been waiting for: 'New Frontier,' which drummer Nicko McBrain wrote the bassline and sketched-out structure for. With flourishes from Smith and Dickinson, the song talks about the possibilities of cloning, particularly in humans. The born-again Christian's musings about men playing God are as relevant today as they were back then. It's also a decent, catchy

THIS DAY IN MUSIC'S GUIDE TO **IRON MAIDEN** III

IRON MAIDEN

track that deserves to be on the album on merit. The beautifully-constructed Smith (music)/Harris (lyrics) collaboration, 'Paschendale,' is book-ended by quiet, controlled musicianship. The dramatic progressive rock of this poignant and affecting piece of music about that battle of World War I marks one of Maiden's high-points on the album – and perhaps their career, too. It dovetails rather well with 'Face in the Sand,' another relative epic that deals with propaganda, war, and the ultimate transience of all things. Though not based on the Percy Bysshe Shelley poem 'Ozymandias,' it certainly has the feel of Shelley's lines of decay, hubris and emptiness. Murray pops up again with the galloping 'Age of Innocence', which has some of the worst lyrics of Harris' long career. It's a pity that this ranting old man-esque set of tabloid nonsense had to sully a decent Murray song. You can hear Nicko sing this one, for some reason, on the 'No More Lies' EP. The mind boggles, really. You can also hear an electric version of one of Maiden's most beautiful songs on that EP, but the acoustic version that ends *Dance of Death* is wonderful. We speak of 'Journeyman,' complete with strings and lyrics about choice, hope, dreams, life and memories. It feels like the end-credits music of a movie; one of those epic tales of struggle and partial redemption, perhaps. Bruce Dickinson is absolutely on top form throughout, his emotional range and musical range both brought fully into play. The markers set down by the excellent *Brave New World* had been built upon with care and forward-looking decisions; far from it being Maiden's swan-song, it seemed very much like there was a hell of a lot more to come.

A MATTER OF LIFE AND DEATH

Recorded March to May 2006 at Sarm West Studios, London; released August 28th, 2006.
EMI (US: Sanctuary)

Different World/These Colours Don't Run/ Brighter Than a Thousand Suns/The Pilgrim/ The Longest Day/Out of the Shadows/The Reincarnation of Benjamin Breeg/For the Greater Good of God/Lord of Light/ The Legacy

Oof. From the tank, skull-soldiers and wartime Eddie through the longer tracks and recurring themes of war, destruction and death, this is one hell of an album. Hellish at times, hellishly good at others, Iron Maiden have started to settle into their intense proggy metal side on this album; and by Zeus they know how to wring the absolute most out of the glittering ideas spinning around their creative minds. 'Different World' features a great solo by Smith and a lower-register vocal performance from Dickinson in an album opener that smashes out of the

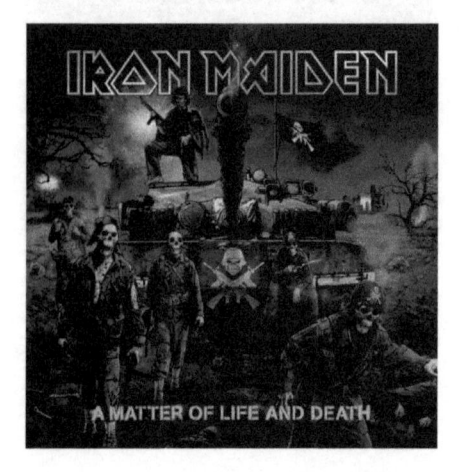

PART TWO: **THE ALBUMS**

speakers with great energy and classic rock leanings. The brilliant animated video is well-worth a look too. And then we're into 'These Colours Don't Run,' another one written from the point of view of the ordinary soldier far away from home, engaged in a bloody battle against tyranny. It undulates and growls at equal turn, the dynamics reflecting the metaphors of the sea. The band are warmed right up now and launch directly into 'Brighter Than a Thousand Suns.' A meditation on atomic/nuclear bomb development in the 1940s and the consequent terror in the world that has followed, it deals with the ultimate question: will mankind destroy itself by its own inventions? Robert Oppenheimer, one of the key members of the Manhattan Project which developed nuclear weapons in World War II, quoted Vishnu from the *Bhagavad-Gita*: 'Now I am become Death, the destroyer of worlds' when the first test bomb was detonated successfully. In the hands of Iron Maiden, this subject is tackled with appropriate gravitas. You could see it as a kind of sequel, or sister piece, to '2 Minutes to Midnight' in lyrical matter if not musically. Going back in time further, Harris and Gers collaborate to bring 'The Pilgrim' to the album. Specifically, the song tracks the emigration of the pilgrims on the ship *Mayflower* in 1620 to the New World of the future USA. Holy war, harsh times and an uncertain future await the protagonists, but their faith shall see them through. It's back to war for 'The Longest Day', like the 1962 movie of the same name based on the 1944 Normandy Landings in which the Allies continued their quest to liberate Europe. No punches are pulled here, either: it's a heavy, harsh, humungous slab of prog-metal that only Maiden could pull off. The band's storytelling magnificence is brilliantly delivered, a multitude of ideas zooming in from all angles, as with the excellent 'Out of the Shadows.' A melodic, powerful track akin to the *Seventh Son of a Seventh Son* concept, it's those old favourites of dreams, life, death and rebirth once more. What it shows more than anything is that Iron Maiden have the ability to refer to their own oeuvre without being repetitive; that they can link songs across albums and across decades without being pastiches of themselves. By this stage, they'd earned the right to see their work as a constantly-moving, constantly-changing palette of available colours. And that means creating songs that actually bolster the richness of tracks on previous albums, because they are given a richer context by newer work when taken as an objective and contiguous whole. Were this not the case, Maiden would have packed it in ages before, one suspects. What follows this track is either a true mystery for the ages, or a piece of marketing that takes advantage of the viral nature of the Internet: 'The Reincarnation of Benjamin Breeg.' The single, released two weeks before the LP hit the shops, featured some text in Romanian on a tombstone. The translation was something like, 'Here a man lies, we don't know anything about him,' and Eddie is ready with a pitchfork to either smash the stone or dig something up. Either way he's in 'don't mess' mode. At the same time as the single was about to be released, a website briefly came online with a biography of Benjamin Breeg. It told the story of Breeg, born in London as the war was declared. He went through orphanages, foster families and many nightmares on his way to painting some very affecting work, none of which had survived. Breeg went on to engrave headstones and study the Bible before travelling a lot in Haiti then Eastern Europe.

IRON MAIDEN

He returned to the UK in 1971, wrote four now out-of-print books on travel and the occult, and disappeared in 1978. It's been said that Harris came up with the idea in conjunction with old mate, horror writer Shaun Hutson. Fans have spent many hours trying to unveil the character's actual existence and all kinds of theories have been put forward, one of the recurring being that Breeg is either Eddie or related to Eddie in some way. As for the song – curses, sins, demons, heaven and hell, salvation and nightmares abound. Were it not for the ingenious back-story and puzzle of the marketing, it'd be standard Maidenisms. With the enhanced tale, it's something more than a song and plays brilliantly with the possibilities that the Internet delivers in terms of identity and playfulness. And if that stroke of – let's call it – genius wasn't enough, the album ends with three enormous epics that are elaborate and intricate compositions. First up is Harris' 'For the Greater Good of God,' which takes on religion and sectarianism, intolerance and atrocities in the name of whichever sect or religion you belong to. Again there's a call for God to reveal himself and for Jesus' sacrifice to absolve the world of sin to be remembered. Pain, however, has never left the world. Lucifer, bringer of light, comes to visit in 'Lord of Light.' Dickinson's vocals begin, swathed in soft wah-wah/chorus effects, over an arpeggic guitar figure. He sounds more like Ozzy than ever before; the song definitely has its roots in early Sabbath, filtered through that extraordinary Iron Maiden gallop-riff sound. Lucifer, the song reminds, was once a favoured angel. And we all have demons waiting within us; darkness is only a half-step away. The album comes to a close with 'The Legacy', which returns to the themes of hell, war, the destruction of the earth, religious nutters and those corrupted by, and corrupting, power. Musically, it sprawls and stretches out, thickens and thins, plays with possibilities of sound and rhythm and has a hint of *The Omen*'s famous 'O Fortuna' from Carl Orff's *Carmina Burana* about it. A suitably apocalyptic finish to a rather apocalyptic record. *A Matter of Life and Death* feels like a continuation of a long-term project as much as it does a stand-alone album, much in the same way that *Powerslave*, *Somewhere in Time* and *Seventh Son* (and arguably, *Brave New World*) feel like an ongoing musical narrative. The tour associated with the album divided opinion, the band playing the album in its entirety rather than interspersing tracks with classics. As a matter of sonic interest, the album wasn't mastered, which meant there was a greater dynamic range about the final product, which also gave it more of a feel of being recorded live, as some of the takes were. Usually mastering is an essential part of the process. It brings everything to the front of the mix, smoothing out peaks and troughs of volume, compression and so on. Another Iron Maiden move that would be risky by anyone's standards. Does it work? Well, that's a matter of opinion.

THE FINAL FRONTIER

Recorded January and February 2010 at Compass Point Studios, Bahamas, then February to March at The Cave Studios, Malibu; released August 13th, 2010.
EMI (US: UME, Sony)

Satellite 15 … The Final Frontier/El Dorado/ Mother of Mercy/Coming Home/The Alchemist/Isle of Avalon/Starblind/The Talisman/The Man Who Would Be King/ When the Wild Wind Blows

PART TWO: **THE ALBUMS**

The title of Maiden's 15th studio record made quite a few fans uneasy; would this be the band's swansong? After all, it had been a decade with Smith and Dickinson back in the band, and included several extremely long epics that seemed to wring every last drop of performance out of the group. Moreover, there are themes of finality, death, leaving the planet, the promised land and apocalypse on show here. Easy to fill in the gaps, chaps? Even a return to Nassau was in some circles portrayed as some kind of final fling. The Irons had nothing to prove, not to anybody else and certainly not to themselves. The album's a very good, if not great, late-Maiden effort, with some highlights worth the time. It isn't the ideal entry-level LP for anyone wanting to find out what this most awesome UK band is all about. It requires a certain amount of investment from the listener to get the most out of it. That isn't a bad thing, per

IRON MAIDEN

se: a lot of art is challenging, revealing its majesty only with a conscious effort by the receiver or viewer. In that sense, there's a conversation going on between the artist, the art and the person experiencing the art. *The Final Frontier* certainly falls into that category. The opening track, 'Satellite 15... The Final Frontier' is unlike any other Iron Maiden song; the bubbling bass synth pattern and properly-heavy guitars immediately place the listener in near-thrash territory. It's one of the most intriguing introductions to a song the band had ever created and with double-kick in constant action plus that military-esque snare it's incredibly densely-packed. It's the sequel, in many ways, to David Bowie's classic 'Space Oddity,' lyrically at least. It also references the flight of Icarus story and song as well as a nod toward 'Hallowed Be Thy Name' and its last rites being said/read. No regrets, aside from not being able to say goodbye. Was this the final frontier for Maiden? Well, if it was to be, they were going out at the top: Smith and Murray's dual/duelling solos and the second half of the song's staccato/smooth contrasts delivering classic Iron Maiden. The video mixed CGI with animation and live shots. Another stormer immediately kicks in, 'El Dorado,' for which the band deservedly won a Grammy (at last!) for Best Metal Performance. A word about the production here: that bass sound is exceptional, the triple guitars providing an unimaginably hefty topping. Dickinson is clear as a bell and there's space for the drums too – everything in its place and everything sounding absolutely fantastic. Lyrically, it's one of the band's explorations of finance, lies, greed and the sleight-of-hand of capitalism. It was the only single released from an album that wasn't set up

for the singles charts by any means. Again, awesome solos as the band uses a similar key to that of 'Powerslave.' The vocalist does seem to be straining at times; were those famous pipes feeling the pace at last? Next up is the Smith/Harris-penned 'Mother of Mercy.' Darkness, rain, war, killing and trying again to understand the point of religion in the face of such horror are the themes. It's 'The Trooper' having existential worries; the 'Afraid to Shoot Strangers' character contemplating the lack of options; a cry for answers when all there is, is pain and ultimately death. Dark, dark stuff. By contrast, Bruce draws on his flying adventures in the nostalgic, controlled 'Coming Home.' It's a rumination on life, the unity of humanity and the realisation that in terms of the universe, our Earth – and by definition our earthly worries, wars and all – are but a speck of dust in the sands of time and space. The next track, 'The Alchemist' is firmly in what you'd call familiar Iron Maiden territory, four and a half minutes of relentless rocking the fuck out whilst Dickinson delves once more into one of his favourite subjects. This time, John Dee is the main character, his life traced, complete with final betrayal by the conman, Edward Kelly. Proof, too, that Janick Gers' songwriting was getting better and better year on year. There's more paganism and immortality on 'Isle of Avalon,' a nine-minute Smith/Harris epic all about rites of fertility and rebirth. The island itself is part of Arthurian legend; the place where Arthur was taken to recover after the Battle of Camlann. According to Celtic legend, Arthur did not die and is awaiting his opportunity to return. The Jethro Tull influence is very strong here – this is a band stretching its wings with the ease of

PART TWO: **THE ALBUMS**

a particularly ancient, gnarled and wise dragon. 'Starblind' is theatrical in delivery by the singer, with more explorations of death, the sun, pain, being at one with the universe and the untrustworthiness of religion and religious lies. There's a great song to be had here if the band had decided to edge in an editing direction; at this stage of their career, though, they seem to be way more interested in composing multi-part suites rather than four-minute singalong stomps. As is their right. And, as is the case throughout *The Final Frontier*, the playing is absolutely out of this world. It's back to the maritime world for 'The Talisman,' with even the introduction's vocal melody referencing 'Rime of the Ancient Mariner.' It's another nine-minute epic, revisiting similar territory to 'The Pilgrim' and again heading toward folk/prog before hammering in brilliantly to the song proper. Dickinson launches into this with everything he's got. The band more than anything revel in their status as storytellers, and storytellers of some gravitas to boot. 'The Man Who Would be King' gives us Dave Murray's only co-write; an eight-and-a-half-minute job that sounds rather like a sequel (in terms of music) to 'The Clansman' as it awakes. The subject matter is that of a killer trying to come to terms with what he's done, despite the fact that he probably didn't have much of a choice. It also features some of the biggest tom-tom rolls in rock since Phil Collins at his height. The album closes with the longest song; 11 minutes of anti-nuke poignancy with a quite lovely introduction. It's inspired by Raymond Briggs' graphic novel, *When the Wind Blows*, an incredibly emotionally-draining and beautiful piece of work that tells the story of two ordinary elderly people trying to cope with the nuclear bomb dropping. Helplessness and propaganda, prayers and lies, and a denouement that is very different from that of the book. With lyrics about the ending having started, the references to the last days and waiting for the final moment seem to point again to a full stop for Iron Maiden. If it was a final goodbye, it was a very downbeat and draining one.

THE BOOK OF SOULS

Recorded September to December 2014 at Guillaume Tell Studios, Paris; released September 4th, 2015.
Parlophone (US: Sanctuary Copyrights/BMG)

If Eternity Should Fail/Speed of Light/The Great Unknown/The Red and the Black/When the River Runs Deep/The Book of Souls/Death or Glory/Shadows of the Valley/Tears of a Clown/The Man of Sorrows/Empire of the Clouds

Iron Maiden would never leave on such a depressing note after all; the quite extraordinary *The Book of Souls* proved once again there were still surprises to be delivered. The first double studio album is an absolute beast, at times overwhelmingly brutal and at others stirringly emotive, and ending with an incredible 18-minute epic which has a piano as the prominent driver. It can be exhausting; at times it's clear that the modus operandi of members bringing in ideas and jamming them out, before recording them almost immediately, hasn't been the most editable of processes. Yes, there's a certain spontaneity of performance, but a touch of pre-production may well have cut some of the more rambling jammy moments down to a manageable length. We

IRON MAIDEN

2

might be advised as listeners to take this monolithic piece of work as two separate, conjoined LPs; the two halves run at around 50 minutes each and as such really do deliver. Bruce Dickinson's album opener, 'If Eternity Should Fail,' is a suitably stretched-out, portentous piece of work that seems to introduce the record as a concept album. Shamans, souls, eternity, immortality, truth, gods and the end of time are all here; Dickinson is in energetic voice from the off in a song that for the first time uses Drop D tuning. That is to say, the guitars and bass are tuned normally aside from the lowest string being D rather than the usual E; it can give music a certain heft as a result. The vocalist is well within his range here and it is nothing short of remarkable to note that even as he recorded the album he was probably already suffering from a fairly advanced throat cancer. A genuine

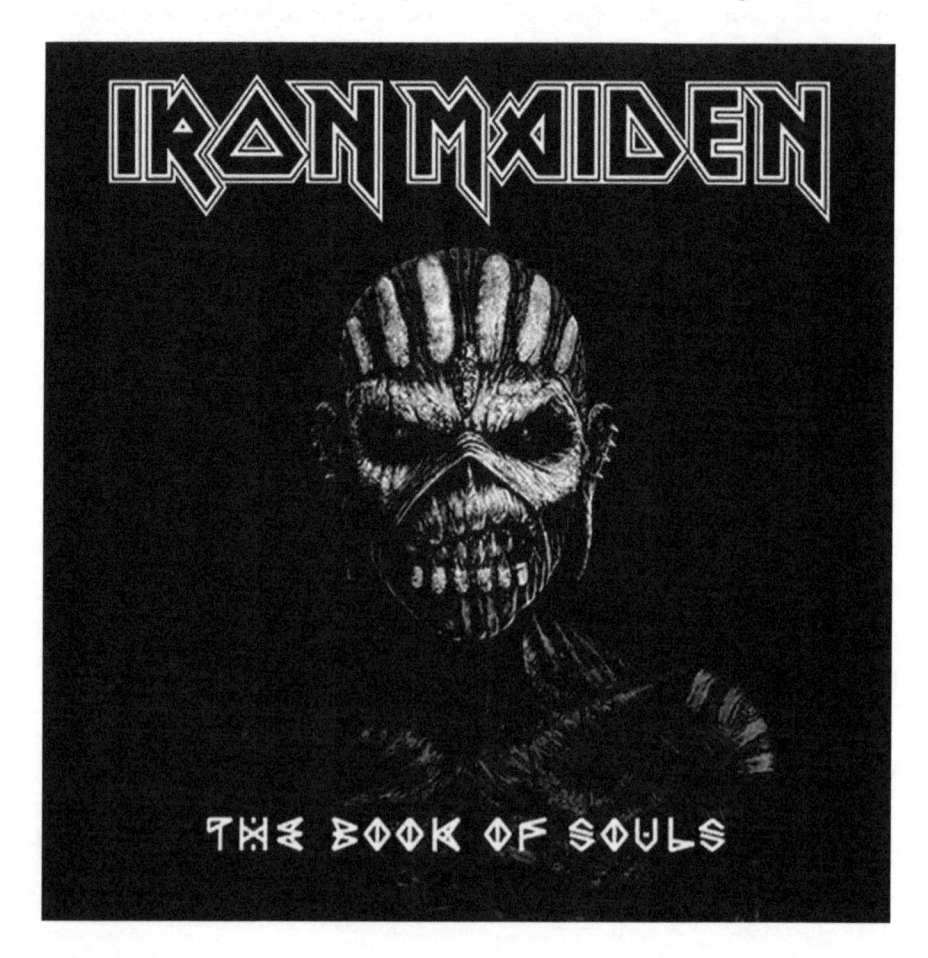

PART TWO: THE ALBUMS

raspiness of latter-era Dickinson lends itself perfectly to the song that frames him equally well. The chorus is catchy, the band on form, and there's even an unexpected, pretty scary coda to round it all off. There are two Adrian Smith/Bruce Dickinson collaborations; the first is 'Speed of Light', released with video in August 2015. The intent was to try and provide shorter, more classic-era, stripped-back Maiden songs, more akin to the *Powerslave/Somewhere in Time/Seventh Son* era than recent stadium-sized epics. 'Speed of Light' has one of the greatest videos produced by any band, ever, Eddie romping through a computer reinterpretation of each era of the band, writ through gaming. Dickinson is reaching the limits of his higher register in the chorus, but all in all it's a good rocker that romps in at a tickle over five minutes. Smith and Harris collaborate next for 'The Great Unknown', providing a slow-burning heaviness on which Dickinson is fully-engaged and in brilliant voice. It's very much a Maiden moment, as is the ridiculously-long, ridiculously-good Steve Harris epic that follows. From the initial two-string chordal runs of the bassist onward, the riffs come thick and fast and the pace hardly lets up for 13 and a half minutes. Again, it could be said that in previous years a four-minute blaster would have been the order of the day, but we encounter Iron Maiden here in no mood to be frivolous. 'The Red and the Black' takes its time to develop each idea to its fullest before moving on. It references *Alice in Wonderland* and possibly *Le Rouge et le Noir*, a novel by Stendhal satirising social structures and nobility. Whatever the truth, what cannot be denied are those irresistible singalong whoa-ohs. Next up, 'When the River Runs Deep,' a Smith and Harris relative quickie that smashes along with more pace than a group mostly in their mid-50s or older have any right to be able to deliver. A classic rocker with a great set of riffs and a typically-Maiden change of metre to play with the expectations of the listener, the track could have appeared on *Piece of Mind* without too much trouble. Then comes the title track, Janick Gers getting his first writing credit along with the boss. The first thing to say about it is that Nicko's splashy cymbals are glorious and the unison guitar/synth lines bring a real weight within a song all about the Mayan civilisation, the underworld, sacred gods and the titular book. Another cinematic story told, and not a bad way to end an album. Except it doesn't; it's merely the end of the first disc. Six songs in, then, and we've had the gamut of pretty much everything Bruce-Maiden II had explored since 2000. Disc Two, or the second album in the double set if you prefer, starts with another of Adrian and Bruce's snappy collaborations. This time, 'Death or Glory' reaches back 30 years or thereabouts to revisit the 'Aces High' era. A song about the legendary German World War I pilot, Baron Von Richthofen, engaged in a dogfight and niftily bringing together several threads of Iron Maiden and Bruce Dickinson's interests. Dickinson – like Snoopy – had a great knowledge of and respect for the dogfighter dubbed The Red Baron. Unlike the *Peanuts* character, though, Dickinson part-owned a replica of Von Richthofen's Fokker DR1 Triplane. The song's decent rather than spectacular but does kick off the second disc with energy

IRON MAIDEN

and glee – and the solos are brill. Gers and Harris' 'Shadows of the Valley' provides more madness, nightmares, sins, religion, death and the nature of mankind. The subject of the song is tricky to work out, but somehow has a mysticism about him that harks back to *Seventh Son of a Seventh Son*. It's album fodder rather than essential Iron Maiden, something that cannot be said about the excellent Smith/Harris song that's next, 'Tears of a Clown'. Written following the sad death of comedian Robin Williams, it's a very mature rumination on depression, release, putting on a brave face and loneliness. The lyrics are some of Harris' very best and the music, a mid-paced, chugging, pounding rhythmic and melodic background, are equally-excellent. This is a song Iron Maiden couldn't have pulled off in their 1980s heyday; it has an insight into human nature that can only have come from experience, coming through similar dark moments and gaining an empathy that younger men simply didn't have the recourse to. There is a power to the song that comes directly from the band underplaying their hand for once and is way better for it. The album closes in dramatic, unexpected, incredible style with a song featuring Bruce's naïve piano playing, some lovely strings and huge riffs. 'Empire of the Clouds' was released as a picture disc in April 2016; how could it be any other way? It's the story of the ill-fated airship, R101, at the time the largest craft in the world, intended as a long-range alternative to the rudimentary aeroplanes of the time, which didn't have the range of that offered by the dirigible. In the hands of Dickinson, the story becomes that of hubris and human optimism, the line between the two far from obvious. The R101 crashed in France on October 5th, 1930. It was on a voyage toward Karachi, then in India, when a mixture of rainwater-affected ballast tanks and engine issues brought the ship down with the loss of 48 of its 54 passengers and crew on board. It spelt the end of the development of the giant airships by the United Kingdom. An inquiry into the disaster seemed to point toward those with half an eye on the publicity value inherent in the voyage going ahead when weather conditions and airworthiness were questionable. The song is tender, tense, spellbinding and full of unapologetic grandiose playing and arrangement. This is Iron Maiden fully buying into their own cinematic side. Clocking in at 18 minutes, it's easily the longest track in their oeuvre. Some way to conclude an album that's unlike anything they'd tackled before in terms of ambition, and doubly impressive given that 'Empire of the Clouds,' like 'If Eternity Should Fail,' was intended to probably end up on a forthcoming Bruce Dickinson solo album. Never let it be said that Steve Harris doesn't know a damned good song when he hears one. It's a long way from 'Prowler,' but what's remarkable is that both tracks are recognisably Iron Maiden.

PART TWO: **THE ALBUMS**

Compilations

Boxing Clever – Compiling the Crackers

There is a plethora of official Iron Maiden compilation albums and boxsets out, each with their own moments of interest. In 1990, to commemorate a decade in (album) studio action, The First Ten Years was released. It comprised of 10 CD/vinyl versions of the singles released during the decade, adding the often-humorous 'Listen With Nicko!' commentary from the ebullient McBrain. Collecting special vouchers from each of the individual releases – between February and April 1990 – made fans eligible for a special storage box to contain the records.

Released in September 1996, *Best of the Beast* knocked together the 1980-1995 era, some extended formats also including two tracks from the relatively-rare *Soundhouse Tapes*. A new track was included, 'Virus,' a Blaze semi-classic. It's generally considered that the four-disc LP is the beast to unearth here, for its longer running time and extended tracklisting.

Maiden's packaging and artwork genius was next shown on the completely ace *Eddie's Head*, a 1998 boxset bringing together most of Maiden's albums up to that date in an enormous 16-disc release. New vocalist Blaze Bayley is only heard on the final disc, a five-part *In Profile* documentary including band interviews. Nothing from *The X-Factor* or *Virtual XI* made it through, possibly because of the relative recentness of those releases in comparison to the enhanced versions of the earlier albums. The CD spines made up that famous *Electric Matthew* shot but the absolute win-win for everyone was the fact that the set came in the shape of Eddie's head. Which rather explains the title, doesn't it? The set – inside the head – is now very collectible.

The compilation soundtrack to the band's *Ed Hunter* video game finally came out in July 1999, by which time Bruce Dickinson was back in the band. Indeed, the US release also included Dickinson singing 'Wrathchild' as a bonus. The three CDs included music plus the game itself.

2002's *Eddie's Archive* came in an embossed box made of metal and comprised not only six CDs (three double albums) but also a family tree and special Maiden shot glass.

The *BBC Archives* and *Beast Over Hammersmith* CDs are in the live albums' section of this book, but the third album *Best of the 'B' Sides* really delivers what it promises. There are many B-sides on here that show the band's influences as they nod to their heroes with various cover versions. Bands including Montrose, Jethro Tull, Beckett, Nektar, FM,

THIS DAY IN MUSIC'S GUIDE TO **IRON MAIDEN** 121

IRON MAIDEN

Free, Led Zep and (kind of) Chuck Berry are reinterpreted by the Maiden boys. And there's probably nowhere else where you'll hear both 'the Sherriff of Huddersfield' and 'Roll Over Vic Vella' in relatively quick succession. Rather good is the *Eddie's Archive* boxset, initially limited edition but re-released as a non-numbered set due to popular demand. If you're not a Di'Anno fan, *Edward the Great* could be your bag; it only includes material from *the Number of the Beast* onwards. The 2002 edition was updated in 2005 with a different tracklisting, encompassing more recent activities.

Now out of print and thus very sought-after is 2005 North America-only Sony release *The Essential Iron Maiden*. Basically, it's more of the same but including everything up to *Dance of Death*. Interestingly, it goes backwards in time – the most recent releases are first, and it ends with 'Iron Maiden,' albeit a version taken from 2005's live album *Death on the Road*. Maiden smashed out a quick *Somewhere Back in Time* album, subtitled 'The Best of: 1980-1989'. Just in case anyone had missed the stuff when it first came out, of course, to ensure maximum singalongability with the tour they undertook of that era's songs. Somewhat churlishly, perhaps, the Di'Anno tracks from *Killers* and *Iron Maiden* were eschewed in favour of current singer Bruce Dickinson's live versions, taken from *Live After Death*. In 2011, Maiden put out *From Fear to Eternity*, a pretty decent roundup of all the albums from *No Prayer for the Dying* through to *The Final Frontier*. And, again, live Bruce Dickinson versions of songs were used rather than those of Blaze Bayley when it came to 'Man on the Edge,' 'Sign of the Cross,' and 'The Clansman'.

Other boxsets include 2012/13's *Picture Disc* collection, for the first seven records of the band on vinyl, and then 2014's *The Complete Albums Collection* 1990-2015, which did the same on black vinyl. Beautiful stuff, though: as collections ought to be done. It's pretty expensive being a Maiden completist ...

Live Albums

Scream for Me, World

Every great band has at least one great live album in its back-catalogue, and Maiden have one of the very best.

The seminal *Live After Death* was recorded at shows in Long Beach Arena, California between March 14th-17th, 1985, plus five tracks at Hammersmith Odeon in London from October 8th-12th, 1984. It's a four-LP bonanza which arguably shows Maiden at the height of their powers during the *World Slavery Tour*, the lengthy and gruelling world-conquering promotional gigfest that boosted their *Powerslave* album. As an intro to the absolutely coruscating live act the Irons were at that time, there is no better document; the vinyl version is wonderful and the 1988 double CD reissue equally so. Best of all may be the 1995 reissue, its three additional tracks including an ace 'Sanctuary' and 'Murders in the Rue Morgue' plus the far-from-essential 'Losfer Words (Big 'Orra)'. Those tracks were taken from B-sides of singles associated with the album.

PART TWO: **THE ALBUMS**

We catch up with Maiden again on *Maiden England '88*, which wasn't given a proper release as audio-only until March 25th, 2013; fans would have already owned the associated VHS video and quite possibly bootlegged tapes thereof (released November 1989). It shows a more mature Iron Maiden and updates the story to all things *Seventh Son of a Seventh Son*. The next live efforts are the dual blast of 1993's *A Real Live One/A Real Dead One*, collectively re-released in 1998 as *A Real Live Dead One*. Produced by Harris, there's a lack of drive about it in comparison to *Live After Death*, both sonically and somehow in energy. It was recorded from a bunch of shows on the band's 1992 European tour; *Dead One* included a load of very early tracks like 'Prowler,' 'Transylvania' and 'Remember Tomorrow,' whilst *Live One* concentrated on more contemporary stuff up to and including the *Fear of the Dark* album. Hot on the heels of the lives and the deads came a grand triple vinyl release, *Live at Donington*, comprising the whole concert of the group's headline appearance at Monsters of Rock in 1992. Released in late '93, it's a better all-round coherent LP than its immediate live predecessors.

Nine long years later, the band put out the lengthy and massive *Rock in Rio*, where they played to one of the biggest crowds ever, around a quarter of a million people. The six-member line-up changes it up considerably, with loads of lengthy songs, including several from the Blaze era. Also out in 2002 were two excellent additions to the canon, both available as part of the *Eddie's Archives* boxset. The *BBC Archives* album features a fantastic 1979 Rock Show session plus a rather brilliant Reading Festival live gig, from August 28th, 1982, a 1980 appearance at Reading and the Monsters of Rock 1988 gig. *Beast Over Hammersmith* was recorded in March 1982 during The Beast on the Road tour; rougher than later releases but with an irresistible energy showcasing what a force the band were about to become.

In 2005, *Death on the Road* came out and brought in tracks from the *Dance of Death* album alongside a clutch of old favourites. But it was *Flight 666* that was to become an essential purchase for Iron Maiden fans. The DVD version in particular was a gem that tracked Maiden on their *Somewhere Back in Time* world tour, piloted around the world by Captain Bruce Dickinson. The film is great, the accompanying 2009 live album boasting the very best performances from a series of gigs from places as diverse as Mumbai, Tokyo, Sydney and Monterrey.

Advances in technology and budget meant

IRON MAIDEN

2

recording was cheaper than ever before; the 2011 tour to promote *The Final Frontier* was thus pegged as another chance to capture the live stuff. The live album was released in 2012, named *En Vivo!* and coming with an associated video release, recorded at the Santiago, Chile show. *The Book of Souls: Live Chapter* followed in 2017, an expansive, hefty piece of work that features 15 tracks across the eras, recorded at various venues, Bruce Dickinson singing to his fans for the first time since recovering from throat cancer.

Again taking advantage of new technology, the concert film was streamed live online for free. The multiple formats available were not free, of course.

As yet, there isn't a live album featuring the best of Blaze Bayley's tenure; he did, however, put out *As Live As It Gets* in 2003, many of his Maiden-era tracks included and recorded with his solo band.

From Long Beach to Cape Town, Montreal to El Salvador and beyond, the live albums capture various eras of Maiden with great aplomb. Followers of the band may find it interesting to compare and contrast tracks over the decades to unearth differences in tempo, singing, key and personnel. A pointless, but excellent exercise which is in many ways the essence of long-term fandom. The blurring between studio and live possibilities in terms of sonic quality is notable across the industry and enables a much more nuanced production to showcase bands live. Which begs a couple of questions: will there ever be a Maiden album without an associated live release a couple of years later? And, of course, what else is there in the vaults yet to be discovered and repackaged for the ever-thirsty ears of Iron Maiden's fanbase?

Bootlegs

Bootlegging across the universe

The concept of the bootleg – the unofficial release of music unbeknownst to the band – has dogged the music industry for decades. Fans sometimes love it, because they get to hear live gigs/alternative mixes/rare songs; record companies and bands tend to hate it because the gigs weren't meant to be released/the quality of recording is shoddy/the band gets no money from it. It is a constant push and pull between two factions

PART TWO: **THE ALBUMS**

and ultimately a copyright violation by the bootleggers.

That all said, like any big band there are numerous unofficial releases out there.

Iron Maiden bootlegs have always been much in demand amongst the rabid fanbase and these days there are countless social media sharing groups devoted to the cause. The Maiden family isn't one to stand for rip-off merchants, though: live concerts are recorded, given excellent artwork and more often than not shared or swapped. People try and make the covers look as good as possible, likewise any artwork on the discs themselves. It's not always easy to tell whether something is an official release or not without recourse to a proper discography.

The thing to bear in mind with any non-official musical release (or, indeed, video) is that the quality may well not be up to scratch. You're as likely to get songs cut off halfway through as you are to hear the surreptitious belching of the audience member who's snuck the recorder into the gig. You delve into this world at your peril, but the very best quality bootlegs will be those either taken from a feed at the sound-desk or recorded from long-lost television appearances, radio sessions and the like. For example, listed online is an unofficial album called *666 – The Number of the Rarest Tracks*. It was apparently 'released' on CD by parties unknown in 2004 and collates the band's 1979 BBC session, tracks from *Top of the Pops*, some live songs from a German festival, Bruce's demo with the band from 1981, and more. Most of this stuff is available online these days, but many people love to have as much about the band they love as is possible (and affordable).

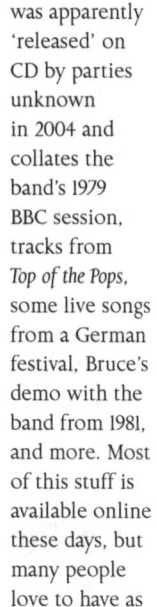

There are many collectors of Maiden product and alternative cover art, releases in different territories, different formats, and picture discs are common. Some of these are official releases but many, particularly before the fall of the Berlin Wall, were sourced from smuggled tapes from the West that were recorded and distributed on underground labels. This meant effectively that people who had no access to Maiden's music any other way could get to hear their heroes on tape (or vinyl, or pressed on to X-Rays. Yes, seriously, look it up). The music just wasn't on the shelves of the officially-sanctioned government stores in those days.

THIS DAY IN MUSIC'S GUIDE TO **IRON MAIDEN** 125

IRON MAIDEN

What is important to be careful about with bootlegs is provenance. And there is one particular bootlegged piece of Maidenology that has been sold, resold and resold again for lots and lots of hard-earned money. That is the vinyl record of *The Soundhouse Tapes*. There is an excellent Facebook site to refer to on this score: www.facebook.com/thesoundhousetapes/ is where you are advised to visit.

Given that there were only around 5,000 made and sold at the time, quite a few of those have fallen by the wayside over the years. Given its extreme importance in launching the career of Iron Maiden, it's also one of the most sought-after records. It represents more than just the music – great though that is. It's a piece of social history; capturing the energy, belief and momentum of a band ready to take it up to the next stage. What you have when you get a copy of *The Soundhouse Tapes* is also an artefact of the Soundhouse era: this is what people were getting off to at the time, a time that can never be repeated.

Some things to look out for in bootlegged copies of *The Soundhouse Tapes* vinyl: fadeouts; wrongly-etched runoff markings on the vinyl; no cut-out on the back cover; coloured vinyl; odd colours in general.

In 2002, 666 CD copies of this seminal moment were released officially to those who collected special tokens. Obviously, there are way more than 666 CD copies for sale worldwide – the numbers simply don't add up. Caveat emptor/buyer beware. It's a murky old world out there, but rumour has it that there are some gems hiding in the dark corners …

The Tapes that Don't Exist

Or do they…?

Not so very long ago, the world of Maidenalia was absolutely rocked to its boots by the release of several short snatches of a rehearsal from 1977. Photographs of the reel-to-reel tape case show a track-listing reading thus: 'Drifter'/'Prowler'/'Another Life' (incorporating drum solo)/'Transylvania'/ 'Floating'/'Charlotte the Harlot'/ 'Innocent Exile' (incorporating guitar solo)/'Iron Maiden'.

The tracklisting was later amended to include 'Burning Ambition', 'Sanctuary'/'Prowler'/'Strange World' and 'Purgatory', the latter developed from 'Floating' ('Rothchild' was also amended to 'Wrathchild').

Other information says it is Iron Maiden, captured two weeks after their first rehearsal at Scarf. The line-up is listed as: Denny (vocals); Terry (guitar); Steve (bass); Tony (keyboards); Me (drums).

The 'Me' is Barry 'Thunderstick' Purkis, owner of the artefact that has become one of the most sought-after pieces of history that has come to light in recent years.

"The tape I own (one I have chosen to call 'The tape that doesn't exist', due to the fact that it is widely believed that the earliest Iron Maiden recordings were The Soundhouse Tapes) is of our second-ever rehearsal, comprising of songs that would

126 THIS DAY IN MUSIC'S GUIDE TO **IRON MAIDEN**

PART TWO: **THE ALBUMS**

later be found on the first two Maiden albums," Purkis says.

So why not put it out for all to hear?

"You ask why it is not being released? Well, on a legal note I own both the recording and my performance on it but not any of the other musician's performances. I could sell it to a dealer/collector without too many problems and what that third party decided to do with it would be up to them. If they chose to release it, I'm sure the might of Iron Maiden's legal team would come to bear on them in no time at all once it was discovered it was out in the public domain.

"I have been told by fans that I should recognise it be some sort of IM 'holy grail', and it would be only right to release it ... OK, and just who would pay my legal costs?"

The likelihood of it being ever officially released, then, seems on the low side.

Dennis Willcock also says he has plenty of material from his era with the band. Rehearsal tapes, plus that notorious Thunderstick/Moore/Wapram/Willcock/Harris concert.

"I will release them as I feel fit. I never asked for them: they were given to me. People have given those tapes to me and they are in storage."

As for these ones seeing the light of day ...

"Who knows?" the frontman teases. "I might turn around, if the path for me was to say I'll release these, then I will. These are before contract; these are nobody's property. There are other stories, but I won't go into that. I won't make any other comment.

"But these are known to exist and basically you don't just get the music, you get all my inter-number commentary. Obviously, I say quite a lot. That cannot be defiled, or say it's wrong, because it's said. Unless I'm a gee-whizz at dropping my comments into a 1976, '77 cassette tape, probably. Yes, we know it can be done but it's the flow of the thing."

Willcock says he doesn't spend an awful lot of time poring through these ancient slabs of Maiden history.

"I have a researcher," he explains. "I don't listen to these recordings. He tells me what's on them, and to be truthful I've got many more things in my life to worry about than what was an old recording. He goes off and says, 'I've spotted that, I've heard this.' He knows when I've said things [onstage], when I've thrown the [original Iron Maiden character] mask away. He can narrow it to the date of the recording."

So when can we hear these valuable recordings?

"One day I will just say: 'Let's get these out'," says Willcock. He also plans to write his own biography at some stage.

"The other plan on certain issues; basically, if I can summon up the effort I will write my own story down. There are many, many other funny things that relate, specially to roadie Vic Vella who became Steve Harris' [assistant]"

It will be entertaining, strident and pull no punches. We all look forward to it.

We wish these ones didn't exist

One bootleg that really never ought have seen the light of day, please God, Zeus, Monkey Magic and the Avengers, is a notorious candid tape that was running during Samson's recording sessions for *Shock Tactics*. Producer Tony Platt recalls it reluctantly.

"I still have a cassette of it," he admits.

IRON MAIDEN

"We were in Studio Two at Battery and somebody kept leaving sweets on the end of the console. I ate this sweet and realised there was a lot of sniggering going on. I managed to coax it out of them that these were fart sweets that somebody had bought in a joke shop."

"In the spirit of the session I finished eating the sweet and indeed they are remarkably good and very functional. What that did was then encourage everybody else to eat one. They really did encourage the juiciest of farts. I put some tape on a machine and a mic in front of it. If you'd come into the session during that particular afternoon, you would probably be treated to somebody breaking off in the middle of a conversation, running across to this tape machine, poising their arse over the microphone, hitting record and letting fly."

"It was in the era of *The Troggs Tapes*, where one of the assistant engineers recorded The Troggs having an argument about a drum pattern. Some of the stuff they were saying was hilarious; it was edited down so you just have the funny bits one after another."

Anyone who's ever heard 'Mission from 'Arry' will recognise that concept. Having a live microphone was useful in other ways, Platt says.

"In that era, people were constantly trying to catch funny things that went on in the control room. Often if we had somebody from the record company coming down we would have a tape recording to catch all the stupid things they were going to say."

At the time, the studio was a playground for the young band and the young producer. They were very serious and professional about the actual recording.

"We were working very, very hard over 12 to 14-hour sessions. You had to have a bit of fun or you'd fall over [...] There were all sorts of bits of candid material; Paul Samson went away and edited it all together and the result was the fart tape."

Surely nobody's that much of a Maiden completist as to want to get a copy?

Then again...

PART TWO: **THE TOP 50 IRON MAIDEN SONGS**

THE TOP 50 IRON MAIDEN SONGS

It's the impossible question, isn't it: what are the best Iron Maiden songs? So, being contrary as we are at TDIM Towers, we thought we'd ask the fans just that. On nearly 50 social media sites we asked for people's top 10 Maiden tracks and collated the results into a master document. This formed the basis of what you see here, according to how many times each song appeared, and in which position. Dates, where applicable, are taken from single release date in the UK. It's important to mention at this point that many people, including your humble author, found it virtually undoable. So we changed the focus a little to What are your favourite Iron Maiden tracks today? With such an incredible back-catalogue that stretches decades and often pulls at the boundaries of genre, the metal gods have always defied categorisation. But we're going to do it anyway. Let the arguments begin...

1 Hallowed Be Thy Name (1982)

Topping the pile is the extraordinary tale of a prisoner's last moments on earth, Steve Harris penning a timeless classic way back in the early 1980s. Not only is it philosophically significant, reflecting on life, mistakes, the passing of time and justice, it also happens to be an immensely catchy seven minutes that showcases each band member in turn. Bruce Dickinson's expressive vocal range is a brilliant introduction to his tenure up front for Maiden; Dave Murray and Adrian Smith's solos are fluid and prickly, and their harmony guitars had never been so smooth;

IRON MAIDEN

Harris drives it along with customary gusto through the different rhythmic changes; Clive Burr holds it all down, working around the kit to give the light and shade. The shadow over the track about songwriting credits has played out over the years. As one of the most covered tracks in the Maiden catalogue, you're quite likely to hear it done by Dream Theater or Cradle of Filth in their sets.

2 Rime of the Ancient Mariner (1984)

Right from the opening chug, it's obvious that here is a band settling in to play an epic. And an epic it is; taking inspiration, and lyrical cues, from the Samuel Taylor Coleridge poem of the same name, it's nearly 14 minutes of hefty, insistent portentousness. Dickinson's voice is confident and controlled, deliciously tackling the words with gleeful gnarliness. The tale unfolds of the mariner sealing his and the crew's fate by shooting the albatross, the multi-part music a typical Maiden exploration, and the ghastly, ghostly middle-eight throws another neo-psychedelic spanner into the works. Planks creak, the narrator whispers and growls, and the song slows. But there is redemption ahead, of sorts. This is Iron Maiden in full flow, unafraid to take on the big beasts of life's narrative zoo.

3 Wasted Years (1986)

Writer Adrian Smith scored a No. 18 spot in the UK charts with this, the lead single from the *Somewhere in Time* album. Its accessible poppiness belies a genesis from those gruelling mid-Eighties tours, whilst retaining an optimism, not least during that ever-singable chorus. A long way from the days of Paul Di'Anno and an indication perhaps that Maiden were ready to explore another sonic space. The self-analysis of the lyrics show a maturity and edge – dare we say wisdom, even – of a band of brothers that has been through some tough, tough times. It's a call to appreciate what you have, when you have it. The golden years won't always last. Amen to that.

4 The Trooper (1983)

If you had one song to play to an alien to explain Iron Maiden to them, this is it. A gutsy, rollocking four-minute Maiden workout that encapsulates the *Piece of Mind* album niftily, and, indeed, is an unequivocal touchpoint for the band themselves. The galloping-bumblebee rhythm is at its apogee here, and the layers of harmonised, phased vocals sit brilliantly on top. The solos are tight and exultant, the harmony guitars pretty much perfect, channelling

PART TWO: **THE TOP 50 IRON MAIDEN SONGS**

Steve Harris' reinterpretation of the Charge of the Light Brigade into the realms of top-class heavy metal. Which, when you think about it, is some achievement. 'The Trooper' has been a staple of Maiden's sets over the decades, and the band has attracted occasional controversy for Bruce's waving of the Union Flag during some performances, a case in point being reported booing of the flag in Dublin in the early 2000s.

5 Powerslave (1984)

The title track of the spectacular album of the same name is an Egyptian-tinged tale of mortality and belief, written by Bruce Dickinson whilst on a reading kick at home. Indeed, the history graduate finds a rich seam of mysticism and mines it superbly with a lyric that has everything from the Eye of Horus – associated with protection, wisdom and prosperity – to the curse of the Pharaohs. The LP saw Maiden absolutely soar into the stratosphere of fame, kicking themselves up several levels by the quality of their songwriting, performance, vision – and a maddeningly gruelling schedule that was to take them on the road for 13 months to nearly 30 countries.

6 Aces High (1984)

Winston Churchill's 'beaches' speech generally introduces this track in live appearances. The single scraped into the charts at No. 20, but then Maiden never really worried much about that kind of thing. What we can say is that this is a fantastic opener to *Powerslave*, tapping into World War II history with a lyric that, despite being written by Harris, clearly resonates with the soon-to-be-airborne Bruce Dickinson. The singer's obsession with everything flight-related came upon him at an early age, and you can hear his absolute commitment to the subject in a fantastic vocal performance that reaches into the heavens itself on a remarkable final octave jump.

7 Phantom of the Opera (1980)

Paul Di'Anno's first appearance in our list, and an early Maiden epic. Rougher all round than what was to follow, be that production or performance, the track nonetheless shows exactly why Harris and company were quickly head and shoulders above other metal hopefuls at the time. The melodic middle-eight, with DiAnno's gruff, attacking vocal answered by Queen-esque vocal harmonies, takes matters to a higher level than the band had showed previously, before things build back into full flow via splendid solo work from Dave Murray and the colourful Dennis Stratton. Hints of what

IRON MAIDEN

was to come can be identified here, from the polyrhythms to the storytelling.

8 Fear of the Dark (1992)

Ending the claustrophobic album of the same name with paranoia and strangeness is one of Steve Harris' treatise on an unspecified, but constant and troubling terror. There's an aggression about the playing – particularly by Harris – that gives the track, like the album, a notable edge. Dickinson, as he does throughout the LP, is also measurably grittier with his delivery than he had been with Maiden up to date. At a time when Grunge was starting to eye up the distorted guitar territory, Iron Maiden were ploughing a furrow they'd already trod in the early to mid-Eighties with a (great) song that could easily have appeared on *Piece of Mind*.

9 2 Minutes to Midnight (1984)

From its Motörhead-esque opening riff to the half-time pre-chorus, this is Maiden in stunning form. Add to this a truly topical – and catchy – chorus about nuclear war and the Doomsday Clock, and you've got an all-time classic of the genre. A co-write between Bruce Dickinson and Adrian Smith, '2 Minutes to Midnight' is yet another absolute belter from *Powerslave*, an album so good it hardly seems fair. Those who bought the 12" single were treated to the notorious 'Mission from 'Arry', nearly seven minutes of an argument between Nicko McBrain and Steve Harris, which was recorded by Dickinson for posterity. Such are the pressures of the road, and such is the sense of humour of Maiden that they were happy to release it as a B-side. Would you do the same?

10 The Number of the Beast (1982)

I think we all know by now it's Barry Clayton doing the Vincent Price-esque spoken word intro, don't we? Well, if not, then now we do. And for a history of how Dickinson came out with that unearthly scream, you are directed toward his excellent autobiography, *What Does This Button Do?* Suffice it to say there's years of frustration, ambition, musicality and technique therein. As for the song, it's strange now to think of how much controversy it caused amongst various religious groups, particularly in the States. Still, one burnt LP means one more LP sale – plus a replacement to burn all over again. A quick read over the lyrics would surely show this is another of 'Arry's weird dream-based efforts, apparently written after watching *The Omen*. And, bands take note, this is how you bring a song to an end properly. Boss.

11 Seventh Son of a Seventh Son (1988)

Synths take their place alongside the vocals on this 10-minute centrepiece of the ambitious, proggy *Seventh Son of a Seventh Son* album, Maiden's – you've guessed it – seventh LP. Harris and Dickinson bonded again over the concept album, taking the band toward the end of a fertile decade in some style. Complex and layered, the track is suitably magick-tinged, with what would be call movements were the band classical performers. It seemed that Iron Maiden were set to explore even further the mystical boundaries of metal, and beyond, the song and album opening up potential new planes of musical existence. As time would show, though, the group would step back from the

PART TWO: THE TOP 50 IRON MAIDEN SONGS

abyss into safer territory, which didn't do anyone any favours at the time.

12 Flight of Icarus (1983)

In retrospect, 'Flight of Icarus' is a surprisingly poppy moment. The lead single from *Piece of Mind*, it's one of Dickinson and Smith's early collaborations, based on the Greek myth of an imprisoned Icarus improvising wings of feathers and wax before flying too close to the sun and therefore to his death. The subtext is of hubris and overconfidence, although in the Maiden version there's also a hint of intergenerational dynamics at play; Dickinson was to note that he'd deliberately made Icarus' father the anti-hero that encourages his son to fly to his demise. The track also introduced the world to the recorded debut of one Nicko McBrain behind the drumkit. Also, check out Bruce's breath control at around the 3.10 mark for a man firmly in the groove. And, truly, is there a better 'hmm-mhmm' in all of rock music than Bruce delivers on this one?

13 Run to the Hills (1982)

What? No. 13? For Maiden's anthem? At least, their anthem according to people who only know one song, and this is it. Maiden fans are an intelligent bunch, however, and we're going to take this relatively lowly placement in our list as testament to the in-depth knowledge of, and appreciation for, all aspects of the band's output. Musically ubiquitous it may be, to the point of cultural cliché, but that's hardly the fault of the band. The song is, by anybody's standards, absolutely brilliant: a soaring, catchy chorus, edgy, roughneck lyrics, historical

exploration and storytelling – and one of the most-recognisable drum introductions of any song, anywhere, any time. In another dimension there's a version of Maiden that imploded in a bizarre coffee-machine incident directly after recording this, and that version of Maiden are still considered absolute geniuses of the genre. Go listen to it. Do it now!

14 Empire of the Clouds (2016)

That 34 years separate this from the previous entry in the list is all you need to really know about the phenomenon of Iron Maiden. This surprising, beautiful, rocking Bruce Dickinson epic based on the story of the ill-fated R101 airship, which crashed with great loss of life in 1930 and put paid to what was previously to be the age of the airship. It was written by the singer, initially on a keyboard he'd bought at a charity auction, then on a Steinway grand piano.

IRON MAIDEN

The vocalist, unaware that he was suffering a life-threatening illness, has a richness of delivery and range that is suitably portentous and grave as it delivers one of Dickinson's greatest lyrics. At 18 minutes, it was the longest in the Maiden oeuvre, stretching out and expanding to fill the ether. The track proved, were any proof needed, that Bruce and Maiden were far from finished yet. Extraordinary on all counts.

15 Dance of Death (2003)

Written by Janick Gers and Steve Harris after the guitarist watched Ingmar Bergman movie, *The Seventh Seal*, this one showcases the power and dynamics available to a group with a triple-guitar line-up. Themes of life and death place it in the same thematic space as 'Powerslave', although the skippy, folky guitar riff that comes in the pre-chorus briefly brings to mind the mandolin break in Spinal Tap's 'Stonehenge'. There's plenty to admire here, though, with all three six-string heroes getting stuck right into the task as the vista unfolds.

16 Blood Brothers (2000)

Nominated for a Grammy for Best Hard Rock/Metal Performance – and that alone is a huge seal of approval for the return of Bruce and Adrian to the Maiden fold for the *Brave New World* album. The lyrics are possibly the most raw Steve Harris ever wrote, coming in the aftermath of losing his father; the song is full of regret and love and Bruce sings with restraint and real sensitivity, controlling a fantastic vocal line. Carried on Harris' fabulous two-string riffing and staccato guitars, synth-pads and the heartbeat-tempo 6/8 metre, this is an exceptional effort.

17 22 Acacia Avenue (1982)

History records that this is inspired somewhat by a track from Adrian Smith's pre-Maiden band, Urchin, called 'Countdown', but revved up alongside Harris and hammered into the stratosphere, pedal truly to the metal. It's another step in the 'Charlotte the Harlot' series, dealing as it does with the same character's nocturnal business adventures. For those idiots who took *Number of the Beast* as evidence that Iron Maiden were somehow in league with the devil, the traditionally-moralistic lyrics are in fact rather sweet, the narrator actually wanting to rescue Charlotte and take her home. The wistful, half-time solos just after the middle-eight are also quite beautiful in their smooth, searching delivery. That said, it's not long before things kick back in with a proper head-banging coda to smack it all right back up to 11.

18 Paschendale (2003)

Some 21 years after the Avenue, Smith and Harris' collaboration was to produce this tale of an unknown soldier at the battle of Passchendaele Ridge. The notoriety of the battles, which took place in 1917 near Ypres in West Flanders, has shocked through the eras as the Belgian mud ran red with wasted youthful blood. The loss of between 500,000 and a million soldiers on both sides is a horrific statistic that deserves never to be forgotten. Maiden's expansive, despondent track is thoughtful, tender, but pulls no punches. Proof that some things retain the power to stun the listener regardless of the era in which they were written; art is nothing if it cannot be provocative and informative, after all.

PART TWO: THE TOP 50 IRON MAIDEN SONGS

19 Infinite Dreams (1988)

A live-recorded single was released in 1989 to coincide with the *Maiden England* video, but it is the album track we're concerned with here. In keeping with the concept of *Seventh Son of a Seventh Son*, it deals with spiritual and other-worldly ideas of sleep, nightmares, mysticism, death and possible rebirth. Musically, it's one of Maiden's galloping-beat favourites, complete with a familiar key change and return and harmony guitars/synths. The anthemic last minute or so is a proper invitation to get those nuts banging again, and again, and again.

20 Alexander the Great (1986)

Not many bands would open a song with a quote from King Philip of Macedonia, but then not many bands can get away with it. Luckily, Iron Maiden can, and so they do. Steve Harris is again responsible for a relatively epic album-closer, although at eight and a half minutes it's a relatively short one by Maiden's standards. If you want an instant education in the Ancient Greek king of the Macedonians, look – and listen – no further. As a bonus, the guitar solo at about four minutes, by Adrian Smith, is stylistically unusual and an absolute corker.

21 Where Eagles Dare (1983)

The fourth studio album by Maiden opens with this bruiser, Dickinson in full high-register, delinquent-opera singer mode. Nicko's drum part is significant, too, reflecting the sound of machine guns in the narrative, based on a 1968 movie. The film, of the same name, is about commandos set to rescue one of their own from incarceration by the Nazis. Musically, this is pure unadulterated early Dickinson-era Iron Maiden, with aggression, power, historical thematicism and quite frankly the sound of a band absolutely enjoying the hell out of their growing career.

22 Revelations (1983)

Also taken from *Piece of Mind*, this song was written by Bruce partly to thumb noses at the daft bastards who'd been burning 'Satanic' Maiden's albums. Indeed, it begins with words written in 1906 by GK Chesterton that are firmly a call to the Lord for deliverance from evil and flawed earthly leaders. Add to this, themes of the tarot and Egyptian mystery and you've got a playful, brilliant take on belief of various stripes. And when Bruce shouts, 'Go' halfway through, the track bloody well does, too. Just ace.

23 Iron Maiden (1980)

The song that's been played at virtually every gig Maiden have done – and beckons Eddie onstage – is arguably one of the punkiest in the band's oeuvre. It's one of the clearest indications that the debut album was recorded so quickly, such is its immediacy and speed. Di'Anno is in his element here, relishing both the gory verse(s) and triumphant lyrics. They will, indeed, get you. Harris' solo break is awesome, and the band is tight as the proverbial nun's proverbial something we won't mention in a family publication. And what a bloody brilliant ending the studio album version has. Top.

IRON MAIDEN

24 Moonchild (1988)

The Smith/Dickinson axis provides this, the fantastic opening to the *Seventh Son* album and as clear an introduction to the concept you can get. It takes its title from the Aleister Crowley novel of the same name, although the book's narrative is very different to that of the song. The occultist Crowley was becoming an interest of Bruce Dickinson's in a creative context, which was later to bear fruit both musically and on film. Back in 1988, though, 'Moonchild' tracks the birth of the seventh son of the seventh son and the misfortunes that are to befall him at the hand of the Devil himself. The singer was later to write that he'd hoped the album would be even more conceptual than it ended up being. Were the LP as consistent to the story as it began, who knows what Maiden could have achieved as the 1990s loomed.

25 The Prisoner (1982)

The story about how Patrick McGoohan, who played the eponymous prisoner in the cult 1960s series, gave permission to use a recording of the show for the intro, is super. And you can read it in both the official history and Bruce's book, so we won't waste space here. The lyrics follow the theme of an escaped convict reclaiming his freedom, and the melodic chorus is a cracking counterpoint to the driving verses.

Clive Burr's tom-toms (based on a Doug Sampson pattern) and Steve Harris' bass intro another iconic classic from the early era. Paul Di'Anno co-wrote it with the boss, and he's noted that it was about his own childhood and teenage years causing strife and chaos all over the place. A perfect song for Di'Anno, then, and a quintessential rebel anthem for all ages. Why should teenagers have all the fun?

26 Killers (1981)

The title track of the band's second album and the only one that has a writing credit for anyone other than Steve Harris. Paul Di'Anno is the man and by Zeus, doesn't he attack the song with his customary grizzled energy. The track zips along on a great rollocking bassline and features some splendid harmonics on the new dual guitar line-up of old mates Dave Murray and Adrian Smith. The sheer amount of ideas jammed into its five minutes or so are quite spectacular and surprisingly melodic, particularly in the middle-eight. Di'Anno has been rumoured to have written the lyrics mere hours before a performance at London's Rainbow Theatre in 1980, refining them for the recorded version.

PART TWO: THE TOP 50 IRON MAIDEN SONGS

27 Caught Somewhere in Time (1986)

Guitar synths? Surely not! But 'tis true, 'tis true. Yes, folks, it's the opening track to the *Somewhere in Time* album, and by jiminy doesn't it set out the stall for the rest of the LP. It fair gallops along once it gets going, the lyrics about time being on the protagonist's side not without irony given the exhausting preceding year on tour. The chorus is instantly-recognisable, both for its crowd-friendly riff and Dickinson's edge-of-register warbling. Repeated listens will reveal some quite extraordinary skilful kick-drum work by Nicko and those Harris fingers working quadruple time on a relentless bassline.

28 Brighter Than a Thousand Suns (2006)

A triple whammy writing time of Smith, Harris and Dickinson provides this beast, a piece of work that is rich, dense and almost Metallica-esque in its verse riffs. Maiden being Maiden, though, there's also a bloody poppy chorus to draw on. The track is a companion piece in some ways to '2 Minutes to Midnight', dealing with the nuclear age once again. The song takes its title from the *Bhagavad-Gita*, the sacred Hindu book from which Robert Oppenheimer – director of the team that developed the bomb - took his famous, fatalistic quote, 'Now I am become Death, destroyer of worlds.' Has any other band featured Einstein's equation of special relativity so heftily? One doubts so.

29 The Red and the Black (2015)

Steve Harris does love his bass chords at times, and he gets an opportunity to whack some bloody heavy ones in here. He also takes the opportunity to give his singer one hell of a mouthful to deliver lyrically, not for the first time it must be said. And, not for the first time, Dickinson smashes it out the ballpark. The contrasts of the red and the black represent light and dark, good and evil, that which is fated and that which is hypocrisy, choices, luck and sorrow. As for that chorus – simply perfect for a stadium-sized call-and-response betwixt band and audience. The 13 and a half minutes make it one hellishly long track ... but not the longest in Iron Maiden's catalogue. To paraphrase John Lennon, it's not even the longest on the album.

30 Sign of the Cross (1995)

Ah! Blaze! We've been expecting you... What an introduction to the new singer this is, too. A doomy, devilish intro soon gives way to a Maiden workout based on the novel *The Name of the Rose*, a murder mystery set in the 14th century. And, come on folks, any metal song with monks chanting is on to a winner, isn't it. Blaze is in grand voice here, not least during that epic-slow-time chorus which gives the new vocalist plenty of space to show off what he can do. Maiden's fifth frontman has a great line in nasty-sounding, scary, close-mic monster-whisper, too.

IRON MAIDEN

31 Ghost of the Navigator (2000)

Janick Gers teams up with Dickinson and Harris on a song that is a cousin to 'Rime of the Ancient Mariner' in its theme. It's tempting, too, to read the lyrics in parts as metaphors for the vocalist's own recent journeys outside and back into the good ship Maiden. But enough of that stuff, what we've got here is nearly seven minutes of modern metal that plays with different rhythms, countermelodies and intricately-confident riffs to good effect.

32 Wrathchild (1980)

One of the oldest songs in the list; tapes exist of this being rehearsed by the 1977 line-up of Wapram/Wilcock/Harris/Moore/Purkis (Thunderstick.) The sound on that is dodgy, the tempo even more so, and it's not likely the full tapes will ever see the light of day. Never mind; the version that eventually surfaced on *Killers* was superb: a romping three minutes with a typically in-your-face vocal from Di'Anno. Hard to believe this is the same band that was to release an 18-minute piano track about zeppelins, really, isn't it? Such is the beauty of Maiden, of course.

33 The Wicker Man (2000)

The first single from Bruce Dickinson's second spell as frontman takes themes of fate, death and helplessness in the face of eternal forces as its subject matter. Draw your own conclusions. Alternatively, you could say it's a genuinely driving Maiden opus which pays tribute to the band's past whilst simultaneously sounding like new vistas of opportunity are opening up.

Good trick, that, by anybody's standards. Welcome home.

34 The Loneliness of the Long Distance Runner (1986)

The well-read Steve Harris delved here into the oeuvre of Alan Sillitoe's rather ace book about a talented youth cross-country runner bucking the rules in prison by deliberately losing a race. Themes of determination, hanging in there, pushing one's self and the relative definition of glory abound. The familiar busy Harris bass here really is reminiscent of feet pounding a track, too.

35 Man on the Edge (1995)

Relative newbies Janick Gers and Blaze Bayley cooked this one up together. By all accounts it's based on 1993 Michael Douglas/Robert Duvall movie, *Falling Down*. The man, indeed, is on the edge – ready to let rip and indulge his frustrations at his life. It's a bloody rocker, too, vamooshing along at a glorious pace. The accompanying video shows the singer in full-on rock star mode, an energised band behind him: Blaze looks every inch the rightful heir to the vocal crown. An underrated classic, which for most other bands would be a career highlight. Maiden, of course, have quite a few of those to call on ...

PART TWO: THE TOP 50 IRON MAIDEN SONGS

36 For the Greater Good of God (2006)

Another Harris rumination on religion, love, life and death. So, perfect for an album called *A Matter of Life and Death* then. Sadly, since 9/11 struck, those themes have been all-too relevant. The confusion felt by the protagonist of the track about life, love and war strike right to the heart of the matter – sentiments that, unfortunately, most people could identify with in the new world of terrorist fundamentalists, reactive warmongers and general paranoia. Jesus died to absolve the sins of humanity, ponders the narrator, so why is it happening all over again? Hefty stuff from the chief.

37 To Tame a Land (1983)

Everyone, quick, flip the bird at the miserable old sod that wouldn't let the band name this song after the book that inspired it. So let's just outline the tale: a foretold king of a sand planet with worms, Fremen and stillsuits. There's the special drug, Spice, which allows second sight. Any takers for which book that might be yet? Clue: the movie was directed by David Lynch. The never-filmed Jodorowsky-planned version wanted Salvador Dali, Orson Wells and Mick Jagger as stars. Anyway, nyurks to the daft Herbert that nixed the title, 'cause the song's boss.

38 The Clansman (1998)

Heavy on the synth-pads and FX guitars, the intro to another Blaze-era banger is suitably portentous; those first two minutes or so sound like the band moving into another creative era. The cries of freedom in the lyrics take on an additional irony in retrospect, which is a shame because this is a damned good Harris vehicle for the soon-to-depart singer. Ridiculously, there was some Internet chatter about whether the song was racist, presumably because of the homonym of the title. The track, of course, is based on the Mel Gibson flick, *Braveheart*. And there's nothing racist about Mel.

39 Still Life (1983)

We may as well have just put the whole *Piece of Mind* album up here really. Anyway, Nicko introduces this one with some backwards text, which is absolute nonsense when you play it the right way round and is designed to wind up the nobbers looking to give Maiden a Satanist label. Bruce channels Paul Di'Anno's gruffer style to great effect on this Murray/Harris contribution.

40 If Eternity Should Fail (2015)

Oh, yes, indeed. Oh yes, oh yes, oh yes. One of Bruce Dickinson's strongest ones, full of doomy atmospherics, references to jesters, shamen and pre/post-history. As the first track on a double album, it kicks open the doors in style. In context with the band's career, it's as strong a statement of intent

IRON MAIDEN

as you can get: we ain't done yet, and time can't hold us in its spell. Dickinson's pipes are in grand shape, rich and forceful and as expressive as ever they were.

41 Death or Glory (2015)

Another from *The Book of Souls*, and one of two Smith/Dickinson collaborations they deliberately set to writing with view to previous shorter, more immediate songs. Indeed, the lyrics hark back niftily to previous dogfight/aerial war tracks like 'Aces High'. The difference this time, of course, is that Captain Paul Bruce Dickinson had more hands-on experience of manipulating aeroplanes, both commercial and vintage.

42 Can I Play With Madness (1988)

As radio-friendly as Maiden will probably ever get, the ultra-accessible chorus singable and memorable, the tone light and melodic. Poignantly, the official video featured Graham Chapman. The Monty Python star, however, was shortly to pass over to his own final frontier. As a song, it's cool; as part of the planned, but only half-realised, *Seventh Son* concept, it's pretty damned stunning stuff. And, Suggs, if you're reading this, please give Bruce a ring – I think we'd all like to see him guest with your mob.

43 Wasting Love (1992)

Arpeggio guitars surround the vocalist on the intro to this Gers/Dickinson-written opus, the third single from *Fear of the Dark*. And dark it indeed is. If one was to take the lyrics at face value, the themes of feeling dishonest but doing your best, long days and roads, loneliness and empty feeling are in line with the downbeat nature of the album. In context with what Dickinson was to do next, there's another layer of speculation to be had as to exactly what – and who – he was singing about.

44 The Evil That Men Do (1988)

Another top-five hit for the boys; their 17th single in all and another crossover toward the mainstream. And good ol' William Shakespeare would no doubt sing along with the chorus – and title – inspired by his famous quote from *Julius Caesar*. We have it on good authority that Shakey plays a mean electric lute at parties, too.

45 Remember Tomorrow (1980)

Those other-worldly guitars, that skilful melodic line from Di'Anno, those drums … is this really the vanguard of the new heavy metal movement? You bet your asp it is. At a time when fast and loud often meant good and better, the band pull this little gem out of the bag. The singer has said that the title was one of the catchphrases of his late grandfather; tomorrow may well bring better things, so hang in there. Sage advice indeed.

46 Out of the Silent Planet (2000)

There's a movie, *Forbidden Planet*, that was released in 1956 and became arguably one of the most important sci-fi flicks of all time. It also arguably influenced this song, although the title is taken from a 1938 C.S. Lewis tale. Either way, the Maiden version

PART TWO: THE TOP 50 IRON MAIDEN SONGS

is dark and desolate as it gets. Death, guilt, demons ... yikes!

47 Children of the Damned (1982)

Inspired by the John Wyndham novel *The Midwich Cuckoos*, this is anecdotally one on which the still-contracted-to-Samson Bruce Dickinson had some kind of input. On the album, it's credited solely to Steve Harris, so legally that's who wrote it and we ain't suggesting anything different, guv. Whatever; it's a bloody ace, bloody, ace, unmistakable early Bruce/Maiden piece of heart-pounding thrillness, so there.

48 Brave New World (2000)

Murray/Harris/Dickinson is a pretty strong songwriting trio, as this slow-burner proves. The heavy irony of the chorus in context and contrast with the desolate verses is palpable; Bruce gives it both barrels in a great performance. Indeed, he has come home, and a brave new world does await.

49 Back in the Village (1984)

The *Prisoner* series continues with the recapture of the protagonist in this ace update from the verdant Smith/Dickinson partnership. The noodly, busy guitars are irresistible, the pace swift and energised, the vocals bang on the button. Incidentally, if anyone can actually work out what the final episode of the Patrick McGoohan series means, please write to us at the usual address.

50 Afraid to Shoot Strangers (1992)

More death and terror, plus a hefty anti-war bit of work from a band not generally noted for taking a political stance. Written by Harris from the viewpoint of a Gulf War soldier, it was a live favourite in the Blaze era. It's powerful, downbeat and absolutely in line with the general feel of that *Fear of the Dark* album.

Bubbling under... Charlotte the Harlot (1980) – unreconstructed sexism that was more prevalent at the time; Heaven Can Wait (1986) – too damn right, we need the boys for a while yet; Be Quick or Be Dead (1992) – politicians in 'lying bastards' shocker; Bring Your Daughter... To The Slaughter (1990) – yes, folks, the No. 1 smash didn't make the top-50 list.

And so comes to a close our top-50, about as scientific as a piece of discarded chewing gum. It ain't half fun, though, to try and put one together. And, we might add, it's an idea absolutely ripe for one of those celebrity talking heads list-based shows that are on constantly over Chrimbo.

Thanks to the superb efforts of Michelle Ferreira Sanches and Brigitte Schön (plus the author), the following social media groups/websites were surveyed during September and October 2017:
Bruce Dickinson Insights; Bruce Dickinson solo; Maiden Family; Iron Maiden Germany; Iron Maiden's Forum, Iron Maiden / Eddie the Head; The book of Lost Souls (Iron Maiden fans); Metal Army Official; The Monsters Of Metal; Iron Maiden Blood Brothers Colombia FC; total iron maiden; Metal Eruption; Iron Maiden England; Iron Maiden's Kingdome; Bruce Dickinson and Iron Maiden - The Great; Iron Maiden

IRON MAIDEN

Argentina; Iron Maiden Brasil; Iron Maiden's Troopers; Iron Maiden fans; Iron Maiden World; Iron Maiden! The Beast and the legacy of they blood brothers!; Maiden Aotearoa; Iron Maiden Belgie; Iron Maiden Fans Forever; 666% Iron Maiden; Heavy Metal; Masters of Rock and Heavy Metal; Metal Seed; Metal Devastation Groupies; Hard Rock forever; Legends of Music; Bruce Dickinson Forever; Adrian Frederick Smith Fãs.

PART TWO: **SOLO CAREERS**

SOLO CAREERS

Some key Maiden members over the years, arranged chronologically in order of date joined. It's not everyone who's ever been in Maiden, because we'd run out of pages.

Steve Harris – The Boss

It's one of life's truisms that the story of Iron Maiden is the story of Steve Harris.

But there's more to 'Arry than Maiden, too. Everyone has to start somewhere, after all. And so it is to Gypsy's Kiss we first turn. Harris was and still is a footy fanatic, and it's easy to speculate that he might well have made it playing for his beloved West Ham United. As a youngster, he was linked with his favourite club, but soon rock'n'roll beckoned, and his life took another turn entirely. Like Bruce Dickinson, his future bandmate, Harris was an aspiring drummer, but it was the bass guitar that won through before too long. He was to quickly join up with his first band, and Gypsy's Kiss drummer Paull Sears, who has one of the sharpest memories in rock'n'roll, takes up the tale.

"It was the spring of 1974," recalls Sears. "I came back to London after working in a band in the East Midlands and got back in touch with an old mate, Roy Middleton, who was a guitarist. Roy told me he was working for the Civil Service and was friends with another guitarist, Dave Smith."

"Dave had a mate who had been playing bass for 10 months. His name was Steve Harris."

Sears and Middleton met Steve at Stratford's Cart and Hoses pub one Friday night in the early days of May 1974. He remembers a band playing that night by the name of Slowbone. Steve (bass), Roy (guitar), Dave (guitar), and Paull (drums) got together the next day to set up in the lounge of Harris' grandmother's gaff.

"[We] played some rock standards by bands like Deep Purple, Black Sabbath, Bad Company and Free," Sears continues. "Myself, Dave and Steve hit it off straight away but they didn't get on with Roy, so we replaced him with Tim Nash on second guitar. Up to that point Dave had done all the singing, but one day he had a cold and couldn't sing. Bob Verscoyle, who until then just hung out with us, said he would give the vocals a try and it worked quite well, so he came in on permanent vocals."

Bob Verschoyle remembers going to Harris' house to bond over their various LPs – or not, as the case may be.

"He was a massive Genesis fan," he says of his former bandmate. "I was a big fan of Emerson, Lake and Palmer, but that didn't go down too well with Steve, because he didn't like organ players. These bands'd have 20-minute drum solos, half-an-hour guitar solos. Steve doesn't have any of that. If someone in Maiden does a solo, it is [an integral] part of the song. He witnessed

IRON MAIDEN

all that in the Seventies and Eighties and doesn't want it."

"He'd been to school with Dave Smith, who could really play guitar. Paull had been gigging for about four years [before Gypsy's Kiss]. He was in the bay window [of Steve's nan's house], set up there. When he started playing we thought, 'Bloody hell, he's like Keith Moon! A proper drummer!'"

"Tim Nash was absolutely brilliant, and that's what the band was, rehearsing there three or four times a week. I'd just go round and not really do anything. Help out with the gear and stuff. We'd all hang around, go to concerts and everything. But that one Saturday afternoon they had to do instrumental songs [Dave Smith was ill]. My dad was always a singer in the pubs and that, and there we were – started going on the road trying to get gigs."

Cart & Horses and Bridge House were two of those venues in those nascent days of the band, whose name, incidentally comes from rhyming slang for 'piss'. It was a little more memorable than their initial choice of name, Influence.

First, though, was also the small matter of a talent show in St. Nicholas Hall, Poplar, London, in July 1974. It has become slightly legendary for two reasons: Firstly, it was arranged by one Dave Beazley (later to become famous as Dave Lights).

"I decided to put on a Battle of the Bands, did the poster myself and put them up with a phone number on it and there was a whole bunch of different bands that came," says Beazley. "The vicar was called Dave Randall and he had a connection with a record company; whoever the winner was would get a one-single deal. Gypsy's Kiss asked to play; they came second to a band called Flame, basically a bunch of kids whose family had spent a lot of money on them. They did places like Butlins and were basically a lot more professional."

Secondly, Steve Harris was, to put it mildly, bricking it, as Paull Sears recalls.

"We were to play three songs," he says, "The first being 'Influence,' then a song called 'What Went Wrong,' and 'The Heat Crazed Vole' to finish."

"Before we went on Steve was very nervous. He had never ever been on a stage in front of people before. He made the mistake of taking a peek around the curtain to see the crowd - the place was packed, and Steve then ran to the toilet," laughs the drummer.

Verschoyle continues: "He was in the toilet and he couldn't get out. He was so, so nervous about this gig. He was always like that when we first started. We played all our own numbers."

Sears takes up the baton.

"Dave managed to get out and we took to the stage. Steve was standing right next to me, so close that a couple of times he hit one of my cymbals with the end of his bass!"

The young Harris' nerves really did get the better of him in the ironically-named second song.

"'What Went Wrong' had a bass intro, but Steve was so nervous that we all thought he was still tuning his bass," the drummer recalls with a smile. "So we missed our cues to come in!"

Verschoyle remembers that members of The Who came down to judge the contest; there were six or seven bands, only one of which had a PA system – Gypsy's Kiss. It was a complete mess, he says, but the band's third song saw them get it back together, the audience responding well.

"We came second to a band called Flame,

PART TWO **SOLO CAREERS**

who were dressed in flares, young kids, dancing as well. It was an experience!"

There were local pub gigs to do, but it was very early days in the career of the band – Paull Sears says they weren't really ready to start with.

"At first we were under-rehearsed," he notes. "As I was the only pro in the band I insisted we had more time to get it right and told the others of the importance of rehearsals. This hit home, especially with Steve. He's the same to this day."

"The vibe in those days was very much Progessive Rock, still a new concept in music. Punk was not far away but this was the age of the supergroup: Zeppelin, Purple, Sabbath, Fleetwood Mac ..."

The band was to last a matter of months rather than years, however. As is often the case, the need to get down and graft at the day-job was paramount. Verschoyle remembers it was only Steve Harris who at the time wasn't employed.

"He took over as leader of the band and would say we need to rehearse. We'd cancel going out or playing football. The worst was that he said, 'We've got a big gig at a working men's club, playing for 45 minutes.' It was on a Monday ... I said, 'You don't wanna do that early in the week, you want to do it on a Saturday.' He said, 'We'll chuck in a load of rock'n'roll numbers.' I said, 'What, learn all that in a week?' I thought, 'I've got no chance of learning 10 songs in a week.' So we convinced him we weren't ready and it wasn't worth it."

"In the end, I thought I couldn't see anything coming of it," Verschoyle says, "I wanted to do other things, had to go to work, so I went round Steve's and said I was going to knock it on the head. Paull did the same a while after – he'd been gigging for five years on and off and needed a rest. Tim had left too, Dave gave up, and it was just Steve."

Sears remembers it well.

"Gypsy's Kiss just faded away," he adds. "I know Bob was getting fed up with the regimented routine [...] and I was beginning to lose my hunger."

These days, Sears and Verschoyle both look back on the experience fondly.

"Steve was there right from the start," says Sears. "He has cited me as one of his influences and his time in Gypsy's Kiss gave him his first taste of rock band life.

"It ignited a fire inside him which still burns bright today."

After some 40 years of absence, Gypsy's Kiss (without Steve) reunited in 2018 for a spectacular performance at BurrFest II, a charity event in honour of Clive Burr and MS charities.

Smiler for the camera

Never one to let the grass grow under his feet, or indeed his footy boots, Harris wasn't ready to give up on this music lark quite yet. He quickly reappeared in the group Smiler, albeit again only for a short time.

Dennis Willcock, who would in due course sing for Iron Maiden, was the vocalist.

"It was a blues/rock band, with Doug Sampson on drums and the Klee brothers [Mick and Tony] – two guitarists. Basically Steve and I knew each other from then," says the ever-strident singer.

Sampson remembers his own experience joining Smiler.

"I saw an ad in *Melody Maker*," he says, referring to a once-essential weekly UK rock paper, "And they were after a drummer. It

IRON MAIDEN

was a bluesy, boogie-sort of band. I rang them up, arranged an audition. [The Klee brothers] were a bit older than me."

"And the bass player happened to be Steve Harris."

They played a couple of numbers – possibly by Savoy and ZZ Top, Sampson thinks – and the rhythm section hit it off immediately.

"We played really well together and got on really well. I got the job. They took a chance on me as I was 17 and didn't have any experience apart from school bands with my mates. It was the first proper band I'd joined. A bit later we auditioned and Den Willcock turned up. He was a good showman, very energetic. He got the job and Smiler was complete."

The effervescent Willcock fronting any band is enough to grab any audience; even more so back in 1976. Basically, there was no social media, hardly any telly, a bit of radio, and a few rock weeklies. So playing live was a way to spread the word, and having stage presence and confidence was a huge advantage.

"When we started doing gigs he had the audience eating out of his hand," Sampson confirms. "People loved him. He had really good communication skills, could talk to them like he was talking to his friends and had really good microphone skills. He could swing it round his head like Roger Daltrey. People could identify with him. He was also a good singer. He had what it took, to take the audience with him."

It was an interesting time for music, with bands proliferating throughout the UK, not least in the English capital, London.

"You sort of knew all the members from different bands. There was a bit of rivalry," says Sampson. "But at the end of the day one bloke would leave one band, join another, it was that kind of environment. There were great bands of all different styles down Stratford, Walthamstow, Leyton. It was a great period to be young and to be around. You had a choice of three or four bands on a Saturday night and could pick and choose who you wanted to go and see."

But Smiler wouldn't be one of those for long. Dennis Wilcock was the first to escape the grinning clutches of boogie-woogie, remembers Sampson.

"It was gonna be a bit of a job to replace him," the drummer notes. "Whilst this was all going on, Steve had decided to leave. He said to me, 'Look I'm gonna go and form my own band. Do you want to come along?' And I told him, 'To be honest I'm having a little break for a while, want to get myself straight [financially]. I was out of work at the time, if I remember rightly, so I had to take a break from rehearsing and everything. Just taking time out."

"And that's when Steve went and formed Iron Maiden."

Iron who?

Logotastic

One thing every band needs is a cool logo. One story is that Steve, a draughtsman by trade, duly designed the famous font so recognisable today. An alternative take is that the logo was designed by Dennis Willcock and a designer called Ray Hollingsworth at his Crowes Art Studio in Rathbone Place, London, in September 1977. A typeface called Metal Lord is often referenced as the classic logo, which has had various tweaks over the years. Another story involves Vic Fair's poster for a 1976 movie called *The Man Who Fell to Earth*, with David

PART TWO **SOLO CAREERS**

Bowie in the title role. Indeed, the original UK-release's poster really does have a very familiar look, font-wise. There is a game called 'Six Degrees of Kevin Bacon' in which people trace themselves to the actor through shared working practices. There ought to be one about David Bowie, too: he seems to crop up everywhere. Check out, too, several album covers by Gordon Giltrap. Hmm.

Anyone for tennis?

In 1991 Steve Harris and Nicko McBrain provided the rhythm section for tennis players John McEnroe and Pat Cash with the Full Metal Rackets. The band recorded and released 'Rock and Roll' by Led Zep as a charity single. Other musicians involved were The Who's Roger Daltrey on vocals, Andy Barnett of FM on slide guitar and the two tennis-ists on geetars. All proceeds went to Rock Aid Armenia, a cause close to the hearts of Maiden. Bruce Dickinson contributed to the charity's 1989 cover of 'Smoke on the Water,' then Maiden's 'Run to the Hills' appeared on the subsequent *Earthquake Album* and *Earthquake Video* compilation releases the next year.

The Lion roars

Harris had been helping a band along in the 1990s, with advice and a kind of mentoring role. They were called British Lion and were after some assistance. Graham Leslie, the guitarist, gave Harris a tape of songs and the outcome was that 'Arry would give them the benefit of his huge experience as a producer, manager and even songwriter. Years went by, Harris obviously quite busy with his main band, but the writing sessions came along when there was downtime. Later, and after some line-up changes, these sessions ended in recording sessions – and those sessions ended up in a full album that hit the streets on September 24th, 2012.

And it's a decent classic rock-esque piece of work, although it's debatable that without the input of Steve Harris anyone would really give it a great deal of attention or not. Hard rock rather than metal, it's got more in common with Soundgarden, Thin Lizzy and – mostly – the likes of UFO than it has with Priest, Purple, Sabbath et al. Singer Richard Taylor has taken a bit of a bumping from some quarters for his sound on it, very much in the 'it grows on you' camp (and let's not forget that lots of different things can grow on someone, including some rather nasty rashes and fungi).

But to the album: 'Lost Worlds' could be a Maiden B-side, were it not for the weedy vocals dragging it down. British Lion tour in smaller venues, which must be a great joy for the Maiden bassist whose gigs tend to attract five and six-figure crowds generally. There's an intimacy to a rock club or smaller venue that you cannot recreate on a huge stage, with enormous zombies dashing about setting off pyrotechnics. British Lion also gives the bassist the opportunity to try out techniques on the bass that wouldn't be appropriate for Iron Maiden: 'Karma Killer' has a cracking syncopated, octave-playful line, for one. More obvious Maiden-y touches are evident in 'Us Against the World' – a super chugging riff and harmony guitars bookending an acoustic-based effort. The project's probably summed up best by one of Harris' co-compositions, the poppy 'The Chosen Ones,' which really does have a hint of 'The Boys Are Back In Town' about it. And why not? The chorus sees Harris have fun up in the higher register. But, please,

IRON MAIDEN

more and bigger reverb on that vocal next time – the boy can sing (any live video shows that, in spades) but he's sounding thin, thin, thin. Or pitch the music down a few steps to his comfortable range.

It's clear that British Lion is a project dear to the Maiden bassist's heart; there's much, much more to come from them and the next albums will be interesting indeed. It's not Iron Maiden, it's not meant to be, and it's all the better for it.

PAUL MARIO DAY – THE VOCALIST

The Day Enigma

Original Iron Maiden vocalist, Paul Mario Day, has long stopped doing interviews about his time in the band. It's understandable; his tenure lasted barely a year before he was ousted in favour of the more theatrical Dennis Willcock. At the time, Maiden were barely scratching around in pubs, still way off the act they were to become. Back in 1975/6 there were no guarantees that any of the bands around at that time would 'make it' as such; you could take yer pick (or your guitar pick) of many.

Still, the Whitechapel-born singer is said to have had more than a hand in writing 'Strange World' during his time fronting the band, which to some makes sense given that track's slightly out-there feel compared to other early material. But without proof, pics, recordings and whatnot there is no way anyone else can claim credit aside from the person legally recognised as the writer on the copyrighted version, and that is Steve Harris.

After Maiden, Day found himself joining More, a blues-rock/metal hybrid that, like the Beatles, cut their teeth in Germany at myriad gigs before returning to the UK. At that point, Day and the ultra-short-timer in Maiden terms, Paul Todd, were drafted into the band. More were some outfit; they recorded a radio session for the influential Friday Rock Show on May 23rd, 1980, which led to a deal with Atlantic Records. Sources suggest AC/DC's A&R man, Phil Carson, was instrumental in the record contract.

Day's vocals can be heard on More's 1981 debut album, *Warhead*. All frantic metally guitars, power chords and Motörhead-y riffs, it's bloody good stuff. Check out the vocals, too: somewhere exactly between Paul Di'Anno and Bruce Dickinson. Day's vocal talent surely should never have been in doubt, and other reasons to get rid of him from Maiden seem nebulous at best. Still, at more than 40 years' distance it's easy to be objective. Bands rarely are, particularly young ones finding their way in the industry. The title track, 'Warhead' is pure 1981 metal, with definite Priest leanings. Definitely recommended. Another coincidence/example of synchronicity is directly after that track on side two of a grand eight-song LP: a cover of 'Fire,' the song made famous

PART TWO **SOLO CAREERS**

by The Crazy World of Arthur Brown, one of the heroes of a young Bruce Dickinson. Whatever happened to him? Elsewhere, More head into Saxon/Samson mode, never a bad thing. An underrated group of their era, and perhaps a lost gem. The band toured with Krokus, Def Leppard, Ted Nugent, Black Sabbath, Foreigner, Motorhead, Saxon and even Maiden, with Day a spotlight-operator for the French leg of the *Killers* tour. Headline tours in their own right followed. More played Monsters of Rock in 1981, but Day was to leave in 1982. Paul Todd had already toddled off by that point.

Next up was his own new band, Wildfire, with whom Day was to record for Mausoleum Records. The 1983 album, *Brute Force and Ignorance* is a mix of hard rock and metal. 'Violator,' for one, romps along, as does 'Another Daymare.' There's a good melodic sense throughout the album, often catchy as a result. It's decent second-wave NWOBHM fodder, although hardly essential. Still, Day got his teeth properly into Wildfire, and went on to record another for Mausoleum, released in 1984, by the name of *Summer Lightning*. It's more accessible than its predecessor; the singalong 'Fight Fire with Fire' is almost maddeningly singable, and the gallop of 'Gun Runner' is about as close to Maidenesque as Wildfire were ever to get. Riffs are strong in the likes of 'Blood Money' and 'The Key,' showcasing a talented bunch of musicians whose time never really did come. Part of it was down to the fact that Mausoleum were a small label based in Belgium; though the audiences loved it, the record company had great difficulty in getting the albums into the shops to coincide with Wildfire's live appearances. Day hung on for another couple of singles in the ironically-named 'Nothing Lasts Forever,'

then 1985's 'Jerusalem,' but that was that for Wildfire. Yet the singer had a bigger opportunity to take care of.

The Sweet made their name in the glam rock era of the 1970s, with hits like 'Block Buster!', 'The Ballroom Blitz', and 'Little Willy,' the double entendre of which our US friends didn't quite notice. By 1985, though, things had certainly slowed down for the group which had split in 1982. Andy Scott and Mick Tucker from the band re-formed the outfit with Day on vocals and set about some serious touring. One of the first major moments was a live album recorded at the Marquee in 1986; the vocalist showing some serious chops upfront for the successful group. It was also to take his life in an unexpected direction: Day married the band's Australian tour guide and moved Down Under, coming back to tour in Europe for the next couple of years. He departed from The Sweet in late 1988.

Things quietened down a touch for the singer in subsequent years, singing in a cover band – Defaced - that did Purple and Zep songs, then formed a duo called The Cryptic. He retired from professional vocals in 1992.

Retired? Nah. He joined a band called Gringos in 2006 and got the bug all over again. Crimzon Lake formed in 2009 and set about touring Australia. Despite recording a decent EP with that band, by 2011 things disintegrated following the departure of a guitarist.

Day has worked in creative media in many disciplines, including video recording and promotions, design and photography. Not a bad career for someone who's only ever asked about one band that he was in ... for about a year, four decades ago.

IRON MAIDEN

DENNIS WILLCOCK – THE SHOWMAN

The man with the bloody mask

Larger-than-life vocalist, showman and bringer of masks full of blood, Dennis Willcock is a significant figure in the Iron Maiden story. The vocalist had already been in bands, including Bearded Lady and Nitro, before joining Doug Sampson, Steve Harris and the Clee brothers in Smiler. He was with Maiden from 1976 to 1977.

When he'd finally had enough of the set-up, Willcock continued to sing with V1, a band formed by Terry Wapram - a fellow alumnus of the Irons.

The new band decided to disassociate themselves from Maiden, not playing any of the Iron Maiden songs they'd worked on in their respective eras of membership. V1 popped down to Spaceward to produce a three-song demo, and one version of the legend states that Steve Harris, on hearing it, praised the production and decided to take the Irons into that same studio for their own debut recording.

V1 fizzled out not long after, but later Willcock joined another group, Gibraltar. Various line-ups included Tony Parsons and Ron Rebel Matthews, also ex-Maiden. The group lasted three years and despite a brief 1984 formation, that was that from Willcock for nearly 30 years.

Cue a Canadian fan browsing the Internet, who contacted Tony Miles of Gibraltar and said record label High Roller may be interested in Gibraltar's songs. As Miles was back in touch with Willcock, it was decided there would be a release of both Gibraltar and V1's demos.

Meanwhile, V1's full-length debut album, *Armageddon: End of the Beginning*, blends old-school 1970s metal with NWOBHM touches and classic riffery; 'Taking You Higher' being a seven-minute epic full of rhythmicism and atmosphere. Wapram now plays with Buffalo Fish.

In June 2018, Willcock was reported as having instigated legal action to claim he had written lyrics for a number of early songs, including 'Prowler', 'Charlotte The Harlot', 'Phantom of the Opera', Prodigal Son', and even 'Iron Maiden'. Also involved in the lawsuit was former Beckett singer, Terry Slesser (also known as Wilson-Slesser), regarding parts of the 1974 Beckett song, 'A Rainbow's Gold', which he said reappeared on 'Hallowed Be Thy Name.'

As a result of Willcock's dispute with Maiden, V1 disbanded in June 2018.

THE ONE & ONLY ORIGINAL
EXCITING, VISUAL & METAL

IRON MAIDEN
ROCK BAND

REQUIRE SERIOUS
TALENTED, TASTEFUL &
ONLY THE BEST

DRUMMER
WITH BIG SET-UP & STYLE

SYNTH/KEYBOARD
RAINBOW/LONESTAR STYLE
PHONE DENNIS 807 5752
EVENINGS, 580 6266 DAYS

"NO IDIOTS"

PART TWO **SOLO CAREERS**

DAVE MURRAY – THE AXEMAN

The nicest bloke in rock music

David Michael Murray is known as an affable, approachable and down-to-earth character, although his early dalliances with gangs and skinheads were a lot more on the aggro side.

After a revelation, guided - as many have been over the years - by hearing Jimi Hendrix's 'Voodoo Chile', Murray took up the guitar. The first band was with his close mate Adrian Smith – Stone Free – and then, briefly, in Evil Ways. He then left to play with the band Electric Gas, then Legend, and on answering an ad from *Melody Maker*, Iron Maiden.

That first Maiden stint began in late 1976 and ended midway through 1977. At this point, timelines diverge somewhat. What we can say is that Murray certainly played on a single by The Secret called 'The Young Ones,' a cover of Cliff Richard's awful twee bollocks track. The 7" is somewhere between a Plastic Bertrand B-side and The Sweet, with thin production and a huge dollop of second-wave, third-rate punking about. Don't go looking for it under his name; he was given the *nom de guerre* Reggie Mental. To put that in context, the singer was Mickey Modern, the drummer Percy Cute, the second guitarist Shrink, and the bassist Benny Leopard. We think these are not the names on their respective birth certificates. B-side, 'Handel A Vandal' is more of the same nonsense. It was released in October 1977, but Reggie Mental had already left.

He became Dave Murray again, briefly joining Smith in the latest incarnation of Evil Ways, renamed Urchin. He played on Urchin's single, 'She's a Roller,' a perfectly serviceable slab of poppy MOR rock. The B-side, 'Long Time No Woman' is more interesting fare, with some nifty controlled single-string riffing evident in a song that builds toward a singalong chorus. It's actually got more than a touch of Rod Stewart about it; whether that's a good or bad thing is debatable.

Murray wasn't to stick around too long, though, as Urchin's Maurice Coyne recalls.

"I remember hearing Dave had joined Iron Maiden, but they were just another pub band in those days," Coyne says. "I saw them a few times at The Cart & Horses and The Ruskin Arms and they were a good band - Dave was always a good guitarist - and they used a lot of gimmicks (Eddie The Head, bubble machines, dry ice, etc.). There was nothing to suggest they would be big at that point. They were playing hard rock / metal, and punk was killing that at the time."

A spell working for Hackney Council followed. But come 1979 the Maiden juggernaut was in sixth gear and Dave Murray has been a constant member since, outlasted only by Steve Harris himself. And doesn't The Blond Bomber look like he's loving every second? He's also guested with a few people over the years, most notably Smith's Psycho Motel, lending his smooth work to 'With You Again'.

You might catch him on a golf course when he's not on tour, particularly if you happen to be around in Maui, Hawaii, where he lives.

IRON MAIDEN

PAUL DI'ANNO – THE BEAST

Taylor? Andrews? Di'Anno!

There is a chap called Paul Taylor, or Paul Andrews if you prefer. He is from East London and we all probably know him better as Paul Di'Anno, the mercurial singer that through a combination of vocal talent, charisma and sheer force of personality became Iron Maiden's first iconic recorded vocalist.

Rewind to the ancient past – OK, the 1970s – and the singer says he used to hang out with his best mate Steve 'Loopy' Newhouse, knocking around the streets. Another mate Clive Adams was in an early band.

"We was like T-Rex in reverse," Di'Anno says. "He played guitar, looked like Mickey Finn and at the time, 'cause I had long curly hair, I looked kind of like Marc Bolan. I couldn't play anything, just bongos. We had a bugger about [playing music] then me and Steve and our mate Davey Wilson, who came over from Australia, used to play a bit. And we started mucking about with bands.

"There was one called Feedback, which is what it was most of the time. Then it all picked up a bit. I played in a punk band called Paedophiles," the vocalist says with a wry chuckle, "That went down rather well … not. It didn't go down well with a women's lib group; I didn't know what that was. Now I know different."

What's evident with Paul Di'Anno is that over the years he has always stepped up to the plate, and these days he steps up to own his past too. He acknowledges his mistakes, and distances himself from some of the attitudes he displayed in his youth; but he does not dismiss them. Whisper it quietly, but there's a maturity about the bloke that on occasion borders on humility. And on others, it doesn't. He is still Paul Di'Anno, for Odin's sake…

"I was in Rock Candy, a band that made a bit more headway. Then Trevor Searle, who was also a mate of Steve Harris, said Iron Maiden were looking for a singer."

We all know what happened next; if you don't know what happened next you have started reading this book in the middle, which is obviously a fine and dandy and altogether punk rock thing to do, if a lot less efficient. But hey, man, that's just, like, my opinion.

Though Loopy always knew him as Paul Taylor, Di'Anno is also known as Paul Andrews officially. He renamed himself as Di'Anno sometime in early 1979, claiming an Italian background. A couple of decades after that he'd give interviews saying his father was Brazilian and he'd go to visit his grandfather in Sao Paolo. Quite the cosmopolitan background, eh? Remember he is still Paul Di'Anno, for the love of Mjölnir …

After Maiden, Di'Anno started a new band called Lone Wolf which morphed into being called, simply, Di'Anno.

"It wasn't long, was it?" he recalls about the short time between Iron Maiden and his newer outfit. "I was getting Lone Wolf together coming out of Maiden. Me and Loopy went to see this band play at the Ruskin who became my band. Then I got my brother-in-law in; I was about to get married. His name is PJ Ward, a great guitar player."

Due to there already being a band called Lonewolf, he decided to do what everybody

PART TWO **SOLO CAREERS**

else was advising at the time and rename the new group after himself.

"I couldn't be bothered with all that [hassle] so thought, 'Sod it,' and though I'd always rather have a band name we were called Di'Anno, which wasn't my choice, to be honest," he remembers. "We were signed to a label in Japan. We demoed a few songs here and there, went to Rockfield Studios - which was absolutely amazing - and had a couple of friends from Sad Café help us out. We got Clive Burr in from Samson. We had a fantastic vibe; it was awesome."

That pesky 'real life' thing got in the way though; Di'Anno had just become a father. Things became something of a blur, he says. The band he'd formed were absolutely doing the business.

"The next thing I knew was that I was out doing publicity in Japan because the album had reached No.1 in their domestic charts. Not the rock charts – I was blown away!"

Paul Di'Anno with his band, Killers, early 2000s

THIS DAY IN MUSIC'S GUIDE TO **IRON MAIDEN** 153

IRON MAIDEN

Typically for Paul Di'Anno, there was to be quite the blast around his stay in Japan. This time, though, it was nature causing the issues rather than self-inflicted adventures.

"I had a really good couple of weeks over there, but it didn't help that the second I got there they had a bleedin' great earthquake! I was on the 19th floor of the Tokyo Prince hotel. They are all built for earthquakes, aren't they, and I felt it go: I was wobbling about in my bed. I thought it was jetlag, 'cause I'd never been that far before. I put on a sweatshirt, jogging pants and trainers and went downstairs to the bar. They were all having a drink like nothing had fucking happened! It was like, 'Hello Paul, fancy a Jack Daniel's?' 'Yeah, a fucking bottle!'"

"We came back [to the UK]. Christine Gorham, Scott Gorham from Thin Lizzy's wife, was on the team and co-managed us. Next thing you know we were on tour with Thin Lizzy, which was awesome."

Everyone was expecting a simple heavy metal album from him, he said, but he didn't want to deliver that.

"Being an awkward bugger, I wanted to do something more like Duran Duran meets Rush," he says, tongue firmly in cheek. "More commercial. The whole idea of being a musician is to try different things. We toured quite a bit, did pretty well."

And although the experience had been a good one, it wasn't a permanent change in direction for the famed metal vocalist.

"I enjoyed it, but it wasn't where my heart is. I wanted dirty rock, metal, kind of thing."

Gogmawot?

In 1985, for reasons best known to himself, record producer and industry wannabe Jonathan King put together a metal supergroup called Gogmagog. The talent was there – Di'Anno, Clive Burr, Janick Gers, Pete Willis, Neil Murray – but again the songs were written by King himself, with the exception of a Russ Ballard cover.

"It was nothing to do with anybody [creatively], which was very strange," Di'Anno says. "My wife phoned me at me mum's and said, 'This bloke Jonathan King phoned up for you.' Next thing I know I spoke to him and he said he was getting the project together. I basically replaced David Coverdale. At one stage there was John Entwhistle [The Who] on bass, Cozy Powell [Jeff Beck/ Rainbow/ Sabbath] on drums, but they all dropped out one by one. They probably knew better than I did."

Bringing such talented folk together and then not letting them write songs seems a surefire way to failure, which Di'Anno still is bemused about some three decades later.

"We had to do the songs that King and Ballard wrote," says the vocalist, who recalls there were plenty of plans and dreams from the production team, but little of actual substance.

"[Jonathan] King had all these ideas, like two characters called Gog and Magog on stage," Di'Anno notes. "He was going around all the record companies asking for something like eight million pounds, eight million dollars to be signed. Then that went down to two million dollars... "

"Anyway, we went and recorded it, thought, 'It's alright,' but nobody's heart was really in it. We weren't allowed to write anything. And that was that." Strange, strange stuff.

Thank the pagan gods of the earth that a proper band followed: the mighty Battlezone. That one lasted for the next four years, coming back briefly in 1998.

PART TWO **SOLO CAREERS**

"It worked out great," Di'Anno says of a band that itself went through several line-ups. "It was thrashy, punky sort of metally stuff. We went flying all over the bloody shop. We played everywhere. North to South, East to West, a week off then back out again. We were out on the road for about three years in the States."

The 1986 debut, *Fighting Back*, is a corker; the follow-up, *Children of Madness*, quality stuff too.

"We burnt ourselves out, basically," Di'Anno says. "Then nothing happened for a while. I took some time out, had a little break. When I work, I do work hard." By the end of 1989 the well had run dry; the final gig was on December 10th in the Netherlands. There was a brief Battlezone resurrection in 1998, featuring a new album, *Feel My Pain*, and a rather excellent tour in Brazil.

Back to 1990, though, and Praying Mantis marked the 10th anniversary of NWOBHM with an excellent reformation gig in Tokyo, with Di'Anno singing and Dennis Stratton on guitar. A quick tour followed that April.

Killing it

Once that all came to an end, Di'Anno had another band – *Killers*. John Gallagher of Raven, Steve Hopgood, Ray Detone and guitarist Cliff Evans completed the line-up.

"The idea was to put together a band of big-name British musicians around [Paul] to create some kind of metal supergroup," Evans says. "It was a good plan. We had US management and Paul was still a major name on the metal front, so we thought there could be a good chance of getting a decent record deal and maybe we could do something.

"John Gallagher and I were living in New York at the time, so we brought Paul and Steve over and started the ball rolling."

A legendary story about Killers, the band, is that they gained their first record deal by playing songs that, um, had kind of already been released, and, um, been pretty bloody successful. Not that the representatives that attended a particular gig were any the wiser, Evans laughs.

"Our manager arranged some showcases and invited all the major labels down to check us out," he recalls. "Only problem was that as we had only just formed the band we had no songs whatsoever. All we could do was play a few Iron Maiden classics and hope for the best."

"Sony and BMG sent their top NY label guys along. Virgin flew theirs in from LA," says the guitarist. "We played our versions of 'Phantom of the Opera', 'Wrathchild' and 'Remember Tomorrow' while they polished off the free drinks and food we had laid on for them." Never a bad move, that. And the gods of luck were smiling on Killers that day too.

"Fortunately, none of the [A&R guys] had probably even heard an Iron Maiden song so they thought the songs were all our own compositions and congratulated us on our writing abilities. They were so impressed that a bidding war started between them. We ended up signing with BMG for $200,000.

"Not bad for a covers band."

You can say that again. A live album followed, including a few crowd-pleasing cover versions.

"My missus at the time was working for RCA Records," recalls Di'Anno. "She said she'd played them some of our stuff and they were interested. We spent about four weeks in New York writing stuff, Nick Burr

IRON MAIDEN

came in and next thing, I nearly chopped my finger off in a car door!" The debut album, *Murder One*, was completed at The Power Station, a New York studio.

"An unbelievable place," says Di'Anno. "And it did alright. It made the record company their money back for them."

Cliff Evans remembers it well.

"We finished recording the album in NY and were all very excited about the finished product we had created. Getting out on the road was the next step so we could promote the album and have a good time.

"The tour started with coast-to-coast shows in the US and then over to Japan for a couple of weeks before heading out across Europe. It was a really great tour and the band was living up to its expectations."

Things were looking good, but there was always the potential of mercurial frontman heading off into Di'Anno-danger territory.

"There were some very dark moments however, which could have ended the band there and then," Evans confirms. "But we managed to somehow get through it all fairly unscathed.

"We knew Paul was not going to be the easiest person to work with so were well prepared for whatever problems arose along the way. Or so we thought. Having Di'Anno in the band would open doors for you but would also cause quite a few to be slammed in your face."

Indeed, the singer's offstage issues were numerous; his marriage broke up, and he was put in jail in Los Angeles, as Evans notes.

"The biggest problem we had to deal with was Paul being banned from entering the US after being convicted and incarcerated in LA County Jail on assault, firearms and drugs charges."

So Di'Anno finally had to return to the UK. *Killers* were based back in Britain by this time and *Menace to Society* came out on Bleeding Hearts Records to a mediocre response, in the UK at least. Audiences of 6,000 went nuts to it down in Brazil.

"We toured all over the place with that, then I mucked about with a punk band for a while, The Almighty Inbreds. I did a demo with them."

Killers had come to a natural end, it seems, Evans describing a wider issue – one that Iron Maiden were also dealing with – as kids were looking to other climes for their distorted guitar thrills.

"Apart from the problem of Paul being unable to enter the US," remembers Evans, "It seemed that the style of traditional heavy metal we were playing was rapidly becoming outdated and was pushed aside almost overnight by the emergence of Grunge. Eighties metal was finished! Denim and leather replaced by plaid shirts and camo shorts." There was a planned reunion of Killers in 2013, but it never came to pass.

Paul Di'Anno and Dennis Stratton teamed up for a couple of albums of varying quality in the mid-1990s, and he had also guested with Praying Mantis for 1991's *Live at Last* LP. There were plenty of other appearances over the next 10 years or so with various bands. Some projects included the Brazil-based Nomad project, where he linked up with Paullo Turin and a Brazilian band. *The Living Dead* album came out of that one, with a DVD recorded in the East London docks. That was an on-and-off project for a lot of the first decade of the new millennium, and with Di'Anno now living in Brazil he toured alongside Jean Dolabella, once of Sepultura, plus two other famed South American players, for the RockFellas group. They toured with a set of rock and metal classics.

PART TWO **SOLO CAREERS**

Banding together

Di'Anno was again jailed in 2011, this time in the UK for benefit fraud, and on his release had the itch to get back up and running in the one place he'd always felt at home: fronting a brilliant band. This time, though, there was an innovative approach to matters.

"My manager at the time, Lea Hart, and me hit upon an idea," explains Di'Anno. "Now every musician's on the bloody bandwagon with it. But to save money, we'd get the best band in the country you were going to play. So I had two fantastic bands playing for me in Brazil, an amazing band in Argentina, one in Mexico ... I was constantly on the road. My Swedish band played. I wasn't recording, but I was on the road."

One of Di'Anno's recent projects – which has since fallen apart – was the bloody excellent Architects of Chaoz, featuring members of his German touring band, The Phantomz. They debuted in 2015 with their debut LP *The League of Shadows*. It sounded immense, absolutely hammering it into the ground. "Joey Siedl is a fantastic songwriter. We hit it off straight away and wrote some great songs," Di'Anno recalls. The Architects have gone on to release new material without him.

And despite saying he was going to retire in around 2013, he couldn't quite keep his promise. Plenty more to come from Paul Di'Anno, for sure. Unless he gets kidnapped, as he did in Argentina not so long ago ...

"It was by the fans," he says. "They wouldn't let me come offstage. I had to stay an extra week and a half just playing show after show after show. I was getting sicker and sicker by the minute; then when I came home I collapsed and was in hospital for eight months. That was in 2015."

"They actually didn't think I was going to make it when I came back from Argentina. I had a massive abscess the size of a rugby ball. I'm pretty lucky to be alive to be honest with you. The mental days are over – a bit.

"[Architects of Chaoz] couldn't wait around for me whilst I was having my knee operation and all that," he explains of the split with his band. "I was a bit pissed off. I thought it was about loyalty and brotherhood. When I start making my new album it'll probably be with my Argentinian band now."

There are many guest appearances to discover; he's hardly the kind of man to stay still for long. Ibridoma – an Italian metal band – featured him on their 2016 album, *December*, on which Blaze Bayley also guested. Airforce, featuring Dougie Sampson, also linked up with Paul, who sang masterfully on their track, 'Sniper', from their EP *Black Box Recordings Volume 2*. Perhaps unsurprisingly, Di'Anno's also worked with the rather awesome The Iron Maidens recently.

So with retirement on hold – as if anyone believed it anyway – Paul Di'Anno survives and thrives into his fifth decade of metal madness. And watch out, world: A brand-new, part-bionic Paul Di'Anno with new knees is in the making. The RoboCops will be quaking in their shiny metal boots ...

IRON MAIDEN

DENNIS STRATTON – THE PROFESSIONAL

In the Lion(heart)'s den with Dennis

The guitarist that played on Maiden's debut, Dennis Stratton, provided not only crucial stability at a time when the group was still faltering but also bags of big-game experience. By the time he joined Iron Maiden he was already a seasoned professional, having toured Europe supporting Status Quo, and was on the verge of stardom outside the confines of Maiden, no matter how upcoming and highly rated the Irons were at the time. Stratton says he was a regular visitor to the musical pubs around Canning Town with his mates in the early 1970s. Though his first serious band was the relatively short-lived Harvest, things stepped up with his next act.

"We put a band together called Remus Down Boulevard," says the axeman. "We did what every band does; got some roadies and started doing the circuit. We built up quite a following in the early to mid-Seventies, then around 1976 we did the Marquee and got signed by Kory management."

That management also took care of Rory Gallagher and Status Quo: one hell of a team to have behind you, for sure. Remus Down Boulevard – RDM – were surely going places.

"We went from the Marquee, out on tour with Quo, playing huge stadiums all over Europe, 60,000 seaters. Quite a step up from the Bridgehouse. It was a good learning experience in a short space of time. You had to grow up overnight, going on stage in front of 60,000 people rather than 600."

The band was signed by UK Records, the label of Jonathan King. At the time, King had a lot of clout in the industry (we won't go into his off-stage activities: suffice to say he has rightly been jailed since). Stratton merely remarks: "We knew there was something up with him, but didn't know what it was."

"We did a live album at the Marquee that never came out; we had 14 songs we'd never recorded. Then King got [himself] a gig on TV doing an American AOR show and the record company folded."

RDM went back out on the circuit, paying their dues many times over before he was asked to join Maiden in early 1979.

Apres le deluge

In the aftermath of that curious and arguably unnecessary parting with Iron Maiden, Stratton was rightly a man in demand. Thus came the group, Lionheart, who immediately started making waves in the industry. A CBS record deal was to follow, things again looking up for the talented musician. But the vagaries of the music industry were to strike a fatal blow to Lionheart, too.

"We were hung out to dry," says Stratton. "We went to America, signed a huge deal, did a brilliant album, a big video and everything. But when you're supposed to go out on tour to promote an album and it's all cancelled there's nothing you can do. We came back from America with nothing and realised the record company had forgotten all about us. Kansas were doing something with their album, Foreigner were recording their album, whatever, so we got let down left, right and centre. By 1986 the band just fizzled out."

PART TWO **SOLO CAREERS**

That LP, *Hot Tonight*, is pretty damned rocking, with hints of Free and a distinct 1980s tinge smashing out the speakers. Fans of Def Leppard will love it, not least the huge-drummed title track. By the way, anyone who's ever seen The Darkness play will recognise exactly where the Hawkins boys nicked their 'Thing Called Love' riff from. Shameless, really. Elsewhere, 'Wait for the Night' blends a load of synthy stuff with sax, cello and 'Final Countdown'-esque anthemic rock. Although that really ought to be the other way around, as Europe's track wasn't released 'til two years later. It's part Meat Loaf, part Queen, and all bloody ace. Another cracker is 'Nightmare,' on which vocalist Chad Brown is in absolutely blinding form. There's also the small matter of 'Don't Look Back in Anger,' mercifully not the Oasis version that was to follow 10 years later.

Lionheart could and maybe should have sold millions of records. All the talent was in place, the production was brilliant, the songs catchy and the harmony guitars classic. But the record business is full of such tales of nearly-weres. Like footballers, it's not always the most talented ones that make it. It's a blend of hard work, persistence, bloody-mindedness and a massive dollop of luck.

After Lionheart, Stratton was contacted by another NWOBHM outfit, Praying Mantis. The band went to Japan to great response, and recorded an excellent LP live in Vienna. The Mantis years were very fruitful for the guitarist and the band.

"I was with Mantis for 15 years. We did about eight albums. It's funny, but 15 years can fly by. But of course, back in England people think you've packed it in, because they don't see you. You're always rehearsing, doing an album, touring."

The Beast drops by

Stratton also collaborated with Paul Di'Anno on three releases: *The Original Iron Men* (1995), *The Original Iron Men 2* (1996) *and Hard As Iron* (1996). Check out 'I've Had Enough' for some proper Saxon/DC riffing. Stratton himself gives the vocal chords an airing throughout the project. Nothing to make too many waves, but some decent material and definitely of interest to Maiden completists. It's surprisingly poppy at times, 'No Repair' being a good example. As a side-project it's decent stuff.

Back to Praying Mantis, though, and unfortunately they too fell through the cracks due to a recession hitting their record company in 2005.

"They shut down, which left us without a record deal," Stratton says. "So it fizzled out again in 2006."

In around 2009, the guitarist began to appear at conventions related to Iron Maiden, he says.

"I was gonna semi-retire; I'd moved to the countryside. But I started working with a couple of other little bands, we got more and more work and then in 2016 were asked to reform Lionheart for a festival [Rockingham 2016, Nottingham.]"

"We had a few rehearsals, and the festival was fantastic. Then we got some songs together, started recording at Steve Mann's studio in Germany. What with the power of the Internet now you don't have to even be in the same studio. So bass was in Grantham, the drums in Heathrow and all my guitars were in Saffron Walden. And there you have it: *Second Nature*. I'm proud of it. It sounds

IRON MAIDEN

good, has great production, I love it. We went to Japan in July 2017 and it was in the charts for six weeks over there, getting to No.3."

So far, so good, right? Not quite...

"We got back over here, and the record company made a complete cock-up of it. They delayed it for two weeks. It was just a shambles. But now it's out we're getting so many good reviews in Europe, out of 52 reviews [at the time of the interview, October 2017] not one mark under eight out of 10. For us at our age to get that out so quickly [is amazing.] You might think I'm in the band, and it's my band [so I have to be positive about the record], but I will tell you, everyone who puts that album on says they love it and it's fantastic."

Lionheart continue to tour and record. The industry can't chew everyone up and spit them out, it seems. Stratton's a survivor – not many people could leave Maiden the way he did and remain so positive. All power to him.

CLIVE BURR – THE JOKER

Burr-illiant man, cruel illness

Clive Ronald Burr, born on March 8th, 1956, was absolutely instrumental in Maiden's first three albums and the sadly-missed sticksman had a long an interesting career before and after his tenure with the Irons.

Like future bandmate Bruce Dickinson, Burr was a major fan of Deep Purple's Ian Paice. Finding he was a talented tub-thumper, he cut his teeth in the band Maya before joining Paul Samson's band. That stint lasted until he joined Maiden in 1979. Leaving the band after *Number of the Beast* was controversial. One line is that Burr was enjoying extra-curricular activities too much, affecting his playing. Another is that the drummer returned home from tour to attend his father's funeral and be with his family. History records that Nicko McBrain stepped on to the drum-seat and has been there to this day.

Burr then replaced McBrain in Trust, drumming on the 1983 self-titled LP and *Man Trap* the following year. He also was part of the horrible Gogmagog project and drummed with a host of NWOBHM-associated acts, including Alcatrazz, Praying Mantis, Stratus Elixir and Desperado, with Dee Snyder.

Multiple Sclerosis

Tragically, Burr was to contract the incurable disease, Multiple Sclerosis, which ended first his drumming career and ultimately took his life at age 56.

Dr. David Jones, in a long career as GP, has seen MS at close quarters. He says the initial stages of the disease can be 'very random.'

PART TWO **SOLO CAREERS**

"[It can include] blurred or distorted vision (eye nerves affected or optic neuritis), random sensation disturbance, usually pins and needles for no particular reason (such as lying awkwardly on your arm or leg), tripping over nothing, dropping things or being clumsy, difficulty walking where before there was no problem, balance problems or falling over for no reason. As a drummer he might have noticed difficulty keeping time or rhythm for instance."

The disease does not affect the mind in some ways, though.

"Intellect is normally maintained as higher function in the brain is not usually affected," Dr. Jones continues. Multiple Sclerosis is a vicious disease that can strike heavily.

"Two main types exist – the remitting/relapsing type and secondary progressive," he says. "The former can become the latter over time. The common type I saw, and that is seen, is the remitting -relapsing type. Effectively you get bouts or acute attacks induced by stress, other concurrent illness, virus infection or bacterial infections– anything that seems to trigger the immune system – with periods of remission. Remission can be without any symptoms or as time goes on accumulative neurological problems."

The basic underlying problem, says the retired doctor, can be thought of as analogous to short circuiting.

"In an electric wire (effectively what a nerve is) there is an insulating cover – a plastic tube in which the copper wire runs. This way you can put lots of wires adjacent without affecting the function of the machine or circuit. If you get a break in the insulation then, this can cause short-circuits and will then affect the function of the electric circuit and system failure."

"Nerves in the brain, spinal cord and the network in the body have a similar covering called the myelin sheath. MS is believed to be a failure of this myelin sheath, thus causing short circuits and system failure – this might be affecting the sensory system (causing pins and needles, numbness, lack of sensation, blindness) or the motor system (causing muscle weakness and twitching, muscle paralysis) – this can be anywhere in the body and usually quite random, not fitting any particular anatomical area or region – a useful clinical sign for health carers to think about MS."

The reasons for this occurrence are not fully understood, but it may be affected by the immune system. The fact that the myelin sheath is disrupted in different areas each time makes treatment so difficult. Antiviral treatments can assist, and prednisolone steroids can suppress the immune reaction, helping with temporary remission. But it is only temporary.

"Sadly, each time the relapse occurs you tend not to go back to where you were before, so gradually over the years your motor and sensory function deteriorate and your mobility and function likewise. Eventually a relapse won't remit, and you are then in the secondary progressive type and downhill slowly thereafter, with no let-up."

And whilst there is always hope of a cure, at the moment the disease is incurable, despite advances in molecular and biological research.

Clive Aid

In 2002, Iron Maiden established the Clive Burr Trust, which helped Burr with medical and living costs. From 2004 onwards, there have been many concerts under the banner

IRON MAIDEN

of 'Clive Aid,' a pun on the famous 1984 Live Aid charity gigs. Robin Guy played in two bands at the 2002 version.

"The Clive Aid gig was fantastic," he says. "GMT (a band I was in with Bernie Tormé – ex-Gillan and Ozzy guitarist - and John McCoy – ex-Gillan and Mammoth bassist) were booked to headline - they'd both played with Clive Burr back in the day, but then Sack Trick got added to the bill."

Sack Trick, should you dare to search, are a band in which Guy plays along with Chris Dale, and a revolving cast of thousands. You may well see them dressed as various animals at their regular One Night World Tour in Sweden each Christmastide. Simply, they are a daft, silly, very daft, very silly and quite brilliant outfit that have released three albums to date.

Sack Trick developed out of the band that worked with Bruce on *Skunkworks*, Dale recalls.

"Me, Alex [Elena] and Alex [Dickson] lived music 24/7 back then," confirms the bassist. "If we weren't working on Bruce's songs, we'd be jamming new ideas, jamming covers or writing even more songs just for the sake of it. When Bruce called an end to Skunkworks, we started straight way on two new projects. One was called Fling, this was Alex Dickson writing and singing some great pop-rock songs. It was a shame that never took off."

"The other was me still writing fun songs. The three of us recorded them with some friends and made the first Sack Trick album, *Mystery Rabbits*. I played the finished album to Bruce and he loved it. He came to our gigs, offered us the support on some UK dates for *Chemical Wedding*, got us on his BBC radio show and yes, guested at some of the Sack Trick gigs. He'd come up and sing one of our songs or a cover like 'Delilah' by Tom Jones."

"The Clive Aid gig at the Royal Standard in Walthamstow was one of those events Bruce came and sang at. He also came to a Sack Trick gig at the Peel in Kingston, where he asked me if a version of Sack Trick could be his backing band for the 2002 festivals."

They are, let's say, unique. Guy remembers their particular brand of madness was a bit tricky for anyone else to get up onstage to play afterwards.

"We all realised that, well, no-one can follow Sack Trick, so we kinda 'headlined' after.

"Bruce Dickinson did the righteous thing, donned his stripes and got up to sing 'Blue Ice Cream' with us - he may have done more but by this point I can safely say we were all rather 'refreshed'..."

Burr met his partner Mimi because they had the same consultant for their shared condition.

"I was a scientist and Sunday School teacher!" she recalls. "I wasn't into that kind of music. We started talking and realised we were in the same neighbourhood. He said he was just over the roundabout but was lying through his teeth when he said he lived in the country. In London, if you've got a tree outside your house it's the country!"

It was clearly meant to be, she continues.

"I worked in Bart's hospital when he was in Smithfield Market working in the meat market for a while," Mimi remembers.

"They started really early and would go to this pub, the Barley Mow. Funnily enough I would go there after work [in the evening.]"

For a drummer, that was terrible timing on his part, no? Also, when the pair did get together, there was still a bit of an issue.

"They would speak this jargon at the

PART TWO **SOLO CAREERS**

market that I couldn't understand ... he'd say so many funny things, 'It's my manor,' for example. But by the end he'd got me speaking cockney rhyming slang... 'Do you want a cuppa Rosie?' and so on."

In 2005 he donated his famous white drum-kit to the Hard Rock Café, who made a donation in return. That, along with the immense assistance of Maiden, enabled a refit of the Burr house that made it much more wheelchair-friendly, with everything electric and adapted specially to make life as comfortable and accessible as possible.

"It's beautiful," Mimi simply states. "Even the doctors and nurses that used to visit said you couldn't tell it was effectively a mini-hospital."

Clive Burr was always larger-than-life, with a personality that was irresistible at times.

"He was a showman. That's why he had that massive cymbal and those tight-fitting leotards that he got from a dance shop in Covent Garden. He was a fab guy. We were together for years and I was lucky to have that time with him. Sometimes he'd be like Ozzy Osbourne, [calling out], 'Miiimes, where's the [remote control]'."

When he did get down, one of Mimi's actions was to put a DVD on of Burr in his heyday.

"If he got upset and angry I'd tell him to be quiet and say, 'Look what good you did," she says.

He also introduced his partner to one of the greatest movies of all time – *This Is Spinal Tap*.

"Every band thinks it's about them," Mimi says, laughing. "But I genuinely think it is Iron Maiden. It's so funny; when you go backstage it's exactly the same.

People getting into skin-tight clothes, just so funny."

As the years went on, bands worldwide would put on concerts to assist. As well as Maiden, musicians would call or call in to see how things were going. They included Dee Snyder, amongst many others.

On March 13th, 2013, Clive Burr died.

"He passed away, next to me in bed," recalls Mimi. "He was the same age as his father was, 56, and his mother also passed in her sleep.

"It seems like only yesterday that we lost him."

Though Burr has left for the great rock'n'roll bistro in the sky, he will never be forgotten by Maiden fans and the millions of people his music touched. Part of a legend forever and sadly missed.

There were many reasons people adored Clive Burr, but Mimi pinpoints one that perhaps brings the most joy as a memory.

"Clive had the most brilliant smile. The most fantastic smile.

"I am blessed to have known him." https://www.mstrust.org.uk/

IRON MAIDEN

ADRIAN SMITH – THE TUNESMITH

Every urchin has to start somewhere

The archetypal urchin of lore is a ragged-arsed street kid with a quick line in patter and even quicker fingers nicking your wallet. Think the Artful Dodger and you've got it (the character in the Dickens novel *Oliver Twist*, not the garage duo of the same name that sadly launched the career of Craaaaaaigggg Daviiiiid).

Around a hundred years, give or take, after the death of Chuck D, another type of Urchin was born, and it was to have an incredible impact on the Iron Maiden story (Chuck D as in Charles Dickens, not the Public Enemy rapper of the same name ... we think).

The very first incarnation of Urchin – the band – was formed at school by twin-guitar nuts and close mates Adrian Smith and Dave Murray. John Hoye was quickly brought in on bass by the duo. At this stage, the project was called Stone Free – after the Hendrix song - and was completed by a rather unusual 'drummer'. Hoye remembers it well:

"In 1972 I was introduced to Adrian & Dave by a mutual friend. Adrian & Dave I think went to the same school but also lived a few doors away from each other near Clapton Pond, London E5. I live by Victoria Park E9. Frank was a friend of mine from school who wanted to play drums but he only had the sticks (he never played). Adrian & Dave rehearsed in Adrian's cellar and Dave's house for a bit when I joined. We rehearsed in my cellar and kitchen much to the annoyance of my neighbours, and a room at the back of Dave's house which I remember was full of equipment with no room to move at all. I remember a small set of drums in my cellar which Dave liked to kick over in The Who type fashion."

A couple of shows at dance nights followed, complete with a Hendrix cover, 'Little Wing'. Even at this incredibly early stage, Murray was showing his talent.

"Dave played it note for note, even getting in the sound of the pick-up change at the end of the song, spot on, it still echoes in my ears," Hoye remembers. "Dave of course, on a couple of songs played the complicated lead behind his head and with his teeth, both perfectly done with no problem (at 15 or so). This was also our first paid gig, it came out of the money taken at the door to fund the dance night. I can't remember how much it was, but it was all in coins.

"Our next gig was a talent contest in a pub called The Earl of Zetland in Hackney. A very big talent contest with big prize money, it attracted many older and professional singers. We were the only band, a very young, scruffy motley crew compared to the well turned-out singers. The pub was packed, we didn't win but were very well received. One of our best songs we played was 'Whiskey in the Jar' and again thanks to Dave he played it note for note and with the exact right sound/tone, it went down a storm."

It's only rock n' roll

After a few low-key gigs in talent competitions and at school, the nascent band looked to bolster their sound, bringing in guitarist Maurice Coyne for a jam (Smith was at this stage the band's singer).

PART TWO SOLO CAREERS

"We were just a bunch of teenagers who loved music and wanted to play it," says Coyne. "I was introduced to John Hoye by a workmate, Chris Malynn, who told me John's band were looking for a guitarist as their current guy was leaving. He knew I was looking for a band so put me in touch - this was early in 1974. I met John and Frank (who was the original drummer - never owned a drum kit to my knowledge but, hey!). I think we met in a pub for a chat, got on well and I agreed to go to John's house for a jam the following week.

"When I got to John's I was ushered down to the cellar, where he'd set up a practice room. A few minutes later the doorbell rang, and Dave Murray arrived. We were introduced, and I gathered he was the one who was leaving the band. We plugged in and jammed on a few numbers and Dave was very impressive. He was a big Hendrix fan and proceeded to play the guitar behind his head and with his teeth. No pressure! After half an hour or so, Adrian showed up clutching a plastic bag with his lead and strap in and his Woolworth's Kay guitar and joined in on a few more songs."

A couple more jams followed but the group – Murray and all – was rehearsing for a talent contest in a local boozer Adam & Eve on Homerton Road in Hackney's High Street.

"That turned out to be Dave's last appearance with them and he went off to join a band called Electric Gas," Coyne recalls. "For that show, they'd acquired a drummer named Peter (I never knew his last name) and Adrian, John, Peter and myself decided to get together at John's old school (Cardinal Pole) on a Monday evening, where we had permission to play in the hall.

"We had a jam session and quickly realised there was some real potential and chemistry, so we decided to form a band. Things didn't really work out with Peter, so we advertised for a drummer. Barry Tyler replied, auditioned and joined. Up until then, they'd been called Stone Free and I think we did a couple of school dances under that name but then changed to Evil Ways, after the Santana song."

Murray, meanwhile, briefly joined a group called Legend alongside Barry Tyler's brother Terry, and Alan Levett, Coyne says.

"They were a good band," declares Coyne. "I remember them doing a great version of 'Summer Breeze' by the Isley Brothers."

Serendipity was to play a part after a fun day/festival-type gig in Daubeney Fields, near Hackney Marshes.

"We found ourselves stranded with our gear but no way of getting home. None of us could drive then," says Coyne. "We met up with Dave Lewis, who offered us lifts home in his van and said he really liked the band and would like to do the sound for us. Dave became our road manager and sound engineer. After rehearsing for a few months, we got our first 'proper' gig at a pub called The Castle in Stoke Newington. We can't have been too bad as they had us back maybe half a dozen times!"

The group was by now getting properly good; playing most nights a week will do that for any outfit. A singer was needed, though, and Dave Hall came in to boost the band's sound and allow Smith to concentrate on guitar.

Management excitement and career disappointment

The band was by now firmly on the circuit, graduating from back rooms of

IRON MAIDEN

pubs to actual venues, including The Brecknock, The Greyhound, Golden Lion and Hammersmith's Red Cow.

"We were spotted at The Greyhound in 1976 by Danny Morgan who, with his boss, Simon Napier-Bell, ran Nomis-Morgan," Coyne notes. "They offered to manage us and get us a record contract and publishing deal. We subsequently signed to DJM Records. Danny and Simon suggested we change the name to Urchin."

The band – as Evil Ways – had recorded demos at various studios, including a session at Chalk Farm plus one in Cambridge's Spaceward Studios as prize for winning Islington Group of the Year.

"It was an overnight session, we met in the pub opposite Dave's shop off Mare Street, Hackney, then drove late afternoon to Cambridge," says Hoye. "[We] recorded through the night and drove back to a café near Adrian's house and had a full English breakfast." Urchin, however, were battling both the rise of punk rock and the perennial lack of cash faced by youngsters entering the world of music. And though the group was now playing college venues, the management wasn't happy with the lads' choice of debut single.

"We went into TPA Studios in Denmark Street to record 'Without Love', one of Dave Hall's songs," Coyne remembers. "It was very poppy and not really representative of the band's sound. I think DJM were less than happy with it, so they sent their A&R guy to one of our gigs. He loved 'Black Leather Fantasy' so it was arranged for us to go into the studio to record that with 'Rock & Roll Woman' as the B-side."

"'Without Love' was shelved and never released. The ('Black Leather Fantasy') single was released on Friday, May 13th, 1977 (an auspicious date!). It didn't set the world on fire but has become a bit of a NWOBHM classic, apparently."

(We must note at this point that Hoye remembers recording '22 Acacia Avenue' – a Smith composition – as the B-side. Memories, of course, at 40 years' distance, aren't always sharp. The song that '22 Acacia Avenue' was based on was called 'Countdown'.)

Alan Levett replaced Hoye as bassist in the band, John leaving to join a band called Headlights. Maurice Coyne also left for reasons financial and personal at this point (the lads have all kept in touch since, he says). Another guitarist was lined up though – one Dave Murray.

"When I announced I was leaving Urchin they auditioned a few guitarists," Coyne notes. "Then Dave left Iron Maiden and he was interested in joining. We agreed I would cover live shows until Dave had learnt all the material and they'd had a chance to rehearse properly, so I stayed on until about January 1978, when Dave took over."

"Dave played on the second single – 'She's A Roller' - but then made his peace with Maiden and went back to them around April 1978. The guys asked me to come back for a while, but I was working by then so couldn't do it." Andy Barnett took up the axeman role instead.

Alan Levett recalls how things were at the time.

"Our recording sessions were primitive by today's standards, and very rushed. We only recorded the two singles and their B-sides in real recording studios. The record producers failed to capture the Urchin sound and I don't think really understood the band. One of them tried to change us, giving the guitars clean chord sounds; I think he was trying to

PART TWO **SOLO CAREERS**

modernise us and punk us up a bit.

"We did loads of four-track demo recordings in our little rehearsal studio in Hackney, which I personally enjoyed much more. Again, they were very rushed and under-rehearsed, but represented what we were trying to do much better. We had control, and we could relax, be creative. There was a brief time when we could arrange and record new songs before we added them to the live set. It was great fun, and this was probably our best studio work."

By now Smith was really progressing as a player, says Levett.

"Adrian was a bluesy soloist back then, with a great feel, and he'd always have tuneful hooks and catchy lines in his solos. His chord sound was fat and powerful; he was a terrific rhythm guitarist. His split lead harmonies with Mo and Andy were really melodic and clever, and often a big feature in Urchin."

Hoye remembers Smith as a 'feel' player.

"Adrian was great, he played from the soul," he says. "Bluesy or rock'n'roll, you name it. On one hand he'd pen a typical rock song and on the other hand a melodic lyrical gem."

Great songs and great sound do not always a career make, of course. Soon enough the management and record company both fell away, and despite interest from WEA Records the band's days were numbered. Levett continues:

"After each gig [WEA would] tell us they wanted to hear a song that would make a good single release, but we really struggled to write a pop-rock song for them, and they reluctantly passed on us. It was after all 1978, and I think all the other recording labels passed on us because punk rock was taking off and seemingly the music press wasn't interested in writing about much else. I think Urchin simply missed its window of opportunity.

"Heavy Metal bands like Iron Maiden managed to fight off punk music and survive beyond the punk era right up to today," Levett muses.

"I think we should have listened to Dave Murray back in the day, he had the right idea."

Urchin split up in March 1980. Smith and Barnett went on to play with Jeb Million and the Broadway Brats. The Brats had some momentum behind them, members including Nick 'Topper' Headon, who went on to join the Clash, and one Nicko McBrain briefly on drums. Ian Richardson, however, was the sticksman by the time Smith joined.

Following quite a few invitations, Adrian Smith agreed to join Iron Maiden as replacement for Dennis Stratton in the latter months of 1980.

Adrian Smith And Projects

Adrian Smith and Nicko couldn't help themselves after the *Powerslave* tour, linking up with H's old mates Andy Barnett and Dave Colwell to get jamming and crack on with the creative side. The project was eventually called The Entire Population of Hackney, and they did a gig on December 19th, 1985. Bootlegs, of course, exist. The band played a host of originals – some from Urchin, some specially written – plus covers of ZZ Top, Bob Seger and, well, Maiden. Though with Harris, Murray and Bruce all joining in for the latter tracks there was more Iron than Hackney at that point, so technically not covers. Still, they rocked the Marquee like nobody's business. Nicko also apparently booked a gig under the

IRON MAIDEN

cockney rhyming slang-naughty moniker The Sherman Tankers.

The band was part-knockabout fun after the serious business of that gruelling world tour, and part-testing ground for some of H's solos. Some tracks also appeared in future projects by Smith; Iron Maiden themselves would pick 'Reach Out', 'Juanita' and 'That Girl' as B-sides on subsequent singles. Nothing's ever wasted really, is it.

And so it came that Smith was to release a non-Maiden record in 1989, with the Adrian Smith and Project LP, *Silver and Gold*. Nicko wasn't able to join the outfit for recordings so one Zak Starkey – son of Ringo and briefly later a member of Oasis – smashed the kit up instead. Smith went back to singing for this one, his gruff delivery somewhere between Bryan Adams and Paul Di'Anno. It's a decent, Def Leppard-ish album from the old gang, although the 1980s synths haven't aged that well. Still, the 1980s haven't aged that well in many respects either. The band played the title track at the Marquee gig in 1985, and several other Hackney tracks were used by ASAP as B-sides. All in all, it's light years away from Maiden in approach, much more soft-edged and poppy. That said, the solos are recognisably Smith's.

An age-old debate: Would they have got signed without the Maiden connection? Regardless, EMI did the biz and we've got a decent and interesting piece of work as a result. A club tour followed throughout the UK and a promotional interview tour in the US, but the contrast with Maiden's sound arguably meant fans of the Irons weren't as enthusiastic about it as was hoped, so ASAP was shelved and Smith set to work on a new Maiden LP.

But he was to become disillusioned at what was happening: *Seventh Son of a Seventh Son* had been another step in the late 1980s' development of the Maiden sound, following on the conceptual footsteps of grand designs *Powerslave* and *Somewhere in Time*. A trio of LPs with thematic material that was coherent per album and in the case of *Seventh Son*, a concept LP in the true sense. However, rather than going further into the creative ether and explore the esoteric and proggy side of the band even further, the decision was to go back to a rawer sound. H wasn't into that, and he was replaced by Janick Gers for *No Prayer for the Dying*. Smith went to live in Canada, putting family life to the forefront and barely picking up a guitar for two years.

You Can't Touch This

But you can't keep a good musician down for long. John Dexter-Jones of the band Jump remembers a key venue in the early 1990s which attracted some rather big names.

"It was The Pegasus at Marlow Bottom in Bucks," Dexter-Jones moiders. "Les Payne, who sadly passed away in 2017, had a Sunday night residency there. He was a great artist in his own right, but he'd also worked on the studio side of things with loads of people and seemed to know everyone."

"Les' band was drawn from a pool of players who were all top people in bands or notable session players and then on top of that he'd punctuate his set with 'special guest appearances', where I got my first little break having moved down to the area from Bangor."

"You'd be standing there singing some standard or one of Les's songs and there'd be Ray Weston on drums (Average White Band, Wishbone Ash, etc.), Chrissie Hammond

PART TWO SOLO CAREERS

(Cheetah, Wakeman etc) on BVs, Davy Paton (Pilot, Fish, Elton John, Kate Bush) on bass, Les, Dzal Martin (The Equals, Roxette, Nazareth) ... on guitar ... and that's just a flavour - I could list loads more. Some of the guests getting up to sing were a bit higher profile than me as well! Fish did a turn. I remember doing 'Knockin' on Heaven's Door' with Les' band one evening and Jeff Beck was sitting in the front row.

"Adrian Smith came to the Peg 'cos Les knew him - Les was friendly and had worked with Martin Birch, I believe - and got up on a couple of occasions to join in. I seem to remember him being a really nice bloke, not in the least bit starry, just plugged in and away he went."

Guest appearances and rough jams are one thing, but once the bug's got you – well, you stay got for life. Enter Jamie Stewart, latterly bass player in The Cult.

"He'd stepped away from Iron Maiden, I presumed permanently," says Stewart, who had left his own band after a tough tour. His and Smith's paths hadn't previously crossed, either professionally or personally; The Cult were more in the alternative rock arena rather than metal."

"The only place we would have crossed paths is at assorted European festivals," he continues. "We just happened to be in the same part of the world, in Buckinghamshire. He got wind of my departure and was looking to do something that wasn't Maiden and just called me up one day. He said, 'Would you like to get together and talk about stuff, would you like to do anything musical?' We got together, and it was an informal arrangement really."

Initially, things were all up in the air, with maybes, ifs and perhaps-es the order of the day as regards writing, gigging and – well, possibly – recording, Stewart continues.

"We said we'd maybe do a couple of pub gigs and see how it goes. We tried to write some songs but didn't really get off the ground; partly because I never really wrote in The Cult. If we'd persevered I'm sure something could have happened, but not in the short term. We did a couple of months rehearsing, seeing what songs might work, just chewing on stuff. Then we did a gig at The Pegasus, just hammering out some tunes. It was funny because we weren't really a band."

John Dexter-Jones recalls it slightly differently.

"Now and again, Les would give the evening over to another band, just to change things up a bit," continues the singer. "Jump benefited from that from time to time and one night he said Adrian was going to come and do a band thing. I used to help Les with setting up his PA on a Sunday lunchtime but on this occasion, he said we weren't needed as Adrian was hiring one in."

And when an ex-Maiden member hires a PA, it's a bloody PA and a half, as Dexter-Jones recalls.

"We got to the Peg in the evening and there was, let's say, a rather bigger rig than had ever been in that room before (it held about 200 at a squash). It was very loud, very tight and an excellent set ... I might be mistaken but think it was their first gig. It was well-received by the audience, only a proportion of whom would've been heavy rock fans ... so it definitely had a catchy edge. Again, I remember them being very pleasant, down to earth guys."

When you get a bunch of musicians together to see what they can do, it can be electric, Jamie Stewart says, and it was a refreshing change from the pressure of being

IRON MAIDEN

in a famous touring band.

"It was odd to be doing covers," reveals the bassist. "I'd not really done that before. We did 'The Boys are Back in Town' by Thin Lizzy, a challenge for bass players, let alone bass players trying to sing. And a song by Canadian singer-songwriter rock bloke Kim Mitchell. Adrian's wife is Canadian, and his wife's brother played keys in the band so there was a connection there. Mitchell wrote some pretty good songs but never really made it out of Canada."

"It was both an experiment and a laugh," says Stewart. "Just something to keep us occupied in music."

Despite the good response, Stewart had assessed his options within – and without – the music industry and concluded that rather than playing for a living, production and engineering was the way forward.

"The music industry is very fickle," he notes. "If you're in, you're in. If you're out you are, 'thank you very much, see you later.' Life moved on; we'd been making waves in America but on the whole Britain wasn't that bothered. I wasn't making any headway in production at that point in the UK so decided to move to Toronto. Even whilst Adrian and I were rehearsing, we knew it wasn't going to be long-term, because I was going to be leaving. It was just whatever we could do in the meantime."

The loose project was called The Untouchables. Stewart assesses Adrian as a player.

"He is very talented in a lot of areas. He plays, he writes, too. Put all those together and he's a very good musician. This was very much, 'Stick every bit of gear we can in Adrian's Range Rover and hike it to the pub.' At the time we were doing it, it was odd. Bands were bands, and this was more of a half-way thing. I think it's more prevalent these days that when you're not touring you'll do something else; acoustic versions, covers, musicians spreading out a bit more. And especially over the last 15 to 20 years in order to survive."

Which is another book in itself, of course. Stewart toddled off to Toronto and was replaced by Gary Leiderman.

Heeeeere's Smithhy

A couple of line-up changes followed, but Adrian Smith now had a project he was happy to pursue further. This time, though, he wasn't going to be singing. The vocalist was to be Hans-Olav Sulli, who had some chops of his own to draw on. At the time, Sulli was in a group featuring Thin Lizzy's Scott Gorham, called 21 Guns.

"I had been with that band for just about a year and we couldn't seem to get a record deal at the time," Solli explains. "My second son was born on September 5th, 1994 and was a bit sick right after he was born. I remember it was one of those days in late September I came back home from hospital and found Adrian's message on my answering-machine."

That message, asking Solli to join a band now called Psycho Motel. As it turned out, there was another link to Smith's past band.

"Apparently Steve Harris had given him the demo-tape I sent off when Bruce left Maiden, with a recommendation," the Norwegian reveals. "The first thing that struck me was the strength of the songs, as well as Adrian's great guitar-playing and singing. I remember thinking, 'Do they really need a singer?' At the same time I really felt the material suited me and laying down vocals on 'Money To Burn' and

PART TWO SOLO CAREERS

'Psycho Motel' really felt good. I did this after Adrian sent me the backing tracks.

"I'll never forget his reaction when he got my versions. I asked if he liked it. He answered: 'Liked it? It's brilliant!' The band was called Skeleton Crew (I think) at the time and Adrian told me they were looking for a new drummer as well, so I suggested Mike Sturgis from 21 Guns, also London-based. So suddenly, half of 21 Guns were in the new band."

The masterplan was to get a record deal and tour heavily in the traditional sense. Smith was bang up for it, Solli notes.

"To me it seemed that Psycho Motel marked a change for Adrian in the sense that he became determined to get back into music business. We worked really hard and had lots of songs written and recorded."

Tantalisingly, and hopefully one day this will be rectified, Solli reveals too that, 'There are still some good ones that have not been released.'

The band's first album, *State of Mind*, came out on Sanctuary and is heavier than the ASAP days, albeit still poppy. Indeed, it also displays some grunge influences alongside the psychedelia and proggy nature of things. The band's song 'Psycho Motel' is absolutely strewn with Hendrix-y riffs and flourishes. Miles from Maiden again, but pretty damned good stuff.

"Recording the album was loads of fun," Solli beams. "The songs were well rehearsed, so it was easy work in the studio. I laid down most of my vocals in the legendary AIR Studios, a big thrill. It also had the advantage that we could use some strings [violin and cello] from the London Philharmonic, who were recording in the same studio. This was for the track 'Western Shore'."

There was also an European tour, similarly great fun although a little short, says the singer.

"We played England and Norway for most parts. I guess the highlight in England was supporting Iron Maiden at Nottingham Rock City in February 1996. In Norway we headlined a big festival way up north at Andøya called *Rock Mot Rus*. It was nice to show the guys the fantastic northern lights up there. We also played my home town, Molde."

Unfortunately, despite the good response Psycho Motel were getting, personal issues meant Solli's time in the band was to come to an end.

"My marriage broke up and I was kind of desperate to get some kind of regular income. It seemed really hard to get the band going in the sense of making income, although we had fantastic reviews from Tokyo to Berlin," says the talented singer.

"I remember a Norwegian newspaper named us as 'Saviours of Heavy Metal' because in their opinion we had managed to merge 'old' and 'new' metal. Unfortunately, not enough people related to that, which I personally think was a good description. However, I ended up leaving the band, a sad decision that seemed inevitable at the time."

Andy Makin was Solli's replacement and that line-up – Sturgis, Leideman, Smith and Makin, went on to record another album, *Welcome to the World*. It's energetic and in parts much heavier than its predecessor, Makin's vocals lending a more atmospheric, heavier edge. The title track, 'Welcome to the World' is certainly a much heftier proposition than much of *State of Mind*, with a tuneful chorus that is pure Smith. Guests on the LP are Scott Gorham and one Mr. David Murray, who steps in to 'With You

IRON MAIDEN

Again' as easily as if he and his old mate had played together the previous day in a band, let alone seven years before. The irony of that title is of course rather obvious. It's also an excellent song, moving and deep as the protagonist recounts the loss of his father. An epic, acoustic-based track, it's emotional, haunting and has more than a hint of Pink Floyd about it. Those twin harmony guitars, though: we had missed you, guys.

Psycho Motel supported Iron Maiden for the British Dates of the X *Factour* tour in 1995, but a phone call from fellow ex-Maiden member, Bruce Dickinson, was to put paid to any further explorations by the Motel.

Smith – like Dickinson – was inching closer to his true home of heavy metal thunder.

Never one to let the grass grow under his feet, even after Smith rejoined Maiden he had side-projects to keep him busy. Technically, Primal Rock Rebellion are still a going concern, although so far the band, on which he collaborates with Mikee Goodman of SikTh, has only released one album, *Awoken Broken*, in 2012. Goodman says he and Smith were already acquainted via mutual friends.

"Adrian's son was a big fan of SikTh and one day I got a call asking us to play Adrian's son's 16th birthday party," Goodman says. "We agreed then went and played, it was cool and Adrian joined us onstage for our 'Wrathchild' cover. A week went by and Adrian called and asked to have a jam with him, so I did and it was amazing. He said to me I had a unique sounding voice and 'you can't buy that'. Myself and Adrian clicked straight away really. It took around six years from that jam to the album coming out, we kept on working on tunes when we were both available, between tours etc. We just made plans as things progressed, becoming more and more exciting. We got on really well straight away, which is very important."

Primal Rock Rebellion is a very different beast to the main projects of the musicians, Goodman adds. And the songwriting process reflects it.

"Two very different creative minds came together, pulling each other in very different directions to create something unique, both taking inspiration from one another. The music that came out sounded innovative and uplifting in many ways. Adrian's solos are classic as ever, it's like he makes the guitar sing. His riffage was heavy, aggressive and experimental. He plays like no other.

"My vocals are way more melodic than ever before, lyrics a lot more honed and poetic also. Then double-kick aggressive drums by Dan Foord. All together a dynamic, catchy and progressive sound."

Adrian Smith's sense of pitch and melody was something of an eye-opener to the SixTh dude, he recalls.

"In the early days of writing he sat there and told me the keys which suit my voice and which he was going to write in. I had never known anything like it. He is very much into huge choruses, but the whole song, new techniques and experimentation are very important to him."

As a songwriter he was actually very open, Goodman continues.

"I came up with a lot of ideas also so it was a very inspiring place to be. Both of us constantly coming up with ideas [and] pulling each other out of our comfort zones. We got Abi Fry in to play viola on the album too, which really inspired him. The funnest album experience I ever been part of making and I really loved the whole experience. He inspired and taught me so much, which has

PART TWO **SOLO CAREERS**

influenced everything I have made musically since then."

The album was very well received on its release, although Goodman does think it would have been taken to another level had they been able to add a live component to the project. As for Adrian Smith as a creative force, Goodman is in no doubt as to the best way to describe the Maiden legend.

"Adrian is a genius," he declares.

"I haven't said that much in any musician I have seen, but he is. He is also the most humble musician I've had the pleasure of meeting, and one of the greatest people I know."

BRUCE DICKINSON – THE RENAISSANCE MAN

Let the Bruce Loose

Paul Bruce Dickinson is one of life's enduring characters. You get the impression that had he been born in the era of the great engineers he could have been a Brunel or a Stephenson; earlier, perhaps an alchemist/poet a la William Blake; in any era his curiosity and relentless drive to wring everything possible out of every opportunity to learn and have fun would have made him a success.

As a musician, he's also had one of the more interesting careers outside Maiden. His first thought was to be a drummer – Ian Paice of Deep Purple was an early hero. At school, the future vocalist would jam with a friend, Mike Jordan, with Dickinson on bongos.

The first real band Dickinson was involved with, now as a singer, was called Styx. Their debut gig was also their last; the Sheffield venue was called Broadfield Tavern, and so the story goes their noise woke up a worker on the night shift. He wasn't a happy bunny, and that was to be the only concert the band played. They split up not long after.

The end of Styx was just the beginning – whilst Dickinson was at university in London studying for a history degree he became part of the entertainments committee, helping with the booking, staging and running of gigs, including Hawkwind and The Jam. Being in close contact with the industry only fuelled his ambition, and the next group was a band called Speed. They played a few local gigs, but it didn't really take off.

The ubiquitous *Melody Maker* was to take a hand yet again; Bruce Dickinson responded to an advertisement for a singer. He duly recorded himself and sent it off to the address, which turned out to be that of Doug and Phil Siviter, who had a band called Shots. Recordings exist of this lot: the track 'Dracula' was later released on disc two of *The Best of Bruce Dickinson*.

Shots played the pub circuit, a rather healthy one at the time. Rob Grain was a significant player in the technical and facilitation side of music and to this day is

IRON MAIDEN

one of the most highly-respected roadies and stage managers in rock'n'roll.

"It was in the Prince of Wales, then the Red Lion in Gravesend," Grain remembers. "The time I saw Bruce was the last time I saw the Shots. They were a great band, and I mentioned them to Paul [Samson]."

Samson was a talented guitarist whose bluesy-rock leanings were showcased by his own band, featuring Chris Aylmer on bass and Clive Burr on drums. When Burr left to join Maiden, he was replaced by Barry 'Thunderstick' Purkis. At the time that Grain and Samson saw the Shots, Paul Samson was singing and playing guitar. Not an ideal way to showcase his undoubted talent on the axe.

"Paul always had a handle on what was going on locally," Grain says. "Even though Samson were getting a name for themselves and playing bigger venues, he'd still turn up to local pubs if there was a band on. We'd talk about local bands, I mentioned the Shots were great and spoke to Paul about the guitarist. The bass player wore a devil's mask.

"Shots had some really good material. Paul used to like to check out the opposition, then tell you afterwards how they weren't as good as he was."

Rob Grain may have been enthusing about the guitarist to his compadre, but it was the young vocalist – at the time in possession of a rather fetching moustache – that really caught the eye.

"Paul turned up to a Shots gig, had a guy with him, a big-built guy with ginger hair, a big denim jacket with the Kiss logo on the back. He introduced me to this guy, his new drummer [Thunderstick]. We had a brief chat about bands and watched Shots.

"Bruce used to do this thing where he'd have a bit of spiel with people; he would say something to them just to get a reaction. The Prince of Wales, where the band played in the back left-hand corner was the entrance to the gents' toilets. Barry went to the toilet, and as he came out Bruce made a comment, a little bit of banter went on."

A couple of months later, Grain went to watch Samson on an outdoor stage at the Red Lion and – lo and behold – there was a new singer.

"The guy out of the Shots came prancing on the stage doing the top hat and cane thing," remembers Grain. "I thought, 'What the fuck's he doing up here?' The previous year Samson had a singer for a short period of time but it didn't work out. Paul always preferred being freed up to play guitar without singing. It all happened very quickly."

Barry Purkis – the masked drummer, Thunderstick – remembers the young singer.

"Bruce, when we first enrolled him into the band, was quite juvenile, because he was," says Thunderstick. "He had come straight out of university doing his degree in history, and was like an excitable puppy dog, unsure of his own abilities but only too keen to try out anything. He doted on all the 'dinosaur' bands - Sabbath, Purple, Zeppelin - but loved abstract vocalists such as Peter Hamill (Van der Graaf Generator), Arthur Brown, Ian Anderson, and various other prog rockers."

Dickinson's living arrangements were rather unique at that time, too.

"He was living in a squat, gaining access through a window rather than a front door (it was boarded up) on the Isle of Dogs whilst everything was being demolished around ready for the complete new building of Canary Wharf."

"He had a moustache and a haircut that

PART TWO SOLO CAREERS

looked as though someone had put a bowl on his head and cut round it. Something his then-girlfriend actually admitted to. Hardly the Rock God he was to become. Vocally he was loud and had great voice projection. Brimming over with ideas. But if you look at the lyrical content of *Head On*, most of those songs were about university life and what it was like to be a naughty student. [That was] something I never really realised until recently, only after playing the album for the first time in years. He could be excitable but at the same time intense, he focused on trying to attain 'something' as long as he could find out what that 'something' was."

He also picked up a nickname – Bruce Bruce – after Paul Samson asked Dickinson his middle name. As Dickinson's full name is Paul Bruce Dickinson, he replied 'Bruce.' So Bruce Bruce he became.

Samson's debut album, *Survivors*, was released before Dickinson joined the band and the group set about writing a new LP as a follow-up. And *Head On* showcased a singer on the up.

The sessions for that album took place at Kingsway Recorders during April and May 1980 for an album released on June 27th, 1980. The record is excellent, and Dickinson's vocals really sparkle. Of many standouts, check out 'Hard Times,' 'Walking Out on You' and 'Manwatcher' for a start, but the best track is the ace 'Vice Versa.'

"For me, *Head On* was Samson at its most adventurous," Thunderstick remembers. "So Bruce has now become a full-time member and Paul, Chris and myself had played enough together to make us all totally at ease with who we were and what we could individually bring to the band. We had a large amount of ideas, as did Bruce."

"The new compositions came about very quickly once we'd started the writing process. Paul with his love of power trios, Bruce at that time a love of the established acts, and me, I embraced anything that pushed the boundaries. Having a love for experimental bands, and Chris the anchorman holding everything down to give the music some kind of foundation."

There was a unique quality about Samson that Thunderstick looks back on wryly.

"Can you imagine what it was like being in a band with three frontmen?" He asks with a glint in his eye. "Paul considered it to be his band seeing as it was called Samson, me because at the time it was my image that was selling it, and Bruce because he was the frontman."

"I stuck out for a 'production' credit because I was the one that did the most work and attendance whilst we were recording. All the crazy stuff on the album was mine, backwards choirs, sound effects ... the whole kitchen sink! I was the one that stayed with our sound engineer whilst we did all Bruce's vocal tracks. I wanted a producer credit because I'd earned it but the others dismissed it. That is why on the album sleeve it reads, 'Additional ideas: Thunderstick'."

There's also the matter of an instrumental, 'Thunderburst.' There has been much talk over the years of this track's similarity to 'The Ides of March,' which appeared on Iron Maiden's *Killers* LP. Indeed, the Samson track adds a Steve Harris writing credit. Here's Thunderstick again with his viewpoint as to the controversy that has grown over the decades.

"Its quite incredible the amount of Iron Maiden fans that have a view about what lies behind both these tracks," he says. "On the one side there's a widespread belief that

IRON MAIDEN

I was robbed of a credit on *Killers* and as a kind gesture should have been recognised for my contribution in the early days.

"Others believe that I had only reworked 'Ides' and therefore was owed no such credit."

"Ironic then that the Iron Maiden version came out a year after the Samson version of 'Thunderburst'. No matter what is said about it - be it here, previously, or in the future - nothing will change unless it's proven one way or another in a court of law. I certainly have better things to spend my money on than coming up against the Iron Maiden legal representation. For me it would be like leading a lamb to the slaughter.

"There have been other ex-Iron Maiden members that have spoken of events and storylines that differ quite dramatically from the official line taken by band historians/representatives, who believe their version of events is the definitive one. Mine's yet another constantly feeding the perpetuation of myth that surrounds the band. All I know is that had I been given a credit on 'Ides of March', financially it probably would have changed my life, but the benefit of hindsight is a wonderful thing."

There you go. Clear as mud.

Samson's issues included management and record company problems, despite the undoubted talent in the band. They did manage to go on and release a follow-up to *Head On*, called *Shock Tactics*. They were at Battery Studios with producer Tony Platt.

"Samson were very good; musically better than Iron Maiden," says Platt. "A tight little band. Paul was a really good guitar player. The problem they faced was that they were in the wrong place at the wrong time. They were more like a British ZZ Top than in this slightly heavier end of the spectrum they were forced in to. When they played they rocked the place, but they weren't getting the exposure that Iron Maiden were getting. It wasn't quite as tribal as Maiden's audience."

The bands could check each other out at close quarters: Maiden were recording *Killers* in the same facility.

"*Head On* was a bit of a mess, quite frankly," says Platt. "I had to do a lot of sorting out; there were tuning problems and various things. The problem with *Shock Tactics* was trying to find a niche they could inhabit within that fanbase that they shared to a great extent with Maiden. Something that wasn't doing exactly what Iron Maiden did but was as satisfying. It wasn't an easy place to find.

"With Samson there was sophistication in the songs, in the lyric writing. Paul studied other guitar players, different tunings and chord versions, so was able to work with me to orchestrate the guitar parts. The combination between Bruce's voice, the backing vocals and all the guitars always had a really good orchestral, anthemic touch to it. That's what gave that particular atmosphere and timbre to the sound."

There was also one thing that nearly put the kibosh on the sessions – and on music for all time.

"We all nearly died during pre-production of *Shock Tactics*," Platt declares.

"We were rehearsing at Easy Hire studios in North London. It was winter time and they had these big gas heaters hanging from the ceiling. We were in there, it was bloody cold, for quite a few hours running through various things.

"I suddenly realised I wasn't feeling all that great, and everybody said, 'I don't feel that great either.' I said, 'I'm just going to

PART TWO **SOLO CAREERS**

get a breath of fresh air. I was falling asleep. I walked outside, the fresh air hit me, and I felt actually quite woozy.

"At that point I realised that one of the heaters was just pumping gas out into the rehearsal room. Everybody was in a very bad way!"

Shock Tactics could and should have been Samson's breakthrough, but management issues stymied any chance of that.

"By that time there were cracks showing," Thunderstick recalls. "The hell we had gone through with management and record company was starting to take its toll. Don't get me wrong, *Shock Tactics* is a great album, but it wasn't the same band. Tony Platt produced it shortly after working with AC/DC and wanted to simple everything down. We went into pre-production with all the material we had written, and it was stripped back and reassembled ready to record."

"It was a grown-ups' album rather than an adolescent offering as *Head On* was. I think *Head On* is the album most Samson aficionados regard as the better of the two.

"Having said that, I think *Shock Tactics* was Bruce's finest hour: he had found his voice. I even think his vocal performance on that album surpasses some of the subsequent Iron Maiden vocal tracks."

'Earth Mother,' 'Communion' and the Russ Ballard cover, 'Riding With the Angels', are testament to the drummer's belief. Great albums don't always make a great career, though.

"By the time the management legal issues had come to end (although it never came to an end – I'm still suffering the fallout from it to this day)," adds Thunderstick, "We were a band in tatters, with no real direction anymore. We were placed on ridiculously ill-matched tours, hauled across the coals legally, completely broke (and broken) both individually and as a band."

"We lost ground so very quickly in comparison to our peers. Iron Maiden, Def Leppard, Saxon, Diamond Head quickly trampled us underfoot whereas only a short while before we had also been contenders for the big boys' league."

Latterly, Thunderstick has been irked by comments made by Dickinson in his autobiography. The singer, says the drummer, was way off the mark with his interpretation of how the recording sessions came together. In particular, the inference that Thunderstick could not play on the record/s in a single take, needing a hundred or more edits to construct an adequate drum track. Thunderstick is very strident about what he thinks of all that.

"[What he wrote was] in my opinion: abhorrent, dismissive, arrogant, and a far more direct 'array of words' if I were able to write them without fear of the IM legal team coming down on me like a ton of bricks," Thunderstick responds. "It's so easy to throw stones when you are hiding behind a wall. The remarks that he made public both in written text and verbally whilst doing promotion for the book made me feel sick. Especially when he [talks about the editing and playing issues]."

Exasperated, the drummer explains that he has plenty of experience in the music biz to draw on, not least working with many different engineers and producers.

"I have managed to make music over a long period of time and [in early 2018, when this interview took place] rehearsing a new line-up to take on tour to promote the album I released last year. I do not know of one producer that would take the time to do a hundred edits on a master tape!"

IRON MAIDEN

This, remember, was in the days before hard disc recording and the ability of programs like Logic, Pro Tools and the like to literally move events around in time, or cut and paste sections to stitch together master tracks. That said, any producer worth their salt would rather have the feel of a consistent take rather than spend hours poncing about with unnecessary edits. Think about it: if a song lasts five minutes, which is easier - spending time finding individual hits and cutting and pasting them into sections where they're needed, making sure the ambience and sound is accurate, or asking the drummer (or whoever) to play that five-minute song again? And this in the digital world; in the early 'Eighties it was literally a case of cutting out, physically, sections of tape, and splicing them into the correct place. Madness.

Thunderstick also takes issue with Dickinson's analysis that his drumming style was a blend of Kiss and The Police.

"I also have NEVER considered my style of drumming to be similar to that of Peter Criss or Stewart Copeland," he says. "A single listen of the *Head On* album would confirm that. On the *Shock Tactics* album my 'style' was taken away from me in the pre- production running up to recording for 'the good of the album'. If a listener were to play the two albums back to back, they would I'm sure be left with the opinion that they contain two different drummers."

As far as the thought that Thunderstick couldn't really play at all, he is even more certain of what his reaction would be if he had the cash.

"If I had anything like the financial back-up the author of this contentious statement writes I would of course contest the comment legally. I haven't and know full well I would be on a hiding to nothing by even contemplating such a course of action. So I can only gain a modicum of satisfaction in the knowledge that I have addressed it in this book."

It is also ambiguous whether Dickinson is talking about Barry Graham Purkis or Thunderstick, his alter-ego when he opines as to the level of skill, he adds.

Finally, Thunderstick says he would like to set the record straight about Samson's actual motivation for doing what they did, in contrast to what he feels was an erroneous overview by the singer in his autobiography (which to be fair, we're doing a good job of selling in this bit. Still, it is worth it).

"As regards to things he has said about the band as a whole, that all we ever wanted was to take drugs and score with women and none of us were really ever serious about the job of making music and it was seen as a 'vehicle' for us enabling those two things - despicable.

"I would've thought a person of his standing within the music business would have had far more dignity than to denigrate people that were once an important part of his career/life. Especially when two of the members of that band will never have the opportunity to redress those comments made [Chris Aylmer and Paul Samson have both passed away]. But apparently not."

From 2018, then, back to our story, and the final big gig for the Samson-Aylmer-Dickinson-Thunderstick line-up was at Reading Festival, 1981. It was released as a live album in 1990 and the group is absolutely smashing the hell out of it. Highly recommended!

That gig was also where Rod Smallwood and Bruce Dickinson had their famous chat about the latter joining Maiden ...

PART TWO **SOLO CAREERS**

2

... fast forward eight years, with Maiden having a year off, and Smallwood brought an idea to the singer: do you want to record a solo song for a film soundtrack? Course he did! 'Bring Your Daughter... to the Slaughter' was duly written with Janick Gers on board. The project developed into an album, which Gers and Dickinson duly produced for a release in May 1990. It is, more than anything, the sound of musicians having that strange thing called 'fun' that had often been missing during the years of hard touring, serious business and all the rest of it. *Tattooed Millionaire* isn't even metal: it's hard rock if anything and has a wonderful cover of Bowie's 'All the Young Dudes' as one of many excellent tracks. The eponymous song was released as a single on April 11th and scored a No.18 hit for Dickinson; more considered and personal than Maiden it was a mile away from swords and dorkery as you could get. The lyrics spoke scathingly of the egos and game-playing of certain parts of the music industry. The title, perhaps, says it all. Further release 'All the Young Dudes' got to No.33. The third single from *Tattooed Millionaire* was the saucy 'Dive! Dive! Dive!' That peaked at No.45 after being released in August. Undaunted, another single finally appeared: 'Born in '58' – because he was – stalled at No.81 in March 1991. Still, it also featured some ace live B-sides recorded during his first solo tour the previous year. Although there is a sense of making it up as they went along to the album, and the solo project, it has a liveliness and self-deprecating humour about it that plays with some of rock's persistent tropes of sex, money, bad behaviour and badass machines. Indeed, it was such a success that Dickinson decided to do it all over again. Initial sessions with *Nightmare/Millionaire* producer Chris Tsangarides and a band called Skin proved unsatisfactory; despite backing tracks having been laid down it was shelved. Bruce nixed the Skin/Tsangarides taoes and refocused his efforts in Los Angeles with a producer called Keith Olsen.

It came about from a 'Manager to manager, or handler to manager' link, Olsen explains.

"It was kind of the way projects came in," confirms the Grammy-winning producer, whose amazing CV includes major work with Fleetwood Mac, Ozzy, Whitesnake, Santana, Foreigner, Journey, Eric Burdon and the Animals, Scorpions, and the Grateful Dead. He says Dickinson was keen to explore different sounds and technologies at the time.

"He really wanted to try some programming of tracks as he liked that sound and freedom," Olsen continues. "So we tried to go really left-field, using a programming guru, Jimmy Crighton, who was in the band Saga. He was instrumental in taking the program Notator to the next level early in its development by the company that eventually came out with Logic. It was very experimental, especially for a singer/heavy rocker like Bruce.

"Maybe for Euro-pop at the time but not for Bruce."

The sessions took place at Crighton's studio in Los Angeles, plus some at Goodnight LA. Olsen says the process of working with the programmer as he worked was 'tiresome,' due to the long-winded process of early digital programming.

"Programming was a very time-consuming process," Olsen notes. "Look at Mutt [Lange] and Def Leppard; it can take months to get it right and we didn't have that kind of time or energy for this experimental project."

IRON MAIDEN

Sometimes the best thing about experiments is when they don't quite work out: at the very least they can provide an indication of what you do not want to do. Such is the case with the Olsen sessions, says the producer.

"I don't think anyone was [happy with it] especially the record company... they thought they were going to get another Maiden album to throw out there," he says. "For me, we tried and failed. I'm sure it was the same for Bruce."

One thing that had dawned on the vocalist was the thought that in order to truly get his yen back for music was to leave a deeply-unsatisfying Iron Maiden behind. So solo he was, free to explore his second album on. He enlisted the fabulously-talented Roy Z for the project, along with Z's band the Tribe of Gypsies. Drummer for the Gypsies was David Ingraham, who recalls how it came together.

"Bruce was doing pre-production work with a producer we were also working with," Ingraham says. "He played Bruce some of our music, Bruce dug it and asked who the main songwriter/leader was. Bruce tracked down Roy and asked if he'd be interested in doing a record with him. In so many words, Roy said, 'If you hire me, you've got to hire my band.' The rest is history: within a few months, I was on a plane to London to record."

At the time Dickinson was in the last throes of his Iron Maiden departure, recalls the drummer.

"We saw his farewell show with them in London right before heading straight into rehearsals a day or two later," adds Ingraham. "I had the impression that, after so many years with Maiden, he was eager to break free from the Maiden formula and experiment with new sounds and styles. I don't recall what the internal politics of Maiden were - I believe he left on good terms - but he definitely seemed ready to try something new.

"I was unaware of whatever had happened with the record before I was brought on board. Whatever the case was before he hired us, it definitely seemed like a fresh start once he and Roy started writing together."

The results of this meeting of musical minds were released in June 1994 under the title *Balls to Picasso*, an old graffiti joke about the artist's cubist period. Two cubes are scrawled on what appears to be a bog wall for the cover. Har de har. Dickinson was later to say he should have called the LP, 'Laughing in the Hiding Bush.' That song title was invented by his young son, Austin, who scores his first credit in the music industry.

David Ingraham assesses the Dickinson-Z duo.

"Although Roy obviously comes from a metal background, he's a very musically open-minded guy so he could switch out his musical hats, so to speak, with relative ease," says the drummer. "I remember loaning him a favourite African record of mine, telling him to check out the amazing guitar-playing. Within a short while, he'd copped the licks to a T and that's where the Tribe song 'Up' from *Standing on the Shoulders of Giants* came from. Roy also has a funky side, hence the heavily syncopated riff on the chorus of 'Laughing in the Hiding Bush.'"

"As a band-leader and writer, I found Roy to be generous and easy to work with. He liked the idea of the music sounding like a band, so was open to other members' input. In the Tribe, he'd frequently have a fully-

PART TWO **SOLO CAREERS**

baked song idea, but he'd let us interpret it and maybe take it somewhere he hadn't envisioned. Other times we'd just start jamming and a song idea would come from that."

"I think Bruce and Roy gelled so well because Roy was well versed in the Maiden style - I know he'd listened to and played a lot of that stuff when he was younger - but Roy was also very much forward-looking, so he had one foot in the past, the history of metal, and one foot in the present/future, and I think that's what Bruce was looking for, whether Bruce was consciously aware of that or not."

The first single to be taken from *Balls* was Dickinson's very resonant 'Tears of the Dragon,' which has been said to cover the subject of his time struggling in Iron Maiden. Lyrics about feeling powerless and wanting to face his fears, to jump into the ocean and feel its power and the mythical dragon tears certainly do suggest an inner turmoil. The tears of a dragon are considered to be the spirit of the waters in Chinese mythology. They are also related to healing and helping the flow of the life-force - the Chi - within shamanic practices. The single reached No.28 in the UK and 36 in the US. Not too shabby a performance at all. There were two CDs released, the second featuring a lovely acoustic version of this great Dickinson song.

Dickinson took his band on tour and released 'Shoot All the Clowns' as a single in August. It sneaked into the top-40 (No.37) and was apparently a last-minute addition to the LP, on the behest of EMI. The track was intended to have an Aerosmith-type vibe and does just that. Not exactly groundbreaking, but at the same time it's proof that the singer now had the confidence to trust his own writing in all manner of rock variants - and beyond.

As the Tribe were still very much a going concern they went off to work on their own stuff, meaning Dickinson had to find new people to work with for what would be his third solo effort. First on board was ultra-talented guitarist Alex Dickson. The rest of the group came together fairly quickly, says Alex Elena, who ended up drumming for the new band.

"Chris [Dale, bassist] and I used to play together in an American London-based band, Machine," says the Italian sticksman. "We heard that Bruce Dickinson was looking for a rhythm section and Chris had the brilliant idea to contact a guitar player (Myke Gray of the band Skin) that played in a band signed by the same management company as Bruce's. We organised a jam session at our rehearsal space in East London and invited Myke. He was totally blown away, went back to the management and Bruce saying he had found the perfect duo for the job. That's how we got the audition. He only auditioned Chris and I ... thank you Myke Gray!

"Imagine an 18-year-old coming from Italy who didn't really speak English too well landing a gig like that. And imagine how lucky I was to also bond a life-lasting friendship with Chris Dale and Alex Dickson. Real brothers, always together."

Chris Dale confirms that the opportunity came about after noting that Dickinson had said in an interview with *Kerrang!* that he needed a rhythm section.

"[We] sent in our demo, biog and photos to Sanctuary Management. Dickie Fliszar and Myke Gray from the band Skin also recommended us to Rod Smallwood, which doubtless helped too. We did a couple of rounds of auditions playing with Bruce and

IRON MAIDEN

Alex Dickson, seemed to get on well and got offered the job!"

As for Bruce Dickinson, Elena says he was great.

"Alex and I lived a few blocks from his house. He rented it to us: me, Alex and the nanny who was looking after his young kids. I would go to his house to cook and hang out. The first time I got drunk on vodka was at his house. He would come get me in the morning to drive to Maidenhead airfield to take me flying with him. I am a lucky guy. I had the absolute best time of my life and learned a lot about the business of music."

At this stage Dickinson was wanting it to be a real band, without his name front and centre, somewhat like David Bowie's Tin Machine phase. The name would be Skunkworks, relating to Lockheed's wartime Skunk Works, a semi-secret development facility in California. The term has been developed to include other innovation incubators in the technology field. The record label, however, were far from keen on keeping the household name of Bruce Dickinson off the artwork, probably sensible sales-wise.

First, though, the band bonded in an incredible way with an extraordinary trip to war-torn Bosnia, where they played a gig in Sarajevo. The experience changed everyone's lives forever.

Scream for Me Sarajevo – the gig

Gigs are powerful events in people's lives. Playing live onstage to an appreciative crowd creates an exchange of creative energy, a belief in the moment, where the visceral is everything. Simply put, the rest of the world melts away. It's just the band, the fans, the music: an amorphous, crackling mass of wonderfulness.

If you're good at music, and people like you, they will ask you to do lots of gigs. Sometimes you even get paid. And if you're really good at it, like Bruce Dickinson, you get asked to do more gigs than you ever have time to fit in.

Sometimes you get asked to play gigs in unexpected places too, and those kind of gigs can change your life.

Such was it in December 1993, when the offer came in to perform in Sarajevo.

Where there was a war going on.

Bassist in Dickinson's solo band, Skunkworks, at the time was Chris Dale.

"I don't think any of us took it too seriously at first. There was a gig booked for us in Sarajevo, Bosnia. We knew there was a war on, but the UN peacekeepers were there and we assumed that meant they kept the peace."

Roland Hyams was working with Dickinson as his PR agent, and also went along on the trip.

"I'll never forget the soldier saying to Bruce, 'Your permit's been withdrawn, you've got no cover, you can't drive to Sarajevo on your own. We advise you to take these boarding passes, turn around, put your kit on the plane and go home.'" There was a flight back to London within the hour, he adds, or the party would have been stuck for three days at the airport. But Dickinson, having come so far, wasn't in any mood to withdraw. Hyams remembers that a possibility soon revealed itself.

"One of the Reuters journalists recognised Bruce and said that in all likelihood we could get through to Sarajevo. As long as we got approval from the Bosnian president. So he tried to telephone him! We were told it'd

PART TWO **SOLO CAREERS**

Photo credit: Alex Elena

take days to get Bosnian approval.

"Bruce just said, 'No. Throw them away. Don't want them. We're going to go in with this lot on a road trip.'"

So what was Hyams' reaction?

"It was, 'Oh, Fuck,'" he recalls, laughing. "Bruce, what have you done? Oh well, I suppose we've got to go along with it. There was this mad outfit called The Serious Road Trip, recognised as neutral by all parties. They volunteered to get us through to Sarajevo with a soft-top seven and a half tonne lorry, all sleeping in the back."

And that's exactly what happened, Hyams continues.

"It was mind-blowing; I'd been reading about [the civil war] there for years, since 1991. We'd heard about horrible, dark things going on, but to actually go into it [was eye-opening]. Every building had no light, had no heat aside from wood-burning stoves. [Sarajevo] was blackened, lots of bombed-out buildings, a war zone. It was a culture shock."

Chris Dale elaborates regarding the journey.

"After we landed at Split airport and began a ride over and mountain range in the back of a truck, things got more and more serious. We could hear distant gunfire. The place was deserted apart from military checkpoints. It got worse in Sarajevo. The city was under siege and in midwinter. The people lived in bombed-out houses, starving in the snow. Everyone there, including ourselves, were in almost constant danger of sniper fire or mortar rounds."

This shit was *real*.

The drummer was Alex Elena, who says simply: "One thing I can tell you. That trip changed my life forever."

The power of music transcends genre, sometimes, and is testament to the enduring human spirit.

IRON MAIDEN

"It was wonderful to be there," Hyams says. "The warmth and the happiness, the vibe of the rock fans in Sarajevo [was incredible.] They had been under siege for three years, so any kind of entertainment was very, very rare. No Western band had ever gone in during the war. Everything seemed heightened; the colours seemed brighter. You felt the edge of everything more. It was like being ultra, ultra alive in a way.

"It is seared into my memory."

As for the concert, Dale recalls it in a unique context.

"The gig itself had a few technical problems, as you'd expect in a war zone, but generally went amazingly well - by that I mean the venue wasn't shelled mid-gig, one of the serious concerns. The people of Sarajevo had a night off from the war, from their daily fears, and got to see a glimpse of normal life at a rock'n'roll concert. We were the only foreign band to perform in Sarajevo during the four-year siege."

The movie, *Scream for me Sarajevo*, will be shown at worldwide cinemas, helping educate fans and non-fans alike as to the significance of the gig amidst one of the most brutal conflicts in modern memory. Roland Hyams adds that initially the concert was to be documented by a legendary and much-mourned journalist, who died in 2009.

"I was supposed to be taking out Steven Wells of the *NME*," he reveals. "Swellsy wanted to go..." Hyams kept a diary of the trip and in there had written that every time Wells spoke with him on the phone in the run-up to the trip, the journalist would make shooting gun noises at him. As it turned out there was only room for Hyams on the plane. The great lost Swells story, no doubt about it.

Alex Elena sums it up succinctly.

"We hear about war," he muses. "We watch movies. We hear stories. But when you are in it yourself everything changes. And it affects you forever, till the day you die.

"In a strange way it makes you into a better person," he concludes. "In my case it instigated my love for photography and storytelling. Going to dangerous places to take photos and tell stories that have relevance."

Sometimes, gigs are way, way more than just a bunch of long-haired people playing songs to other long-haired beer-drinking people. Sometimes they can change everyone's lives.

Such is the force of this thing humans call art. Indeed, perhaps art is mankind's greatest achievement. Perhaps art is the achievement that will save us all, ultimately. There is always hope.

Back to the studio...

A double CD album of tracks was to be created, entitled *Alive in Studio A*. It was intended as a radio session which didn't come through, the new line-up performing tracks from the first two albums.

Album recording began at The (Linford) Manor, a residential studio in Milton Keynes, Buckinghamshire.

"Recording was incredible back in those days," recalls Elena. "No computers to fix mistakes. You had to play for real. Alex and I even brought some of our furniture since we had given up our flat in London. I had 10 days just to track all the drums. What a luxury.

"We had a Victorian style living room with a snooker table, four gigantic windows

PART TWO **SOLO CAREERS**

overlooking a private park and a record player. I would do a few takes on the drums then chill, smoke, have some wine, then back recording.

"After a few days one evening I got so stoned and buzzed I demanded I wanted to record drums NOW," he continues. "Bruce and Jack Endino (the producer) tried to convince me I should just go crash ... Cut a long story short, I managed to get them all in the studio and nailed the first song in one take. They all looked at each other from the control room and asked: 'Do you wanna do another one?' 'Hell yeah!' was my answer and most of the drum tracks were cut that same night!"

Chris Dale adds that the whole experience was great, not least the opportunity to work with the ex-Maiden vocalist.

"He's obviously a great singer and that tends to make gigs generally a pleasure to play. He's very relaxed to work for, he gave us pretty much complete creative license in our playing. As a person, he's very quick and intelligent, constantly thinking. His mind simply doesn't take a rest. He takes his music and his flying very seriously but that's not to say he wasn't up for fun and japes along the way."

There were many funny moments, adds Dale. "My memories of those years are of travelling the world and laughing almost non-stop. Most of those stories are unrepeatable!"

Skunkworks was released on February 19th, 1996 and surprised fans with its much more alternative rock/grunge leanings; producer was Jack Endino, who has also worked with Nirvana, Soundgarden, Mudhoney, and loads more. He provides one laser-sharp piece of insight into Dickinson's studio requirements. Here's one for the gear geeks:

"Bruce is a great singer," says Endino. "I remember when we were working on *Skunkworks*, and it was time to start recording the final vocal tracks. I had to decide what mic to use.

"Rather than waste time, I asked Bruce straight-up, 'What mic did Martin Birch use for your vocals?' Because if it ain't broke, you don't fix it! He said it was usually a Neumann U87. From my experience, this mic can sound a little nasal on some singers, so I was wary. But I set up an 87, and we got going, and I immediately knew he was right. There it was, THAT VOICE!"

There it was indeed.

Engineer Andy Griffin was there for the tracking process alongside Endino and then returned for the mixing sessions at Mayfair and Landsdowne Studios in London.

"The sessions were all good, I seem to remember," says Griffin. "I think Jack was happy to try different studios to get the mix he wanted. He even checked out Ridge Farm, where Tim Palmer mixed [Pearl Jam's debut album,] *Ten*."

"I saw Maiden in 1987 at Manchester Apollo so was already a big fan and nervous about meeting Bruce. But to be honest, and I know it's a cliché, he was so unassuming and down-to-earth you just couldn't help but like him. He did me a drawing of Steve Harris' studio set-up, which I wish I still had! I remember thinking he was a nice, nice guy. He also introduced me to the Internet on this dial-up PC they had set up upstairs."

"It seemed very different from a Maiden album," Griffin concludes. "Bruce had more control; the band were his, they had done stuff like the trip to Bosnia and were tight [as a unit]. Good vibes all round."

Good vibes within the camp abounded.

IRON MAIDEN

But *Skunkworks* marks, in retrospect, the furthest point from Maiden that Dickinson's solo career would reach. It's one that has also divided fans of the Irons over the years. The writing process, says Chris Dale, went a bit like this:

"Alex Dickson wrote and demoed all the songs instrumentally. He gave the cassette demos to me, Alex Elena and Bruce. Me and the two Alexes jammed the songs into shape and Bruce wrote lyrics and melodies over them. Interestingly, rather than call his demos Song #1, Song #2 etc, Alex gave them rough 'Spacey' titles such as 'Innerspace,' 'Space Race,' Solar Confinement,' 'Faith', 'Octavia', etc. Bruce often took these demo titles and worked them into the lyrics of the completed songs, giving the album its vague spacey concept. This was of course back in the day when bands made albums the old-fashioned organic way. We rehearsed the songs, played them live at gigs, rehearsed them more. Alex, Alex and I would be in rehearsal all day, Jack Endino the producer was in rehearsals too, honing the songs down. Bruce would come in and try out the lyrics he'd been working on. It was a very productive time."

"[We] were there solidly for six weeks. We didn't leave. All day every day was music for us, playing, recording, listening, mixing, cooking ... yes, we even cooked music! Bruce of course is a busy guy, he had press to do, business meetings, a family to raise and flying exams to study for, so he was there less than us but still put down very impressive performances.

"I think the vocals Bruce put on that album are some of the best of his career. You can really hear the full gamut of his range, from whispering soft melodies to screaming in anger. There's so much going on in a Maiden song that Skunkworks gave him space to spread out like he never had before."

Live concerts were 'mental,' says Elena. "The first proper show I played with him was at the Bol D'Or bikers' festival in the South of France. Approximately 45.000 people! I go on stage first, sit behind the drums, stretch my arms and all of a sudden everybody has their arms in the air. 'Jesus, that's what it feels like to be a leader,' I thought."

"I do it again and the same thing happens! I close my eyes, big smile on my face, and start playing. Bruce gets on stage and after a short period of time puts his foot on the monitor and goes, 'SCREAM FOR ME!'"

"That's when the dream became a reality. I used to fall asleep to *Live After Death* when I was 12 years old in my little room in Rome, dreaming - and now the dream is real. I can't even begin to describe that feeling; I get goose-bumps even now. And once again I was sooooooo lucky to have Chris and Alex as my bestest friends, making sure I stayed humble and on the right track."

It wasn't all plain sailing, of course, with the odd minging moment along the way.

"I farted on stage during a show at the Paradiso club in Amsterdam and pooped my pants," admits Elena, with refreshing honesty. "The first tour in the American Midwest was pretty funny. Chris and I would go walking around and couldn't quite understand that American accent. We would have a blast testing Americans on their lack of Historic and Geographic skills – 'Is Scotland an island off New Zealand?' one person said."

Groupies were also involved, kind of, on occasion. Although the Italian Stallion Elena was not...

PART TWO SOLO CAREERS

"I convinced a girl in Missouri to take me back to her place, so I could make pasta (American food was making me sick)," laughs the drummer. "I made the pasta, ate, and took a taxi back to the hotel.

"She just stood there by the door speechless."

Interesting though *Skunkworks* was, it didn't sell as well as hoped, says Dale.

"There were a number of factors involved in this. I think basically it came down to the fact that most Iron Maiden fans did not want an alternative rock album, while most alternative rock fans did not want an album by the singer of Iron Maiden.

"Bruce realised that if he wanted to sell records, they would have to be more in the style of Iron Maiden. Alex Dickson in particular was against repeating heavy metal cliches and instead wrote more alternative style song ideas for a follow-up album to *Skunkworks*, which Bruce already wanted to call *Accident of Birth*. Bruce didn't like Alex's ideas. From there it was only a matter of time before the split came.

"Bruce called a meeting at a pub next to the old Sanctuary management offices. He told us straight that he didn't want to do the band with us anymore. He said he already had studio time booked with Roy Z in LA and had asked Adrian Smith to be involved again. He gave us a bit of money to go away with, wished us all the best and served us termination of employment contracts. It was all done in a very fair and amicable way. I had no hard feelings.

"We had spent two years, touring the world, making an album I'm personally very proud of and we got paid for. What's not to love?"

Another release worth getting a hold of is *Skunkworks Live*, an EP that came out in October 1996 in Japan, featuring four live tracks, including an excellent rendition of 'The Prisoner.'

Bruce was closing back in on metal; the follow-up to *Skunkworks* is a cracking little piece of work that does indeed feature Smith, initially as a guest. The Tribe of Gypsies were back on board and Dickinson was writing with Roy Z again. David Ingraham remembers it well.

"Well, first of all, we had one record with Bruce under our belt, so recording *Accident* was slightly less nerve-wracking," says Ingraham. "And we did that one at the legendary-yet-sadly-now-defunct Sound City in Van Nuys, San Fernando Valley, about 10 minutes from where I lived at the time, so it was nice to be able to hop out of bed and just drive down the street every day.

"But beyond that, the process was similar: Bruce and Roy would write together, record the demos, Roy would present the music to the rest of us, we'd give it a good listen and maybe chart it out, and then we'd start rehearsals a few weeks before, shaping and modifying the songs. Although the music was largely pre-written, Bruce and Roy were always open to the other band members' input. If someone had a good idea that worked, we'd go with it."

Accident of Birth came out in May 1997, complete with Derek Riggs-drawn cover art. The title track was released as a single and scraped up to No.54 in the UK charts. The subject matter is way more Maiden-ish, too: a family lives in Hell, a son is born into the world, but he doesn't want to return to his family in Hell. Is it too much of a stretch to read into this, thoughts about returning to Maiden? Speculation is always fun. The tour ran from April to the end of November that year, taking in Europe, North and

IRON MAIDEN

South America. A bumper 81 dates made it the longest jaunt since his days with 'Arry's Army. *Accident* was much better-received than its predecessor, with second single 'Man of Sorrows' returning to Dickinson's interest in Alisteir Crowley. Indeed, it was originally intended to be part of a movie called *Chemical Wedding*.

The movie would take a while to come to fruition, but the title would be used much quicker for a swift follow-up to *Accident*. The line-up was the same, remembers Ingraham.

"We now had two records under our belts, so the confidence and comfort levels just kept growing," he recalls. "Everybody knew the basic modus operandi by that point, so it was business as usual: we knew what our jobs were and made it happen. And of course, we all knew each other that much better by that point, having toured the world together with *Accident of Birth*, so we were a well-oiled machine by then."

Chemical Wedding is partly inspired by alchemical themes and partly by William Blake. It was incredibly well-received by the world of rock and metal; a heavy and furious piece of work that spikes and burns at the corners of the world. Given Maiden's relative travails at the time, many have pegged this one and to a lesser extent its predecessor as better Iron Maiden albums than the actual band were delivering in the Blaze days.

Certainly the reaction of the fans was still very special in the live arena; the 1999 live album released on Dickinson's own Air Raid records entitled *Scream for me Brazil* shows that in spades. By 1998 it was a matter of course that Dickinson would deliver several Iron Maiden tracks as special treats and/or encores; 'Powerslave,' '2 Minutes to Midnight' and 'Flight of Icarus' just three of the songs the fans lapped up alongside the excellent solo material.

There was talk at the time of a possible Samson reunion for a celebration of NWOBHM in Japan. Dickinson was involved in the idea and seemed to be leaning toward rejoining Paul, Thunderstick and Chris for the special event. But with *Chemical Wedding* knocking down many doors back in the world of metal, there was growing momentum for Bruce the heavy metal singer to return to his most successful style. It had not gone unnoticed by the Iron Maiden camp either.

Thus it came that Rod Smallwood, Steve Harris and Bruce got together in a pub and sorted out the details of him returning to Maiden.

"By the time *Scream for me Brazil* was recorded," says David Ingraham, "We'd heard the news and knew that was the end. Needless to say, it was bittersweet because it'd been a great ride, but I knew it was a business decision for Bruce and Adrian —and a wise one at that— so we knew it was nothing personal. All good things must come to an end, right?"

Indeed so. In 2002 Dickinson brought the band back together (more or less) for a tour to support his solo compilation *The Best of Bruce Dickinson*. It was, Dale says, a lot of fun.

"Bruce told me he had a few European festivals to play, would I want to do it and could I get a band together. So we had Alex Dickson on guitar again, Pete Friesen (The Almighty/Alice Cooper) on second guitar and Robin Guy from Sack Trick on drums. It was in support of his *Best Of* album and he said it was just for fun really, so there was no alternative rock theme, it was just heads down heavy metal. Let's please the fans and give them what they want."

"So me and Bruce sat in a pub and wrote

PART TWO **SOLO CAREERS**

a rough setlist together. We decided on one per solo album, plus a few extras and some Maiden tunes. It was great to be able to pick which Maiden songs to play. We wanted to choose songs that Bruce wrote that Maiden (at that time) did not play in their setlist. I tour-managed those gigs too, which again just meant I could schedule it around comfort and fun. We did about six European festivals, all the big ones - Wacken in Germany, Sweden Rock, Graspop in Belgium, etc. The whole thing was good metal fun, as you can see from bits on YouTube. It was just a shame we didn't do more.

"Little known fact - we had another unconfirmed gig added at the end in South Korea. Pete Friesen wasn't available for that one as he had commitments with Alice Cooper, so I asked Ace from Skunk Anansie to do it. He said yes, and had just started learning the set when we heard the gig was cancelled ... what would that have sounded like?"

Robin Guy is an extraordinary drummer and was absolutely filled with joy when he got the nod to do the 2002 tour.

"Bruce is incredible to work with," Guy notes. " He seemingly never tires and always has something on the go - be it a radio show (he had his own show on BBC6 Music), a commercial flight (we all know Bruce is a pilot), Maiden, some aviation business, writing a book (he's a published author), being a husband, a father, a fencer, a solo artist, inventing beer ... it's ridiculous how he fits it all in!

"I remember one rehearsal (we did three with just the band - to get the arrangements, structures and solos sounding good, then three with Bruce), had got there 'early' (I think around 11am) and already gone through the set once - maybe twice, when Bruce walks in around 1pm and one of us taps his watch and jokingly goes, 'Nice of you to turn up, Boss...' to which Bruce turned apologetically and said: 'I'm so sorry I was late, guys - I had a flight simulation exam at 7am this morning at Gatwick Airport." Needless to say the room fell instantly silent, and all of us looked at the floor.

"Another time, after a triumphant show on top of a mountain in Greece, the Lycabettus Theatre, Athens, we retired backstage, dripping with sweat, and reaching for a cold beer from the fridge, I offered Bruce one, to which he replied: "No thanks - I have to do a commercial flight at 4am."

There were many memorable moments on that short tour, Guy says.

"I can pretty much say that all the time spent with that band was a high point," he continues, not unreasonably. "However, a day I often refer to as 'The Best Day In My Life', was headlining Wacken Open Air festival in Hamburg to 40,000 crazy metalheads! It was such a special concert - not only because we were headlining the biggest metal fest in Europe, but also because we went onstage in daylight and saw a huge audience as far as the eye could see, and then during the set it became twilight and the stage lights kicked in, and by the encores it was night-time, all the lights and smoke were in full effect, plus we could see, piercing the audience shrouded in blackness, loads of little fires being lit around the periphery of the festival - it looked spectacular, and magical.

"Also, every time Bruce went, 'Scream for me ... *insert name of festival/ country,' I would basically lose my mind, as it instantly took me back to being a kid listening to *Live After Death*: 'Scream for me Long Beach...!'"

As well as working with Maiden,

IRON MAIDEN

Dickinson continued to write alongside Roy Z; the results were 2005's *Tyranny of Souls*. Listening to it in a contemporary context, the moments of piano and acoustic were absolutely non-Maiden at the time but given the Irons' continued development as songwriters such things really do serve to look forward in time. 'Mars Within,' and 'Power of the Sun,' however, are pretty much Maiden songs. The LP as a whole isn't up to the standard of *Accident of Birth* and *Chemical Wedding*, but as a stop-gap after Maiden's *Dance of Death* it does the trick nicely. A particular highlight is 'Navigate the Seas of the Sun,' based on barmy Erich von Daniken's books about ancient aliens: typical Bruce Dickinson fare, and all the better for it.

Dickinson has said he plans a solo record sometime in the late 2010s; that is, if Steve Harris doesn't nick all his songs for Iron Maiden again, of course ...

NICKO MCBRAIN – THE BLASTER

Thumpingly good stuff

When William Henry McBrain joined Iron Maiden, he already had many years of experience behind him. Indeed, the drummer had already played with covers act Peyton Bond, Wells Street Blues Band and then Billy Day. By that stage, McBrain had picked up the name of Nicko, apparently named after a teddy bear he'd owned. Standard.

The first big breakthrough for Nicko was joining Streetwalkers in 1975, set up by former Family members Roger Chapman and John Whitney in 1973, first under the name Chapman, Whitney, before the name change on signing to Phonogram in '75. The band's vaguely funky rock stylings haven't aged that well, although 'Downtown Flyers' provides a kind of Roogalator-ish sub-Hendrix romp. Chapman's vocals are in fine fettle on the 1975 LP, also called *Downtown Flyers*, to be fair, but there's not much here for the Maiden fan. The closest is probably 'Raingame,' which has a hint of Zep about it. Another album was released in 1976, *Red Card*, for which a tour of UK footy grounds was arranged. It was a good bill – Sensational Alex Harvey Band, Little Feat, Outlaws, Streetwalkers, and The Who. The album was a reasonable success, reaching No.16 in the UK. It's more blues-rocky than its immediate predecessor, first track 'Run for Cover' bridging the gap between T-Rex and AC/DC. Chapman's vocals on the cover of 'Daddy Rollin' Stone' never sounded more like Bon Scott – never a bad thing. Needless to say, Nicko's solid on both releases, as on the Peel Session they did in '76.

Nicko left Streetwalkers prior to what was to be their final album, *Vicious But Fair*. The band was talented as performers, but the raw energy and realness of punk rock had struck by 1977 and blown the old guard

PART TWO SOLO CAREERS

out of the water. McBrain jumped ship to work with Pat Travers, an upcoming blues/hard rocker, and smacked the kit about in due course on *Makin' Magic*, the 1977 Polydor release. Travers was highly-rated in the industry but similarly made to look outdated by the punk explosion; the LP, along with its successor *Putting It Straight*, are more than decent mid-Seventies hard rock. Fans of Paul Samson would no doubt love what the group provides. Nicko is also much more energetic within a much more driving outfit than Streetwalkers ever were. On leaving Streetwalkers, Nicko popped up drumming for Jenny Darren on three tracks of her *Heartbreaker* LP, as well as joining rather interesting French band, Trust. Bass player Martin Connolly is a long-term friend and musical collaborator of the drummer.

"I first met Nicko in 1979 when we both went to audition for a band called Fury," says Connolly, explaining that the audition took place in a rehearsal studio at Lots Road in Chelsea. "We both got the gig and went on to play with different artists – Peter Sarstedt and Cheetah - but Nick left to re-join Trust and the band never achieved success."

His drums are unusual enough. It's like a percussion den. He had to have his Sweep (Sooty and Sweep) glove puppet on the front of his kit!

Jeff Williams, ex-production manager, Iron Maiden

Trust blended metal, rock and elements of punk, led by vocalist Bernie Bonvoisin. McBrain's skills are lent to the 1981 LP, called *Marche Ou Creve* in some territories, *Savage* in others, including the UK in 1982. It's very much an AC/DC vibe from the outset, not least opener 'The Big Illusion'. There's even a tribute to Bon Scott on album closer, 'Your Final Gig'. But bigger things were beckoning.

Clive Burr was leaving Maiden. And the band were looking for someone to take over. Given Maiden had toured with Trust in 1981, they would have been well-aware of the talented sticksman giving it everything. So Nicko McBrain was drafted in to the Maiden camp in 1982. Burr was to later accept an invitation by Bonvoisin to join Trust, squaring the circle nicely. As Connolly notes, "It was during his stint with Trust that Steve Harris saw him play, and the rest is history as they say."

Beastly stuff

Over the years, McBrain has been in much demand to pass on his knowledge to up-and-coming artists. Martin Connolly recalls many an occasion in which the drummer and the bassist worked with sponsors to do just that.

"The drum clinics were set up by Paiste cymbals and we did a couple of out-of-town shows then a weekend at the Olympia Trade Fair," he explains. Those successful masterclasses were to lead on to something even more formal.

The results are still there for all to see on the rather excellent *Rhythms of the Beast* video that came out in 1991. It's rather different from Maiden; Dave Murray is also involved in the project, pulling out an excellent solo on the title track of the VHS (it has since reappeared on DVD in limited edition).

IRON MAIDEN

"Nicko had been threatening to do a vid, so got some funding from [drum manufacturer] Paiste and [microphone manufacturer] Beyer, and I'd previously worked with him before he joined Maiden."

The music on the video, by the way, is quite different: as well as the affable sticksman talking viewers through tuning, warming-up, choice of gear, soloing and miking, there's a live performance featuring Murray and Connolly. Mike Moran completes the main line-up on keys, as well as taking responsibility for adding saxophones and trumpets to the sound. The results are intriguing.

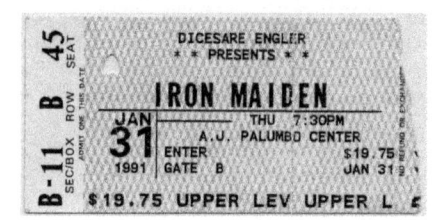

"Nick had always loved the big band sound, so Mike Moran organised the score for the horns and we recorded it 'live' one Sunday, to around 150 fan club members," recalls Connolly.

Another fantastic project was 2011's WhoCares, which brought together Ian Gillan, Tony Iommi, Jon Lord, Jason Newsted, and Mikko Lindstrom alongside Nicko to put out a charity single. Proceeds went to the relief efforts for a music school in Gyumri that had been badly damaged by a devastating earthquake in Armenia. Iommi and Gillan had found out about the school's plight whilst visiting the country as a follow-up to the 1989 release of 'Smoke on the Water,' the Rock Aid Armenia single that featured Bruce Dickinson. A 20th anniversary remix and video was released in 2009.

Apart from Maiden, Nicko also plays with McBrain Damage – covering all sorts of songs, including those of the Irons. It's an offshoot, in many ways, of 1985 project, The Entire Population of Hackney, something of a fun knockabout with musical mates from far and wide (in Hackney), after the mammoth *Powerslave* tour.

Connolly sums it up.

"In my opinion Nicko is one of the best drummers Britain has produced [and] his talents extend beyond Heavy Metal," says the legendary bass player, who has been in the music biz four decades, including stints with Rick Wakeman and Scarlet. "The two Streetwalkers albums will support that."

"I will say as I consider him a friend first and foremost, we have always worked well together," concludes Connolly. "As for the Maiden phenomenon? I see Adrian Smith often as we live near each other and share a passion for fishing - and even he has been amazed how they have gone from strength to strength."

"My current band Vardis are finding it hard at the mo: I may have to call in some favours!"

Nicholas McBrain also has a pilot's license; famously he was instrumental in Bruce Dickinson's first endeavours in the skies. Since 2009 he has been a partner in the super BBQ restaurant, Rock 'N' Roll Ribs, now a stop off for any Maiden fan anywhere near Coral Springs, Florida. Indeed, a local paper named their ribs the Best of 2012. Lovely. He underwent

PART TWO **SOLO CAREERS**

a transformational experience in 1999 at a church near his Boca Raton house and found himself to be called to the Christian religion, something that informs his life. You might well see him pop up on telly in other forms – whether driving his custom Jaguar XKR-S, playing golf or most likely watching snooker, a real passion of his.

Chief passion, of course, is the drums. To that end, he partnered with Craig Buckley, formerly of Premier Drums, to take on a longstanding drum shop in Manchester's Trafford Park. The new store, Nicko McBrain's Drum One, took over premises from previous business Manchester Drum Centre. In-store events, drum clinics and of course sales were all promised. Never still, those stick-wielders, are they?

Playing that famous kit – and setting up that stage

Jeff Williams knows the Maiden set-up better than most, having served in various capacities over the years. He has first-hand experience of the monster, after years of experience with other acts.

"I had spent my whole career working as a drum tech, for WASP, Prong, Kylie, BB King, Helloween, Bruce Dickinson's Skunkworks, Adrian Smith's Untouchables etc, but when I was asked to join Maiden, it wasn't as Nicko's drum tech," he says.

"My role was as head of stage production. I managed and ran the stage-set, operated the moving parts such as the Wickerman and drawbridge (including finding and recruiting the virgins for each show), huge moving Eddie heads behind Nicko, the backdrops and zip wires, the flame boxes and runways, flags and all the other props."

A day in the life...

"A typical day would involve Dickie Bell shouting us up out of our bunks on the tour bus if we'd been night-rolling and straight into a huge empty arena, bull-ring, skating rink, or football stadium and meeting our local crew, who by then have already been unloading catering, lighting and PA trucks, the riggers would be putting up the motors in the roof and the production office is being established and set up. We'd have a look around, find out where everything was, where we were, who was who, whilst the lighting crew filled the stage and got their rigs up in the air, then the soundcrew fly their rigs while we bring in our production trucks and direct the locals to unload this here, that there."

"As soon as everything was up in the air, we went into a build frenzy like you wouldn't believe. It's a very well-oiled machine and everyone is at the top of their game. The stage-set goes up in a few hours and then the backline trucks unload onto the stage. We'd usually finish soundcheck and have an hour or two before doors, so I'd take a couple of crew out to help source the virgins for the Wickerman, while some guys would just watch a movie on the bus or sleep."

Drumming to the masses

"Nicko chose a guy who had no drum-tech experience and couldn't play the drums. Was it so he could mould him into what he wanted rather than have someone come in telling him how things should be done? Probably!

"Anyway, my job included playing Nicko's kit for up to an hour every day whilst front of house soundman Doug Hall did his thing

THIS DAY IN MUSIC'S GUIDE TO **IRON MAIDEN** 193

IRON MAIDEN

out front, and then with Gonzo we'd get Nicko's monitor mix set up. We'd often do the soundcheck for the band ourselves, occasionally in front of thousands of their fans if it was a festival. That was a big buzz.

"If you've never played a kit like Nicko's onstage at Madison Square Gardens with a full house or at Rock in Rio in front of a 250,000-strong crowd and had them screaming wild with your every hit, stick it on your bucket-list! That shit is raw power!

"It's just fucking immense. AKA: indescribable."

MICHAEL KENNEY – THE COUNT

Yes, he's not an official member. But it seems churlish to leave out a dude who's played on albums and toured with the band for so long, doesn't it?

Count on me (The Count on keys)

For a long time, the sixth member of Iron Maiden, keyboardist Michael Kenney, is now the seventh member of Iron Maiden.

The Californian has had many different jobs over the three decades or so he's worked with Maiden, including being Eddie in the video for 'Women in Uniform' way back when. He's also the long-time tech for Steve Harris, making sure all is well onstage and off technically for the bass man to bring the low end in his inimitable way. Since 1980 he has had a myriad of jobs, first taking over from Vic Vella on the UK tour after Vella knocked his ankle. Kenney stepped in as Dave's tech and continued to do so on their European tour with Kiss.

After that, he returned to Los Angeles until July 1982, when a call came in from soundman Doug Hall that Harris was after someone to look after his bass gear on the road. So a short filling-in job became an extremely long-term one. Luckily, Harris prefers to retune on stage, and tends not to swap basses too much, which since 1988 freed Kenney up to his second job. He is a talented musician in his own right, as well as an excellent sound engineer, but it is as keyboardist that Maiden fans know him best.

Once Maiden really got stuck into matters in terms of keys and progginess, which would be around the *Seventh Son* sessions, Kenney also took on live keyboard duties. Since *Brave New World* the keyboard parts on the LPs are generally credited to Steve Harris. Kenney – named The Count due to his wearing of a large, black cloak-like coat – continues to play in his own right on downtime in LA, with such acts as Happenin' Harry and the Haptones. He has also guested alongside long-term Bruce Dickinson cohort Roy Z at charity gigs, as well as with the Iron Maidens on their *Route 666* DVD.

No surprise to find out that The Count collects organs … but it's not as gruesome as all that. He's a fan of vintage Hammond

PART TWO **SOLO CAREERS**

and Leslie organs. Anyone who's ever been to the end of a UK pier will recognise the sound immediately. They're heavy, heavy things. Well, you try picking one of them up sometime.

JANICK GERS – THE STYLIST

Hartlepool's finest export, Janick Robert Gers, has been a guitarist in demand since he began his career in the mid-Seventies. And it's been quite the ride to get to his current status as one-third of the most vaunted guitar attack in metal, too.

The first project Gers is mainly known for is hard rock act White Spirit, formed in his hometown in 1975. It took the group a few years to get some traction, but eventually Neat Records sorted them out a single deal. The lead track was 'Back to the Grind', with 'Cheetah' on the flip. Both songs would appear on the rather ace 1980 self-titled MCA-released album. Check out lead track 'Midnight Chaser' for an awesome blend of Deep Purple progginess with Saxon-esque riffs and up-front guitars. Indeed, the band's comparisons with Purple are not misplaced on an LP that has become something of a collectors' item over the years. 'Red Skies' opens with a guitar lick that Meat Loaf/Jim Steinman would have been proud of before settling into another riff-and-keys-hefty stomp; in a pre-echo of his later work there are dual guitars picking out a smooth lick, first in unison and then in harmonies. Course, it's easy to see these links in retrospect; back in 1980, the NWOBHM was just getting into gear – there were few guarantees that anyone would break through, regardless of skill or artistry.

Talking of which, 'Way of the Kings' is a bloody stormer and keyboardist Michael Pearson has a splendid little space-rock Doctor Who-esque interlude in the middle. It's boss.

White Spirit were one of many Maiden-connected groups to appear on a *Metal for Muthas* compilation, albeit on the less-influential Volume II, with the mid-paced, slightly epic 'High Upon High'. Muthas Pride, a terribly-named EP based on a pun with a popular brand of bread loaves (seriously), had the Spirit's 'Red Skies' on it; a far choppier and more satisfying romp by anybody's standards. White Spirit's arguably highest point was 1980's Reading Festival (then known as Reading Rock) appearance; that brilliant line-up included everyone from Maiden and Whitesnake to Rory Gallagher, Def Leppard, Samson and – on paper – Ozzy Osbourne's new project, Blizzard of Ozz. Famously, Slade stepped in and absolutely rocked it to pieces; an EP was later released of Slade's performance. White Spirit themselves only got a spot on the bill after Q-Tips withdrew, one of many bands billed but not appearing when it came down to it. A few bootlegs exist of various performances – sadly not White Spirit, but Maiden (from the audience) and quite a few by the good ol' BBC for broadcast, and in the case of Gillan, released on BBC

IRON MAIDEN

Enterprises/Raw Fruit. You are advised to head to http://www.ukrockfestivals.com/reading-80-recordings.html for more on these bits and bobs. Suffice to say that quality of recordings – Maiden's is rubbish – is patchy, but as a record of the time they are of interest.

White Spirit toured during October as one of two supports to Gillan on the *Glory Road* tour; something that was to prove rather good for Janick's career, if not White Spirit's. Impressed by this young, dynamic, kinetic and skilled guitarist, the Deep Purple legend was to ask Gers to join him in his new band.

Gillan calls

Ian Gillan's influence on many bands in this book, including Bruce Dickinson as a singer and as a musician in the incredibly important Purple, cannot be underestimated. Simply put, without him (and his bandmates) one could say it was unlikely that Maiden would have sounded the way they did, or even formed at all. And in the early 1980s he was in the odd position of being something of an elder statesman for the NWOBHM set, despite being only in his 30s. Looking back, the singer explains that Gers had an energy and vibe about him that was palpable. Just the man, indeed, to replace recently-fired Bernie Torme in the band.

"We crossed paths a few times," Gillan says, "[Us] and White Spirit being on the same circuit. My thoughts were very appreciative of his style. He was enjoying himself so much and that was very infectious."

"For a musician, especially a banjo player, he is a wonderfully uncomplicated man. You know where you stand with Janick; reliable too. These are rare qualities that contributed hugely to the human chemistry of my band."

One comparison that has been attached to Janick Gers over the years is that he resembles Richie Blackmore at times, onstage and stylistically. Ian Gillan, for one, is not buying it, as he stridently tells the author.

"Which comparisons? I never read that kind of crap," asserts the Purple frontman, adding, not unreasonably, that, "Fact is we all go through our formative years and then find our voice, so to speak. I wonder what influenced Ritchie, eh?"

Janick's two albums with Gillan are interesting and stand the test of time quite well. *Double Trouble*, originally released in 1981 as a double album that features two sides of studio, two sides of live tracks. Gers is in fine form on 'Men of War' – as is the vocalist, for that matter, the familiar screaming high notes and rough-arsed distortion bringing musicianship and feel together in truly fantastic style. Gers gets a co-writing credit for 'Sunbeam', his guitar heralding a fair old blend of hard rock and softer-edged keyboard pads. Some great vocal harmonies lay atop solid riffing throughout, as you'd expect. Proof that Ian Gillan knew a thing or two when it came to pulling a group together. That said, you ask him about how Gers approaches his instrument, and sonic spaces, at your peril, as the author found out in the interview for this book.

"I don't know how he approaches it, those things don't interest me," Gillan says. "All I know is that he delivers the goods ... Oh come on, please! He puts together all the right chords and rhythms, then plays the right solos. Sonic Space? Give me a break."

Point made strongly and taken on board.

The second LP Gers played on with Gillan

PART TWO **SOLO CAREERS**

was 1982's *Magic*, on which he co-wrote 'What's the Matter' alongside the singer and bassist John McCoy, plus 'Bluesy Blue Sea', a collaboration between Gers and Gillan. The former is an absolutely triumphant, fast-paced stomper – standing up against much of the extensive and often wonderful back-catalogue Gillan can draw on and with a 'Black Night'-esque squeal to boot. The second track has one foot in blues and one in hard-rock riffing; two sides displayed by all the musicians which they show with skill and genuine affection for their craft. As regards songwriting partnerships and creative possibilities in bands, Ian Gillan has no truck with over-analysis.

"Sorry mate, this is not science," he says. "If you could analyse it successfully and come up with a formula, it still wouldn't work, because everyone would be doing it and whatever 'it' is would become incredibly boring.

"This is all about human chemistry, talent and application, plus a little bit of magic."

Some things are timeless and ineffable, clearly. Back to 1982, however, and the *Magic* album was to be the swansong of Gillan, the band. Unfortunately, Ian Gillan's packed schedule had taken its toll on his distinctive voice, and due to damaged vocal cords, he had to take time off to rest. Gers, like the rest of the band, would have to find other ways to explore their sonic spaces (sorry, Ian). In the downtime he now had, Gers studied for a degree in sociology.

Gogmagollocks More Like

It must have seemed a good idea at the time; bring together some of the best musicians in the country to try and crack the charts, make some cash and a bit of noise along the way. That was the intent of the supergroup Gogmagog, put together by Jonathan King – at that time just a record producer. Janick joined ex-Maiden members Paul Di'Anno and Clive Burr, Pete Wills (Def Leppard) and bassist Neil Murray on this strange and doomed idea in 1985. If only King had taken the advice Ian Gillan gives above and left well alone, perhaps the band would have had a chance. As it was, King insisted on writing two of the songs himself, with the third from Russ Ballard (whose 'Riding With The Angels' was covered by Samson in 1981 and Bruce Dickinson's solo band live a decade-ish later).

Gogmagog was named after a giant in British folk literature; it's a legend of the founding of the country itself. Typical hubris; the band was great as musicians, the songs were not. Ballard's 'I Will Be There' is a surprisingly passionless run through a track originally released in 1981 on Ballard's *Into the Fire* LP. As for the two King tracks, they are 'king awful. Yukky stuff all round, a horrible project both in conception and delivery. It was, at three decades' distance, an exercise in the worst capitalist excesses of the pop industry, driven by one of pop music's most odious characters. But who could know that at the time? And, of course, there's always the 'off' button. Nobody mourned when Gogmagog fizzled out without troubling the charts. The musicians, of course, had proper careers to turn to. For Janick, that meant linking up with Iron Maiden's lead singer, and mate, Bruce Dickinson. The project was centred around a track for *A Nightmare on Elm Street 5: The Dream Child*. Dickinson's 'Bring Your Daughter... to the Slaughter' went down so well that the record company Zomba asked for a whole album. Thus, *Tattooed Millionaire* was born, more of which you can

IRON MAIDEN

find in the Bruce Dickinson solo section. The album was largely written by the pair, more for fun than in expectation, but by gum it's a good 'un; perhaps for those exact reasons. As it turned out, of course, Maiden were to nick Dickinson's song for their own (and get a number one with it). Janick's links with Maiden were getting stronger ...

Into the deep

First things first, though. Gers' next major project was an intriguing, very solid link-up with none other than Fish. The ex-Marillion frontman was embarking on his solo career, having left that band in 1988. The Scottish singer, actor and all-round dude was working on *Vigil in a Wilderness of Mirrors*, eventually released in 1990 but ready to go long before that.

"I knew Janick from his work with Gillan," remembers Fish, "And previous *Kerrang!* type of events, Marquee, and his work with Bruce's solo stuff. We lived just down the road from Bruce and used to bump into him quite a lot. Janick was up for doing some writing and came up to the rehearsal studio, where we started working on 'View from the Hill' together.

"For me at the time it was a blank canvas; I could do anything I want and work with anyone I want. Janick came up for two or three weeks, we got on really well and played with ideas. 'View From the Hill' was perfectly suited to what I wanted to do with him. I wanted something a bit rock-y, something a little bit harder. It has an anthemic quality at the end, a great rock song. The way it picks up and goes through the gears is well-suited to Janick.

"He is a really lovely guy, I really like his attitude and character," concludes Fish.

"I think we were both kind of in the same situation; he was finding himself as well. Ian Gillan [had come] off the road, Janick was kind of looking for stuff to do and I was looking for another foil to work with."

Indeed, Gers played at Fish's first ever solo gig, remembers the singer.

"He came onstage and we played 'Big Wedge' – at a cinema in Lockerbie, a charity gig for the disaster. Hal Lindes was involved, John Keeble... a fantastic line-up. And there was Janick, swinging his guitar around his neck. I wasn't used to that flamboyant behaviour!"

It was a short period of creative collaboration, Fish recalls, with Hal Lindes and Frank Usher mainly playing on the album.

"He came in and played 'View from the Hill' – I was there in the studios and it was a quick in-and-out with John Giblin on bass and Mark Brzezicki on drums."

Gers was busy with Bruce at that time, recalls the Marillion man, which impacted on his availability.

"He was considered for the [solo] band but was too tied up with Bruce, who was doing world tour vibes at the time. I was just getting my solo career together. We went out on a tentative first solo tour at the end of 1989, and Janick was really embroiled with Bruce. The monster machine Bruce had behind him was very different to what I had.

"He is a great guitarist, but I wanted a twin-guitar setup [...] I didn't want to get drawn into just copying the Marillion sound. Frank [Usher] was already going to be in the band as principle guitarist, so I needed a second guitarist, which is where Robin Boult came in.

"Janick is more of a solo guitarist, and so is Frank Usher. I needed somebody to come

PART TWO **SOLO CAREERS**

in who was more of a rhythm guitarist and felt that Robin fitted more than Janick did. Bruce was more reliant on Janick than I was. I had a lot [more] musicians to draw on."

So it was more a moment in time for the Fish/Gers linkup; quite the moment, though. It's well worth looking out for the album.

Bruce Dickinson may have been messing with solo stuff, without really taking it as a serious career move at that time, but in 1990 Adrian Smith had left Iron Maiden.

Janick Gers was drafted in to replace him in short order. It was in many ways an obvious next step and three decades later, give or take, the Hartlepool lad is still in the band.

BLAZE BAYLEY – THE PHENOMENON

A firestorm called Blaze

Birmingham, England is often known as the Second City; outside of London it's the most populated place in England. That population increased by one, and a very significant one at that, on May 29th, 1963.

Bayley Cooke is the name of the gentleman concerned and he spent his teenage years on the night-shift listening to heavy metal to get him through the dark hours. Cooke, who picked up the nickname Blaze Bayley along the way, soon found he had a talent for singing in his own right and along with his mates formed a band called Wolfsbane in 1984. Back then it was all about hard work, persistence, talent of course, and a whole lot of hitting the road spreading the word.

"We had a van and some demo tapes, got our own T-shirts printed up," says Bayley. "We had just had a couple of lines in *Kerrang!* magazine, with a small photo. That was enough that we could get in touch with a very small [booking] agency and we managed to get our first paying gigs."

The band toured extensively and picked up fans very quickly throughout the mid-Eighties.

"We could play to 300 people and we were unsigned! We were the biggest unsigned heavy metal band in the UK," Bayley explains. "Live, we were just crazy. We meant every word of what we did and would stick around [after gigs] to sign things for fans. And we considered ourselves fans."

Significantly, Bayley analyses some of the appeal: does this remind you of anyone?

"We were kind of the everyman band: four working-class guys that never tried to be anything else apart from have fun being a band and write the best music we possibly could. And that's what we stuck to."

The afore-mentioned Wolfsbane demos managed to get into the hands of mega-producer Rick Rubin – not something that happens every day to every band. In fact, it is rare as hen's teeth.

"I have had a lot of luck in my professional career," Bayley says. "OK I've had ups and downs, but a lot of breaks,

IRON MAIDEN

coincidence and pure luck. Our agent in London built us up to a point where we got some great support slots. We supported Motörhead as an unsigned band, and supported King Diamond, an absolutely great bloke, at Hammersmith Odeon."

The review of that latter gig also mentioned Wolfsbane, and in being placed opposite a review of thrash megastars Slayer gave Blaze et al significant kudos. Rubin read it, wondered who these upstarts were, and found he was a fan of Wolfsbane's output. Off they then went to Los Angeles, although they felt more Ramones than Van Halen, the singer laughs, so would have preferred to record in New York City's grittier environs.

"We were off and recording our first album in Sound City Studios [where the likes of Dio, RHCP, Nirvana and even Johnny Cash also laid down tracks]. We worked with some absolutely top people, and that was the [1989] album *Live Fast Die Fast*."

Indeed, Wolfsbane had a long-term contract with Def American – five albums – but as it turned out the rest of the States didn't share Rubin's enthusiasm.

"It didn't sound much like Wolfsbane live," Bayley explains. "It didn't have the energy of the demos: something was missing from it. He hadn't captured a part of the band that we all felt very important. It wasn't until we released the EP 'All Hell's Breaking Loose Down At Little Kathy Wilson's Place' that we felt we sounded how Wolfsbane actually sounded. The sound of the album didn't capture us.

"It was dull. If you listen to the AC/DC and Metallica albums [Rubin produced] they do not sound exciting to me. Those albums worked great for those artists, but it didn't for us. It wasn't a part of what we were about."

Nobody's fault; if the vibe and feeling isn't right, or the passion isn't there, Blaze adds, it's not going to work. But find the right person, and you're flying. A more live-sounding, faster-recorded record may have suited Wolfsbane better. It also kept the band away from their natural environment of hard-gigging in the UK, which didn't help a group widely considered to be one of the best upcoming metal groups in many a year.

That more authentic-sounding EP came out around the same time as Wolfsbane snagged an amazing support slot: backing Iron Maiden on the UK leg of the *No Prayer on the Road* tour in 1990.

"We had something we believed in, it sounded like us, and we were on our way," Bayley says of *All Hell*. "It had a great video, a good song, 'I Like It Hot', and we got selected to play 33 sold-out shows in the UK. It was the last time Maiden would ever play shows of that size in the UK and was a thank you to the fans. It was fantastic.

"We got encores every night."

For a support band, that is a huge deal. But Wolfsbane's record company didn't build on the momentum by sending them on tour

PART TWO **SOLO CAREERS**

with the EP; instead they were in the studio recording another album.

"By the time we came back," says Bayley of the unnecessary delay in activities, "We had lost all the impetus and popularity and interest from supporting Iron Maiden. All that had dissipated."

The band was also facing down the grunge music explosion.

"I knew Soundgarden quite well; I'd met them in LA and went to see them in the UK. They did nothing [at first] and played to a half-empty Marquee. Then a few years later they were selling out a whole tour! Then Nirvana came out.

"Wolfsbane were happy, good time [type of band] and grunge was miserable, look-at-your-shoes music," he continues. "Grunge was the antithesis of what we were. You had to like grunge and not like anything else. That was the new bible of rock and it made things very difficult. At the start in Wolfsbane we thought it was great – we never for a minute thought it would exclude us. You were then just fighting for your life [as a band] really."

Bayley and Wolfsbane were often misunderstood by the people they worked with on an industry level, he says, with all sorts of people putting their oars in. One particular trope was constant suggestions from record companies that songs ought to be named after the most often-repeated words.

"I am a lyricist and a poet," he continues. "You don't always want the chorus to be the title, because you want to ask a question, sometimes. You want to give the song a title that will ask a question and the answer is the journey within the song. Well, I'm sorry, but we aren't pop. We aren't doing that. Pop is another discipline. Yet, they would say that how many albums they would press depended on the chart position and we are going, 'Well, what chart position? We're a heavy metal band! We're going on tour, we're trying to build a career like Iron Maiden: album after album, not single after single'."

So the vista changed again and Wolfsbane's time had been and gone. For the singer, though, greater things were on the way. That support tour with Maiden – on which Bayley had sung with them as a guest in an encore or two – was to have huge repercussions.

Bruce Dickinson left. Maiden auditioned singers. Blaze Bayley got the job. The best Christmas present ever ... or so it felt at the time.

Andy Griffin was the engineer on Wolfsbane's self-titled album and recalls the mixing sessions after Blaze had left for pastures new.

"He came to see Simon one day," Griffin recalls. "We were working with a band called Big Boy Tomato and they offered him a beer. He said, 'No,' he was under orders. You could tell that Maiden had told him to get into better shape. He was excited, though.

"I think he wanted Simon to produce his vocals on the Maiden record, was happy to sit in the studio and scan through the porn.

"I thought it was a good fit [Blaze joining Maiden] and didn't blame him at all for taking his chance."

Nobody would turn that kind of opportunity down, and if anyone says they would you can call them a silly sausage and a fibber. And a daft cunt.

IRON MAIDEN

Solo again

Blaze set about getting a new band together almost immediately after his departure from Iron Maiden; he had a clutch of awesome material originally intended to be for his third Irons LP and was absolutely rabid to get that out into the world. The results were collated with his new band, titled Blaze, as the exceptional album, *Silicon Messiah*. Somewhere between Metallica and Blade Runner, the album is beefy, melodic and absolutely excellent. Just whack on 'Ghost in the Machine' to hear Blaze Bayley in his natural environment; it's arranged around his voice rather than him struggling to compete with guitars and high-register, 17 million notes a second bassing.

"Everything I'd learnt in Iron Maiden [I drew on for Blaze that's Blaze the band," he says. "I'd really enjoyed working with the two guitars and the different things you could do with that. I put my ideas together for my own album, did my own thing."

It is one of metal's great lost LPs in many ways, not least because the vocalist's luck was firmly out by this stage, being saddled as he was by a record company that made some extraordinarily bad choices.

"If I'd got that album out before Iron Maiden released their new album, which would of course be huge [2000's *Brave New World*], I would have a lot of interest from some of the fans," Bayley continues. "And that might be just enough to start me off. I got the band together, got the album ready.

"But I didn't get a record deal in time."

Timing is one of the things that is crucial in keeping momentum, as the singer's Wolfsbane experiences had shown. Any delay at this point was going to be crucial, and so it proved.

"When I did get a record deal the album came out the same week as *Brave New World*," Bayley says, shaking his head. "I did not have a proper booking agent at the time so there were no shows booked. The manager looking after me was not very good. No tour dates were booked for the release of my album. So *Silicon Messiah* was still-born really."

"It got great reviews, but they were all in the same magazines as *Brave New World*, so nobody was interested in it."

Ten years later Bayley did tour the album for its anniversary, headlining across Europe's smaller venues.

"It went absolutely great," he confirms.

Back in 2000-2001, Blaze the band were not going to be daunted by the industry. But there was another kick in the teeth waiting.

"I had a record deal, I battled on. We were getting gigs now, and a few festival offers. I was preparing a concept album, *Tenth Dimension*. I spoke to the record company and asked what the best time to release an album was. They said, 'February is the absolute best time [...] because all the magazines have got nothing to write about, have done their Christmas editions. So if you release in February you might get a front cover or at least some good coverage, because there's not much going on.' So I said [to my manager] I would do that and he said, 'How?' and I said, 'It's called *work*. I can do it.'

"The management I had at the time said it had to be July and I said, 'That's weird because I spoke to the record company and they said I could release in February.' And he said, 'No, July.' So I had to rush that album. So what happened was that all the summer festivals, all the momentum I'd built by battling on through *Silicon Messiah* was gone. By the time *Tenth Dimension* came out I could not capitalise on the popularity I'd gained

PART TWO **SOLO CAREERS**

2

by the end of that *Messiah* release. And in the end it didn't come out until February because of delays and problems. It was horrible.

"First album: stillborn; second album: smothered. The third album was a live album: *As Live as it Gets*, which came out fantastic."

The fourth Blaze album was the more personal *Blood & Belief*, in 2004. It was the last for SPV/Steamhammer, and the final one with that band line-up. Blaze Bayley is open about how things were going for him at the time.

"I was suffering from depression," he says. "I had suffered from depression for years but didn't really know it until I'd been to the doctor's. He put me on some medication and I started to see things differently. As soon as you know there's a word for this turmoil that you go through, called depression, there is a label you can put on and you don't feel quite so crazy mentally anymore. It's been a long, long road from there to here [2017].

"I am very lucky because I made it through. A lot of people don't. I am as fine as you can be when you've got this problem. A lot of the songs [on *Blood & Belief*] were about depression, and what I was going through. I had given my whole life and all my energy to music. And I never had any control over it.

"It was always somebody else's decision: the record company, the management, somebody else. I felt like I had no control over the direction and no matter what you did, no matter how hard [you worked] or good you were made absolutely no difference whatsoever. You go and give of your best, pour out your heart night after night to hardly anybody: in the end it starts to eat away at you."

Bayley Cooke then spent time earning some actual money; the band and the name Blaze was on the back-burner as he re-entered the world of employment, outside of the music industry.

"You go to a factory job – and I have had factory jobs since *Blood & Belief*, since Maiden – you go to a regular job, work eight hours a day and you get paid at the end of it. 'Bloody hell, you get paid at the end?' I had been working for nothing. I had been working my guts out and I had nothing. Now I was doing an ordinary job, as millions of people do – and I got paid at the end of the week! I feel I can live, I can go to the chip shop, I can buy a bottle of Newcastle Brown!

"It was a terrible time, really. That whole time coming round *Blood & Belief*. At the time of that album I was working as a taxi driver, doing long jobs around airports. And I worked sometimes 60 hours a week just trying to keep my house. After that job I went straight into the writing process for *Blood & Belief*. I worked intensely on the lyrics for that album. Hours and hours. I was living with my brother. He said, 'Won't you take a break?' and I said, 'No, it's finished when it is done, not when I'm tired.'

"There is a lot of pain in there, a lot of truth, but it is some of my favourite stuff I've ever done."

The album also marked the final time that Bayley had a traditional record deal.

"After that I just never cared about it," he says. "I tried to get something going occasionally, but, *pfff*. That was it. It was enough. Then I had some odd things I'd do for people, who wanted a guest singer or some to come and sing some Maiden things. And I just did that for a little while."

IRON MAIDEN

2

The story continues

Broken, battered, relatively skint and chewed up by the industry, it could have been the end of the singer's career and conceivably worse. But, fortunately, the story does not end there. The artist had way more to offer and wasn't going to go away quietly. This time, it would be on his own terms though.

"I was foolish enough to try again," he says, laughing. "I got the Blaze Bayley band together. We did two fantastic albums: *The Man Who Would Not Die* [in 2008] where many of the lyrics were about the situation I'd had at the record company, being blackmailed, feelings around that. It is a big album. The main guys with me on that album were Larry Patterson, a huge Motörhead fan who used a lot of double bass drums, a great drummer, David Bermudez on bass, his brother Nico on guitar. An incredible talent: a creative talent. The parts he created were brilliant."

"So we had all this energy to do something new. I'd been to Plastic Head Distribution without much hope at all, telling them I wanted to do my own record company and was wondering if they would distribute it. They just crunched the numbers of how many albums I'd sold with Iron Maiden and said yes. Suddenly I was a record company. We borrowed money to make the album."

The follow-up was *Promise and Terror*, which Bayley says is full of 'dark energy.' Old mucker Jase Edwards of Wolfsbane came in to produce, as he had with *The Man*. The band toured, but events in Bayley Cooke's life that he understandably wanted to keep personal in our interview intervened. His whole world view had been shaken to the core and the singer was in a very dark place indeed.

"We just had reached the limit of where we could go," he says of the subsequent dissolution of Blaze Bayley Band. "It was a sad ending. That nearly killed me to be honest. I was having suicidal thoughts at the time and I didn't want to carry on at that point.

"I often thought that after *Blood & Belief* I should have retired. If I could go back to that point I shouldn't have carried on. I was so close to the edge. And I almost never made it.

"I did carry on. But I think I was stupid to carry on. It's like a curse. Sometimes if you do this it just takes over you. I just kept going. I couldn't stop myself. It's like some sort of horrible addiction."

As the 2010s dawned, Blaze Bayley came back to music yet again. This time, though, an opportunity was offered with an acoustic angle to explore.

"A young classical guitarist called Thomas Zwijsen was going a project called *Nylon Maiden*, taking Iron Maiden songs and making his own arrangements on classical guitar. He asked if I would be a guest singer, so I said I wouldn't mind singing that again. We had a lot of fun and then got together to jam a few ideas; a couple of writing sessions went well and that was the start of me coming back."

The result was the 2012 album, *The King of Metal*.

"The music on it is great but the production and mastering got messed up," says Bayley, who for the first time was in the producer's seat on his own. "I was responsible for that but didn't do a good job. I learnt a lot from it, and stand by the songs, but it's not an easy album to listen to."

There was also a Wolfsbane reunion in 2011, a couple of tours along with fellow ex-Maiden singer Paul Di'Anno and a Best Of compilation in those early days of the

PART TWO **SOLO CAREERS**

new decade. Entitled *Soundtracks of my Life*, the double CD marked his 30th year in the business and included two new tracks. Bayley then teamed up with Manchester band Absolva.

"We did the *Soundtracks* tour and the anniversary for *Silicon Messiah*. Then decided to write for a studio album."

It was the first foray into a trilogy of records under the *Infinite Entanglement* banner, a concept linked to a book Bayley is writing. The records, the concept and the story are the most ambitious he has tackled in his career and bring together all his experience as a musician, a man and a seeker of wider truths.

"I wanted to do one original song for the *Soundtracks* album. I was compiling it with Rick Plester and we wrote and recorded a song together. While we were doing that we had another idea. That was called 'Eating Children.' The idea was that the sun at the centre of our solar system will one day die, and because it's a yellow dwarf it will become not a supernova but a red giant. It will become so big that it will consume other planets in the solar system.

"When that yellow dwarf formed, the planets are made of the debris left over from it. The yellow dwarf eats its own children. So if you know the sun will die and you have enough money you will go to find another planet.

"Who knows what we will discover in our own backyard, galactically-speaking?"

That concept is at the heart of *Infinite Entanglement*; the uber-rich will be seeking new planets to live on.

"They won't be having any heavy metal singers or journalists on that mission," Bayley counsels. "They are going to be very carefully selected. In a darker way, they are going to be the super-rich secret rulers of the world. They have to be persuaded to part with a great deal of their wealth."

There is also an incredibly insightful and intriguing layer to the project, he explains. It is related to the weird and wonderful world of quantum physics.

"The idea at the root of quantum physics, which makes no sense to anybody, is that two electrons are related and instantly know the position of its partner electron. So if atoms are comprised of electrons, particles are comprised of atoms, molecules are comprised of particles. So human beings have all this in them. So if two people are connected, if two people are deeply, deeply in love and connected, wouldn't they sense what was happening to the other person? Isn't that possible?"

And that is *Infinite Entanglement*'s kernel of narrative. Bayley says he was supposed to be writing sleevenotes for the compilation album but was working on what he thought was initially a short story. And that story became the concept for an album. And the album became a concept trilogy based on this sci-fi set of ideas. And the trilogy will become literature.

"I am planning to get the book out," Bayley explains.

The World is Not Ours

The artist and thinker signs off with an absolute zinger. The world, he assesses, has its priorities all wrong. And we are all suffering because of it.

"This is The Great Government Lie. Business, oil producers, whoever is behind it: the terrible lie that they fed us. That one per cent of people in the world control most of the wealth. In reality, if you just take our

IRON MAIDEN

small island as an example, the UK is the richest country in Europe – in wind.

"We have wind on our North Sea coastline. We have got stronger and more consistent waves on our coasts than anywhere in Europe. There are companies trying to develop wave power and tidal power; none of them are funded by the Government.

"The Government is not interested in free power. The Government is not interested in renewables until it becomes political. Windmills are turned off and they stop collecting power because it is too expensive to turn a gas or coal-fired power station on and off. There are no batteries to collect the power from wind turbines, so they turn them off.

"Basically, the clean energy that can be gathered from the environment is stopped. It is not used [...] Elon Musk has invented the batteries. Why isn't the Government buying them?

"This is the great lie. We can have [clean energy] but it is the political will [that is stopping it].

"The people in charge of the wealth in the world in my belief, if those people see their grandchildren gasping for breath they will do something about it."

A metal singer with intelligence? Someone who explores the possibilities of technology, energy and the future? Not so rare as you might think.

Indeed, not as rare in Iron Maiden circles as is often thought.

Viva Blaze. Long may his fire burn.

THE NEARLY-MEN – AUDITIONEERS

I was a teenage Maiden hopeful... how to audition for the biggest band in the world

It was the plum job; the pinnacle of any vocalist's ambition.

It was the position of lead singer in Iron Maiden.

Bruce's announcement of his parting with the band back in 1992 led to an absolute deluge of cassettes landing at Maiden HQ, all full of the work of hopeful singers looking to make the shortlist. It took a while to sort the wheat from the chaff, but sort it Maiden did and so the camp set about drawing up a shortlist of realistic candidates to fill the boots of the Air Raid Siren.

The Scottish Force of Nature

One of those was Douglas 'Doogie' White, whose extraordinary pipes had appeared as member of La Paz and a returning Praying Mantis for a Japanese tour. During March 1993, he recalls, he was in Belgium recording an album with an unnamed UK band.

PART TWO SOLO CAREERS

"[That band's] management were trying to have me sign a long-term, tie you in knots, forever and a day, I give you nothing, still you ask for more, kinda contract that I really did not want to sign," he says. "I was being put under a huge amount of pressure from the band and management but after previous management deals it was, for me, not going to happen.

"The matter was finally put to bed when I got phone calls from a couple of friends who told me that Bruce was leaving Maiden later in the year and that perhaps I should send a tape to Sanctuary and see what happened. I thought it was a brilliant idea. It made the rest of the recording a bit more difficult though."

White already knew Janick Gers and Bruce Dickinson, he said, but hadn't met Steve Harris. On his return to the UK, the singer delved into his back-catalogue for a handful of tracks that 'would give the powers that be an overview of what I could do.'

"I mixed them down onto a tape and added a wee picture, so they could see what I looked like, with a note saying who I was and what I had done and sent it in ... and waited and waited. I heard nothing. No acknowledgment that the tape had arrived. Nothing. For ages."

Then as he was getting ready one Friday night to catch a bus to visit family in Scotland, the imposing figure of Dickie Bell turned up at the door of Chez White, as he remembers.

"'Where the bloody hell do you think you're going, Scotsman?' he roared. I explained what was going on. 'Not bloody likely,' he replied as he handed me a tape and a book of lyrics. 'You will be singing with Iron Maiden on Monday. I will pick you up at 11am. Don't make me wait.'

"Two days in which to learn a bunch of songs I had never sung and some I barely knew. That was my mission and I accepted it. Of course, I had been working in secret, on my own, in the background just in case I got the shout. Still - listening and learning is NOT the same as singing and doing.

"Dickie picked me up at 11am prompt and quizzed me all the way from Chiswick to Steve's place in Harlow. Had I any criminal history? Drug convictions? A passport? Any outstanding management issues or contractual obligations? When we arrived, I was shown in through to the kitchen where the band were having tea, Hobnobs and Jaffa cakes. I was introduced to everyone, including crew, gardeners. Everybody. It was all very relaxed and friendly."

The band, says White, had the two recent live albums to draw on: *A Real Live One* and *A Real Dead One*, which he and the boys ran through dutifully in Steve Harris' studio/barn.

"They were set up in a circle and the vocals were to be done with me standing in the middle. That was odd for me as I had always had a set-up as if the band was on stage. I did not know where to look or who to turn my back on," says the singer.

"I settled with the drums behind me, so I would have some sense of normality and could watch the others and take any cues from anyone who offered them. It was loud and very powerful and must have been strange for them to hear someone who was not Bruce singing these songs for the first time. I was first to audition [that day] - and also the last. So, I was very aware of that. I was also concentrating on coming in at the right moment in the songs. 'Number of the Beast' caused a few moments of hilarity as I just could not find the start point. Arguably

IRON MAIDEN

their most famous song and I fucked it up. Not once, but twice."

A quick break followed, during which Harris and White had A Conversation (in capital letters...)

"Steve as cool as ever and me a sweaty nervous wreck. I thought I had done okay but now came the 'interview'.' It was very informal and friendly, but he was trying to get a bit of a handle on who I was, where I had been and what I was doing. He asked questions and I probably just babbled, such was the high I was on. I don't really remember much about that but do remember our birthdays are just a day apart, although in different years.

"After tea and Hobnobs we ran a few more songs. Then I was shown the bar and thanked for coming along and that they had more people to see but I would hear later how I had done and if I was successful or not.

"Dickie Bell ran me home and said I had done well ... 'for a Scotsman.'"

A second audition followed a while later, complete with more tea, more biscuits and more rocking out.

"Nicko did have a bruise on his head as he had played a gig the night before and banged his head on a mic," White says. "We ran the songs again and I was a little less uptight. I had been asked back. That was a good sign, right? Right? There was no indication from the band, crew or indeed the gardener as to how it was going or how I had done. I would just have to wait like everyone else to see which of us would be the next singer of the greatest metal band in the world."

History notes of course that Blaze Bayley was chosen for the coveted position a while later in the year.

"Steve called me personally and said how well I had done but they were going to go with Blaze Bayley as he had more the type of voice they were looking for," recalls the Scottish legend. "He was polite, thanked me again for my interest, the work put in to learn the songs and wished me luck in the future."

What neither of them realised was that White's path was to lead to glory regardless.

"[M]y future in the world of rock'n'roll was to take a dramatic turn with a phone call from the greatest of guitar players and my all-time hero (after Bowie). Ritchie Blackmore."

White subsequently joined Rainbow and has since worked with a number of high-profile rock and metal acts, including Yngwie Malmsteen's Rising Force, Tank and Demon's Eye. You can also hear his vocals on Maiden tribute album *666 The Number One Beast* and *A Tribute To Iron Maiden - Celebrating The Beast Vol. 1 (The Evil That Men Do)*. He rocks the fuck out of it, needless to say.

The Prog Star

Another auditionee was Damian Wilson, the Surrey-based singer of Landmarq and Threshold. He remembers that the series of events that led up to his own audition was one full of coincidence and mutual contacts.

"I first read about Bruce Dickinson leaving Iron Maiden in a tabloid paper I found lying on a tube train, as I headed to a band rehearsal in Acton, London. It was an article that mentioned their PR man Roland Hyams. I remember reading it and having a strange feeling I would be approached somehow," says Wilson.

"Bizarrely that evening I was playing an acoustic gig in Streatham. Roland, who I had never met before was there. When I came

PART TWO SOLO CAREERS

off stage he introduced himself to me and I mentioned I had read the announcement he put out that day. It all seemed such a coincidence to bump into him. We spent some time chatting and he suggested I'd be a great replacement for Bruce. He even pointed out the name Damien was an anagram of Maiden. On my birth certificate my name is spelt Damian, but my Mum commonly used to write my name with an 'e'.

"As Roland helped me get my DAF Variomatic car going, which had broken down outside the venue, he said he'd put in a good word for me."

Again, the trail went cold for several months before Wilson received a letter out of the blue from Dickie Bell, which asked him to contact Sanctuary Management. Later, Wilson received a phone call from who he thought was Landmarq's keyboard player.

"He was called Steve and lived in Dagenham and expressed he was trying to organise a meet-up at his place. I probably didn't come across as too enthusiastic as I was living way over the other side of London and beyond. As he started explaining how I was going to get to his place, I became confused. I knew exactly how to get to Steve Leigh's house - I'd been there many times before. Then the penny dropped and I realised this wasn't Steve from Landmarq I was talking to, but Steve Harris from Iron Maiden. I didn't let on, and we finished our conversation.

"Walking into the kitchen I put the kettle on to make a cup of tea and a big smile came across my face. I couldn't help thinking wow, that was Steve Harris asking if I'd like to jam with Iron Maiden. Then the phone rang again. I picked it up and I heard the voice on the other end say, 'Hi, this is Steve Harris here'. I said, 'Hi Steve, everything ok?' He said, 'Yes ... are you actually interested in joining Iron Maiden?'

"I had obviously come across as so blasé I think Steve thought I wasn't interested."

Wilson got on well with Bell, even meeting his wife at reception, before the party decamped to the house of Harris.

"I recall the fleet of Jags pulling up outside. Everyone was very accommodating, Steve was lovely and I had already met Nicko a few months prior in LA at the Foundation Forum, where I was playing with my band. I found myself chuckling at his rendition of events in Burbank as he informed his bandmates, that's why I looked so familiar to him.

"Being at Steve's place was a very special memory. I was thrilled to see his pub, football pitch, etc, but to play with the guys was amazing. I had been given a specially-prepared tape and a long list of songs to learn. As we played through them I remember getting to the end of 'The Trooper' and asking if we could play it again, which they obliged. It was simply such a blast to be singing those songs with Iron Maiden. A day I will never forget. They were just good decent guys and I warmed to every single one of them."

Of course, the media interest in the job was unparalleled, and Wilson agreed to stay tight-lipped and not talk to the press.

"So I kept as quiet as I could about the trip to everyone," laughs Wilson. "However, later that evening, in a bikers' pub, I found I couldn't help myself when a great-looking girl came up to me and asked me why I looked so tired. I told her I was exhausted, to which she responded, 'Why, what have you been doing all day?' I replied, 'Singing with Iron Maiden'.

IRON MAIDEN

"She simply let out an expletive and wrote me off as a liar."

Wilson's vision for the band, had he got the job, was to 'be [him]self, to own the stage, to get on with the guys, and do a great job.'

"Iron Maiden played Wembley Arena (May 17th, 1993) not so long after it was announced Bruce would be leaving. I had no tickets and no pass, but still managed to walk backstage and sit on a flight- case right outside Bruce Dickinson's dressing room door. I guess I just looked like one of them. He left it quite late to arrive for the show that day, but I wished him luck as he went on stage. A small part of me secretly thought, I could be running out with Iron Maiden next time they play Wembley."

Wilson spoke to Harris the day before Blaze Bayley's unveiling as the singer, although that fact was still being kept under wraps.

"He said they had decided on a replacement and sadly it wasn't me. I asked him who they had chosen, but he said he couldn't say," says the musician.

"I had a gig that night at the Mean Fiddler in Harlesden. I remember feeling a little deflated but when I heard the next day who they had chosen, I thought they had made the right choice.

"At the time, Blaze was really something on stage. My bandmates would go to Wolfsbane shows and would come back, blown away by how incredible he was. He'd toured with Maiden and although I may not be an authority, I believe Steve Harris wouldn't have looked anywhere else, had he thought that Blaze was up for it and available. I was very pleased to hear he got the job."

Wilson's adventures since then have included touring with Rick Wakeman, singing on several Ayreon albums, and solo work. He has also sung on Maiden uniteD releases; acoustic versions of Maiden's famous songs.

The Shortlist

Other vocalists that were said to have made the shortlist were Steve Grimmett from Grim Reaper, who has told reporters he was in the top-five (Grimmett declined to be interviewed for this book); Andre Matos, the Brazilian singer of Angra, who has subsequently said he wasn't ready for such a task; James LaBrie of Dream Theater (who declined an offer to audition); and Michael Kiske of Helloween. Kiske has, though, been very strident in noting that there was no truth to it. Apparently, Harris told a French magazine Kiske was one of only a few people he could imagine fronting Maiden, but aside from sharing the same management that was as far as it went. There were also rumours that Paul Di'Anno himself would rejoin – rumours shut down very quickly by Di'Anno himself.

As time has passed, a great many of these singers have recorded or played Maiden tracks live. A visit to time-sucking work-wrecking rabbit hole YouTube will bring up many, many videos of what the band could have sounded like had they chosen anyone other than Blaze Bayley. Pointless, of course, but a hell of a lot of fun ...

Photo credit: Ami Barwell

PART THREE: MAIDENOLOGY

IRON MAIDEN

3

"Music can bring back long-lost hope. I live with hope that humanity will realise that there is no beauty, or real satisfaction, in destruction but in creation instead".

Jasenko Pasic, writer, Scream for me Sarajevo

PART THREE: **MAIDENOLOGY**

PART THREE: MAIDENOLOGY

ROD SMALLWOOD

The Sheriff of Huddersfield

Rod was the catalyst that allowed Maiden to move into the big time. Using his experience and connections in the business he was able to break down barriers that many up and coming acts can't get through. He also used his own money during the early days while the band were waiting for record company advances for touring. I think without Rod, Maiden could still have done well, but not in the same timeframe and not to the same extent. Rod created the masterplan(s) that helped the band get to where they are. He dealt with the financial and legal aspects and kept the scammers away. He and Steve forged a formidable and successful partnership.
Keith Wilfort, former Iron Maiden fan club supremo

Roderick Charles Smallwood is what every band needs: a manager that will listen to them and implement what they need whilst protecting them from being taken advantage of. Moreover, any manager provides a vital buffer between ideas and practicality – the job can be anything from appearing on stage in an Eddie mask in the early years to developing potential aircraft-based world tours. These days, Smallwood oversees the vast Maiden empire and brings his experience and knowledge to every part of the music business. You name it, he's been there, done it, designed the t-shirt, sold it and reissued it 10 years later as a legacy limited-edition release.

Simply put, Maiden could not have envisaged the career they've had without a great manager; and Rod Smallwood is exactly that. The Yorkshireman met his future professional partner Andy Taylor whilst at university in Cambridge's storied Trinity College. The pair went on to book a host of acts for university events, including the rather awesome MC5. After spending some time in Paris, Smallwood worked for a booking agent and ended up managing Steve Harley & Cockney Rebel. The experience wasn't always a happy one – but no experience is ever wasted on the bright people, and Smallwood certainly falls into that category.

After the Harley job, a brief stint working with Gloria Mundi followed, but the prospect of returning to finish his degree in law took centre-stage in the late 1970s. That was blown out of the water, though, when Smallwood went to see a band playing in a smallish pub. This may have been on a recommendation from bass player Mark Percy, who insists he put the management team on to the band, but it must also be said that Maiden were making all kinds of waves at the time.

IRON MAIDEN

1

He is a powerhouse. He is a man of vision and boundless energy. He certainly doesn't suffer fools gladly. The drive of the band is all Steve Harris. It's his baby. He radiates it. Rod will go right out on a limb to make things work. It is a very powerful combination.
Roland Hyams, former Iron Maiden PR agent

Famously, that concert was somewhat stymied by singer Paul di'Anno, who inadvertently brought some equipment home from the job he was doing at the time. To whit: a rather large knife. Subsequently arrested, Di'Anno was to miss most of the gig and left Steve Harris to attempt the vocals. Never the best idea; talented on the low-end and the vision he may be, but singer not so much. Nonetheless, Smallwood saw enough in the group to get involved and duly became manager in 1979. He wasn't everyone's cup of tea, however, as guitarist Dennis Stratton explains.

"I found him a bit painful; a bit young for a manager," says Stratton, who joined the band based on the songs and played on the debut LP. "But he was serious, knew what he wanted, as was Steve."

As the 1980s progressed, Maiden's success did too, Taylor and Smallwood handling ever-more high-profile tours, gigs and events. The management company – Sanctuary – took on additional clients and continued to look after all aspects of the business. It floated on the Stock Exchange in 1998, expanded into a record label, booking agents, merchandising, artist management and contracts, and went from strength to strength. Notably, during Bruce Dickinson's solo spell, Sanctuary continued to manage the vocalist while Merck Mercuriadis was more hands-on with the day-to-day contact.

Smallwood is a savvy operator, adds Tony Platt, producer of notorious mis-step single, 'Women in Uniform.'

"Iron Maiden, when they put a single out, put out four or five versions of it on different colour vinyl, things like that," says Platt. "He was playing the system and as a result Gallup – the chart people at the time – stopped [people from putting out multiple versions that were all chart-eligible.]

"He had identified the fact that Maiden's fans can be at the completist end of the spectrum, and a large proportion would buy all five different versions. So he multiplied the sales quite dramatically.

"Rod Smallwood made Iron Maiden," he concludes. "He is the guy that actually put them on the map. His marketing strategy was absolutely brilliant."

Timing is also an extremely good knack to have; the release of 'Bring Your Daughter... to the Slaughter' on December 24th, 1990 made it eligible for the charts of the week following Christmas. This traditionally dead time for singles sales blew away all competition under the ferocious loyalty of Maiden fans' purchasing power (of course, a rather ace track from Bruce and Janick helped). Nonetheless it is another stroke of organisational genius that brought the group their first No.1 single.

There are few bands that have had such little mainstream attention yet have managed to inspire countless bands and still remain relevant some 30 years after their inception. But it's not just their music that has influenced other bands but also their fierce independence, their respect for their own fanbase and the mini-empire they have created with the people around them, such as manager Rod Smallwood.
Neil Daniels, journalist and author

PART THREE: **MAIDENOLOGY**

In 2006, Smallwood left the group to form Phantom Music Management with old pal Taylor, concentrating on Maiden and Maiden alone once more.

There aren't many rock managers that have songs written about them, but Smallwood certainly does. The 1986 single, 'Wasted Years' had a B-side called 'The Sheriff of Huddersfield' – a reference to the manager's move to Los Angeles. And there's even a rap from the man himself.

Suffice to say, some people are born singers, and some people are born managers.

EDDIE

The Death and Life of Edward the Great

The sixth (or seventh, these days) member of Iron Maiden is simply an icon that transcends even the music.

We speak, of course, of Eddie. The monstrous, larger-than-life dude has been a part of Maiden's aesthetic for 40 years now, appearing first on the cover of the band's 1980 debut album. The punky, challenging figure that stares out of that LP cover was created by artist Derek Riggs. It was inspired by the wasted youth of the punk scene in the tail-end of the 1970s, Riggs – who these days has his own website at www.derekriggs.com - wanting to portray the nihilism of the streets. Initially, the character was called Electric Matthew; the painting's name was *Electric Matthew Says Hello.*

As the story goes, the management of Maiden was looking for a striking image that would make the band's LP as memorable as possible. Riggs had made a cover for Buckinghamshire keyboardist Max Middleton, which caught the Maiden camp's eye. They duly met with Riggs and selected the *Electric Matthew* pic. At this juncture, Iron Maiden were already an established act, as was the prop known as Eddie the 'Ead, created by the pyrotechnics-obsessed Dave 'Lights' Beazley to cover the stage in blood and then smoke. Essentially a mask on a background, it became a signature of Maiden's act and was an obvious choice to extrapolate on to the new lead character; hence Matthew became Eddie, and a cult was born.

Dave Lights takes up the story.

"When Maiden went along for their first deal with EMI they saw a lot of people's artwork. The first album cover, from what the guys have told me, they saw [the Derek Riggs artwork] and said, 'Whoa, fuck me, it's Lightsy.' I had spiky hair and would dye it back then, and that's one of the reasons they went with Derek."

Dougie Sampson, drummer, remembers the trials and tribulations of having a head spitting blood all over you when you're trying to play gigs.

"When Maiden had Dennis [Willcock] in the early days he was very theatrical," says

IRON MAIDEN

Sampson. "He had blood capsules; blood everywhere pouring out of his mouth. Proper theatrical stuff that you'd use on TV plays and that. When he left there was a big hole in the stage act. It was not Di'Anno's thing – he was not gonna start dripping blood out, no way. It wasn't for Paul, that sort of act.

"Dave Lights came up with a rectangular box with 100-watt bulbs all the way round it. There was a mask and the name 'Iron Maiden.' Attached to it was a windscreen wiper pump from a car. That was [wired up to] the [mixing/lighting] desk; when you pressed a button all the lights would come on and flash, during the song, 'Iron Maiden.' And blood would come out of its mouth."

"Generally it would come out all over my head, because I was sitting under it."

It didn't have a name at the time, says Sampson, but there was a much bigger prop to follow which spelt out the band's name in mosaic, mirrored glass.

"It didn't do the blood, much to my relief. Smoke came out of it, and it was quite impressive. The next stage, Eddie got born."

The name was associated with an old joke: a kid is born, healthy but no body. Just a head. He grows up, does what he can, gets to school and all that. Just a head: no body. No arms, legs, torso: nothing. Just a head. But he does alright. It gets to Eddie's 18th birthday and his mum says, 'I've got you a present,' and Eddie opens it with his teeth before saying, 'Ah not another fucking hat.'

Quickly, Eddie took form, first appearing on stage courtesy of members of management dressed simply in a mask and jacket. By *The Beast on the Road*, Eddie had grown to about 10 feet tall and would totter around on stage; as the band's budgets improved, so did the ability of the band to create ever-more-elaborate versions.

The huge walk-on Eddie was inspired, Dave Lights says, by an exposition at Earl's Court in 1981 or 1982.

"In the early days Rod Smallwood used to come out with the Eddie mask on, get on the stage, then we wondered where we could take Eddie from there."

"I went to a thing at Earl's Court, a big theatre place with [important, professional] people in the theatre showing off what they could do with backdrops and stuff. There was a theatre show on with massive, big animals as part of it. I suddenly saw this guy's artwork there, he had one of these massive big furry things, and I thought, 'That would be great for Eddie. That would be fantastic as the Iron Maiden walk-on.'

"They still use him today, the same ideas I originally came up with back in the day. They still follow that pattern. It's nice to see they can't come up with better ideas!"

Maidenology being what it is, there are many different versions of what is accepted as 'the truth' – Dave Lights is happy to set the record straight as to the initial inspiration for the walking Eddie.

"It wasn't *Jack in the Beanstalk*," he says, firmly.

"[The Internet often perpetuates stories that are] incorrect but once it's out there...

"I did see a theatre show, but the story was elaborated on. It was an exhibition with people showing what they could do, at Earl's Court; I can't remember what it was, but it was a huge animal basically."

Now Eddie was on the artwork, on stage and part of the set itself.

"I designed the *Powerslave* stage-set and came up with the idea of 'Eddie-on-a-stick'," Dave Lights remembers. "The one that came out over the drum-kit. I was told [by

PART THREE: **MAIDENOLOGY**

other lighting engineers] I couldn't do that and asked why not, as usual. It's a cherry-picker, which people use to change street lights, with a bucket on it. I got Charlie Cowell, who did all the stage-sets for me, and we made that. If someone says I can't do something it makes me want to do it all the more. Then there was the fibreglass Eddie head – it came in four bits and was 27 feet high. It was massive!"

"The *Powerslave* tour was mega, theatrically and visually, a massive, 75ft-across rig in sports arenas. After a few months on that tour you were like a robot on remote control. So I started designing and coming up with ideas for the next tour. I would sit there thinking about how to make Eddie even bigger, and that's when I came up with the idea of turning the whole stage-set into the Ed Monster. I was involved in the concept of where Eddie was going: should we do it Egyptian, you know."

"I worked quite closely with Derek Riggs. The band would come up with the idea of what the album was going to be about, then Rod would go to Derek for the artwork, then I'd get Derek to produce work for me for the construction of the different elements. I'd take that to people who made backdrops, inflatables and so on. Derek a lot of the time was given a brief, which he'd follow through and send back, then he'd be asked to [tweak things or] change it. On my side he'd do drawings for the construction or backdrops. I put loads of Egyptian books and the late Dave Perry came up with loads."

"On the *Somewhere in Time* tour where Eddie fights with Bruce and there's all the pyrotechnics, I came up with all the ideas for that as well. Generally, when the band would start the tour certain songs wouldn't flow one into the other, so I'd say, "Ah, this would work if you did it this way instead," and the band might change the position in the set so [the production] worked better. It's like a movie: the beginning of it you want the audience to go, "Whoa!" so the first three songs are full-on and then you take it down slightly, change the look or the backdrop, then another few numbers that are "Whoa!" and you have a beginning, a middle and an end: you take the audience through the highs and bring them down again. You have to keep the audience interested and can't go full-on all the time."

THIS DAY IN MUSIC'S GUIDE TO **IRON MAIDEN** 217

IRON MAIDEN

Eddie's able to carry the artwork of the band on his desiccated shoulders, his development over the years following closely the aesthetic of the music. *Powerslave*, for example, has a definite hint of Ancient Egypt about it and Eddie appears as an enormous Sphynx on the cover. The concept has carried on throughout the band's career, although Riggs stepped back in the early 1990s from creating Eddies. Other artists/modellers include Melvyn Grant, Mark Wilkinson, Hugh Syme, Tom Adams, Tim Bradstreet, Anthony Dry and David Patchett, while animated Eddies have been created by Bob Cesca for various videos. Riggs went on to work with Bruce Dickinson's solo work *Accident of Birth*, on which the character Edison was first shown. Edison, a kind of Mr. Punch gone badly gnarly, can also be read as ... Eddie's Son. Surely a coincidence. Riggs has also worked with The Iron Maidens and a host of other bands over the years. Another member of Eddie's family popped up courtesy of Aces High, a Vegas-based Maiden tribute band. Designed by Riggs, the character bore a definite family resemblance – but different – and is named Teddie. The artist also designed much of the backdrop and stage-sets for the band, who played as support to Paul Di'Anno in January 2011.

There is much to be discovered in Maiden artwork. *Somewhere in Time* is possibly the most famous example; Easter Eggs abound – the gatefold sleeve in particular has a plethora of Maiden quotes, song references, cultural shouts out and jokes to discover. Just the thing for a rainy day listening to records and musing on life's strange beauty.

The ever-moving Eddie is also a rather good piece of controversy-generating fodder: the 'Sanctuary' and 'Women in Uniform' singles featured Margaret Thatcher, first being loomed over by a knifed-up Eddie, then the Iron Lady lurking to wait for her nemesis to get revenge. The *Twilight Zone* single drew criticism for its alleged misogyny; *Maiden Japan* originally had Eddie holding up Paul Di'Anno's decapitated head. That was withdrawn, so the tale goes, because the singer was likely to be let go from the band soon after the 1981 tour and EP release. That didn't stop Maiden skewering the similarly-departing Bruce Dickinson on the front of 1993 live single, 'Hallowed Be Thy Name,' of course. Ed also had something to say about Robert Maxwell on 'Be Quick or Be Dead' and hangs out with Jessica Rabbit on one of the 'Bring Your Daughter ... to the Slaughter' singles. Well, who wouldn't? Roger was punching way above his weight there for sure.

It was *The Number of the Beast*, though, that really got under the skin of some nobhead Yank religious nuts. Essentially it shows Eddie pulling the strings of the Devil himself, who is in turn pulling the strings of a mini-Eddie. This was alleged 'proof' of the band's Satanism; but hey ho, ya know. Who's pulling whose strings? It's art. And, yes, it ain't half good publicity for a band trying to break America. Again, who is pulling whose strings?

It's impossible to think of Maiden without Eddie. He's not only an excellent t-shirt-selling image, but a character you can play on computer games. He might be one day lumbering around the stage, trading blows with guitarists, then appearing on the tail-fin of Ed Force One. And, brilliantly, Eddie has won a Metal Hammer Golden God Award in his own right: 2008's 'Icon' Award.

For a No Future-esque punk once named Matthew, the zombie has had quite some career. Long may he reign...

PART THREE: **MAIDENOLOGY**

I Was a Teenage Monster: Confessions of Maiden's Stig ...

Eddie is famously taciturn, preferring to make his point by displaying his pleasure – or displeasure – through the band's artwork. Think of the 'Women in Uniform' single, 'Number of the Beast' 7", or, indeed, the mega-intricate references of *Somewhere in Time*. However, he does appear onstage in every gig the band do. We asked ex-Maiden head of stage production Jeff Williams to intercede with Eddie on our behalf, as he knows the monstrous hoodlum of metal better than most. From the inside out, you might even say.

Being Eddie

"Yes, it's true - I was Eddie on every tour between about 1995 through to late 2001. When I left Maiden, I was the only Eddie who had never fallen over! It did come close at one or two shows. Janick used to run through my legs then jump up and hit me in the face with his guitar."

"One particular show, the stage rake was pretty severe and a slight knock sent me stumbling towards the front edge, where my foot hit Bruce's monitor wedges. You can't see your feet inside that thing and I was flailing inside that contraption and knew I was going over. My eyes were fixated on the barrier, just about in the right place for a broken neck. Wally Grove grabbed a bunch of security in the pit to get ready to catch me, but Janick, my dancing partner, ran under me and wrapped an arm tight around my leg and held on long enough for me to regain my balance. Love that guy!"

What's it like inside Eddie?

"It's heavy, it's hot, and it's hard work. I had to go out to a farmhouse where Hangman create all this stuff, and they had me stand in front of a giant grid where they took photos from every angle, measuring legs, arms, even head size. From that, they built the Eddie around me. Amazing stuff. I went back for a fitting some weeks later, they made some adjustments, then came to production rehearsals and the first few shows, making adjustments and refinements along the way. Then we were away. I'd never walked on stilts before, never mind doing it wearing the body weight of two or three other people whilst walking on stilts! That took some practise. We had a great team. We had The Eddie House upstage, far stage right. A big metal framed tower draped in blackout cloth. Inside were three staggered platforms at various levels to enable me to get my stilts on the guys dressing me to access Eddie head to toe. By the time the head went on, you were already soaked through with sweat. It's like an oven in there."

Where can Eddie go?

"It was pretty much up to me where I went, but obviously you're not going to go stand in front of Bruce at the front. I think it only took a couple of gigs for us all to settle into a loose routine, so we knew where everyone was on stage. It's safer that way, the bridge would open, I'd walk on and stop as if I was deciding which one to go at, the crowd go wild and you take a few steps towards Dave and take a swipe at him. Bruce would run past and I'd take a swipe

IRON MAIDEN

at him and he'd run up the drum-riser and onto the rear platform out the way. Then me and Jan would get down the front for a fight. I'd swipe at him and duck, he'd run through my legs, hit me in the face with his guitar, etc., then hold his guitars up for Eddie to strum."

But what a thrill, right?

"Yeah, that was such a strange but exhilarating feeling. To walk on stage and have 100,000 people roar and cheer with every gesture you make is indescribable, but then it's strange because it's not actually anything to do with you. They're all looking right at you, but all they see is a 14ft monster!"

THE KILLER KREW

Killing it backstage

Every band needs 'em. Indeed, without them, the gigs would never go ahead, at least not if you have anything of a stage show. Lights, technicians, front of house, monitors, heads spitting blood, driving, loading in, loading out, changing strings, cooking meals, changing hotel rooms, taking care of blown tweeters and finding green Smarties at 3am in the middle of nowhere ... it's all about the background staff.

The crew that travels with Maiden these days is necessarily large - trucks full (and sometimes jumbo jets). Sets need building; Eddies need animating; everything has to be exactly correct way before soundchecks are done – and the crew even takes care of ensuring the band members' signature sound and set-up are spot-on too.

Iron Maiden's family of workers is known as the Killer Krew, and their hard work and skills are intrinsic to realising the vision of the band. Loopy Newhouse was a member of that early gang of reprobates and miscreants.

"The original Killer Krew was me - drums, Pete Bryant - guitars, Vic Vella - front of house sound and Dave Beazley - lights," recalls Loopy. "As the band became bigger, we employed a lot more staff, but I can't remember a lot of them or their jobs.

"Most days would usually start with a long drive somewhere, followed by setting up and sound checking. Then it was time to try and find something to eat or hit a pub and fill up with crisps.

"Show time and taking down came next, followed by the long journey home. Of course, as the shows got bigger, we were ferried to and from each venue. Load-in times were usually around 8am and the load-out was usually done by about 1.30-2am. The bit in between remained pretty much the same routine. It wasn't as glamorous as people might think, and we didn't have much time to get drunk, due to the hours we had to work."

Sounds a pain in the proverbial, doesn't

PART THREE: **MAIDENOLOGY**

it? No sleep, loads of heavy lifting, no time to see the countries you're in aside from tour buses, the odd hotel room if you're lucky, and the inside of cavernous venues. So why do it? Loopy sums it up with six simple words:

"I wouldn't swap it for anything."

Dave Lights really gets his teeth into it when you ask him about what's involved, logistically.

"I designed all the stage-sets, special effects and lighting rigs from *The Number of the Beast* onwards," he recalls. "We rented that equipment but after that I decided that if we were going to be touring this much we'd be better off owning it, then I could design stuff that I wanted, stuff nobody else had done.

"Everybody had the same stuff in the lighting world. Nobody was doing anything different. On *Piece of Mind* was when we owned lighting and started buying our sound equipment. It gave us the opportunity to do things other lighting companies weren't investing in. They were quite happy having the same old shit, sending it out year in, year out and making money on it. Soon as I started designing new stuff, putting rigs on grips, which nobody else had done, other bands would go to the companies and want what Iron Maiden had. Then the lighting companies had to start spending money on upgrading their old stock.

"There were some bands out there doing stuff differently – Judas Priest for instance, with The Open Road and Wilson from Medialights, who we rented our gear from originally. Priest were doing bits of extra lighting that nobody had at the time and that's where I took my inspiration, plus the Motörhead bomber which moved up and down. Kiss also had a theatrical show. I wanted to do something nobody else had done.

"The way people did it back then was with a SuperLift Genie, originally used on building sites to lift pallets of bricks onto scaffolding – you'd take the lighting rigs up that way. You'd get up on there and focus each individual lamp where you wanted it. When I was up doing that I thought there had to be a better way of doing it. So we came up with a ground support system along with The Open Road and Wilson from Medialights. It had a grid, a solid metal structure, that you lifted up on legs, and underneath that I had lighting trusses I could put into different shapes, like triangles on the *Piece of Mind* one.

"All the lamps in that were actually pre-focused, so I didn't have to get up there and focus them individually. They all had motors on them, so each triangle had three motors and I could move them up and down in the show [and get the right focus]. When we had a backdrop up, the lighting rig would be flat up to the top of the ceiling, then on other songs with a black backdrop I could drop in the lighting from different angles and get different focuses. You could move it around and have as many focuses as you liked. Also, it looked spectacular, having two, three, four tons of aluminium and lighting moving around, smoke, dry ice – it just looks great and no-one else was doing it at that point."

"I remember people saying, when I came up with the ideas to do this, it couldn't be done. I said, 'Well, who said that? Who's going to tell me what's possible or not? Just because it's not been done before doesn't mean I can't do it' It was the same when we used different lamps in the actual light itself – like an ACL, basically an aircraft landing light – and you'd put eight of those together."

IRON MAIDEN

Life on the Edge

You can find out a lot more about what's involved with what these brilliant guys do as a matter of course on a bonus disc with the *En Vivo* DVD. Behind every great band, there's a great stage crew. Behind Iron Maiden, perhaps there's the best there's ever been. Hard-working, creative, able to be flexible where needed: just a few traits needed. Being a decent footballer may help, too.

It's also a gruelling ol' business. Dave Lights remembers being taken right to the edge by the ludicrously-long 1980s' tours.

"I took so much on, so much stress, employing people on those tours – and it took its toll on me. I left in '87, '88 and they were still doing massive tours. The shortest was 10 months, then there was a couple of 12 months and a 14-month tour. They basically toured for 10 years with just a three-month spell off between each. With the *Powerslave* tour we went around the world twice. I was only actually in my house in London for one or two days, which was Christmas.

"It was fucking hard work, and obviously drugs came into it a lot, drinking and all that. In America we were doing one-nighters, not two or three shows at each venue. We were literally going in, putting up the show, doing the show, taking it down for six days of the week and the seventh day was meant to be a day off. Which it wasn't, because there would be a thousand-mile drive. There was no way you couldn't take stuff to just be able to do that. Not just me, the majority of the crew as well.

"I also got divorced, which didn't help my mental state. It took its toll on us. We had crew members just saying they couldn't do it, it was too long; we replaced quite a lot of backline guys, sound people, not just the lighting. It was gruelling. I look back on it now and wonder how the fuck we ever did it. The only person left from the old days is Mike Kenney. Nobody else is there anymore."

Dave Lights was in talks to return for the first tour with Blaze, but the damage had been done after he parted ways with the Maiden camp in 1988, two weeks before the end of the *Somewhere in Time* tour.

"They are ruthless," he says. "Absolutely ruthless. Once you're out, you're out. You're not part of the family.

"I worked for Prince after Maiden, and Sabbath, Dio, lots of stuff, TFI Fridays, the Hampton Court Festival for nine seasons. I lit the Palace up with over 2,000 lamps, lighting up gargoyles, chimneys and the whole lot. I did house lighting at the London Astoria for years. Loads of stuff - Princess Diana's memorial, the Millennium Dome."

Oh, and if you ever want to know how to spend a hundred grand in the last four minutes before Maiden take the stage, Dave Lights Beazley has a great tale of inflatables to tell ...

Anyhoo, next time you see one of the Killer Krew looking in need of a refreshment, please buy them one. In their absence, there'd be no enormous Eddie, no amazing light show, no stage-sets, no cauldrons, no decent sound ... and no legendary gigs. Big up da Krew!

Boys on Film

Iron Maiden have always had an eye for the visual. From the very earliest blood-spattering antics of Den Willcock and the notorious head-backdrop all the way through to their massive stage-sets, walking Eddies and ace videos, the pictures have been very important to the package.

PART THREE: **MAIDENOLOGY**

As you'd expect then, there are many videos, DVDs and live performances authorised by the group, some of which are essential and some ... well. Beauty is in the eye of the beer holder, and all that.

The band's first released video was *Live at the Rainbow*, recorded on December 21st, 1980 at a gig by the lads at, well, the Rainbow Theatre in London. It was released on EMI's video division, titled PMI (i.e. Picture Music International, rather than the EMI acronym which was Electric and Musical Industries, fact fans). Back in 1981, when the video was released, it was cutting edge technology and not everyone had access to a video player. It was a pretty brave move – or perhaps a confident one – by a group plugging their debut album. The seven songs on there include 'Killers,' on which Paul Di'Anno is more or less making it up as he goes along, plus the dual blast of 'Phantom of the Opera' and 'Iron Maiden'. Those latter two tracks had to be re-recorded due to technical problems in the show itself. At a touch over 31 minutes, it's a bit of a short sharp shock, but for fans not old enough to have been there in those halcyon days/too drunk to remember those halcyon days it's excellent, not least for the fact that it's the only live video officially released with Clive Burr on drums. You can also see this on disc one of *The History of Iron Maiden – Part 1: The Early Days*, released in 2004.

By 1983 the band was absolutely flying and had started to build up a repertoire of promo videos. In these days of instantly-available work by any band, anywhere, on any number of visual formats, it's hard to believe it was necessary to buy or even rent something like *Video Pieces*, Maiden's 1983 release of four videos. For your money you got 18 minutes and four songs: 'Run to the Hills,' 'The Number of the Beast,' 'Flight of Icarus' and 'The Trooper. As with the majority of Maiden's promo videos for songs, there's a whole lot of live footage, or staged live footage as the case may be. Moments captured forever for the young band, for whom Bruce Dickinson was now up front and Nicko McBrain introduced for 'Flight' and 'Trooper.'

A year later, Maiden stepped things up considerably with *Behind the Iron Curtain*. It was, and is, a ground-breaking look into the band behind the songs, with footage offstage and interviews with band members. It was also ground-breaking in another sense: not many groups from Western Europe would tour in countries of Eastern Europe at that time. The so-called 'Iron Curtain' separated the Eastern European states annexed under the communist/fascist rule of the then Union of Soviet Socialist Republics, and the democratic states that were truly independent following the Second World War. An extended version of this one was broadcast on MTV but unavailable commercially until the release of the *Live After Death* DVD in 2008. Speaking of which ...

There are awesome live albums, and there are legendary ones. Think of *Live at Leeds* by The Who, Deep Purple's *Made in Japan*, Thin Lizzy *Live and Dangerous*, Motörhead's *No Sleep Til Hammersmith* or the gory *The Osmonds Live* as examples (maybe not the last one, but hey ho). Iron Maiden took their place in the pantheon of greats with the absolutely stonking *Live After Death*, released as a beautiful double LP in an astonishing gatefold sleeve where Derek Riggs' art is at its finest. The songs were recorded at Long Beach Arena between March 14th and 17th, 1985, plus five at London's Hammersmith Odeon from October 8th to 12th, 1984. The

IRON MAIDEN

songs featured are from the albums up to and including *Powerslave* and show the band absolutely at their best. The DVD version, 23 years later, also included an hour-long documentary continuing the history, the full MTV *Iron Curtain* doc, a 1985 gig at the first day of Rock in Rio, where Maiden supported Queen, and a great little quarter-hour candid video of soundchecks and interviews in San Antonio, Texas, from 1983. Cor.

The band kept up the pace the next year with another release, *12 Wasted Years*, which made even more of the now-ubiquitous VHS format. A blend of promo videos, live and *Top of the Pops* appearances, German TV shows and interviews, there's a lot for fans to get their teeth into. It even includes the promo video for the ill-advised 'Women in Uniform' cover, a rare mis-step for earlyish Maiden. If you squint, you might just be able to spot a soon-to-be-booted-out Dennis Stratton on that one. This release was unavailable until 2013, when it was released as part of the DVD version of the next entry in our series, 1989's *Maiden England*. Speaking of which (again) …

Another breakthrough of sorts came courtesy of Steve Harris' utter commitment to getting everything absolutely right as regards the band. Previously, the lads had been only lightly involved with the production side of their videos and Harris wanted to rectify that by both directing and editing the next one. It was an attempt to capture the experience of a Maiden fan at a gig, and Harris spent a good six months working on it at home in Essex in his specially-installed edit suite. Again, it was re-released – as *Maiden England '88* – as part of a reissue in 2013. Part three of the *History* also appears on that 2013 disc.

Next up was the November 1990 *The First Ten Years: The Videos*, which is exactly that; it was re-released in 1992 for the American market to include five new tracks from *Fear of the Dark*. And then we're back to purely

live stuff with *Donington Live 1992*. The gig was attended by about 80,000 people in August that year and the video also features a guest appearance from recently-departed guitarist Adrian Smith, on 'Running Free.' It's probably the best document of the Dickinson-Gers-Murray-Harris-McBrain line-up and shows not a hint of disunity. Maiden always stepped up to the plate when it mattered most and are at full throttle throughout. By the time we got to August the following year, Dickinson's imminent break with the band was out there for all to see. And to mark his leaving, Maiden decided to put the singer in a prop Iron Maiden,

PART THREE: **MAIDENOLOGY**

doing away with him forever courtesy of Simon Drake, a stage magician. Elsewhere in the concert, Dave Murray got his hands chopped off and several crew members were similarly erased from existence, or at least that's how it looked. No animals or metallers were harmed in the making of *Raising Hell*, of course, which was recorded at Pinewood Studios and first broadcast by MTV in America, and live in the UK on pay-per-view telly. A shade under two hours, *Raising Hell* kind of harks back to the Willcock days in spirit, although the budgets were obviously much bigger in 1993.

Millennium Big

Something a little classier was the 2001 edition of *Classic Albums*, a series that ran on UK television for around 20 years. The shows brought together the production, engineering, sonic and management team along with the musicians responsible for the albums. They'd go back to the studio, often the one where it was recorded, and listen again to the master tapes. This both revealed the way songs came together as well as brought up a few surprises from long-lost extra layers of tracking that may have been left off the original, released mixes. Previous participants in the series had included Paul Simon, for his *Graceland* album, The Jimi Hendrix Experience (with one obvious exception) for *Electric Ladyland* and The Who, who checked back in with *Who's Next*. The blend of ace music, analysis and interviews was built on open dialogue with the full participation of the bands themselves, and as such provides excellent insight into exactly how these seminal pieces of work were made. In Maiden's case, the group looked at *The Number of the Beast*. It's a stormer, this one,

with footage from an Autumn 1982 show as well as plenty of chat with the band – and Clive Burr, who announced publicly for the first time he had MS. As an entry point for anyone to the classic era of Maiden, this can't be bettered. Seek it out.

Maiden's millennium efforts have been ever-more intricate, the DVD format allowing for bigger, better and deeper adventures into the blend of the sonic and visual. Dean Karr was hired to direct the group's concert at Rock in Rio, the last show of the *Brave New World* tour. Karr had previously worked with Maiden on the video for *The Wicker Man*, and used 18 cameras to make sure things were hunky-dory. That said, equipment does have a mind of its own sometimes; many shots of Adrian Smith and Dave Murray were lost along the way. No matter. Despite not wanting to initially take care of the edit, Steve Harris decided to step in when things started going awry. It took him a while, but *Rock In Rio* is suitably huge as a result. Extras include interviews, a day with Maiden, shots by Ross Halfin, and more.

The promo videos were collated once more for 2003's *Visions of the Beast*, plus some animated additions and extras accessed by ... well. Look, we have to keep some things mysterious. But it's fairly easy. Regardless, you wouldn't want to buy this plus either of the preceding collections of videos that came out: one is probably enough, unless you're a completist. Los Angeles filmmaker, critic and movie expert Brian Wright put the release into context. "In 1992, the seminal director of photography film *Visions of Light* debuted, featuring 100 years of ground-breaking, important cinematography," says Wright. "No Iron Maiden videos would make the film. However, the East London metal

IRON MAIDEN

Photo credit: Ami Barwell

band could make a counterpart, sub-genre documentary, focusing on their live shows and music videos featuring their own brand of 40 years of heavy metal, titled *Visions of The Beast*.

"This is, essentially, what the visuals of this band amount to - possibly the most potent audio/visual combo in music or cinema, showcasing Eddie the Head, Iron Maiden's mascot. There is no Maiden without Eddie, which is to say the sound is he, he is the sound. A culmination of sorts took place in the band's 2015 genre-bending music video for 'Speed of Light,' which is a must-see for any fan of the band/music/cinema/gaming/you-name-it."

In 2004 things stepped up again with the much-anticipated *The History of Iron Maiden – Part 1: The Early Days*. It brought together loads of ex-members for the first time in decades to discuss the nascent days of Maiden, with all the line-up changes, difficulties, triumphs, disasters and hilarious moments. With four concerts from 1980-82 included, the release hit home on every level. There were also *Top of the Pops* videos, promos, photos, artwork and even a 1981 documentary called *20th Century Box*. This, along with the *Classic Albums* release, is essential for anyone interested in the band at any level.

Three guitarists, and now a triple DVD: *Death on the Road* came out in 2006. Again it included a documentary, this time tracking the band recording the album *Dance of Death*, with plenty of interviews, tour insight, fans' viewpoints and crew chat to keep people up to speed. It's clear from the performances alone that Maiden had definitely got new momentum from the return of Dickinson and Smith, and the six-piece band was also finding ways to successfully accommodate the additional guitarist. Moreover, promo videos from 'Wildest Dreams' and 'Rainmaker' were available, making it another excellent package for those who couldn't get there and a superb addition to the memories of the fans who did attend.

Something entirely different is *Flight 666*, the amazing 2009 release that tracked dates on the *Somewhere Back in Time* tours of 2008. Indeed, each track was recorded at a different venue and the consistency of

PART THREE: **MAIDENOLOGY**

excellence is astonishing. With Captain Paul Bruce Dickinson at the helm of the flight deck, this is an unprecedented piece of work that transcends genre. Whilst some band-related movies can be unintentionally boneheaded and quite hilarious (cf. *Some Kind of Monster*) and others gritty tales of striving against all odds (cf *Anvil! The Story of Anvil*) the Maiden camp brought together every single shred of talent to create a timeless piece of work. The group plays like demons, the cinematography is beautiful: no wonder it won awards, including the '24 Beats per Second' for best music documentary at South by Southwest Film & Music Festival in 2009. In contrast to the *Early Days* documentaries, this was a view of how things had progressed into the stratospheric heights of fame. That it is – more or less – the same band is mind-blowing. A huge, huge hit.

The band have of late started to create mirror releases for their official albums in the form of subsequent live LPs and DVDs, as proved by 2012's *En Vivo*, which tracked the tour for *The Final Frontier*. The *Flight 666* team were taking care of the tech for this one, which comprised scenes from the Santiago, Chile gig as its main source material. Another one-and-a-half-hour documentary, *Behind the Beast*, features interviews with band and crew, with the intent to showcase the logistics of getting the enormous show set up and successfully delivered. The amount of moving parts involved in the process is a real eye-opener; that Maiden felt confident enough at this stage to break the fourth wall and let the audience into their world is notable. The next year, the *Maiden England '88* DVD was reissued.

Finally (at the time of writing) *The Book of Souls: Live Chapter* came out in 2017, comprising live versions of the group's tour to coincide with the enormous double album that surprised even many long-term Maiden-heads. Again, tracks were recorded at different venues worldwide and showed audiences from Donington to Buenos Aires headbanging; Tokyo crowds and Tristese music fans having the time of their lives; Montreal and Canada separated only by geography. The clever juxtaposition of venues speaks loudly to the transcendent nature of heavy metal, and specifically to the worldwide family that makes up an Iron Maiden crowd.

As Brian Wright put it, "Maiden's live show videos seemed to have struck an ever-deeper chord than their music videos by offering fans a deeper, more intimate look into not only their impressive live shows and world tour, [but] also the consistency and talent these guys as players (and people) have. What crosses cultures, in both the UK and US, is the idea of a blue-collar band sticking to their guns, not selling out, bringing their unique brand of metal and mayhem to every single fan at every single show.

"*Flight 666* proves it on the world stage, *Maiden England* for the home crowd, and *Rock in Rio* in one of the great music cities of the globe, Rio de Janeiro, Brazil. The pattern in all the live show videos is: show up, level the crowd, keep going. We're now 40 years into their music, with over 100 million records sold, and in some ways it seems like we're just getting started."

IRON MAIDEN

THE CHEMICAL WEDDING

The Beast, reborn

In 2008, *Chemical Wedding* was finally released. The movie had been mooted for several years and had passed through the hands of many different producers, including Terry Jones, of Monty Python. Finally, it ended up with Bill & Ben Productions and Focus Films, in conjunction with Duellist Film Production, Motion FX and E-Motion.

The movie, something of a Hammer horror homage, is based around the story of a Cambridge scholar, Oliver Haddo, possessed by the late Aleister Crowley following an incident in a Virtual Reality chamber. Crowley/Haddo starts to find ways to meddle with occult forces he doesn't understand. It meanders around through various theological, physical, scientific, alchemical themes, not stopping for a moment in its bizarro trip round the inside of a strange and wonderful mind.

All in all, LA filmmaker, journalist and critic Brian Wright says the film may not have made anyone's lists as top movie of the year.

"But it was an inspired effort that expanded the palette of all Maiden fans," he says. "To be fair, it's profoundly better than fellow metalhead Dee Snider's *Strangeland*, the Twisted Sister singer's first foray into film a decade earlier."

Other rock and metal artists have had a crack at this movie business, says Wright of the Simon Callow-fronted picture.

"Rob Zombie, creative force behind White Zombie and a half-dozen highly-stylised goth-horror genre pictures, may have set the tone for talent coming from metal to movies, but even he's batting about .500. Where Snider may have gone for gore and relied too heavily on shock value, and Zombie on quick cuts and hand-held camera work (and also over-gore), at least Dickinson reached into the rich real-life history of famous English occultist Aleister Crowley.

"Kudos to him for even trying to put pen to paper, and finding a heck of a director (Monty Python alum and *Life of Brian* editor Julian Doyle) and a healthy independent budget of $3.5 million."

Dickinson himself has a couple of cameos in the final movie, as you'd expect. The soundtrack features songs by a number of musicians, from Maiden and Dickinson's solo stuff to Handel, Debussy and Mozart. There's even a place for a song called 'Fanlight Fanny' by gore-thrash bloodthirsty monster of

PART THREE: **MAIDENOLOGY**

demonic black metal, George Formby.

You can see the madness and magic alike for yourself by seeking out the DVD, released in the UK on September 8th, 2009. Keep the popcorn handy...

SCREAM FOR ME SARAJEVO – THE MOVIE

In 2012, Chris Dale wrote multiple columns for *Metal Talk* about his experiences at the Sarajevo concert. One reader was Jasenko Pasic, a Sarajevan actor and stage producer, who had the idea of making a movie about the trip. The result? An award-winning documentary that is raw, dangerous, funny, tragic and incredibly important. This is living history, folks, and comes from an angle that had never been taken before. Pasic ended up writing the movie.

"I called Tarik Hodzic, who directed the film, and he agreed it was an amazing idea. Alex Elena and Chris Dale gave me additional courage on this, saying they will support me with all I need," says Jasenko. "A year later I was in UK working on a theatre performance, and met Chris, who organised my first meeting with Bruce Dickinson. Before we met with Bruce he was telling me about this lady who he got in touch with that might be great help for the project.

"That was Tatjana Bonny who ended up, besides being a great friend, associate producer. Bruce said he loved the idea and we should continue working and he will be part of it. At this point Adnan Cuhara, producer of the film, came along with resources and contacts, so he made all our ideas reality. After all is said and done, it was the best four years of my life. Even now, friendships that were made through the process are priceless. Arts can do wonders."

Tatjana Bonny agrees.

"At the time, none of us knew the documentary would materialise," she adds, "But the belief was so strong and the people got along so well, that we really had all the ingredients to push it forward. [...] I had some TV experience from Kosovo and Montenegro working as a BBC fixer/translator, so for me a documentary was a logical option.

"It was beyond me how the stories would unfold and how much it would be collected - bit like a domino effect. What the crew in Sarajevo and namely Jasenko did with assembling this is still beyond me. In short, personally, the more I got to find out about it the more it was developing a sense of duty to get this story told."

Banging the drums

Alex Elena was drumming for Bruce's band at the time and remembers the project well. "Jasenko Pasic was a kid during the war and heard countless stories about this band of crazy people that, while everyone was trying to leave Sarajevo, came into the city to play a show," says Elena. "He told me he was interested in making a documentary about the show we played but also portraying how music and the arts in

IRON MAIDEN

general can turn an abnormal situation into a 'normal one'. Telling stories of life during the longest siege in modern history."

Around a year of logistical planning

Photo credit: Ami Barwell

took place and the aim was to film on the 20th anniversary of the gig, in 2014. Bruce Dickinson was firmly on board, Bonny says.

"His encouragement and attitude were amazing, and once you have this in your hand you better not screw up, which was also a source of significant amount of motivation. Adnan and Prime Time in Sarajevo got fully on board for producing it, so the rest is a miracle you can now see on screen."

It's hard to describe the importance of this movie; Pasic notes that in his mind it is 'one of the most important films made ever on the topics of both war and music.'

"The message that the film brings with it is, unfortunately, always relevant in this crazy world," he says. "I live my life with hope that there will be a time when art will be able to change the people and the world, and that *Scream* will be part of that change."

Tatjana Bonny adds, simply: "One of the phrases we used quite a lot throughout was, 'We need to get this story out'."

Trevor Gibson was the UN officer at the time and provided footage for the movie and the gig itself, says Pasic.

"I was well prepared for everything, as I have heard a lot of stories working in Sarajevo War Theatre and by preparing for the film," he notes. "But, not to spoil anything, Trevor Gibson destroyed me with footage he sent me for the film and with story he backed it with. Till this day I can't say I am fully recovered from it."

The power of the movie resonated during the first phase of filming, says Bonny.

"When Alex, Chris, Martin [Swan, also a UN soldier at the time] and Trev were brought back to revisit the situations, they were incredible. I wasn't there during the war itself, so keep saying I have learned a lot from this. We all have different emotional journeys and they still go on."

Shocking news

The movie process, however, was held up by some shocking news, remembers Alex Elena.

"Chris and I were already in Sarajevo waiting for Bruce," he says. "Everything was planned for a full day of shooting. [Bruce] was going to fly himself from Paris very early in the morning and get to Sarajevo. The

PART THREE: MAIDENOLOGY

camera crew, director and everybody was at the hotel having breakfast.

"I wake up super-early and incredibly hungover (them Bosnians can drink) and checked my email. There was one from Bruce that said [he had to cancel due to a 'medical situation' that needed tests, and that all his commitments were cancelled as a result.]

"I was the one who had to deliver the news. Nobody panicked or freaked out … we knew it had to be something serious for him to cancel. We just went on with the day and filmed other stuff for the documentary."

Pasic adds that Bruce was 'just brilliant' on his recovery from cancer.

"Yes, his illness came just when he was about to come to Sarajevo to be filmed. He cancelled but told us to be patient and to trust him that he will come back and do his part in the film. Exactly one year later he was here filming as if nothing had ever happened. The strength that man has is just out of this world."

Since *Scream for me Sarajevo* has been released it has gathered incredible reviews and affected many people across the board. For the filmmakers, it was, as Bonny says, a 'dream come true.'

"There were ups and downs and this sounds like a cliche but everything is possible with a mutual support and belief. As Jasenko states often, the best compliment for the film is when it was said that it is the best document for the siege ever made, so for me having played a part of it was both a great pleasure and achievement."

"I hope the film will be seen by as many heads possible, and people learn something from it. I hope it also serves as inspiration to those who are not necessarily pushed with big film budgets to seek inspiration in the story itself and gain strength from it."

Alex Elena went to a screening of the movie in Sarajevo during 2017. Chris Dale was there as well as Elena's parents. He describes the experience.

"We all had a blast and it is incredible to see the effect of an action done 22 years ago still resonating into people's hearts," says Elena. "During the screening there were tears of joy, tears of laughter and an overall sense of accomplishment. It has been defined as the best documentary ever made about the siege of Sarajevo by the people of Sarajevo. That was the biggest accomplishment.

"We did it for them. It's their story that is relevant. Not us playing a show."

Jasenko Pasic concludes that looking at life, history and events from a different perspective can still bring positivity to a world often beset with the negative and the unthinkably horrendous.

"Music, and this is a fact, can heal and bring back long-lost hope," says the writer.

"I live with hope that humanity will realise that there is no beauty, nor real satisfaction, in destruction but in creation instead."

The movie was distributed to cinemas in the UK and abroad on April 17th, 2018. Many of the screenings also featured a Q&A with Bruce Dickinson, filmed at Vue Cinema in London's West End during a special screening on April 11th. The United States and Canada saw the movie released from May 10th.

It continues to gain awards and looks set to be a significant historical document in its own right.

IRON MAIDEN

MAIDEN BOOKS

There have been millions of words written about Iron Maiden over the years, and the irony of adding to that pile isn't lost on us. We've had a sweep through what's out there and picked out a few selected tomes of interest. This isn't a comprehensive list. There are loads more out there of varying quality and only of interest to completists. There's even a 'Maiden-inspired' colouring book, ffs ...

Official publications

First port of call has to be Mick Wall's authorised biography, *Run to the Hills*. With unparalleled access to the band and the structures around them, it's a comprehensive account of the group's career. The original 1998 edition was boosted by a 2004 update, and as you'd expect from a journalist and writer of Wall's standing, it's a great read. And, obviously, overdue another update. Garry Bushell and Ross Halfin, photographer, put together the first Maiden biog, *Running Free*, back in 1984. It retains a kind of roughneck charm and certainly captures the essence of the moment Maiden became the behemoth they subsequently were. Another journalist, Neil Daniels, has contributed two decent ones: *Killers: The Origins of Iron Maiden, 1975-1983* and *The Ultimate Illustrated History of the Beast*.

Another official book worth the time is Bruce Dickinson's 2017 autobiography, *What Does This Button Do?* It tracks the singer's life and career through music and art, planes, trains and automobiles. Bruce's hyperactive approach to life was never more entertainingly-written, the vocalist displaying a light touch and a willingness to take the piss out of himself on regular occasions. As the saying goes, take what you do seriously, but not yourself. Never more appropriate than for the Air Raid Siren. It has attracted mild criticism for its relative lack of rock'n'roll shenanigans, but as Bruce says in the pages of the tome, there are plenty of anecdotes – but they aren't to be had therein. So, we await part II with bated

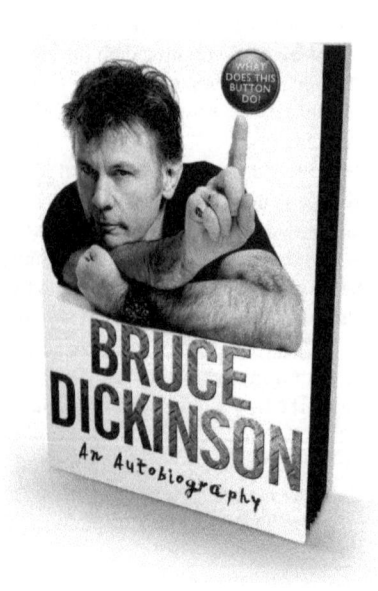

PART THREE: **MAIDENOLOGY**

breath but little expectation of anything humungously revealing.

Bruce's adventures into fiction were most notoriously presented in the early 1990s, with the dual publication of *The Adventures of Lord Iffy Boatrace* and its sequel, *The Missionary Position*. Taking a kind of scatalogically-daft angle on the novels of Tom Sharpe, the dual tales of toffs, fucking and intrigue must have gone down well on the tour buses at the time, but won't win many awards for anything else. The books are collectible; silly prices are being asked online, so do shop around. Bruce returned with *Chemical Wedding* in 2011, a co-write with director Julian Doyle and a tie-in with the Crowley-based movie the pair cooked up to good effect. A mad rush through science, esoterica, quantum effects and the 'rebirth' of the wickedest man in the world await. All very serious stuff, albeit with something of a twinkle in its eye. As curious as the movie, and indeed the subject thereof.

Not to be outdone is Paul Di'Anno, whose 2010 autobiography, *The Beast*, is as gnarly as you'd expect. Drugs, violence, prison and Maiden: you'd anticipate nothing less. In recent years Di'Anno has cast a little doubt over some of the contents of 'his' book, and perhaps it ought to be taken with a large pinch of salt as a result. An updated edition would be grand though, his story continually throwing up new challenges and triumphs. To the typewriter for you, Paulo...

The Man Who Would Write 100 Books

Delving into the world of the unofficial, and occasionally unruly, brings up some rather interesting books and some even more interesting characters. Which is where we come across one Stjepan Juras, a journalist and writer who is the driving force behind Maiden Croatia (which can be found via www.maidencroatia.com). And Juras is nothing if not ambitious.

"My plan is to publish 100 books about Iron Maiden in next 15 years," declares the writer. "It is not a joke and you can

IRON MAIDEN

see that right now because in 2017 my 10th book about Iron Maiden was published. This is a record which will not be broken in the future of the world. Iron Maiden will be band with more than 100 books about them."

So far his output has included books on various Maiden albums, biographies of Steve Harris and Adrian Smith, a fan-centric opus that tracks the worldwide characters that love Maiden, and the ace *Iron Maiden for Maiden Kids*. The latter is part narrative, part picture book, part encyclopaedia and part history book. It's targeted at ages 7-15 and seeks to inform its readers through questions arising from Maiden's songs. Given the group's obsession with history (and the future), there's plenty to talk about there. Though the original run sold out very quickly, Juras has plans to revisit the idea.

"I am ready to print and publish 2000 [copies of that book] and I am ready to give 100% of profit to a charity for children's cancer. I am 100 per cent behind my words. Also I helped many charities with my books and I will do that often in future."

Juras grew up in what was then Yugoslavia, first getting into Maiden around 1986 in a way familiar to many of us.

"I remember when the salesman in a CD store put few albums on the desk in front of me and he told me, please choose one," recalls the writer. "My mum was there just to pay for my cassette, but the choice was mine. I looked Judas Priest, Whitesnake, Motley Crue and Iron Maiden album covers and picked Iron Maiden. I didn't know their music, their lyrics (I just started to learn English) but when I saw the beautiful cover artwork for *Somewhere in Time* I just fell in love with Iron Maiden forever."

He also fell in love with great design;

without exception the Maiden Croatia/Juras books have excellent covers that draw inspiration from the music, art and context in which the album/projects of Maiden sit. As for those 100 books, well ... why set such a goal?

"First, I love Maiden so much and I want to write about them and teach old and new fans about their huge legacy, music, lyrics, members and everything else," he says.

"But also, I believe and I can say I know that Iron Maiden are not just a band. Iron Maiden is huge project and big part of their official history is some kind of heavy metal fairy tale. Well, I am a huge fan and many of my buyers too, but they deserve to see whole picture about Iron Maiden, positive and negative things, hidden truth, etc.

"On the list of my buyers are some of the most know Maiden fans worldwide, huge collectors, traveling fans, old school fans from the early days, etc., and all of them love my books and I received a thousand of emails and also info for book. They love my style, they love to read about alternative truth and I think that's why almost every book is sold out in the pre-sale period."

Juras points out that many books rely on extant material available on the Internet, but he prefers to get stuck right into the project.

"I love to dig, explore, I am happy as a baby if I find something new and when I talk personally with some Maiden member, ex-member, crew-member etc. In my interview with Neal Kay on more of 40 pages you can find the whole history of NWOBHM etc. said by iconic person who really knows the thing. You can also find speculation and brave conclusion in my books. In every of my book on its first page you can read this:

PART THREE: MAIDENOLOGY

That is why I'm proud to conclude: this is not an official book, nor is it intended to act as such, it does not feature insider info, and neither is it trying to pile up all of the available Wiki articles and Maiden-related fan sites info. It was not written encyclopaedically, factually, statistically, it's not trying to create a timeline of all the shows, bootlegs, various album editions, awards, interviews and everything else.

"At the end of the day, I want to show realistic, but positive picture about Iron Maiden and fans love that. My work about Iron Maiden will stop on over 25,000 pages of my books and this is a huge project."

All About The Words

Brigitte Schön is an academic and metal fan who in 2015 released a remarkable analysis of Bruce Dickinson's lyrics, entitled *Bruce Dickinson: Insights*, which you can order via http://www.troubador.co.uk/bookinfo.asp?bookid=3528

Why write about Bruce's lyrics?

A friend of mine asked me to translate some lyrics of *The Chemical Wedding* album. He wanted to know what Bruce was singing about. The first step to accomplish an excellent translation is to understand the meaning of the text in the foreign language. Reading the lyrics of the song 'Chemical Wedding', I didn't understand much, though. This is why I had to take a look at its background. By this time, I didn't have the foggiest notion of the themes of Bruce's lyrics. To start with, I read the album sleeves of *The Chemical Wedding* album. Then I did web research about *the Accident of Birth* album.

The subjects were absolutely new ground for me as I heard the names William Blake or Aleister Crowley for the very first time. I didn't know anything about occultism or alchemy. Being fascinated by the profundity and complexity of Bruce's lyrics, I was keen to bring light into the darkness - like playing Sherlock. Therefore, I continued interpreting Bruce's lyrics for my own pleasure and occasionally posted short interpretations in a German Iron Maiden forum. After two years of work my husband came with the idea to publish my efforts as a book. He was persuaded that other Bruce or Iron Maiden fans would also be interested in what Bruce expresses with his songs. It was to take another year and a half until I was satisfied

IRON MAIDEN

enough with my interpretations to publish them as a book.

What are the main themes?

There is a clear development in Bruce's lyrics over the years. The main theme of his first album is sex. Later, the subject matter becomes more and more elaborate. All in all, Bruce often sings about personal freedom. According to him, it is necessary to transform yourself into the person you really are. This seems to be one of his most heartfelt desires. Many of the main themes are associated with it: Aleister Crowley, occultism, alchemy, William Blake, flying. Even the lyrics containing criticism of misinterpreted religion (as for example in 'Trumpets of Jericho') can be related to the subject of individual freedom.

What was the public response?

Thankfully, I had got fantastic feedback. As my husband supposed, many people had been fascinated in Bruce's ideas. An Italian woman translated parts of the book in Italian for her thesis. My friend Michelle translated it into Portuguese for her own pleasure. Now her translation will soon be released by a Brazilian publisher. There is a very little amount of people dissatisfied with my book. The reason for their disappointment mostly is that they expected something else: my book is not a biography. It is a collection of my interpretations of Bruce's lyrics owing their credibility to references to a variety of background literature and, of course, Bruce's own statements. Nevertheless, I love people sending me their own ideas about Bruce's songs. In this way this lyrics and interpretations stay sort of active.

Talking of Bruce

The first ever biography of Iron Maiden's singer came out in Farsi, published in 2001 in Iran by Shervin Siami and Amir Reza Noorizadeh. The book sold 3,000 but was banned by the regime soon after. Next up was the awkwardly-titled *Flashing Metal with Iron Maiden and Flying Solo*, the first English-language look at Dickinson's musical career, written by Joe Shooman, the author of the book you now hold in your hand. It came out on Independent Music Press in 2007 and was updated in 2009. To date it has been published in Brazil, Bulgaria, France, Germany, Greece, Poland and Sweden. A brand-new version, retitled *Maiden Voyage* and including 25,000 words of new interviews with the likes of Blaze Bayley and Paul Di'Anno among many others, was released in 2016 by Music Press Publishing, bringing the story up to date and adding new information that had come to light following its initial publication.

Looping the Loop

Steve Newhouse, better known by his nickname, Loopy, was at school with Paul Martin/ Andrews/ Di'Anno and even played in a couple of bands in the early days. However, his trajectory was always about the background stuff and he became a valuable member of the Maiden crew for many years in the 1970s and early 1980s. His book *Loopyworld – The Iron Maiden Years* stands up as a hilarious, brutally-honest addition to the Maiden canon. Loopy says he never thought of putting pen to paper initially.

PART THREE: **MAIDENOLOGY**

"I was approached by Steve Goldby from Metaltalk.net in 2012 and asked if I wanted to write a column for the site," Loopy notes. "Up till then, the idea hadn't even crossed my mind. Although I was never told the numbers, the column was apparently successful, which prompted a guy from Belgium to ask if I could write a book about the early days.

"I started work on it straight away, but only had the column to work from. Then, by a complete stroke of luck, my wife found my old diaries in a box in the wardrobe. The column was done from bad memory and I thought it was all the right way around, but with the new information, the book is now chronologically correct. The guy from Belgium and I couldn't agree on a format, so we parted company. I was then contacted by a guy based in America, an acquaintance of Derek Riggs. This guy financed the book and Derek did the artwork. The book was finally released in September 2016."

The book is still available and responses have been great, says Loopy. You can grab a copy – and we advise you do so because it's awesome – via http://loopyworld.co.uk/ Steve has also recently released a novel, Justtin, which you can get at www.pegasuspublishers.com.

The comprehensive membership rundown

To say Maiden fans are an interested bunch is the understatement of the century. Step forward Erwin Lucas, a fan from Holland whose amazing research skills are put to the test in his fantastic book *Outside Iron Maiden*. Simply put, it's a collection of details on all releases by any member of Iron Maiden, past and present, with cover art where available, members of bands, release dates, guest appearances and ... well. It's an incredible piece of work and as definitive as you can get (although there are plans to put out part two). A compilation album was also released, with all profits going to MS Action Fund.

Hi Erwin. Uh – why?

The main reason why I wanted to write *Outside Iron Maiden* is because I had so many papers lying around with detailed information about solo projects by (former) Iron Maiden members, that I lost track of all the information I got. Scrapbooks filled with sticky notes, photographs, catalogue numbers, etc. I started collecting Iron Maiden stuff in 1986, and when Adrian and Bruce [had solo works] in 1989 and 1990 I became more interested in collecting that stuff also. That's when it really started. Collecting Iron Maiden releases is probably a lifetime job. There is so much, you can't get it all. Then there is the solo stuff, side-projects, bands before, during and after their time in Iron Maiden. The source is inexhaustible. The main idea of writing the book came in 2012. First I had to go through all my notes, then I had to go see if I was missing something. Halfway through 2014 I saw light at the end of the tunnel and started to think about getting it published.

What were the difficulties you faced?

When I got all the information the way I wanted it, writing the book was pretty easy. It took me some time to figure out how to get all the information in the book. By year? By (ex) member? In the end I figured out

IRON MAIDEN

it was best to do it alphabetically by band/project. Next thing was getting it published. I found a publisher but he wanted a very big part of the income. That was not what I wanted, I wanted to make something by a fan for other fans and not make a lot of money out of it. So I started my own publishing company, *MaidenHolland Books*. I found a company that wanted to bind and print it. Only problem I had was getting the money to start. That's is where social media helped me out. I announced my plans on Facebook by telling what my idea was, what it was going to look like, what the costs would be, etc. By promising to make it a special release for the first few buyers I drew the attention I wanted. The first 100 copies of the book were hardback and numbered copies and the first 50 buyers got their name in the book and a special limited edition *MaidenHolland Outside Iron Maiden* patch. So, I basically sold an idea. The first 50 copies were sold within two weeks and the second 50 went in the six weeks after that. This gave me enough funds to start the project, get the book to the printer, get Baz Crowcroft to draw the cover picture and do some more promoting. As I said, I was never in this to make money or get rich. All the funds I got went straight back in pressing new books.

Bob Sawyer in 2017. Photo credit Bob Sawyer

And the triumphs?

There were so many triumphs. Just after publishing the book I got a message from Buffalo Fish (with ex-Iron Maiden guitarist Terry Wapram). They were planning to take a trip to Amsterdam as some kind of team-building thing, and asked if I would like to join them. I didn't think twice, immediately said yes, arranged them a small gig in a pub, and we had a great weekend. Next thing I know, a few weeks later I was in London, staying with Terry. Met Tony Moore in his radio studio in Soho, where I actually got to meet my *WatchOut Records* companion Andy Holloway for the first time too. We had an afternoon beer-drinking session in the backyard of Ron 'Rebel' Matthews, where also Bob Sawyer was present. After a few hours we got picked up by Dennis Willcock to go to the *Origins Of Iron* release party, where we got to meet Doug Sampson, Terry Rance, Dave Sullivan, Barry Graham Purkis, and also Bob Sawyer and Tony Moore showed up. Eight ex-Iron Maiden members in one place! And to top it off, we got to meet Dennis Stratton, Tony Parsons and Steve 'Loopy' Newhouse the next day.

Another triumph is that we got both Doug Sampson and Barry Graham Purkis back behind their drum-kits. When we invited Doug to the release party, he responded: 'What would I do there, no one is waiting

PART THREE: **MAIDENOLOGY**

for me.' But you could see the surprise in his eyes when he showed up and saw all the fans there. On one of my later trips to London I got to meet Joanne Purkis, Barry's wife. We never met before but when we met she gave me a big hug, thanked me, and told me how happy she was to see Barry playing again. And now both Barry and Doug have released albums in Thunderstick and Airforce (on our own *WatchOut Records* label).

And the compilation?

During all the conversations I had with [co-founder of *WatchOut* Records] Andy Holloway through Facebook an idea surfaced to try and get a compilation album out with ex-Iron Maiden guys playing on it. The proceeds would go to the MS Action Fund that helped Clive during the last stages of his life. That would be a dream! But when we started talking with Chop Pitman (Airforce guitarist) things got in another perspective. Airforce was willing to give us a track. With that in our back-pocket, we went shopping, two guys asking artists if we can get a track for our compilation album. Not totally for free but for close to nothing. We asked Tony Moore, Bob Sawyer, Baz Morris from Lizard, Paul Mario Day in Australia, Chris Declercq, who made a track with Blaze Bayley, on vocals, Andreas Ballnus from Architects Of Chaoz (with Paul Di'Anno on vocals), with all willing to donate a track for the album. When we contacted Barry Graham Purkis for the possibility to get an old Samson track he put us through to Rob Grain but also gave us a track from Thunderstick. Rob Grain provided us with an old Samson demo track, with Clive Burr playing on it. We could fit nine tracks on the CD and eight on the vinyl so used the instrumental track by Bob Sawyer as some kind of intro on the CD.

Pressing the CD was easy. We had someone to design the cover, and that was fixed in a few weeks. The vinyl version was more difficult. The pressing company had major problems with delivering the final product to us, but in the end we got it all done. The response we got was good, although we hoped it would become a bigger success. The die-hard fans bought it and we got some money for the charity.

Tell us about Burr-Fest

A very large triumph was probably organising Burr-Fest in 2017. After the compilation album we wanted to do a charity event for the MS Action Fund. We talked to Airforce, Lizard (with Terry Rance), Thomas Zwijsen (ex-Blaze Bayley), Cris Martin (ex-Thunderstick) and V1 (with Dennis Willcock and Terry Wapram), who all played for free and got a venue in London, The Lounge, for a good price. After we got approval from Mimi Burr (Clive's wife) we started promoting and in a few days sold half the tickets! We sold out weeks in advance. It was a night to remember. Afterwards Andy and I looked at each other and couldn't believe what happened, so proud of what we achieved. The next day was the first of two Iron Maiden concerts at the O2 in London and it was good to see an occasional Burr-Fest shirt in the audience. And we are making this event an annual event. In 2018 Burr-Fest was a two-day event, with March 9th a pre-party with three bands at the birthplace of Iron Maiden, the Cart & Horses pub, and March 10th at the same venue as 2017, with seven bands.

IRON MAIDEN

The revival

But the biggest triumph I think is that Andy and I, with help of a few dedicated fans like Mike Chudleigh, Darren Witt, Bruce McLaren, Phil Cole and many others, stood at the beginning of the revival of the ex-Iron Maiden members. Suddenly everything fell into place:

Doug Sampson started playing again and got back in Airforce. They released a compilation album and are writing and releasing new material.

Barry Graham Purkis took his seat behind the drum-kit and reformed Thunderstick and also released an album with new songs and re-recorded tracks.

Dennis Willcock got on stage again with GVI, the demo tapes of VI and Gibraltar got released. He and Terry Wapram started with VI again where they left off so many years ago reforming VI, writing new songs and also releasing an album with new and re-recorded tracks.

Terry Rance is back with Lizard, playing original tracks after being in a covers band for years.

All the ex-Iron Maiden members got more interest and exposure for their releases and projects

www.watchoutrecords.net/
www.maidenholland.com/

Art attack

The work of Derek Riggs cannot be underestimated: his picture of the punky Eddie (at that time named Electric Matthew) for the band's debut album is as iconic as it gets. Eddie's mutations and developments over the years have been a feature of the amazing Maiden artwork, as well as inspiring musicians and artists alike worldwide. Journalist Martin Popoff pinned down the rather reclusive Riggs for *Run For Cover: The Art of Derek Riggs*, which contains about 200 graphic images from the sketchbooks, easel and mind of the man himself. Your *This Day in Music's Guide to Iron Maiden* author had numerous large-sized posters featuring Riggs' artwork on his bedroom walls in the 1980s, and continues to be a fan. Popoff, by the way, also wrote *2 Minutes to Midnight: An Iron Maiden Day-By-Day*, which does exactly what the title suggests it oughta. Up to 2013, that is, when it was published.

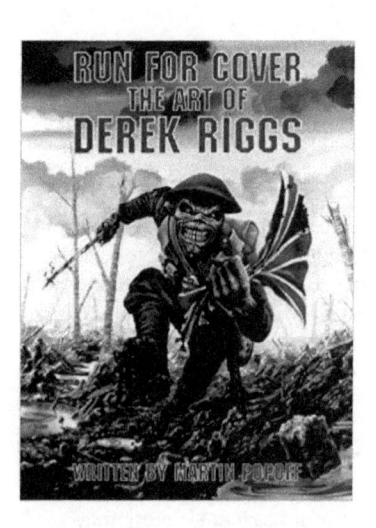

Long-time photographer with the band, Ross Halfin, also contributed to the books canon with *Iron Maiden: A Photo History*, originally released in 2006. The foreword is written by Steve Harris and the photos are of awesome quality. As good a photo-documentary as you're likely to get. A newer book, *On Board Flight 666*, features the work of John McMurtie, official photographer, tracking the band on that famous Ed Force One Boeing 757 piloted by Captain Dickinson himself. There are 600-plus shots from tours, including *Somewhere Back in Time* and *The Final Frontier*, with plenty of snippets and anecdotes to boot.

PART THREE: **MAIDENOLOGY**

MAIDEN VIDEO GAMES

Virtual Maiden

The beast's legacy on your video screens

Media crossover is ever-more important for any creative artist, and Iron Maiden have always had a roving eye. Over the years, the group has appeared in many different computer games – not just their music, but also as playable characters such as Eddie in *Tony Hawks Pro Skater 4*. Best of all for any fans, there have been official games released by the band themselves.

That said, it wasn't all plain-sailing: a mid-1990s proposed game called *Melt* was finally cancelled after not coming up to the required standards. We asked respected games journalist – and metal fan – Mike Diver to cast his expert eye over all things virtually Maiden.

Can you give some idea as to why games - like Melt - get cancelled?

I see that the band issued a statement to the effect of: it sucks, so we're not releasing it. Which leads me to believe: it really must have been bad, because the late 1990s didn't witness the same levels of quality control we have now. All manner of terrible games came out. They still do now, but more so through Early Access schemes, and indie publishing platforms that weren't really around in the 1990s. I suspect what was *Melt* was repurposed as *Ed Hunter*, rather than scrapped, a new game built from the very ground up - some of the ambition dialled back, and this much more modest offering released. Even for the 1990s, a linear rail shooter, as *Ed Hunter* is, wasn't cutting any edges.

As for why games get cancelled: a whole number of reasons. You'd need another book. It can be that rights aren't acquired, so the developer and the publisher can't release the product with those characters. Might be that the game simply won't come together to the standard its makers - or more pertinently, often, its financial backers - expect. It's hard to make a game, and the bigger that game is, the more dazzling its visuals and innovating its gameplay, the harder and harder that becomes.

But it's common that elements are retained, and repurposed - imagine working on something for a year, two or three even, then it's done with no end result. You want to at least pull something out of that mess and take it forward. This happens in gaming - what was *This Thing* ultimately becomes *That Thing*. For example, Blizzard had been working on a game called *Titan*, that never

IRON MAIDEN

came out - but some designs from it, some of the assets and design ideas, eventually became *Overwatch*, a game that is massive today.

Sometimes it's just a sad case that the money runs out. As well as being hard, making games can be extremely expensive.

You've written extensively on the relationship between Heavy Metal and video games, not least for Kerrang!

Metal has a bit of an on-off relationship with games - probably because we're still told it's such a niche genre (looking at you, Mercury panel). There have been games released with Journey in them, Aerosmith, Motley Crue, Queen, Kiss - then games that lean on metal for their soundtracks, too, like DOOM and Quake. The games that feature the artists - they're really aiming for that fanbase, the listeners. Those that use metal for atmosphere, for adrenaline - well, get those drums pounding and the heart speeds up too, doesn't it? Used properly, a metal track can make a gaming set-piece, just as it can a movie scene, or the best night out of your life.

Your thoughts on Ed Hunter?

Very much one for Iron Maiden fans first, and gamers second (obviously, its target market being the middle of that particular Venn diagram). In 1999 we got *Silent Hill*, *System Shock 2*, *Shenmue* - three-dimensional, fully-explorable worlds that felt alive, like you could reach into the screen and touch them (and immediately wash your hands). A game that played basically like *Operation Wolf*, an arcade-shooter dating from 1987, was never going to set the gaming world alight.

Speed of Light was a big step up, wasn't it?

It was deliberately retro-flavoured - perhaps a nod to the band's legacy, or longevity. But that art style - throwback, but underpinned by newer tech - was very much on trend in 2015 (and arguably still is [in 2017]). What you get is actually a much slicker game than *Ed Hunter* - by not over-emphasising the visual side, it doesn't feel dated, and the gameplay is more classic platformer (in the *Donkey Kong* style) than stiff rail-shooter, which is always likely to be of greater general appeal. I mean, compare a series like *Sonic* to *House of the Dead*. Both are by Sega, but you needn't be a walking gaming encyclopaedia to know which has shifted the most units and meant the most to people growing up.

Legacy of the Beast is another kick upwards.

It is probably the best-designed Maiden game, in terms of how it plays. Turn-based role-playing has been around since forever, but this is a pretty cool take on it, being able to swap around your Eddies for best advantage in battle. The mobile model though, and the need to encourage in-app purchases, does blur the lines between entertainment and exploitation. I wonder - or rather, I dread - how much money truly hardcore fans with money to burn have invested in it. I was impressed enough by it at preview to feel optimistic and compared to some mobile games it's not too in your face with the Buy More Shit stuff. It could be a lot worse - and really, from a games critic's perspective, that's the main takeaway. A lot of games hooked on a movie release, a TV show, a popular toy line, and so on, are total garbage. This ... isn't. It's always, always cool to explore places that you've only previous seen, or heard about, in a passive capacity. One of the greatest joys of a modern *South Park* game, for example, is to go into the TV, and walk around that town. If you've lived

PART THREE: **MAIDENOLOGY**

Maiden for years, being able to step into that world, through a game, is super-cool.

So what's next? Virtual Reality?
Speaking to a Virtual Reality (VR) developer recently, he told me VR is dead. Which, given Eddie's whole undead vibe, might be perfect. But honestly - the best way for Maiden, or any act out there, to dabble in the games world is to target platforms with the biggest possible user base, maximising your audience across both existing fans and, maybe, newcomers. Phones make sense. PC and browser games, too. Consoles can be expensive - I'm not expecting to see an Eddie game appear on PlayStation soon. And VR? Until six out of ten people on the street have it in their home, until it's reached that tipping point, I'd leave it alone.

MAIDEN ALE

Hallowed Beer Thy Name

These days, bands like to spread their wings and diversify into many different markets. Maiden, of course, are experts at this. And with Bruce Dickinson a genuine Real Ale aficionado, it was an obvious step for the band to move into the frothy stuff. The well-known Robinsons brewery thus came on board with the release of Trooper ale in 2013, Eddie resplendent on the label and a surprisingly awesome beer in the bottle.

We asked Adrian Tierney-Jones, the British Guild of Beer Writers' Beer Writer of the Year 2017, for his expert views.

"Beer is pretty fashionable and on trend at the moment," says Tierney-Jones. "And it makes sense for a band to link up with a brewery, especially as their fans probably enjoy beer — rock, especially heavy rock, has always been more about beer and cider than Chivas Regal or Crystal.

IRON MAIDEN

"I suppose it's an echo of heavy rock's original working-class background," continues the award-winning writer. "I'm thinking Black Sabbath for instance. Bands are also more savvy in the way they present themselves as a brand. Merchandise has long been important with bands, but the linkage with a brewery and a beer brand is a different avenue from the t-shirt.

"I remember when I was young how Mateus Rose suddenly became fashionable when Rod Stewart was drinking it on stage with the Faces; then there was Southern Comfort with other bands and cocktails with Duran Duran. But brewing your own beer with a company is a clever and totally different way of presenting the brand."

Dickinson was involved in the process, as a fan of such ales as Abbot Ale, Leffe, Fuller's ESB and Robinsons' own Unicorn and especially the multiple-award-winning Old Tom, named Best Beer in the World twice as well as Champion Winter Beer of Britain by the Campaign for Real Ale. Thus armed with taste-buds prepared, Dickinson spent time tasting the various iterations of Trooper before its release. But why Robinsons?

"I wonder if the fact that Robinsons are a solid, traditional family brewery was a draw," muses Tierney-Jones, who has also worked for NME. "And as Bruce Dickinson said he liked Old Tom, there's a reason why people collaborate - they share values."

But is it any good?

"I think you would find it difficult to get a craft beer geek to stick their thumbs up, unless they did a blind tasting, but those drinkers that are objective would probably come down on the positive side, Robinsons aren't still in business because they can't brew. In the pub they provide something that the bar person can talk about with the drinker; there's a story behind the beer, but the beer does have to be good."

Quite so. And the writer of this book can attest that the Trooper family of beers is very drinkable; Trooper 666 being a personal favourite. Other beers in the Robinsons/Trooper/Maiden family include the Belgian-style blonde-ish beer, Hallowed, and a limited-edition porter, Trooper Red 'N' Black. Those latter two pack rather a punch, having over 6% alcohol by volume. In February 2018, Light Brigade Beer was created to support the Help for Heroes charity, assisting British Armed Forces members who suffered illness or injury on duty.

As for the beer industry, is it being challenged by band-branded beers, or is the market just thinning out to accommodate these new ales?

"I think that if Iron Maiden beers get non-beer drinkers (especially if they are metal fans) to start thinking about drinking the beers, that would be positive on the market," says Tierney-Jones. "But I don't know if it has impinged on other breweries' beers. However, the plethora of music band beers (*also including Elbow, Madness, New Order, Queen, Status Quo and Super Furry Animals*) suggest breweries have thought it was a good idea, even if Maiden's beers seem to have been the most successful.

"After all, who remembers Status Quo and Marston's' collaboration?"

It certainly wasn't rockin' all over the world, that's for sure.

PART THREE: **MAIDENOLOGY**

MAIDEN ON THE BALL

Footy footy

As well as blasting out the tunes, Maiden are also somewhat obsessed with soccer – and that comes from Steve Harris.

Harris has a full-sized footy pitch in his home, and regularly plays charity matches alongside a host of huge names in the football world. Indeed, had things taken a slightly different turn he could have played for his beloved West Ham United. But how good is he? Gypsy's Kiss singer Bob Verschoyle says football has always been important to Harris. And it's also a revealing insight into what drives the bassist.

"We used to all go round his place to play Subbuteo," says Verschoyle. "He'd always win, all the time, cause he'd just practise, practise, practise.

"It was the same with football; he wouldn't just be right-footed, left-footed, he can kick with both feet and take a corner from both sides. He can score goals, bang in 30-yarders. He still plays on tour. Until he moved to Bahamas [in 2003] he used to play with our veterans' football team. He was a good player. Used to score loads of goals all the time. He's still pretty fit now."

Steve 'Loopy' Newhouse knows better than most where the Maiden band members' loyalties lie, at least as far as soccer is concerned.

"Back in the really early days, Dave [Murray] and Doug [Sampson] couldn't care less," he says. "I think Dave was more of a Spurs fan. Den and Clive [Burr] were both West Ham fans, and I think Adrian is a Spurs fan, but no one really cared. Bruce is a Sheffield United fan, but doesn't care and Janick supports Hartlepool. Nicko don't care for footy much either."

Famously, Harris was also on the books of West Ham as a kid. Rumour had it that ex-guitarist Dennis Stratton also played for the Hammers, but that simply wasn't true, says Stratton.

"People get this all wrong. I've got a football photo of my first school team that won everything," he explains. Leslie Stratton – Dennis' uncle – was a very talented footballer who played for Great Britain at the 1952 Summer Olympics, as well as for Walthamstow Avenue as a club side. Dennis' dad was also a semi-professional footballer.

THIS DAY IN MUSIC'S GUIDE TO **IRON MAIDEN** 245

IRON MAIDEN

Photo credit: Ami Barwell

PART THREE: **MAIDENOLOGY**

"I played from about age seven and when I was 11 we won everything at primary school. What happens in East London at the time, is that in the six weeks between [junior] school and secondary school, West Ham FC runs a Boys' trials. Each child that's any good at primary school gets to go to those trials in the six-week holiday, so I went.

"But when you get there you notice you're not as tall as the other kids, and some of them are brilliant. You knew who was going to go through and get picked for West Ham's youth team. I did the trials and didn't make the grade."

His secondary school side also won everything, though, so he can't have been half bad.

"I started playing guitar when I finished school," he says of his career. Steve Harris also had to decide between playing for West Ham's youths - having been picked at his trial – and music, beer and girls. Obviously the latter won out, otherwise this'd be a section about how Steve Harris, footballer, could have made it in music. But was he any cop at soccer?

"Steve is a brilliant player," Stratton confirms of his one-time bandmate. "He has kept himself fit; I played with him when I was in Maiden, and he still plays now. I see quite a lot of Steve when he comes over from the Bahamas or Portugal, wherever he's been living. He's always playing football.

We meet for a drink and he has got to play football. He is a very good footballer and obviously a very keen West Ham fan, as I am."

Loopy also agrees that Harris is one hell of a footballer.

"Steve was a great player and could play anywhere in midfield or forward," says the legendary tech. "He was offered a place at the West Ham Academy, but preferred music and women. He was still training with the first team up till earlier this year, as Slaven Bilic is a close personal friend.

"Steve used to play for a team years ago called Melbourne Sports. I went with him a couple of times, before heading to the Soundhouse in Kingsbury. Don't remember any of the games though. So long ago."

Being super-fit obviously helps Harris with his on-stage stamina and effervescence; the countless charity matches over the years are also testament to that. Indeed, it has even been said – with some tongue in cheek, of course – that at one stage the Iron Maiden crew was selected not for the individuals' technical ability in the music industry, but for their skill as a footballer in a particular position on the pitch.

(We must add for the record here that both Rod Smallwood and Bruce Dickinson are on record as saying they are people who prefer odd-shaped balls. Meaning, of course, fans of Rugby Union, and nothing else. What?)

IRON MAIDEN

3 FEN-SINGER

En garde!

One of hyperactive vocalist Bruce Dickinson's other loves over the years has been fencing. (That's the sport where you face off with kinda swordy things, not the other kind of putting up garden fences. Though we're sure he's a dab hand at that too.)

He began at his Oundle school at around age 13 and found the blend of physical and mental stimulation – plus the drama involved – rather to his liking. He even became captain of the school team by age 15. Rock'n'roll was to intervene and it wasn't until 1983, with Maiden beginning to really hammer the touring schedule, that he returned to the sport. Henceforth Dickinson trained wherever he could and would compete in tournaments where the schedule allowed.

Fencer Jed Houghton explains that there are three weapons in the sport: foil, epee and sabre.

"Foil and épée require you to stab the opponent with the tip of the blade to get the point. Sabre is a slashing movement with the side of the blade. Foil and épée require a bit more finesse and patience, while sabre is a bit more slash the opponent and hope for the best," says Houghton.

"Foil traditional is the starter weapon for new starters so it makes sense he started on that weapon. Once you have learnt foil you should have the skills to go on to épée or sabre. In foil the target is the smallest as it's just the torso, with everything else off target (no point). Épée the target is all over the body so hit anywhere on the body and you get a point.

"This is where it gets complicated. Foil has a right of way system which means only one person can get a hit at one time. If you attack your opponent by moving forward and extending your arm and you both hit each other, the person attacking will receive the point. However, if your opponent was to parry you while you were attacking and you were both to hit each other, the person who was parrying would receive the point. With épée there is no right of way. This means if you both hit each other, you would both receive a point."

In 1985 Bruce trained with Zsolt Vadaszffy and in downtime between *Powerslave*'s tour and the *Somewhere in Time* recording sessions, was advised to switch from right to left-handed stance.

"Changing stance from right to left is very unusual," Houghton adds. "I've been fencing 11 years and could not change stance. Only a few people can do it effectively. I think it depends on the person. This could be useful as there are fewer left-handed fencers, which means less training against them for

PART THREE: **MAIDENOLOGY**

[your opponents to] practise."

The singer really had the bug at this point and would fence competitively wherever possible, training all the while and dashing to gigs in between. Following the recording of *Seventh Son of a Seventh Son* Dickinson based himself in Bonn, training at the (then) West Germany National Centre, a six-month spell which enabled him to climb to 18th in Britain by 1988. Following the tour associated with that album, he climbed as high as (appropriately) seventh in the UK rankings. His discipline was men's foil. The rankings may have been slightly skewed by the fact that many of the 1988 Seoul Olympic UK team were taking a rest after their exertions, but the record books will show forever that he was indeed one of the top fencers in the country. That was evident when his club side Hemel Hempstead Fencing Club were UK representatives in the European Championships. Not too shabby! He also was part of an equipment company called Duellist Limited, which supplied fencing gear to fellow swordsmen. The UK's James Williams was sponsored by the company at the 1996 Atlanta Olympics. Dickinson is also a qualified trainer.

As a shorter guy, Dickinson's style was always to draw taller opponents into mistakes – he's described it as an aggressive defensive style. He, plus fellow fencer and mate Justin Pitman, travelled Europe a great deal in the Eighties going to and from tournaments.

"There are a few key skills you need to be a good fencer," Houghton says. "That's not to say you need them to fence but you need them to be good at the sport. Hand-eye coordination and agility are definitely needed as the blades move so fast. You need patience and knowledge of the sport, especially with foil and épée.

"Bruce Dickinson seems to be quite good at fencing," concludes the expert. "He seems to be suited for épée by waiting for the best time to attack."

Bring your author to the slaughter

Stuart Bailie is a renowned journalist, scriptwriter, broadcaster, author and fervent music supporter. He's written for many major magazines, including *The Times*, *Mojo* and *NME*, where he was assistant editor for three years. His acclaimed Thin Lizzy biography came out in 1997, and he's also penned and narrated TV series.

He also challenged Bruce Dickinson to a fencing showdown in 1994, through the pages of *NME*.

As you do.

"I fenced at school in Belfast and was Irish Intervarsity Sabre Champion [in 1982]," Bailie explains. "I was a Northern Ireland Schoolboy International."

He had also been at various fencing tournaments, he recalls, and even saw the Maiden frontman in action ... without realising it.

"I actually didn't know who he was at first, 'cause he was wearing all the [fencing] gear," recalls the writer. "And [somebody said], 'That's Bruce Dickinson.' And he wasn't very good; he was OK. He didn't have a lot of finesse, you know, he was a strong guy bashing away.

"What I found quite amusing was the record company/PR spin, which was that he was great and potentially amazing ... you know, suggesting he was near international standard. So we challenged him to a duel in *NME*. There's a picture of me [in fencing

IRON MAIDEN

gear] throwing down the gauntlet, saying 'Let's do it.'"

Eventually, around 18 months and another challenge later, the word came back: the fight was on.

"We had a bout in St. Paul's Public School and it was a two-page feature in *NME*. My mate Jonny Davies was an international fencer [competing in foil at the Summer Olympics in 1988 and 1992], and he was the [referee]."

Skill is part of any sport, for sure. But fitness will always be key, too, says the music journalist.

"Unbeknownst to me, rather than a short bout [Davies had] set it up like a tennis match, so it would be 25 minutes, half an hour. At that stage I was very rock'n'roll, doing all rock'n'roll things, so had no fitness whatever."

Unsurprisingly, it transpired that despite Bailie beginning the bout in good form, the singer was in much better shape physically.

"His physical energy prevailed," recalls the Northern Ireland writer. "It came down to the last hit, *La Belle Touche*, which was probably a bit of showbiz, and he beat me - to my eternal shame."

The two-page spread in the weekly music paper also featured pictures by Pennie Smith, whose photographs had adorned album covers by The Clash.

"I thought, 'This is great – she's going to make me look like Joe Strummer,'" laughs Bailie. "But I just looked like a fat Paddy in fencing kit."

The headline in NME? *Bring Your Author to the Slaughter*.

The paths of Dickinson and Bailie crossed a few times subsequently, as is inevitable in music.

"He's a nice, affable gentleman," says the journalist. "But to be good at a sport like that you really have to start young and concentrate [on it fully]. European fencing is so sophisticated and dedicated.

"Bruce Dickinson is a great enthusiast who writes books, will do his fencing and fly his planes, so he's almost that old-fashioned Biggles character who's handy at a lot of stuff. You've got to admire that."

Dickinson has stepped back from competitions since his heyday but often still pops up in challenge match-ups, including a televised 2001 battle with Peter Vanky – at the time No. 6 in the world - and a 2013 session with Bartosz Piasecki, who was the Olympic champion. Piasecki praised Dickinson's speed, calling it his best weapon. His energetic, supple movements on stage are testament to the conditioning an elegant sport has given him. He now fights in the épée discipline mostly.

As it turns out, fencing was also directly related to another of Dickinson's passions, dating back to when he was stranded after a competition and forced to hitch a ride with Nicko McBrain in the aeroplane the drummer was learning to fly. That got Bruce thinking of the skies. Yet that is, as they say, another story.

PART THREE: **MAIDENOLOGY**

FLY TO LIVE

Bruce Dickinson began his flying career by default – basically hitching a lift with Nicko McBrain and his flight instructor on the way back from a fencing competition in France. That plane, a PA-28 Cherokee, was piloted by McBrain. The drummer inadvertently set Dickinson's never-still ambitious and playful nature on yet another path and he duly got the flying bug.

His first official lesson cost $30 and took place in Kissimmee, Florida. And from there he began to work his way through the levels. It's quite the commitment, says William 'Merm' Mermelstein, operating manager and founding partner of Aviation Management Services Cayman.

"On average if you can dedicate three days per week, [a first licence takes] about four months," Merm explains. "[In all the cost is about] £6,000 - £8,000 for a private pilot licence."

Dickinson went through more training in New Zealand, in a Cessna 150 Aerobat, then in the UK at Leavesden. He subsequently bought a Turbo Aztec, much later investing in a Cessna 421 that cost him in the region of £170,000.

On parting with Maiden he found he had more time on his hands and set about gaining both flight instructor and commercial pilot licences.

"The commercial rating requires 250 hours as a licensed pilot," says Merm. "Most pilots who want to get this rating with the intention of becoming a professional pilot (career path) can log this time in about three to four months. It's not that difficult. You learn a few more skilled flight manoeuvres, and an instrument rating."

Merm adds that those 250 hours comprise 100 in powered aircraft, of which 50 must be in an aeroplane; 100 hours of pilot in command time [responsible for operation and safety onboard a multi-crewed aircraft]; 50 hours in aeroplanes; there must be also 20 hours of training, including with hood/vision-limiting devices; retractable gear; cross-country flights at day and night; solo flights and more. Not for the faint-hearted, for sure. And not for the more financially-challenged, either.

"Altogether to go from *Ab Initio* to commercial-rated pilot is about £19,000," Merm explains. "This would include all the training, classes, books, equipment, and so on."

Commercial pilot licence duly attained, he began flying Air Atlantique Twin Pioneer, then ran into a captain at British World Airlines, who signed Dickinson up. After flying 20 sectors, he moved to Astraeus, flying Boeing 737s and 757s. And the idea came: why not lease a plane from Astraeus to take Maiden around on tour?

Why not indeed. The 757 was given a makeover – the band's name and Eddie prominent – and renamed Ed Force One.

IRON MAIDEN

3

You can find out loads more about the 2008/9 adventures of *Somewhere Back In Time* on the documentary *Iron Maiden: Flight 666*. Another tour, this time to coincide with *The Final Frontier*, saw the band change the livery to accommodate the new album's artwork, which is evident in the documentary *Behind the Beast*. Finally, an ex-Air France Boeing 747-400 jumbo was supplied by Air Atlanta Icelandic, customised to carry more equipment by Volga-Dnepr Gulf. That plane was flown by Captain Paul Bruce Dickinson on *The Book of Souls* world tour.

Logistics

The logistics of playing a major tour, flying and planning flights are taxing, says Merm. Not many people would even consider it; but Bruce Dickinson is hardly someone to take no for an easy answer.

"This is a very large burden. The pilot in command must perform all their flight planning, weather, amps/charts, collecting frequencies, filing flight plans, get the required duty rest periods, no medications or alcohol within the regulations," Merm explains, adding that there's an, 'Old time saying: eight hours from bottle to throttle for an 8oz glass of alcoholic beverage'.

"Add all this to playing in a band and moving around, moving equipment, running a business, and so on."

There are also numerous restrictions on flight time yearly (1,400 hours) and daily (eight hours for a single pilot; 10 for a two-person crew). Minimum rest period between flights is 10 hours and duty period is 14 hours. Dickinson has been in the news many times, whether on mercy missions to rescue UK citizens from Lebanon and Egypt, or more fun adventures, including taking Rangers and Liverpool to European football games in Israel and Italy. He also flew with Buffalo Airways to Yellowknife, Edmonton in 2012 as part of TV series, *Ice Pilots NWT*.

Not content with being the vocalist for the greatest heavy metal band in the world, plus flying some of the heaviest metal around the world, Dickinson also set up his own maintenance business, Cardiff Aviation, in 2011.

"The requirements of maintenance are actually two-fold," Merm says, lending his many years of expertise to the conversation. "The legality of keeping records and complying with all the requirements, airworthiness directives, service bulletins, and tracking all the required maintenance is a huge task. Then the planning of when to accomplish all the maintenance while still having the aircraft available to fly when it's required to, safely, is a whole set of issues as well."

Cardiff Aviation has supported other airlines such as Air Djibouti, and as well as

PART THREE: **MAIDENOLOGY**

offering flight training the company provide what they call an 'airline in a box' service. Things haven't always gone smoothly; 2017 saw financial issues surface briefly.

Back to the skies, though, and Dickinson became part-owner of an SA Bulldog and World War II biplane – the Bucker Jungmann. In this, he's been able to indulge his skills in another way; the Jungmann is famous for its aerobatic abilities. Cue loop-the-loops, rolls, and so on. He also owns a Fokker DR1 replica, which he flew at Duxford Air Show in 2014. He was praised by one Gary Coleman (not that one) for an emergency landing at RAF Halton in 2015 in the same DR1, a replica of the craft the infamous Red Baron used in the First World War.

"Each airplane has its own unique flight techniques and requirements," Merm adds. "Actually, a pilot with different type of aircraft flown is generally a better pilot than someone who only flies a limited number of different aircraft." Dickinson has said if it were up to him, he'd add aerobatic flying to flight training in general. He really does live to fly. But why do people go above the clouds at all?

"It's the freedom and simple thrill of flight," Merm concludes, "And escaping the Earth's surface. Being in total control of your destiny."

THE FANS

Gonna get you...

Iron Maiden are a band with some of the most loyal fans in the universe. Even Ironus Maidenizkaliba of the planet Tralfamadore cannot compete with the absolute belief and love followers of Maiden are rightly feted for. Year after year, tour after tour, over band line-up changes, through good times and bad, you've got the holy trinity: Steve, Rod – and millions of fans ready to rock the fuck out.

Loopy still follows Maiden wherever he can and knows first-hand how incredible strong the bond between band, fans, crew and each other is.

"I spent three weeks travelling the country with fans, and they are incredible," confirms the Killer Krew original. "Everyone knows each other, and they regard each other as brother or sister. We stayed in hotels full of fans, so there were many late nights. I met hundreds of people who all knew exactly who I was, and on more than

IRON MAIDEN

one occasion I was called royalty.

"I had never experienced anything like it and would happily do it again. Maiden fans think of themselves as family, and I was happy to be part of it."

Metal journalist Raziq Rauf says the band goes beyond mere songs these days and is way more than simply six (or seven) guys jumping about on stage.

"Nobody goes to see Iron Maiden because they just heard the new single on the radio or a mate dragged them along," he points out.

"They go to see Maiden because Maiden is a spectacle that never, ever disappoints and it's a beautiful thing. You know the songs are great - they've been great for a large portion of your life - and you'll learn the words to the new songs because ... well, it's Maiden. Of course you'll learn the words."

The merchandise and the look are also central to many fans' outlook, says Rauf.

"Massively important is the fact that a Maiden tour means a new Maiden t-shirt and it's always a wonderful thing identifying another Maiden fan walking down the street or through Marks & Spencer's, maybe giving them a knowing nod.

"A Maiden tour means a massive night out with Maiden-loving pals, and you're all wearing your favourite Maiden t-shirts. No need for that nod tonight, though. It's easy to take it for granted that there will be another Maiden tour and you will go because you won't spend a moment considering your attendance. You're going. It's part of your blood. It's just a thing you do every year or two, and you love it."

It's not a coincidence that Iron Maiden FC exists – football shirts to show your allegiance to the band (even in West Ham colours, should you wish). It's a far cry from the early days, says Keith Wilfort, who ran the fan club almost by default. Indeed, he caught a very early gig back in 1976, and loved the band so much he literally made the T-shirt. Wilfort's DIY clobber is thought to have been the very first of its kind.

"The idea of the T-shirt came to me one day, walking along London's Oxford Street," he explains. "There were lots of little shopping arcades alongside the big department stores and fashion stores. One of these was called Marbles arcade and there was a stall there that put iron-on transfers on t-shirts. I thought: why not do a Maiden one? It was a plain blue shirt and had *Iron Maiden* in black lettering on the top line, *See 'Em Bleed* on the middle line in red lettering and finally on the bottom line, *Hear Them Rock* in gold metallic lettering. Quite a colour mix, but it stood out."

The reaction, recalls Wilfort, was fun.

"The band loved it, but thought I was mad," he notes.

The next t-shirt he created was a pale blue one with *Charlotte Rules OK* in black letters, inspired by the recent addition of 'Charlotte the Harlot' to Maiden's set.

"Both shirts were based on slogans the band were using to advertise their gigs," he says. "The last self-designed t-shirt I did was all white with a picture of a Viking and his scantily-clad woman on the front, *Invasion* above it and *Iron Maiden* on the back, all in black lettering."

Once Paul Di'Anno joined Iron Maiden, things were hotting up to such an extent that Wilfort had a cracking idea, which he first mooted to the bassist and driving force.

"I suggested to Steve that maybe they should start a fan club where people could sign up and get exclusive band news and advance notice of shows," he begins. It

PART THREE: **MAIDENOLOGY**

didn't initially grab the goolies of the nascent Maiden, though.

"At that time, they didn't really think it was worth it or would be too costly, but I would keep nagging them. Eventually, after they signed with Rod Smallwood and turned pro, Steve mentioned my ideas to Rod and he called me to his office for a meeting. [He] asked if I was interested in running an information and mail order service from home, initially on a part-time basis."

Just before the lads' debut album dropped in March 1980, Wilfort was taken on as a full-time employee.

"I would run the fan club and mail order, sell merchandise at gigs and also be Rod's assistant," he says. "The band were always close to their fans and were determined that the fan club would be run properly. They wanted to make sure it was run on a non-profit basis and to make sure the content was informative and that letters from fans got answered promptly. As the club grew they would give their free time to help with interviews, competitions, and so on, and also answer letters themselves. At all times they kept a personal eye on fan club operations. They also found it a valuable resource for getting the views of their fans."

A company called Bravado came in during 1982, to take over retail, touring and mail order operations as well as the fan club, under the supervision of Smallwood and the band. These days, the Internet is a fantastic tool, says Keith Wilfort.

"Fans can get news about and from the band almost instantaneously, which certainly helps with promoting music, tours and merchandise. However, on the downside you have the trolls, rip-off artists and fake news. By and large though, the good outweighs the bad. Maiden and their management saw the potential and we developed an online strategy early on. When the Internet and social media explosion happened they were ready to go, while others lagged behind. A solid Internet presence has helped solidify and expand the fan-base into a worldwide Maiden family."

Finally, he points to something crucial in that strong glue that holds the band and fans together. It is, he says, a matter of several factors.

"The band have stayed true to their roots. The music has evolved to a degree, but it's always been undeniably Maiden. They have refused to compromise. The stage shows and merchandise are incredible. People who aren't even into the music love the merchandise. Maiden have a long stable management set-up behind them. They have one of the most incredibly loyal and long-lasting fan followings, with Maiden lore being passed from generation to generation. They are loyal to their fans, always listening and keeping tabs on what the fans feel. They are always willing to meet the fans and despite now being multi-millionaire celebrities are basically the same people they've always been."

Tony Miles has another spin on it.

"Steve Harris, if nothing else, is all about consistency and that, plus finding the right manager at the right time, meant they stood out from their contemporaries by keeping it simple and keeping it straight," he says.

"Apart for the odd member change here or there, they really haven't changed from the first album to now. That's probably why they've built up such a following. There are far better bands in terms of music in my opinion, but Maiden are almost unique in the level of tribalism they've created in the heavy metal genre. It's basically a club for

IRON MAIDEN

the everyman (and woman). They've defied fashion and remained consistent."

Dave Lights has a different view entirely. "I can't believe that Iron Maiden are still doing what they do after all this time," he says. "For example: Steve did the tour last year then straight after went out with his own band and did two weeks more. It must be like he can't do anything else: the only life he has is being on the road and playing that bass guitar [...] It's impressive that they can still go out there and do it, but I can't possibly believe they're enjoying it."

IRON WHO?

There's only one Iron Maiden, right? Wrong. There have been several completely unrelated bands with the same name over the years, and actually they're not too bad.

The Only Way is Essex

Take Iron Maiden for example, a band formed in Essex around 1968. The group went through a series of line-up changes over the years (sounds familiar) but the classic four-piece that eventually emerged recorded the rather excellent album, *Maiden Voyage*, which was recorded between 1968 and 1970, with tracks appearing on various compilations and singles at the time. Gemini Records are the long-forgotten label. The master tapes were dusted off after a small surge in interest and released as a coherent LP in 1998.

The eight-song opus is pretty good, too. Think Sabbath without distortion, Led Zep with added hippy, and what's been called a kind of hybrid of prog, blues, psych and early metal. 'Falling' is a cracking little number, for one. Barry Skeels' intricate bassing and Trev Thoms' guitars are rather interesting, and though some of the material hasn't aged too well, there's no doubt this lot could have built on a promising debut, had the cards fallen for them. The group supported The Who and Amen Corner, but by 1972 had packed it in.

Meanwhile, in Bolton

At around the same time as the Essex lot were making a small belch on the music scene, up north in a Lancashire town something was also stirring. After a few line-up changes (sounds familiar) and name changes, the band formerly known as Ways 'N Means, Kincade's Wood and later Birth decided on a much more hard rock-sounding Iron Maiden, apparently overhearing an elderly lady cleaner come

PART THREE: **MAIDENOLOGY**

out with the phrase in a cinema. In a previous incarnation, the Bolton band even played a song called 'Running Free', sadly never recorded.

The band settled down as a three-piece and toured around the North West. In 1972, guitarist Beak (Ian Boulton Smith) laid down harmony guitars on the track 'Crawl Crawl Nightcrawler.' Other intriguing times included playing the Cavern in Liverpool, and members of Black Sabbath coming to a gig to check them out. Beak passed away after a battle with cancer in 1976, but there was a reunion of sorts in 2006 to raise money for Cancer Research and MacMillan Cancer Care. Now known as The Bolton Iron Maiden, they continuing to raise cash for charities, with details via their http://theboltonironmaiden.com/ website.

Indeed, there's a link between the Bolton chaps and the better-known Iron Maiden. The latter have been very supportive of their fundraising exploits, carrying news about how to get involved on the official website. The Bolton band list Led Zep, Free, John Mayall and Cream among their biggest influences, and have released two CDs - *Maiden Flight*, which mixes four studio tracks with several demos, and covers album *Boulton Flies Again*.

Across the Pond

Iron Maiden were formed in Seattle in 1970 and played many venues in the American Northwest over the next three years. After a few line-up changes (sounds familiar) they settled down as a quartet. The all-female band also made it down as far as Northern California, Idaho, Montano, Colorado and more for the next three years. They called it a day in 1973 and though photographs exist online no recorded music was available at the time of writing.

The Politician

A hideous monster, cruel of eyes and dangerous of visage, stalking the streets and terrifying the souls out of all who crossed their path; it was difficult to know whether the being was living or dead, such was the dark, inhuman nature of the beast. Able at any time to pivot from one mood to another and cause serious, serious damage, this horrendous creation of a particularly twisted Dr. Frankenstein was full of malice, capable of foul deeds and entirely without conscience. The 1980s were so scarred by the experience of this creature that the UK has never been the same again.

But that's enough about Margaret Thatcher, milk snatcher and murderer of retreating Argentinian soldiers for one book, isn't it?

Long live Eddie, and may the other unmentionable never grace the pages of this book again.

IRON MAIDEN

3 THE TRIBUTE ACTS

Sadly, there just ain't enough Maiden to go around. The behemoths play the biggest venues possible, which means the maximum amount of people get to see them at one time. There's nothing like being in a crowd of a quarter of a million to make you feel part of the family ... but, conversely, that's one hell of a big family, isn't it.

So for all of us who failed to see Maiden in more intimate venues in the early days due to complications such as not being born, or being born in another country altogether, or simply coming later to the Irons' party, we have to be creative about it. So creative are some Maiden-heads that they perform as tribute acts. There are countless worldwide tributes to the mighty originals – of varying quality, it must be said – but as a flavour of what's out there we've had a good rummage in the under-crackers of the Internet to come up with a selection of groups keeping the flame alive at grass-roots level.

The Iron Maidens
USA

Possibly the best-known tribute act out there, this LA-based hard-touring act (found via http://www.theironmaidens.com/) have been bringing the good stuff to the world since 2001. With three well-received albums to draw on and a brilliant angle on the Maiden sound, the group continues to wow crowds across the globe. But don't take our word for it, here's the brilliant band in their own words.

What inspired you to start the band?

Linda (Nikki McBurrain, drums): "I was looking for a bass player for my band, Phantom Blue, and was invited to a show of an Iron Maiden tribute with a female vocalist and bass player. With the intention of enjoying some Maiden tunes and recruiting a new bass player that night, I was introduced to the world of tribute bands and told the singer and bassist were wanting to turn the project all-female, ending up recruited to a female tribute to Iron Maiden just in need of a drummer and guitarist to complete the line-up, which became The Iron Maidens."

Wanda (Steph Harris, bass): "Back when the band was first formed, we were all in other bands and projects and were just looking for a fun thing to do on the side. Since we were all Iron Maiden fans and wanted to do something more musically challenging than what was already out there (as far as all-female tributes), Iron Maiden was a good fit. The original plan was to play out for fun in local bars about once or twice a month but, after the first few shows, we started getting inquiries from other states, then from other countries. The band,

PART THREE: **MAIDENOLOGY**

originally started as just a fun side-project, now keeps us all pretty busy."

Have any Maiden members seen you or even played at a gig with you?

Linda: "Steve Harris and Bruce Dickinson have seen us play in Mexico City, and Steve gave us kudos after the show. He was so kind, with a twinkle in his eyes. What an exciting moment that was. I still can't believe that happened! We actually played 'Alexander the Great' that night. Michael Kenney has also joined us on stage several times on keyboards, allowing us to do songs like 'Seventh Son', 'Blood Brothers' and others with dominant keyboard parts."

Wanda: "Steve Harris and Bruce Dickinson saw us play at the Hard Rock Café in Mexico City a few years back. We were on the same bill as Steve's daughter, Lauren, so they were already there for her, staying for our set as well. We were all very nervous seeing them there, especially since our backline wasn't that great, but I think we pulled it off because, after our set, Steve let us know he liked the show. Things really can't get any better than that! A few years prior to that, a couple of us got to play a song with Nicko at a jam in Hollywood. He was super-sweet, and a good time was had by all. Definitely a night to remember."

What is your masterplan/ ethos?

Linda: "Don't let the party die! Haha! I'm just having a blast playing this amazing music for fellow Maiden fans around the world. Iron Maiden is a huge reason I started drumming to begin with and I never imagined I'd be playing in a tribute band to Maiden someday, going on 16 years so far. There is no masterplan other than continuing to have joy performing and bringing smiles to others through music. When the joy fades, I'll call it a day and move on."

Courtney (Adriana Smith, guitar): "Masterplan? This band is not a job for us, we're just having fun and get to rock out with Maiden fans all over the world. I always say if I wasn't onstage, I'd probably be in the audience! We are very humble and are definitely blessed by the success we've achieved. I look forward to seeing where this crazy ride takes us."

Kirsten (Bruce Chickenson, vocals): "Our ethos is simply to deliver the best show we can, paying homage to Iron Maiden. We strive to keep it fun, both for us and the crowd. Lots of smiles, laughter, and high jinks throughout the show!"

Wanda: "We just want to have fun and deliver the best show we can for as long as people still want to come and see us."

Best and worst moments in your band?

Linda: "Best moments include traveling and touring to so many places to share the love of Iron Maiden. One of the most memorable being a trip to Iraq for our US troops. They thanked us for letting them forget where they were for that one hour of their day. It was really a life-changing

IRON MAIDEN

experience. Worst moments would have to be crap transportation and promoters who think we possess a superhero ability to function without any sleep. Haha!"

Courtney: "The best moments are every time we walk onstage. Playing to a small crowd, large crowd, to one person sitting at the bar during soundcheck (ha) ... it's all the same to me. You find what you love to do and never work a day in your life. The worst moments are probably the days involving lack of sleep, which we're faced with most of the time on the road. The show must go on though ... lack of sleep, shower, meal, and so on ... Rock'n'roll!"

Kirsten: "I echo Courtney's sentiment; it's all about the joy we see on people's faces when they hear songs they love and grew up with, singing along and air-guitaring/drumming in near-ecstasy! Playing Maiden tunes night after night never gets old to me. The worst moments in this band are when we we can't find a decent (sanitary) bathroom at the venue. Let's just say we've had to get creative sometimes and leave the rest to imagination, haha... (eww)."

Wanda: "Best moments are during shows, because they are so much fun! Worst moments were getting robbed in Turkey and locked in a building in Mexico until someone coughed up $1500 (the promoter took care of it, but still)."

Final words?

Linda: "We all know how lucky we are to have the opportunities we've had with The Iron Maidens and never take any of it for granted. Our gratitude and respect to Iron Maiden and all their fans is very, very high. We are fans too. Long live Maiden!"

Courtney: "Up the Irons!"

Kirsten: "We are eternally grateful to Iron Maiden for creating such incredible, timeless musical masterpieces that enthral audiences and spawn legions of multi-generational fans all over the world!"

Wanda: "We feel lucky to be able to do this and are grateful to Iron Maiden and all their fans. Thanks for the support and up the Irons!"

The line-up is completed by Nikki (Davina Murray).

Iron Maidnem
HUNGARY

This six-piece (http://ironmaidnem.hu/) have been playing since 1996, putting on 30 shows a year in Europe, including Germany, Hungary, Austria, Romania, Slovakia, Ukraine, Croatia, Serbia, Poland, Switzerland, Norway, Denmark and Belgium. They've released several albums, their soundalike nature pretty remarkable. Guitarist Mihaly Beviz told us more.

"In 2008, we released *10 Wasted Years*, well received both by Iron Maiden fans and the media. A live DVD, *Brave New Tour 2010*, was also released. We play around 60 Maiden songs, among them titles the band never played live, like 'Alexander the Great', 'Flash of the Blade', Déjà vu', and 'Back in the Village'. You can enjoy all the classics as well, including brilliant songs like 'The Trooper', 'Aces High and 'Hallowed Be Thy Name'.

"We liked Iron Maiden from the beginning. We even started to learn to play

PART THREE: **MAIDENOLOGY**

guitar by learning their songs. Two guitarists of the band started their first band together and played two Maiden songs at their first concert. So, Maiden has always been part of our lives. We played in different bands later but stayed in touch and when we got together we always played Maiden. After a while, we decided to play only Maiden songs—just for fun. We didn't hear about tribute bands back then. We just came together to play our favourite songs. We gave the DVDs of our live performances to Maiden members personally. We do what we like best. We try to play the songs as accurate as possible and be faithful to the album versions. However, we love to play live. The biggest thing is to play these songs in front of the people.

The best moment was when we played in Belgrade in front of 12,000 people. That was like a real Iron Maiden gig. When the 'Aces High' intro started and the audience commenced to scream, that really sent shivers up and down our spines. Also, when we met Steve Harris and showed him our Eddie puppet and he grabbed its face with a smile. That was one of the best moments, too. Worst moments? When we run out of beer.

The Duellists

ITALY

Naples-based The Duellists (http://theduellistsmaiden.wixsite.com/theduellists-website) formed in 2007 and like many of the bigger tribute acts they set great store in not just looking and sounding like their heroes but also providing visuals and stagecraft to enhance the experience. Here, they tell us all about it.

"Iron Maiden has always been the soundtrack of our lives, although having different ages among our band members. We reproduce - note by note, with accurate backgrounds, sounds, voice, and costume - the whole live Iron Maiden tours. We don't play with other bands because the project absorbs all our energies and passions. We are so proud to diffuse Iron Maiden to those who did not know them, or the ones who knew them only thanks to their name or for the most famous songs.

"We are so sorry to not be able to satisfy requests from all over the world, because different countries want us so they can enjoy our Iron Maiden experience.

"Beautiful moments? When the common passion between us and our audience brings great enthusiasm to our shows. Funny things? "When people confuse our music with the real Iron Maiden!"

Best Maiden Tribute

BRAZIL

Featuring a three-metre-high Eddie, this Brazilian outfit (http://www.maiden.com.br/) are quite the experience. They've been going for over a decade and have even played with two former Maiden vocalists as quality backing bands to the singers' solo tours. BMT continue to produce high-quality musicianship – you have to, really, to get those songs across properly. Here, they let on more.

"Everybody in our band is a Maiden maniac. We all started our life in music learning Iron Maiden songs, trying to emulate every single aspect of each Maiden musician. So, it was really natural to gather six guys and start the band.

"Actually, we are the supporting band for Blaze Bayley in South America. He is our

IRON MAIDEN

friend since 2013. We also had the pleasure to play some songs with Paul Di'Anno. Another great experience for us. In 2008, we did a show in Sao Paulo and some crew members of Iron Maiden and also Steve Harris' daughter, Lauren Harris and her band were there.

"We just want to keep playing and spread Heavy Metal and Iron Maiden songs to as many places as possible. We do it because it's really fun and we can meet a lot of people and make new friends every time.

"We're always having great moments. We try to keep things professional, but without pressure. But the best moment was when Blaze chose us to be his supporting band in South America. There are a lot of other tribute bands in the world and he decided to choose us. The worst moment was when we were about to start a tour with Blaze and Di'Anno but unfortunately Paul had some health issues and got hospitalised. The Di'Anno part of the tour was cancelled but we did all the dates with Blaze.

Powerslave

SOUTH AFRICA
(Pretoria-based five-piece https://www.facebook.com/PowerSlave.TheTribute/) that firmly has its feet in Bruce-era Maiden. Gregory Wall, who played in Gunship, explains more.

"I was doing a Metallica tribute at the time, and thought that being huge Maiden fans as well, we should definitely do that too. So, I put together a different band altogether for that. We all grew up on their music, and it's a lot of fun to play."

So the reasons are the same for a lot of people worldwide, it seems. As are, it must be said, the pitfalls of being in any band.

"Our bassist moved to Australia," Wall sighs. "which ultimately dissolved the band."

Powerslave, as our friends across the pond might say, are therefore currently on hiatus. Come back soon, gents!

And there's more...

The more eagle-eyed among us will have noted that sometimes when Iron Maiden ain't on tour a certain Nicko McBrain appears with his own covers act, the McBrainiacs. Often, they play gigs to raise cash for charity, and quite rightly too. Splendid chaps. A long-standing act is Hi-On Maiden, who appear on ace tribute LP, *666 The Number One Beast* and have performed at Maiden conventions and on Iron Maiden Fan Club tours. Over the years, most of Iron Maiden have joined Hi-On Maiden onstage. Then, there's the small matter of the quite wonderful Attick Demons (http://www.attickdemons.com/v3/). Not a tribute band, but a bloody awesome Portuguese metal band with a sound of the Iron Maiden juggernaut circa 1985-ish. The pipes on vocalist Artur Almeida are an uncanny match for the Air Raid Siren himself at times, and tracks like 'City of the Golden Gates' and the brilliant 'Let's Raise Hell' are simply amazing songs. Keeping the flame alive since 1996, this lot's energy, power and sheer forcefulness are unbelievable. All Maiden fans are heavily encouraged to seek them out. And, no, we are not getting paid for this ad. We just love 'em.

Tribute albums

As you'd expect, bands of all stripes have paid tribute to the Irons over the years, with numerous cover versions and collections

PART THREE: **MAIDENOLOGY**

recorded, released and/or whapped on the front of metal magazines. The more the merrier, we say. Always great to get another outfit's take on a familiar track, and there are some surprises to be had too. Alongside the sterling efforts of the tribute bands themselves, many of which have released albums and singles of their own interpretation, standalone projects often give a short sharp shock of new stuff too. Here's a list of a few different angles people have taken.

The 'What Might Have Been' Approach

Examples: *The Maiden Years Volume 1 – Tribute to Iron Maiden* (1996, Sum Records), *The Maiden Years Volume 2 – Tribute to Iron Maiden* (2001, Sum Records).

Method: assemble famous names to take on Maiden's classics. Include former singers (Paul Di'Anno) and auditionees for the Bruce job (Steve Grimmett, Doogie White). Stay close to the blueprint and provide an insight into an alternative world in which said vocalists either stayed with, or joined, the band. These two albums are both bloody great, too.

The 'Famous Mates' Approach

Examples: *Numbers from the Beast* (2005, Rykodisc), *Slave to the Power: The Iron Maiden Tribute* (2000, Meteor City).

Method: assemble a host of mega names from bands, including Anthrax, Testament, AC/DC, Motorhead, Black Sabbath, UFO and D well, Paul Di'Anno's on NFTB as well. Get these people playing in the studio together on different tracks. Light the blue touchpaper and stand well back. Some really amazing performances to be had here.

The 'Famous Other Bands' Approach

Examples: *A Call To Irons* (1998, Dwell Ministries), *A Tribute to the Beast* (2002, Nuclear Blast), *A Tribute to the Beast, Vol. 2* (2003, Nuclear Blast), Various Magazine Cover-Mounts Over the Years, e.g. *Maiden Heaven Vol.1* (2008, Kerrang!) and *Maiden Heaven Vol.2* (2016, Kerrang!).

Method: invite a host of metal acts to interpret the magic of the Irons, filtered through their own style. Thrash, Death, Power and Black Metal versions of Maiden tracks await the brave listener. Sometimes the songs get murdered. Sometimes that's not a bad thing. Sometimes they're so heavy they fall out of the speakers and crash through the foundations of metal. Cover-mounted CDs (and, in the past, tapes and flexidiscs too) are given away free on the front of magazines. Often they're themed around a particular band, especially when there's an anniversary to be had. Bands love them 'cos they get to play Maiden songs. Management of bands love them because they get to be on the front of the magazine. Magazines love them because bands give them tracks to put on their compilation and make the mag more appetising for readers. Readers love them because, well, it's free music innit. Everyone's a winner, baby!

The 'Weird But Brill' Approach

Examples: *Food for Thought* (2005, Book of Hours Entertainment), *The Piano Tribute to Iron Maiden* (2005, Vitamin Records), *Mind the Acoustic Pieces* (2010, Maiden UniteD), *Across the Seventh Sea* (2012, Maiden UniteD), *Remembrance* (2015, Maiden UniteD), *Powerslaves* (2003, Angelmaker), *The String Quartet Tribute to Iron Maiden* (2003, Anatomy of Evil), *The Hand of Doom Orchestra Plays Iron Maiden's Piece of Mind* (2006, Vitamin Records), *Hip Hop Tribute to Iron Maiden* (2007, Koch Entertainment).

IRON MAIDEN

3

Method: Throw the traditional cover style out the window and rework the music in vastly changed style. Hence the Food for Thought LP has jazz, disco and country versions and the Piano Tribute is played on Sousaphone. Only joking, it's on piano, obviously. It's often said that a good song transcends genre and the proof of that is to be had on these and similar releases. The Maiden UniteD acoustic tracks are very cool indeed and have featured Paul Di'Anno, Blaze Bayley and Thunderstick as guests. Damian Wilson – who auditioned for Maiden after Bruce left – handles Maiden UniteD's vocal duties with great skill and nuance, as you'd expect from someone of his talent. The Powerslaves collection is an electro reinterpretation of Maiden tracks, and as out there as you get. That said, Mr. Paul Di'Anno is there on the cover giving it his blessing. Cor, he gets around a bit, don't he? Not so for the rather crappy Hip Hop Tribute, or, indeed, the odd MIDI bleepyballs of the sadly-missed Anton Maiden's Lunacy Records bedroom singalong karaoke. RIP amigo.

The 'Who??' Approach

Examples: Numerous we're not going to single anyone out here for paying tribute to their idols.
Method: Start band. Play Maiden songs. Release recordings of your band playing Maiden songs. And/or – Start label. Find new acts and unknown musicians. Release recordings of these bands playing Maiden songs to introduce them to the world. There's literally thousands of these type of things knocking about. Maybe not thousands, but certainly quite a few. And they're worldwide; sometimes with translated lyrics, sometimes not. Again, loads to discover here, including potential new favourite bands. Go forth and search, fiends, for treasures await (and a load of donkey shite as well, to be fair. Still. Love's like that, isn't it.).

The 'We Used to be in Maiden' Approach

Examples: Origins of Iron (2015, WatchOut Records)
Method: This is a doozy, this is. Assemble tracks from subsequent projects led by or featuring ex-members of Iron Maiden. Origins of Iron thus has rare cuts from Crimzon Lake (featuring original singer Paul Mario Day), Architects of Chaoz (Di'Anno's Brazilian band, briefly), Chris Declerq (includes Blaze Bayley and Michael Kenney), Airforce (Doug Sampson): a real treat for fans. The Chaoz and Crimzon tracks in particular are absolute belters. WatchOut Records are also responsible for the awesome Outside Iron Maiden encyclopaedia of band members' various projects, and, indeed, can be said to have reignited the passion of various ex-members who subsequently brought themselves back into the music biz. We are all better off for it. We salute you!

PART THREE: **MAIDENOLOGY**

IRON MAIDEN: THE NEXT GENERATION

It's Maiden, Jim, but not as we know it...The inexorable passing of time is one of life's only certainties; whilst it is only possible to make sense of things in retrospect, the future is full of hope and dreams, creativity and potential triumph. Maiden's musical legacy is secure – those songs, the albums, the videos and all the rest of it will always be awesome and in centuries to come will turn on new generations of interplanetary garglers, who'll bang several of their proto-heads to the eternal riffery.

In the meantime, the Maiden camp has also produced a few talented sons and daughters to keep the flame alive, presented here in no particular order, because we don't have favourites at TDIM Towers ... well, none we'd admit to easily.

The Raven Age

Formed in London, 2009 by Dan Wright and George Harris – Steve's lad. Harris the younger is a six-string beast rather than bassist, and the music channels the likes of Trivium and Mastodon rather than NWOBHM, but they ain't half good. George and Dan (now involved on the management side) are, however, fond of the occasional guitars-in-harmony moment. It's a boost when you're able to support both your dad's bands, obviously, as this lot did on 2014's tour with British Lion and then the big one – The Book of Souls World Tour. They've also backed Anthrax, toured extensively in their own right, and released their debut album in 2017 too. A bright future ahead... or, rather, the opposite: that first LP is called *Darkness Will Rise*. New vocalist Matt James, late of Wild Lies, joined in early 2018 in time for some serious touring. Website: https://www.theravenage.com/

Lauren Harris

Steve's daughter started out demoing with the legendary Russ Ballard, doing pub gigs before linking up with Grammy-nominated producer Tom McWilliams. Between 2005/8 Lauren and McWilliams wrote together and played some enormous festivals, including Rock Am Ring in Germany and the legendary Download (formerly Donington). She played a couple of gigs on the *A Matter of Life and Death* tour, then *Somewhere Back in Time*, plus supported other huge names, including Alice Cooper and Mötley Crüe. After releasing the LP, *Calm Before the Storm*, she put together

IRON MAIDEN

a new band, Six Hour Sundown, and set to recording in Compass Point Studios, in the Bahamas. Despite some great performances and festival triumphs, the sun went down on the project in 2012. Lauren went on to work with Dave Stewart (Eurythmics) on new project, Kingdom of I. A graduate of the Oxford School of Drama, Lauren is also a well-regarded stage actor and her debut movie, *Adrift in Soho*, was released in 2017. Website: https://www.facebook.com/LaurenHarrisOfficial/

(The) Catherine Wheel

During the 1990s the world was treated to the rather lovely shoegazey stylings of Catherine Wheel, a band fronted by Rob Dickinson, cousin of Bruce. His voice is gentle and hypnotic rather than loud and airline-bothering, which is entirely appropriate these days as he reaches out to the world as a soloist. Catherine Wheel debuted on vinyl in 1992 with *Ferment*, reaching No. 36 in the UK charts; a second LP a year later was produced by famous alternative producer, Gil Norton. The Pixies producer's work on *Chrome* produces rather an edgier sound, guitars-wise; grunge is definitely going on around this one, which is a highly-recommended LP. Norton also produced *Happy Days*, the band's third record. The content was harder still and approached an alternative metal sound in 1995, via Soundgarden-ish riffery and even a guest vocal by Tanya Donnelly of Belly, Breeders and Throwing Muses. The fourth album, *Adam and Eve*, was a textured, layered, dynamically-interesting set of tracks on which such luminaries as Tim Friese-Greene of Talk Talk played keys and Bob Ezrin (Pink Floyd) had production hands. The band's final (for now) album was 2000's *Wishville*, which hammered out the rock and smashed heads in with in-your-face single, 'Sparks Are Gonna Fly' – which sounds somewhat like something The Birthday Present might have gnarled out in their time. Rob returned as a soloist in 2005 and toured in his own right. The tinkering-with-machines gene is clearly strong in the Dickinson family – Rob has a company called Singer Vehicle Design, which restores Porsche 911s and in particular the 964 Carrera models. Websites: https://www.facebook.com/TheCatherineWheel/ and http://www.robdickinson.com/

Halide/Rise to Remain/As Lions

A. Dickinson leads metalcore band Rise to Remain, who morphed into As Lions in 2015. That's Austin Dickinson, Bruce's eldest. Indeed, Austin first gained a rock'n'roll writing credit at the age of four – his Lucy In The Sky-esque moment coming when he informed his daddy he was 'laughing in the hiding bush'. That became the title, chorus and inspiration for the song of the same name on Bruce's *Balls to Picasso* album. When Austin reached the enormous age of 16, he joined a group called Halide, before that project morphed into Rise to Remain from 2008 onwards. Austin is way more of a gnarly growler than his pops; Slayer more than *Seventh Son*, for sure, with elements of Mat Heafy too. The band won a *Metal Hammer* Golden God award for Best New Band in 2010 and also *Kerrang!*'s Best British Newcomer that year. Support slots with Korn, Funeral for a Friend, Bullet for my Valentine and Hatebreed followed, as did a debut record with Colin Richardson, notable for his work with BFMV, Slipknot,

PART THREE: MAIDENOLOGY

Trivium, Napalm Death and many other hard metallers. Things took on more momentum in the new decade, the band appearing on the *Final Frontier* tour with Maiden in several countries during 2011. Supports with Trivium and In Flames followed but – echoes of the Irons here – a major line-up change stilled progress and put paid to a planned tour with Machine Head. The boys regrouped and played the famous Vans Warped Tour in June and July 2012. A planned second album was shelved and the group split in 2015. Austin, plus bandmates Ben Tovey and Will Homer (originals from the Halide days) went on to form As Lions and have since toured with Shinedown, Five Finger Death Punch, Alter Bridge and old mates Trivium. As Lions' debut LP, *Selfish Age*, was released in 2017 and lead single, 'Aftermath' had some radio success. Incidentally, does anyone else reckon there should be a tribute band to that lot called British As Lions? No? Hello? Come back ... Website: https://www.facebook.com/risetoremain/ and http://aslionsband.com/

SHVPES

Brummies with attitude SHVPES are so in your face they don't even spell things properly. Take that, Letter A! You Bvstvrd. It's Griffin Dickinson up front for this bunch, albeit that he only joined the party in 2015 on the exit of original singer Joby Fitzgerald, who fronted the group's previous incarnation as Cytola. SHVPES are signed to Spinefarm Records, which will give you some idea of where their sound lies, as names like Babylon Whores, Anti-Flag and Children of Bodom are their stablemates. The band's debut LP, *Pain. Joy. Ecstasy. Despair*, landed in 2016, Griffin displaying a similar approach to his brother on the mic. And – surprise, surprise – they supported Trivium in 2017. The band have been tipped as ones to watch for a few years now on the metalcore circuit; SHVPES' music is more than Cookie Monster vocals and melodic interludes, though: 'Two Minutes of Hate' has more than a hint of Rage Against the Machine about it, for one. Lots to come from these chaps, for sure. Expect a Maiden support slot in due course. Website: http://www.shvpes.com/

Justin McBrain

Nicko's lad is an accomplished drummer in his own right. If you have a quick search on YouTube you can see why he's so highly-rated. Based in Boca Raton, Florida, Justin's worked with Track Nine. They formed in 2016 so it's early days for 'em. Website: https://www.facebook.com/pg/TrackNineMusic

Nicholas McBrain

No prizes for guessing whose son this is either. And no prizes for guessing the instrument he plays. And some prizes for guessing he has smashed the kit for a band called Die Kult (please note that there are no prizes in actual fact).

The Wild Lies

Bassist Dylan Smith brings the big frequencies to the table for The Wild Lies, who released their debut album *Prison of Sins* in 2017. Their riffs are bloody enormous; check out 'Can't Carry On' for some exceptional metal madness interspersed with portentous verses. The band played

IRON MAIDEN

Download 2016 as well as plenty of other European venues, their sound one foot in the classic metal era and one bang up to date. Incidentally, the video for 'Save Your Breath' was directed by Adrian's wife, and Dylan's mum, Nathalie. It's a banger, too. Website: http://thewildlies.com

WEBSITES

It's pretty easy to find official and unofficial Maiden sites – they are the biggest bloody band in the world, after all. Here's a few of our interviewees to look out for, too.

Adrian Tierney-Jones: http://maltworms.blogspot.co.uk/

Airforce: www.watchoutrecords.net

Alex Elena: http://www.alexelenaphotography.com/

AMS Cayman: https://www.ams.ky/

Blaze Bayley: www.blazebayley.net

Brigitte Schön: https://www.facebook.com/BruceDickinsonInsights

Damian Wilson: www.damian-wilson.net

David Ingraham: www.davidingraham.com

Dennis Stratton: www.dennisstratton.com

Derek Riggs: www.derekriggs.com

Doogie White: www.doogiewhite.com

Doug Sampson https://www.facebook.com/OfficialDougSampson/

Erwin Lucas/Maiden Holland: www.maidenholland.com

Evil Ways/Urchin: www.evilways-urchin.webs.com

PART THREE: **MAIDENOLOGY**

Fish: https://fishmusic.scot/ www.fishheadsclub.com/

Ian Gillan: www.gillan.com

Jack Endino: www.endino.com

Jump: www.jumprock.co.uk

Mikee Goodman: https://www.facebook.com/mikeewgoodman/

Neil Daniels: www.neildanielsbooks.com

Paul Di'Anno: www.pauldianno.com

Raziq Rauf: https://www.facebook.com/downwardgrog

Robin Guy: https://www.facebook.com/robinguydrummer/

Roland Hyams: http://www.workhardpr.com/

Sack Trick: https://www.facebook.com/sacktrick/

Scream for Me Sarajevo: https://www.facebook.com/screamformesarajevo/

Steve 'Loopy' Newhouse: www.loopyworld.co.uk

Stjepan Juras/Maiden Croatia: www.maidencroatia.com

Thunderstick: https://www.facebook.com/thunderstickofficial/

Tony Moore: https://www.facebook.com/tonymooremagic

Tony Platt: http://www.platinumtones.com/

UK Fencing: http://www.britishfencing.com/

Gibraltar/V1: http://v1rocks.com/site/history/

Samson: http://www.paulsamson.co.uk/

The Soundhouse Tapes site: www.thesoundhousetapes.net

IRON MAIDEN

Eddie, as interpreted by a young Michael Kiske, when he probably should have been listening to his schoolteachers rather than making intricate drawings of Heavy Metal monsters. Still, we know who's had the last laugh... credit: Michael Kiske

PART THREE: INDEX

INDEX

Symbols
2 Minutes to Midnight 52, 53, 76, 95, 96, 113, 132, 137, 188, 240
12 Wasted Years 224
22 Acacia Avenue 52, 92, 93, 134, 166

A
Accident of Birth 187, 188, 190, 218, 235
Aces High 53, 81, 95, 96, 119, 131, 140, 218, 260, 261
Acoustic 9, 55, 92, 97, 99, 100, 101, 110, 112, 147, 170, 172, 181, 190, 204, 208, 210, 263, 264
Adrian Smith 3, 9, 45, 51, 55, 59, 60, 62, 70, 91, 93, 95, 96, 100, 101, 119, 129, 130, 132, 134, 135, 137, 151, 164, 167, 168, 169, 170, 172, 173, 187, 192, 193, 199, 224, 225, 234
Adrian Smith and Project 168
Adrian Tierney-Jones 5, 243, 268
Afraid to Shoot Strangers 80, 102, 116, 141
Airforce 157, 239, 240, 264, 268
Alan Levett 5, 165, 166
Alex Elena 5, 181, 183, 184, 186, 229, 230, 231, 268
All the Young Dudes 179
A Matter of Life and Death 76, 114, 139, 265
Andy Griffin 5, 185, 201
Andy Taylor 213
A Real Dead One 123, 207
A Real Live One 123, 207
Arthur Brown 23, 149, 174
Artwork 10, 11, 76, 81, 92, 98, 102, 106, 108, 121, 125, 182, 215, 216, 217, 218, 219, 226, 234, 237, 240, 252
Auditions 18, 25, 30, 36, 181
Austin Dickinson 266
Aviation 6, 189, 251, 252

B
Back in the Village 53, 95, 96, 141, 260
Balls to Picasso 180, 266
Barnyard Studios 100, 102, 104, 106
BBC Archives 121, 123
Beast Over Hammersmith 121, 123
Beer 5, 74, 80, 81, 95, 184, 189, 201, 223, 238, 243, 244, 247, 261
Behind the Iron Curtain 53, 223
Benjamin Breeg 76, 112, 113
Be Quick or Be Dead 62, 102, 141, 218
Best of the Beast 67, 121
Best of the 'B' Sides 121
Black Sabbath 5, 70, 75, 76, 93, 143, 149, 244, 257, 263
Blaze Bayley 3, 5, 60, 64, 65, 67, 68, 69, 104, 121, 122, 124, 138, 157, 199, 201, 202, 203, 204, 208, 210, 236, 239, 261, 264, 268
Blood Brothers 80, 108, 109, 134, 141, 142, 259
Bob Sawyer 19, 20, 23, 24, 238, 239
Bob Verschoyle 5, 143, 245
Book of Souls 28, 82, 84, 86, 117, 124, 140, 227, 252, 265
Books 2, 4, 6, 11, 62, 666, 86, 99, 105, 114, 190, 217, 232, 233, 234, 235, 238, 240, 245, 249, 250, 251
Bootlegs 3, 11, 53, 124, 125, 126, 167, 195, 235
Boxset 121, 122, 123
Brand 8, 27, 43, 64, 67, 71, 78, 80, 81, 86, 93, 95, 157, 162, 195, 226, 227, 236, 244
Braveheart 107, 139
Brave New World 71, 72, 74, 108, 109, 110, 112, 114, 134, 141, 194, 202, 225
Brazil 6, 54, 81, 155, 156, 157, 188, 227, 236, 261
Brian Wright 5, 105, 225, 227, 228
Brigitte Shoen 5
Bring your Daughter... To The Slaughter 59, 60, 77, 100, 141, 179, 197, 214

IRON MAIDEN

Bruce Dickinson 3, 5, 8, 11, 12, 48, 49, 50, 51, 52, 53, 55, 56, 59, 62, 63, 64, 65, 70, 71, 75, 76, 77, 78, 80, 81, 83, 84, 86, 92, 96, 97, 100, 102, 103, 104, 108, 110, 112, 118, 119, 120, 121, 122, 123, 124, 129, 131, 132, 133, 136, 138, 139, 140, 141, 142, 143, 147, 148, 149, 160, 162, 172, 173, 175, 178, 181, 182, 188, 190, 192, 193, 194, 196, 197, 198, 199, 201, 207, 208, 210, 214, 218, 223, 227, 229, 230, 231, 232, 235, 243, 244, 247, 248, 249, 250, 251, 252, 259

C

Canada 46, 62, 71, 72, 77, 86, 168, 170, 227, 231
Cancelled gigs 72
Cancer 75, 81, 82, 83, 84, 119, 124, 231, 234, 257
Can I Play With Madness 57, 98, 99, 140
Cart and Horses 18, 21
Charlie Borg 17
Charlotte the Harlot 32, 89, 90, 126, 134, 141, 150, 254
Charts 35, 42, 43, 49, 53, 55, 57, 58, 60, 61, 62, 666, 67, 71, 76, 78, 80, 99, 100, 101, 102, 111, 116, 130, 131, 153, 160, 187, 197, 214, 252, 266
Chemical Wedding 4, 162, 188, 190, 228, 233, 235
Children of the Damned 49, 92, 93, 141
Chris Aylmer 174, 178
Chris Dale 5, 162, 181, 182, 183, 185, 186, 229, 231
Classic Albums 71, 225, 226
Cliff Evans 5, 155, 156
Clive Aid 73, 161, 162
Clive Burr 3, 40, 41, 50, 51, 73, 75, 76, 77, 90, 91, 94, 130, 136, 145, 153, 154, 160, 161, 162, 163, 174, 191, 197, 223, 225, 239
Collaboration 666, 67, 72, 74, 95, 101, 112, 134, 197, 198, 244
Como Estais Amigos 106, 108
Compilation 37, 67, 71, 73, 77, 80, 121, 147, 188, 195, 204, 205, 237, 239, 240, 263
Computer game 67, 71, 106
Court Case 52

D

Damian Wilson 5, 208, 264, 268
Dance of Death 73, 74, 110, 112, 122, 123, 134, 190, 226
Dave Lights, 7, 11, 16, 17, 19, 22, 26, 32, 35, 40, 44, 45, 48, 144, 215, 216, 221, 222, 256
Dave Murray 3, 17, 20, 23, 24, 29, 30, 31, 32, 39, 45, 60, 71, 86, 90, 95, 98, 101, 102, 103, 106, 109, 110, 111, 117, 129, 131, 136, 151, 164, 165, 166, 167, 191, 225
Dave Sullivan 16, 17, 18, 20, 238
David Ingraham 5, 180, 187, 188, 268
Dean Karr 225
Death 24, 53, 54, 63, 68, 73, 74, 76, 77, 91, 94, 95, 96, 98, 100, 101, 109, 110, 111, 112, 113, 114, 115, 116, 117, 119, 120, 122, 123, 133, 134, 135, 137, 138, 139, 140, 141, 164, 186, 189, 190, 215, 223, 226, 263, 265, 266, 267
Death on the Road 74, 122, 123, 226
Dennis Stratton 3, 5, 38, 40, 41, 42, 44, 90, 131, 155, 156, 158, 167, 214, 224, 238, 245, 268
Dennis Willcock 3, 5, 18, 19, 20, 22, 23, 24, 28, 29, 30, 31, 44, 63, 127, 145, 146, 148, 150, 238, 239, 240
Depression 120, 203
Derek Riggs 55, 62, 92, 98, 102, 108, 187, 215, 217, 223, 237, 240, 268
Dickie Bell 193, 207, 208, 209
Different World 77, 112
Doctor 161, 195, 203
Documentary 49, 74, 78, 80, 121, 224, 226, 227, 229, 231, 240, 252
Donington 59, 77, 81, 100, 123, 224, 227, 265
Donington Live 1992 224
Doogie White 5, 263, 268
Doug Sampson 5, 29, 30, 31, 32, 33, 34, 38, 39, 41, 136, 145, 150, 238, 240, 264, 268
Download 77, 84, 265, 267

PART THREE: **INDEX**

Drifter 34, 39, 90, 91, 126
Drink 16, 23, 28, 51, 82, 90, 154, 231, 247
Drug 46, 139, 207
DVD 17, 74, 76, 77, 78, 80, 86, 111, 123, 156, 163, 191, 194, 222, 223, 224, 225, 226, 227, 229, 260
Dylan Smith 267

E

East End 7, 25, 41
Eddie 4, 5, 8, 10, 11, 32, 49, 51, 52, 54, 55, 74, 75, 76, 77, 79, 81, 84, 86, 92, 98, 102, 104, 105, 106, 108, 111, 112, 113, 114, 119, 121, 122, 123, 135, 141, 151, 193, 194, 213, 215, 216, 217, 218, 219, 220, 222, 226, 240, 241, 243, 251, 257, 261, 270
Ed Force One 77, 78, 79, 84, 86, 218, 240, 251
Ed Hunter 67, 71, 106, 121, 241, 242
Edward the Great 73, 122, 215
El Dorado 79, 114, 115
Electric Lady Studios 53
Electric Matthew 121, 215, 240
EMI 37, 38, 40, 42, 57, 59, 70, 90, 92, 94, 95, 97, 98, 100, 102, 104, 106, 108, 110, 112, 114, 168, 181, 215, 223
Empire of the Clouds 84, 117, 120, 133
Erwin Lucas 5, 237, 268
Evil Ways 5, 151, 165, 166, 268

F

Facebook 126, 238, 239, 262, 266, 267, 268, 269
Fan Club 5, 22, 48, 63, 76, 192, 213, 254, 255, 262
Fear of the Dark 62, 76, 77, 102, 110, 123, 132, 140, 141, 224
Fencing 53, 55, 58, 59, 96, 248, 249, 250, 251, 269
Festival 43, 48, 50, 54, 59, 61, 77, 86, 123, 125, 159, 165, 171, 178, 186, 189, 194, 195, 202, 222, 227, 266

Fire 10, 26, 94, 95, 145, 148, 149, 166, 183, 197, 206
Fish 5, 150, 169, 198, 199, 238, 268
Flash of the Blade 53, 95, 96, 260
Flight 666 78, 123, 226, 227, 240, 252
Flight of Icarus 51, 86, 94, 95, 116, 133, 188, 223
Football 26, 58, 65, 104, 145, 193, 209, 245, 247, 252, 254
For The Greater Good of God 86, 112, 114, 139
From Fear To Eternity 80, 122
From Here to Eternity 62, 102
Futureal 67, 68, 106

G

Gangland 49, 92, 94
Gary Bushell 58
Genesis 15, 25, 93, 130, 143
George Harris 265
Gibraltar 5, 19, 30, 36, 38, 150, 240, 269
Gogmagog 154, 160, 197
Grammy Awards 109
Griffin Dickinson 267
Grunge 61, 62, 69, 132, 156, 171, 185, 201, 266
Gypsy's Kiss 5, 7, 15, 143, 144, 145, 245

H

Hallowed be Thy name 50, 72, 75, 76, 92, 94, 116, 129, 150, 218, 260
Hammersmith Odeon 54, 59, 122, 200, 223
Hans-Olav Solli 5
Hartlepool 195, 199, 245
Health 68, 81, 84, 161, 262
Heaven Can Wait 56, 97, 98, 141
Heavy Metal Soundhouse 6, 34
Hell 19, 32, 37, 40, 42, 45, 54, 57, 58, 63, 666, 68, 75, 94, 98, 99, 108, 112, 114, 135, 137, 144, 158, 177, 178, 185, 187, 200, 203, 207, 210, 225, 247, 258, 262
Helloween 5, 9, 10, 193, 210
Holy Smoke 60, 100, 101
Hooks in You 60, 100, 101

IRON MAIDEN

I

Ian Gillan 5, 8, 192, 196, 197, 198, 268
If Eternity Should Fail 117, 118, 120, 139
India 77, 78, 120
Infinite Dreams 60, 98, 99, 135
Infinite Entanglement 205
Innocent Exile 90, 91, 126
Iron Maiden (album) 46, 666, 69, 234
Iron Maiden FC 254

J

Jack Endino 5, 185, 186, 268
Jamie Stewart 5, 169
Janick Gers 3, 59, 60, 62, 72, 100, 102, 111, 116, 119, 134, 138, 154, 168, 179, 195, 196, 199, 207
Japan 46, 50, 61, 62, 76, 77, 79, 153, 154, 156, 159, 160, 187, 188, 218, 223
Jasenko Pasic 5, 212, 229, 231
Jethro Tull 110, 121
Jimi Hendrix 151, 225
John Dexter-Jones 5, 168, 169
John Hoye 5, 164, 165
John McCoy 41, 162, 197
John Northfield 17
Jonathan King 154, 158, 197
Journeyman 110, 112
Judas Priest 7, 8, 9, 10, 42, 50, 70, 221, 234
Jump 5, 52, 65, 131, 168, 169, 181, 219, 268
Justin McBrain 267

K

Keith Olsen 5, 179
Keith Wilfort 5, 22, 48, 63, 213, 254, 255
Keyboard 23, 24, 25, 27, 84, 102, 133, 194, 196, 209, 259
Killer Krew 4, 5, 34, 220, 222, 253
Killers 5, 10, 32, 44, 46, 48, 50, 60, 77, 90, 91, 101, 108, 122, 136, 138, 149, 155, 156, 175, 176, 223, 232
Kiss 5, 7, 9, 15, 23, 44, 45, 48, 143, 144, 145, 174, 178, 194, 221, 242, 245

L

Laughing in the Hiding Bush 180, 266
Lauren Harris 77, 78, 262, 265
Led Zeppelin 7, 41, 55, 92, 110
Legacy of the Beast 86, 242
Live After Death 54, 77, 122, 123, 186, 189, 223
Live At Donington 123
London 2, 7, 11, 17, 21, 24, 25, 28, 31, 34, 36, 37, 40, 43, 44, 45, 49, 59, 79, 86, 89, 90, 92, 110, 112, 113, 122, 136, 143, 144, 146, 152, 156, 162, 164, 171, 173, 176, 180, 181, 182, 184, 185, 199, 200, 208, 209, 222, 223, 225, 231, 238, 239, 245, 254, 265
Lord of the Flies 666, 104, 105

M

Maiden Japan 218
Management 6, 9, 10, 22, 23, 36, 38, 42, 43, 48, 51, 58, 60, 63, 78, 83, 155, 158, 165, 166, 167, 176, 177, 181, 187, 202, 203, 207, 209, 210, 213, 214, 215, 216, 225, 251, 255, 263, 265
Man on the Edge 666, 68, 104, 105, 122, 138
Margaret Thatcher 218, 257
Marillion 5, 198
Marquee 24, 37, 38, 149, 158, 167, 168, 198, 201
Martin Birch 43, 45, 49, 61, 91, 102, 104, 169, 185
Martin Connolly 5, 191
Mask 16, 19, 22, 32, 51, 127, 150, 174, 213, 215, 216
Maurice Coyne 5, 151, 164, 166
McBrain Damage 192
Melody Maker 16, 24, 31, 36, 145, 151, 173
Merchandise 35, 72, 244, 254, 255
Metal for Muthas 37, 38, 41, 42, 67, 195
Metal Hammer 57, 218, 266
Michael Kenney 3, 60, 102, 194, 259, 264
Michael Kiske 3, 5, 9, 10, 210, 270
Mick Wall 51, 232
Mike Diver 5, 241

PART THREE: **INDEX**

Mikee Goodman 5, 172, 268
Mimi Burr 5, 50, 51, 73, 239
Monsters of Rock 59, 62, 77, 100, 123, 149
Motorhead 9, 148, 149, 263
Movie 5, 59, 75, 78, 79, 90, 93, 95, 96, 101, 105, 107, 110, 111, 112, 113, 134, 135, 138, 139, 140, 146, 184, 188, 193, 217, 225, 228, 229, 230, 231, 233, 242, 266
Multiple Sclerosis 73, 160, 161
Murders in the Rue Morgue 68, 90, 91, 122
Myke Gray 181

N

Napster 69
Nassau 51, 73, 78, 94, 115
Neal Kay 34, 37, 234
Neil Daniels 5, 214, 232, 268
New Wave of British Heavy Metal 37
Nicholas McBrain 192, 267
Nicko McBrain 3, 51, 52, 59, 63, 74, 94, 110, 111, 132, 133, 147, 160, 167, 190, 191, 193, 223, 250, 251, 262
Nightmare on Elm Street 59, 60, 102, 197
Nirvana 62, 185, 200, 201
NME 57, 184, 244, 249, 250
No More Lies 74, 110, 111, 112
No Prayer for the Dying 60, 61, 100, 122, 168
Number One 60, 100, 101, 198, 208, 262
Nunnery 7

O

Out of the Silent Planet 72, 108, 110, 140
Ozzy Osbourne 57, 58, 76, 163, 195

P

Paschendale 74, 110, 112, 134
Patrick McGoohan 93, 136, 141
Paul Cairns 5, 31, 34, 35, 39
Paul Di'Anno 3, 5, 8, 14, 31, 32, 33, 34, 35, 36, 37, 42, 45, 46, 47, 50, 63, 89, 101, 130, 131, 136, 139, 148, 152, 154, 156, 157, 159, 168, 197, 204, 210, 214, 218, 223, 233, 236, 239, 254, 262, 263, 264, 268
Paull Sears 5, 143, 144, 145
Paul Mario day 3, 5, 7, 8, 16, 17, 36, 63, 90, 148, 239, 264
Paul Samson 128, 160, 174, 175, 178, 191
Paul Todd 35, 36, 148, 149
Phantom of the Opera 26, 39, 42, 89, 90, 131, 150, 155, 223
Piece of Mind 9, 24, 51, 52, 77, 94, 95, 96, 110, 119, 130, 132, 133, 135, 139, 221, 263
Plane 77, 78, 80, 84, 86, 180, 182, 184, 251, 252
Powerslave 6, 10, 53, 55, 77, 95, 96, 100, 110, 114, 116, 119, 122, 131, 132, 134, 167, 168, 188, 192, 216, 217, 218, 222, 224, 248, 262
Praying Mantis 5, 36, 37, 155, 156, 159, 160, 206
Primal Rock Rebellion 5, 172
Producer 5, 42, 43, 45, 49, 55, 666, 72, 91, 104, 127, 128, 147, 154, 175, 176, 177, 178, 179, 180, 185, 186, 197, 199, 204, 214, 229, 265, 266
Psycho Motel 5, 151, 170, 171, 172
Pub 16, 17, 18, 19, 20, 25, 27, 34, 36, 39, 89, 143, 145, 151, 162, 164, 165, 166, 169, 170, 173, 187, 188, 209, 213, 220, 238, 239, 244, 265
Purgatory 46, 91, 92, 126
Pyrotechnics 16, 19, 44, 54, 77, 86, 147, 215, 217

R

Rainbow 5, 45, 49, 55, 136, 150, 154, 208, 223
Rainmaker 74, 110, 111, 226
Raising Hell 63, 225
Raziq Rauf 5, 254, 268
Reading 23, 28, 40, 43, 48, 50, 57, 93, 123, 126, 131, 140, 152, 178, 183, 195, 196, 208, 235
Rehearsing 10, 15, 16, 17, 25, 26, 27, 67, 144, 146, 159, 165, 169, 170, 176, 177
Remember Tomorrow 47, 50, 89, 123, 140, 155
Remus Down Boulevard 39, 158

IRON MAIDEN

Revelations 93, 94, 135
Rhythms of the Beast 5, 191
Rick Rubin 60, 199
Rick Wakeman 5, 192, 210
Riding with the Angels 177, 197
Rime of the Ancient Mariner 54, 88, 95, 96, 117, 130, 138
Rob Dickinson 266
Rob Grain 5, 173, 174, 239
Rob Halford 7, 72
Robin Guy 5, 162, 188, 189, 268
Rock in Rio 54, 72, 73, 81, 123, 194, 224, 225, 227
Rod Smallwood 4, 36, 41, 43, 45, 48, 57, 63, 64, 178, 181, 188, 213, 214, 216, 247, 255
Roland Hyams 5, 56, 57, 61, 64, 182, 184, 208, 214, 268
Ron Matthews 15, 16, 18, 20, 21
Ross Halfin 225, 232, 240
Running Free 38, 39, 40, 41, 42, 54, 89, 90, 224, 232, 257
Run to the Hills 9, 49, 50, 51, 54, 73, 75, 92, 93, 133, 147, 223, 232

S

Sack Trick 162, 188, 268
Samson 5, 8, 37, 41, 43, 44, 48, 91, 92, 109, 127, 128, 141, 149, 153, 160, 174, 175, 176, 177, 178, 188, 191, 195, 197, 239, 269
Sanctuary 10, 20, 38, 43, 72, 90, 91, 112, 117, 122, 126, 171, 181, 187, 207, 209, 214, 218
Sarajevo 4, 5, 182, 183, 184, 212, 229, 230, 231, 268
Satanist 62, 93, 139
School 9, 10, 15, 144, 146, 150, 162, 164, 165, 173, 192, 216, 234, 236, 245, 247, 248, 249, 250, 266
Scream For Me 4, 5, 122, 182, 184, 186, 188, 189, 212, 229, 231, 268
Seventh Son of a Seventh Son 56, 57, 80, 98, 100, 108, 113, 120, 123, 132, 135, 168, 249
Shakespeare 666, 110, 140

Shock Tactics 127, 176, 177, 178
Shots 30, 106, 116, 173, 174, 225, 240
SHVPES 267
Sign of the Cross 67, 68, 86, 104, 105, 122, 137
Silicon Messiah 70, 202, 205
Skunkworks 5, 162, 182, 185, 186, 187, 193
Smiler 15, 18, 145, 146, 150
Smoke on the Water 15, 31, 147, 192
Somewhere Back In Time 77, 122, 123, 226, 240, 252, 265
Somewhere in Time 55, 57, 97, 100, 101, 114, 119, 130, 137, 168, 217, 218, 219, 222, 234, 248
Soundgarden 62, 147, 185, 201, 266
Sounds 27, 35, 36, 37, 38, 41, 42, 55, 57, 58, 69, 82, 88, 90, 101, 108, 109, 114, 117, 159, 166, 179, 180, 220, 231, 256, 257, 261, 266
Spaceward Studios 31, 166
Speed of Light 84, 117, 119, 226, 242
Status Quo 39, 45, 158, 244
Steve Harris 3, 7, 11, 14, 15, 16, 17, 18, 20, 21, 23, 28, 30, 31, 32, 34, 35, 36, 39, 41, 43, 44, 45, 47, 51, 52, 54, 56, 59, 60, 666, 73, 76, 78, 79, 86, 90, 95, 99, 100, 101, 102, 104, 105, 106, 107, 108, 109, 111, 119, 120, 127, 129, 131, 132, 134, 135, 136, 137, 138, 141, 143, 144, 145, 146, 147, 148, 150, 151, 152, 170, 175, 185, 188, 190, 191, 194, 207, 209, 210, 214, 224, 225, 234, 240, 245, 247, 255, 259, 261, 262
Steve Newhouse 236
Stjepan Juras 5, 233, 269
Stranger in a Strange Land 55, 56, 97, 98, 106
Strange World 32, 37, 89, 90, 126, 148
Streetwalkers 190, 191, 192
Stuart Bailie 6, 249
Studio 16, 30, 31, 33, 38, 41, 42, 43, 48, 49, 60, 64, 65, 72, 78, 81, 84, 101, 102, 108, 109, 110, 115, 117, 121, 124, 127, 128, 135, 135, 146, 150, 156, 159, 166, 167, 168, 171, 179, 184, 185, 187, 191, 196, 198, 201, 205, 207, 225, 238,

PART THREE: **MAIDENOLOGY**

257, 263
Styx 173
Support 31, 42, 44, 50, 51, 57, 65, 76, 77, 162, 188, 192, 200, 201, 218, 221, 229, 231, 244, 260, 265, 266, 267

T

Tatjana Bonny 5, 229, 230
Terry Rance 5, 16, 18, 20, 238, 239, 240
Terry Slesser 47, 150
Terry Wapram 5, 17, 21, 24, 25, 27, 29, 30, 31, 150, 238, 239, 240
The Angel and the Gambler 67, 106
The Beast 5, 31, 46, 49, 50, 53, 67, 72, 75, 76, 77, 86, 92, 93, 121, 122, 123, 132, 134, 142, 152, 159, 160, 191, 207, 208, 216, 218, 219, 221, 223, 225, 226, 227, 228, 232, 233, 241, 242, 252, 257, 263
The Beatles 38, 148
The Book of Souls: Live Chapter 86, 124, 227
The Bridgehouse 18, 27, 29, 39, 158
The Clairvoyant 59, 99, 100
The Cult 57, 79, 96, 136, 169
The Duellists 6, 53, 95, 96, 261
The Entire Population of Hackney 59, 167, 192
The Essential Iron Maiden 122
The Evil that Men Do 58, 76, 98, 99, 140, 208
The Final Frontier 79, 80, 81, 114, 115, 116, 117, 122, 124, 227, 240, 252, 267
The First Ten Years 121, 224
The Green Goddess 28, 37, 39
The History of Iron Maiden – Part 1: The Early Days 74, 223, 226
The Ides of March 26, 90, 91, 175
The Iron Maidens 6, 157, 194, 218, 258, 260
The Irons 10, 55, 57, 60, 74, 75, 76, 77, 81, 111, 115, 122, 150, 158, 160, 168, 186, 190, 192, 258, 260, 262, 263, 267
The Loneliness of the Long Distance Runner 97, 98, 138

The Number of the Beast 49, 50, 67, 72, 75, 76, 77, 92, 93, 122, 132, 218, 221, 223, 225
The Red and the Black 117, 119, 137
The Reincarnation of Benjamin Breeg 76, 112, 113
The Ruskin Arms 38, 151
The Soundhouse Tapes 33, 37, 39, 93, 126, 269
The Sweet 8, 20, 42, 89, 128, 149, 151
The Trooper 52, 75, 94, 116, 130, 131, 209, 223, 244, 260
The Who 7, 52, 57, 67, 144, 147, 154, 164, 190, 223, 225, 256
The Wicker Man 71, 86, 108, 109, 138, 225
The X-Factor 666, 67, 68, 69, 121
Thin Lizzy 18, 20, 147, 154, 170, 223, 249
Thomas Zwijnen 204, 239
Thunderburst 91, 175, 176
Thunderstick 5, 21, 24, 41, 126, 127, 138, 174, 175, 177, 178, 188, 239, 240, 264, 269
Tokyo 123, 154, 155, 171, 227
Tony Moore 5, 24, 25, 26, 27, 238, 239, 269
Tony Parsons 5, 36, 38, 150, 238
Tony Platt 5, 43, 48, 666, 127, 176, 177, 214, 269
Transylvania 38, 39, 79, 89, 90, 123, 126
Trivium 265, 266, 267
Trooper Ale 80, 243
Twilight Zone 46, 92, 218
Tyranny Of Souls 190

U

Untouchables 5, 170, 193
Urchin 5, 20, 30, 36, 93, 134, 151, 164, 166, 167, 268

V

V1 5, 17, 29, 30, 31, 150, 239, 240, 269
Vic Vella 22, 122, 127, 194, 220
Vincent Price 93, 132
Virtual XI 67, 69, 106, 109, 121
Virus 40, 67, 81, 102, 121, 161

IRON MAIDEN

Visions of the Beast 225, 226

W

War 53, 62, 666, 96, 101, 102, 104, 105, 107, 108, 112, 113, 114, 116, 119, 131, 132, 139, 140, 141, 155, 182, 183, 184, 196, 223, 229, 230, 253
Wasted Years 55, 56, 97, 130, 215, 224, 260
Wasting Love 102, 140
West Ham United 143, 245
What Does This Button Do? 132, 232
White Spirit 59, 195, 196
Wildest Dreams 47, 73, 74, 110, 111, 226
Winston Churchill 53, 131
Wishbone Ash 16, 39, 168
Wolfsbane 5, 60, 64, 666, 199, 200, 201, 202, 204, 210
Women In Uniform 43, 44, 45, 67, 194, 214, 218, 219, 224
World Slavery Tour 53, 56, 97, 122
Wrathchild 32, 90, 91, 92, 121, 126, 138, 155, 172

Z

Zomba 43, 197

JIMI HENDRIX
THE DAY I WAS THERE

For more info, visit www.thisdayinmusic.com